REGULATION, INNOVATION AND COMPETITION IN PHARMACEUTICAL MARKETS: A COMPARATIVE STUDY

This book explores the fundamental and inextricable relationship between regulation, intellectual property, competition law, and public health in pharmaceutical markets, examining their interconnections and the delicate balance between the various interests and policy goals at stake.

Although pharmaceutical markets are heavily regulated and subject to close antitrust scrutiny, there is a constant requirement for existing rules and policies to tackle a number of persistent, complex issues. The variety of anti-competitive practices occurring in this sector, the worrying rise in drug prices, and major, far-reaching concerns over the accessibility of medicines are sources of frequent controversy in academic and policy debates. Understanding the unique features and dynamics of the pharmaceutical industry requires a tailored and multifaceted approach.

The study is enhanced by the adoption of a comparative perspective, tracing convergence and divergence between EU and US systems through the analysis of relevant applicable rules, significant cases, and policy choices. Pursuant to this rigorous approach, the book provides an original and thought-provoking critique of the challenges of regulating pharmaceutical markets.

Hart Studies in Law and Health

Series Editors

Tamara Hervey, City Law School, City University of London
Thérèse Murphy, Queen's University, Belfast

Hart Studies in Law and Health aims to publish the best existing and upcoming voices in scholarship on law and health. Viewing law as a broad church, the series welcomes a range of methodologies from the doctrinal to the critical and including regulation and governance, and law and ethics approaches.

Titles in this series

Compulsory Mental Health Interventions and the CRPD: Minding Equality
Anna Nilsson

The Interplay of Global Standards and EU Pharmaceutical Regulation: The International Council for Harmonisation
Sabrina Roettger-Wirtz

Healthcare, Quality Concerns and Competition Law: A Systematic Approach
Theodosia Stavroulaki

Regulation, Innovation and Competition in Pharmaceutical Markets: A Comparative Study
Margherita Colangelo

Regulation, Innovation and Competition in Pharmaceutical Markets

A Comparative Study

Margherita Colangelo

•HART•
OXFORD • LONDON • NEW YORK • NEW DELHI • SYDNEY

HART PUBLISHING

Bloomsbury Publishing Plc

Kemp House, Chawley Park, Cumnor Hill, Oxford, OX2 9PH, UK

1385 Broadway, New York, NY 10018, USA

29 Earlsfort Terrace, Dublin 2, Ireland

First published in Great Britain 2023

A catalogue record for this book is available from the British Library.

A catalogue record for this book is available from the Library of Congress.

Library of Congress Control Number: 2022950665

ISBN: HB: 978-1-50996-551-9
ePDF: 978-1-50996-553-3
ePub: 978-1-50996-552-6

Typeset by Compuscript Ltd, Shannon

Acknowledgements

I WOULD LIKE to thank Professor Vincenzo Zeno-Zencovich for his constant encouragement and valuable advice over the years, and the Editors of the Hart Studies in Law and Health Series, Professors Tamara Hervey and Thérèse Murphy, for their confidence in this study and for hosting the book in the Series. I am also grateful to Professor Spencer Weber Waller and the Institute for Consumer Antitrust Studies of Loyola University Chicago School of Law, for having given me the opportunity to conduct part of this research as 2020/2021 Non-Resident Research Fellow, and the numerous colleagues with whom I have discussed the various topics of this book. Finally, I owe a special thank you to Federico, Simone and my family for their unique support and trust.

Contents

PART II

PART III

Introduction

I. THE DIFFERENT FACES OF PHARMACEUTICAL MARKETS

THE PHARMACEUTICAL SECTOR has long proved to be fertile ground for research, as it is characterised by an uncommon intersection of regulation, intellectual property (IP) and competition law, which makes it rather unique.

Being an innovative and high-technology industry representing a significant part of the global economy and essential to public health, different concurring interests within this sector coexist. On the one hand, the indispensable function carried out by pharmaceutical activities for human health has led to the creation of a large sectoral and particularly pervasive regulatory system. The life cycle of new drugs, the nature of demand for drugs and the dynamics of competition in the drug market over time are all shaped by regulation. Regulation in this sector pursues different goals. It aims at ensuring a high quality of pharmaceuticals, including their safety, efficiency and efficacy, while promoting innovation and medical research. In most industrialised countries, various models of price regulation are also in place. In others, noticeably the United States, this approach to pricing is rejected. On the other hand, the uncertainty of research and development activity and the high costs of bringing new products into the market have rendered necessary the creation of a legal framework of rewards and incentives, typically in the form of barriers to entry through the tools provided by IP law, but also through other regulatory exclusivities. The pharmaceutical sector presents difficulties in reconciling these goals, which are distinct from those in other high-technology industries.[1]

Competition law, whose scrutiny in this sector often comes at the intersection of IP law and regulation, plays a fundamental role. Due to *sui generis* features characterising the industry, the nature of competition is peculiar too. The evolution of the market and of medicinal products has led to important changes over time. The emergence of biotech and generic companies challenging the traditional dominance of large multinational originator firms, together with the shift towards vertical specialisation and mergers, has had a fundamental impact on the market's structure.[2] Moreover, categorisation between types of firms

[1] MK Kyle, 'Competition Law, Intellectual Property, and the Pharmaceutical Sector' (2016) 81 *Antitrust Law Journal* 1, 32.

[2] MK Kyle and F Scott Morton, 'Markets for Pharmaceutical Products' in MV Pauly, TG Mcguire and PP Barros (eds), *Handbook of Health Economics* (Oxford, Elsevier, 2012) vol 2, 764.

operating in the sector have been blurred by the tendency of firms to combine business models and the type of products to manufacture and/or market – for example, innovative companies also produce generics, some biotech firms have invested in small-molecule products too and some generic firms have started working on the development of novel compounds.

The rate of innovation by companies in the sector is constantly subject to inquiry, particularly with regard to the high prices of prescription drugs. Originator companies are recurrent targets of fierce criticisms for the decline in innovative research, often based on public funding, and for aiming their major efforts on slight variations of existing drugs and the development of the marketing side of the business. Recent literature has also connected lower innovation rates to the tendency of incumbent pharmaceutical firms to implement strategies of acquiring innovative targets and terminating their projects in order to pre-empt future competition.[3] Thus, the contraposition between innovative and generic medicines no longer provides an exhaustive picture of the pharmaceutical markets. Despite this, it still represents a fundamental viewpoint for observing anti-competitive behaviours by pharmaceutical firms, which are traditionally subject to antitrust scrutiny with regard to practices developed by incumbent originator companies to prevent or delay generics' entry, often artificially extending patent protection to unduly preserve their market power.

Generic entry is generally sustained by governments due to the reduction in prices that it brings and the consequent savings for health systems and consumers in general. Patents, as the main tool – together with regulatory ones – granting exclusivity to the holder, have been typically considered the main cause of skyrocketing prices. However, recent practice testifies that extraordinary prices may also concern medicines that are not covered by patents, in particular when therapeutically equivalent drugs are lacking and there is no competition despite the absence of IP barriers. In addition, the existing experience shows the dissemination of several practices leading to a significant number and variety of antitrust infringements.

Prescription drug costs represent the most complex and controversial problem in health policy. Still, there is significant disagreement as to which measures are most appropriate to employ in this regard and who should be responsible for implementing them. When considering high drug pricing, one cannot also disregard the inevitable public health dimension of granting access to medicines. This issue is particularly urgent and compelling in the case of developing and least developed countries, which typically lack both the capacity to manufacture the drugs (or to otherwise obtaining the active ingredients) and the bargaining power to buy them at affordable prices. However, in a different way, it also concerns developed ones, as testified by the heated political debate in the US with regard to the growing number of relatively poor citizens who cannot afford

[3] C Cunningham, F Ederer and S Ma, 'Killer Acquisitions' (2021) 129 *Journal of Political Economy* 649.

life-saving medications and by the threats the tight public budgets of several states, including in the EU, have to face.

By and large, this brief overview shows that this is an area where intersections between different fields of law and related (often conflicting) interests occur.

II. PURPOSE AND SCOPE OF THE ANALYSIS

Although pharmaceutical markets are heavily regulated and subject to close antitrust scrutiny, there is a constant requirement for existing rules and policies to tackle a number of persistent, complex issues. The variety of anticompetitive practices occurring in this sector, the worrying rise in drug prices and major, far-reaching concerns over the accessibility of medicines are sources of frequent controversy in academic and policy debates.

This book concerns the means by which several legal disciplines intervene in pharmaceutical markets with the aim of securing a better outcome for society. It aims to analyse the interconnections between the various relevant areas of law from a substantive point of view, in the perspective of investigating the full implications of policy choices in this field.

The balance within the structural tension of the various interests inherent in the pharmaceutical sector is typically found in the interplay between competition, IP and regulation. As a general issue, such interfaces have been the subject of large body of literature. Therefore, some preliminary clarifications on the premises of this work are due.

Besides the recent attention devoted to digital markets, the pharmaceutical sector has traditionally been one of the main areas of investigation by antitrust enforcement. Competition law promotes rivalry as a means of organising economic behaviour. The main substantive provisions of competition law address anti-competitive agreements, unilateral behaviour and mergers. This study deals with the first two cases, ie joint conduct and single-firm conduct restrictive of competition. This choice is driven by the fact that these two areas provide the most significant room for discussing the intersections at the core of this book.

With regard to the IP/competition interface, this study will not attempt to trace the general debate on this topic.[4] For the purpose of this book, intellectual property rights (IPRs) – in particular, patents – are primarily intended to provide

[4] See, eg RD Blair and D Sokol (eds), *Antitrust, Intellectual Property, and High Tech* (Cambridge, Cambridge University Press, 2017); SD Anderman and A Ezrachi (eds), *Intellectual Property and Competition Law: New Frontiers* (Oxford, Oxford University Press, 2011); MA Carrier (ed), *Intellectual Property and Competition* (Cheltenham, Edward Elgar, 2011); M Maggiolino, *Intellectual Property and Antitrust. A Comparative Economic Analysis of US and EU Law* (Cheltenham, Edward Elgar, 2011); SD Anderman (ed), *The Interface between Intellectual Property Rights and Competition Policy* (Cambridge, Cambridge University Press, 2007); J Drexl (ed), *Research Handbook on Intellectual Property and Competition Law* (Cheltenham, Edward Elgar, 2008).

their owners with *ius excludendi alios*, ie the right to exclude anybody else from using and reproducing the protected inventions as the power to decide over their utilisation.[5] The relationship between competition rules and IP has at times been framed in terms of tension and even conflict. At first sight, the concern to maintain access to markets appears inevitably opposed to the exclusivity provided by patents. However, the most common reading is that of a complex and dynamic interrelationship between two complementary fields of the modern industrial policy, which aim to improve innovation and consumer welfare.[6]

In pharmaceuticals, a great asymmetry occurs between innovation costs and imitation costs. Under current systems for regulating entry, innovators incur most of the expenses for clinical testing to prove that a new molecule is both safe and efficacious for the treatment of certain diseases, whereas, once that information is disclosed, it becomes available – absent IP and regulatory constraints – at minimal cost to would-be generic imitators. Here, the intersection between IP and competition deals with the objective of preventing the use of unworthy IP-based obstacles – albeit lawful under IP law – to free competition, including a series of practices recurrent in this sector, from various forms of 'strategic patenting' and 'evergreening'[7] to misleading ways to obtain IP entitlements, in addition to the atavistic problem of the granting of 'poor-quality patents'. Such practices give rise to an uncontrolled proliferation of IPRs, in contrast with the assumption that the exclusivity guaranteed by patents corresponds to a reward for the costs incurred by the holder and must be matched and counterbalanced by a deserving innovative effort.[8] The issue of where to draw the line between competition law provisions and the exercise of IPRs is at the core of their interface as it becomes

[5] Certainly, the right to exclude goes hand in hand with the freedom to choose which third parties to include in the exploitation of the protected intangible assets. See G Ghidini, *Rethinking Intellectual Property. Balancing Conflicts of Interests in the Constitutional Paradigm* (Cheltenham, Edward Elgar, 2018) 10–12 (explaining that the 'core' exclusive protection afforded by IPRs per se consists in nothing more than the power to forbid economically significant free riders to access the protected intangibles, and the related right to include – eg co-venturers, licensees, distributors – is itself an expression of the right to dispose of one's own right).

[6] A Jones and R Nazzini, 'The Effect of Competition Law on Patent Remedies' in B Biddle, JL Contreras, BJ Love and NV Siebrasse (eds), *Patent Remedies and Complex Products: Towards a Global Consensus* (Cambridge, Cambridge University Press, 2019).

[7] The term 'strategic patenting' refers to a series of heterogeneous practices essentially aimed at extending the breadth and duration of patent protection and to delay or block the market entry of generic medicines (including patent thickets/clusters, secondary or follow-on patents and defensive patenting). The term 'evergreening' is generally used to indicate the practice of filing for new patents on secondary features of a particular product as earlier patents expire. For details, see Part II of this book.

[8] The link between intellectual property and innovation is debated. Some scholars have questioned the idea that patents serve to increase innovation and productivity, and have argued that empirical evidence does not support this view but rather that 'while patents can have a partial equilibrium effect of improving incentives to invent, the general equilibrium effect on innovation can be negative': M Boldrin and DK Levine, 'The Case against Patents' (2013) 27 *Journal of Economic Perspectives* 3; see also M Boldrin and DK Levine, *Against Intellectual Monopoly* (Cambridge, Cambridge University Press, 2008). Others have pointed out that in practice the differences between individual sectors are very marked, so that a differentiated analysis of the relationship

crucial to understand how to manage the conflict arising when competition rules prohibit behaviour that IP law permits.[9]

Extensive literature has been devoted also to the interface between competition and regulation, discussing similarities and differences between the two and their relationship in terms of complementarity or alternativity.[10] Different stances have traditionally characterised the US and European approaches to the issue.[11] In general, competition law and regulation often apply in different settings and the latter is usually considered more intrusive as it intervenes more deeply in market mechanisms than competition law.[12]

The pharmaceutical sector provides a unique showcase for the observation of this relationship and the related issue of the need for antitrust oversight in

between innovation promotion and patent protection is required. See, eg JR Allison, MA Lemley and DL Schwartz, 'Our Divided Patent System' (2015) 82 *University of Chicago Law Review* 1072, according to whom 'owners of patents in the pharmaceutical industry fare much better in dispositive litigation rulings than do owners of patents in the computer and electronics industry, and chemistry patents have much greater success in litigation than their software or biotechnology counterparts'. Others have claimed that, for most businesses today, patents fail to provide predictable property rights and produce costly disputes and excessive litigation that outweigh positive incentives: only in some sectors, such as the pharmaceutical industry, do patents work properly and bring their benefits outweighing the related costs. See J Bessen and MJ Meurer, *Patent Failure. How Judges, Bureaucrats, and Lawyers Put Innovators at Risk* (Princeton, Princeton University Press, 2009). However, the presence of multiple patents to protect one product and an overly fragmented patent rights structure potentially imply difficulty for innovating firms to access the existing knowledge of other patent holders, resulting in an impediment to innovation: see MA Heller and RS Eisenberg, 'Can Patents Deter Innovation? The Anticommons in Biomedical Research' (1998) 280 *Science* 698.

[9] Both in the US and the EU the problem of where to draw the boundary between antitrust prohibitions and the assertion of patent rights has been controversial. IP rights are not subject to special competition rules or principles and do not immunise their holder from the application of competition rules.

[10] See, eg T Prosser, *The Limits of Competition Law* (Oxford, Oxford University Press, 2004); J Tapia and D Mantzari, 'The Regulation/Competition Interaction' in I Lianos and D Geradin (eds), *Handbook on European Competition Law-Substantive Aspects* (Cheltenham, Edward Elgar, 2013) ch 14; C Kirchner, 'Competition Policy versus Regulation: Administration versus Judiciary' in M Neumann and J Weigand (eds), *The International Handbook of Competition* (Cheltenham, Edward Elgar, 2004); G Monti, 'Managing the Intersection of Utilities Regulation and EC Competition Law' (2008) 4 *Competition Law Review* 123; P Ibáñez Colomo, 'On the Application of Competition Law as Regulation: Elements for a Theory' (2010) 29 *Yearbook of European Law* 261; K Coates, *Competition Law and Regulation of Technology Markets* (Oxford, Oxford University Press, 2011); N Dunne, *Competition Law and Economic Regulation* (Cambridge, Cambridge University Press, 2015); H Shelanski, 'Antitrust and Deregulation' (2018) 127 *Yale Law Journal* 1922. It is worth mentioning that most of the debate on the relationship between competition and regulation concerns utilities and network industries, subject to liberalisation processes. As clarified at the beginning, regulation of pharmaceutical sector derives from different reasons.

[11] In brief, it is well established in the EU that the competition rules continue to have almost full application within regulated markets. In the US, antitrust deference towards regulation has been affirmed, especially in the wake of the *Trinko* and *Credit Suisse* rulings, relying on checking whether the regulatory regime acts as 'effective steward of the antitrust function': *Verizon Communications Inc v Law Offices of Curtis V Trinko*, 540 US 398 (2004); *Credit Suisse Securities LLC v Billing*, 127 S Ct 2383 (2007); *Pacific Bell Telephone Co v linkLine Communications Inc*, 555 US 438 (2009).

[12] Economic regulation 'typically refers to government-imposed restrictions on firms' decisions over price, quantity, and entry and exit': W Kip Viscusi, JE Harrington Jr and DEM Sappington, *Economics of Regulation and Antitrust*, 5th edn (Cambridge, MA, MIT Press, 2018).

industries with complex regulatory systems. This occurs in particular for the presence of the conditions for regulatory gaming behaviours, which find fertile ground in sectors (as the pharmaceutical one) subject to government approval for market entry.[13] As a matter of fact, regulation of pharmaceutical products, which is also a fundamental source of exclusivity in addition to IPRs, gives companies the opportunity to profit from market distortions and abuses. The number of cases brought against companies in the pharmaceutical sector for practices such as strategic use and/or manipulation of IP systems, product hopping and excessive pricing testify how such practices may involve conduct that can be plausibly within the letter of the regulatory regime but aims at results that are at odds with the spirit of the underlying legal framework, thereby corrupting it.[14] In such cases, the regulatory framework within the market is an integral element of the wider context to an alleged competition violation.[15]

This book analyses the role of antitrust intervention in selected cases concerning prescription drugs, taking into consideration not only the substantive perspective (content of the rules), but also the institutional one (enforcement of the rules), namely the interplay between different institutions. Competition authorities, patent offices and medicines agencies, according to their respective mandates and goals, generally operate at arm's length from each other. Whether the resulting disconnect and (potential or actual) inconsistencies might be mitigated and the realisation of objectives pursued by concurring regimes in the field of prescription drugs might be improved by new forms of enhanced coordination is an issue that deserves attention.

The flexibility of antitrust law, which allows it to capture several and new practices creating harm to competition, has led to the question of whether it may also work as a tool to pursue objectives beyond those based purely on economic efficiency considerations. Due to the fundamental role of the pharmaceutical sector in goals related to the fundamental right to health, it represents a perfect testing ground to investigate whether broader public policy considerations and non-price parameters should be integrated in antitrust assessment. The idea of using competition law tools in the wider issue of the full realisation of the right to health is not entirely new. High drug prices and access to medicines have been always a controversial issue in human rights and international trade debates.[16] This is, of course, a compelling problem in the case of developing and least developed countries. However, the unstoppable rise of costs for prescription

[13] 'Regulatory gaming' has been defined as 'behavior that abuses a neutral or procompetitive regulatory structure and wields it as a tool to accomplish exclusionary results': SL Dogan and MA Lemley, 'Antitrust Law and Regulatory Gaming' (2009) 87 *Texas Law Review* 685, 708.

[14] N Dunne, 'The Role of Regulation in EU Competition Law Assessment' (2021) 44 *World Competition* 287, 301.

[15] ibid 291–92 (explaining that in such cases 'antitrust proxy wars' may occur, as competition enforcement is not merely concerned with a defendant's behaviour, but also with dissatisfaction with the way in which the pre-existing regulatory framework has been designed or is being administered).

[16] In general, see, eg H Hestermeyer, *Human Rights and the WTO: The Case of Patents and Access to Medicines* (Oxford, Oxford University Press, 2008).

drugs is a difficult topic to be tackled by developed countries too, and is among the hardest problems for health policies.

Recently, in the wake of the challenges to the mainstream conception of antitrust, as concerned primarily with economic efficiency, proposals of rethinking boundaries and parameters of competition policy have been put forward. The book illustrates approaches envisaged in the literature discussing the intersection between competition law, IP rules and the human right to health. Moreover, it takes into account views discussing the inclusion of public non-economic interests in competition law, as proposed in the scholarship in the past and as currently re-read in the context of broader narratives (including, for example, a rights-based approach or sustainable development goals). By doing so, it considers the boundaries of competition law from a normative standpoint critically questioning the extent to which it might and/or should protect non-economic health-related interests and whether these interests can be incorporated in antitrust analysis without stretching its scope beyond its core focus.

III. METHODOLOGY

As a premise, this book is grounded on the functionalist method of comparative law,[17] which – although variations, alternatives and criticism have been elaborated in the doctrinal debate on methodology – remains a fundamental starting point in this field.[18] In line with this 'nondoctrinal' approach, the analysis

[17] The functionalist method is generally ascribed to K Zweigert and H Kötz, *An Introduction to Comparative Law*, 3rd edn (T Weir tr, Oxford, Oxford University Press, 1998). But see J Husa, 'Comparative Law, Legal Linguistics and Methodology of Legal Doctrine' in M VanHoecke (ed), *Methodologies of Legal Research* (Oxford, Hart Publishing, 2011) 209 (tracing the first origins of the functional method in comparative law back to E Rabel, 'Die Fachgebiete des Kaiser-Wilhelm-Instituts filr auslhindisches und internationales Privatrecht' in HG Leser (ed), *Er Rabel Gesarnmelte Aufsdtze*, vol 3 (Tilbingen, Mohr Siebeck, 1967)); EK Banakas, 'The Method of Comparative Law and the Question of Legal Culture Today' (1994) 3 *Tilburg Law Review* 113, 118 (tracing functionalism to M Rheinstein, 'Teaching Comparative Law' (1938) 5 *University of Chicago Law Review* 615). This approach is 'one of the best-known working tools in comparative legal studies': M Graziadei, 'The Functionalist Heritage' in P Legrand and R Munday (eds), *Comparative Legal Studies: Traditions and Transitions* (Cambridge, Cambridge University Press, 2003) 100. It flows from the assumptions that law has a function – ie that it serves to rationally solve certain social problems – and that only law which fulfils the same function can be compared.

[18] Functionalism has enjoyed a long-standing reputation as the basic methodology in comparative law. See U Kischel, *Comparative Law* (Oxford, Oxford University Press, 2019) 87ff (explaining that 'The vast majority of comparative studies follow this method, whether consciously or not, and the quality of any given comparative law study is often judged according to its principles'). At least eight different interpretations of the 'functional method' in comparative law have been identified in the literature: R Michaels, 'The Functional Method of Comparative Law' in M Reimann, R Zimmermann (eds), *The Oxford Handbook of Comparative Law*, 2nd edn (Oxford, Oxford University Press, 2019) 350. Other authors have adopted a more pragmatical approach, considering functionalism as a 'rule-of-thumb', eg J Husa, 'Functional Method in Comparative Law – Much Ado About Nothing?' (2013) 2 *European Property Law Journal* 4, 17; see also J Husa, 'Metamorphosis of Functionalism – Or Back to Basics' (2011) 18 *Maastricht Journal of European & Comparative Law* 548; for a comment, see JM Smits, 'Taking Functionalism Seriously: On the Bright Future

intends to focus not only on rules and doctrinal arguments alone, but on their effects and consequences.[19] The basic assumption is that selected legal systems may be compared by considering their various responses to the same problems in the light of their functional relation to society. Comparative analysis allows a study of the EU and US systems to be conducted with the aim of showing the extent to which they can both learn from each other and questioning which rules and policy choices may better fulfil their function.[20] To this end, the functional method is supplemented by a holistic view, aimed at understanding the interactions between the various elements and partitions of the law relevant for the study of prescription drug markets.[21] Rather than analysing the different subfields of law on their own, the book explores the inevitable and inextricable relationship between them through the study of the evolving case law, legislation and regulatory process.[22]

Moreover, the book is inspired by the field of comparative law and regulation.[23] The adoption of this perspective aims at delineating legal convergences and divergences among the selected jurisdictions, the rule-making and the reform process driven by political and legal actors, including regulatory oversight and enforcement. This comprises a comparative institutional analysis, which takes into account the pros and cons of related choices, the allocation of competences between different and concurring public authorities, and their relationship with private actors. In addition, the comparison between the EU and

of a Contested Method' (2011) 18 *Maastricht Journal of European & Comparative Law* 554. For further comments and criticism to functionalism, see also E Örücü, *The Enigma of Comparative Law: Variations on a Theme for the Twenty-First Century* (Leiden, Springer, 2004) 19ff; Kischel, *Comparative Law*, 90ff; J Gordley, 'The Functional Method' in PG Monateri (ed), *Methods of Comparative Law* (Cheltenham, Edward Elgar, 2012) 107; E Örücü, 'Methodology of Comparative Law' in JM Smits (ed), *Elgar Encyclopedia of Comparative Law* (Cheltenham, Edward Elgar, 2012) 442; M Siems, *Comparative Law*, 3rd edn (Cambridge, Cambridge University Press, 2022) 15, 31.

[19] Michaels, 'The Functional Method', 347.

[20] It should be noted that the use of comparative analysis in its functionalist role has been supported in health law as a tool to 'support the search for a "better" solution to domestic legal problems, either a legislative reform or as judicial reasoning/advocacy and argumentation': TK Hervey and D Orentlicher, 'Editors' Introduction' in TK Hervey and D Orentlicher (eds), *The Oxford Handbook of Comparative Health Law* (Oxford, Oxford University Press, 2021) 2. Similarly, the functional method has been advanced also in comparative studies of competition law. See, eg R Van den Bergh, *Comparative Competition Law and Economics* (Cheltenham, Edward Elgar, 2017) 10.

[21] V Zeno-Zencovich, *Comparative Legal Systems. A Short and Illustrated Introduction* (Rome, Roma TrE-Press, 2019) 104.

[22] 'Comparative law, generally, is not about static legal situations but about processes in which rules interact and bring about a certain result': V Zeno-Zencovich, 'Lessons from a Traffic Light. A Juridical Scherzo' (2016) 3 *European Journal of Comparative Law and Governance* 3 (affirming that 'Metaphorically, [comparative law] is not about photographs but about documentaries').

[23] In comparative law and regulation, regulation is defined as 'a form of governance designed to address complex social, environmental and economic problems that relies heavily on rules, enforced against market actors, and administrative authorities': F Bignami, 'A New Field: Comparative Law and Regulation' in F Bignami and D Zaring (eds), *Comparative Law and Regulation. Understanding the Global Regulatory Process* (Cheltenham, Edward Elgar, 2016) 1, 3 (also discussing the use of the functional method at 30–35).

the US in prescription drug markets constitutes an interesting example showing the implementation of public intervention and the different conceptions and models of the welfare state.[24]

The role of competition law constitutes the *fil rouge* linking the various disciplines and topics analysed in the book. Competition law research is frequently done in a cross-jurisdictional manner, either analysing one main jurisdiction and referencing solutions found in others, or directly focusing on the comparison of legal issues in two or more jurisdictions. These features can be found in the acknowledgement of a discipline of comparative competition law too.[25] The focus on the US–EU comparative perspective considers differences between these systems (those at the level of micro-comparisons are even more profound than those at the level of macro-comparisons) and similarities. Such analysis is much needed in the current context, where the global influence of the European model of competition law is discussed.[26]

Finally, due to the role that economics plays in competition law and policy, the book integrates the comparative law perspective with the consideration of main relevant insights deriving from economic approaches to antitrust issues under investigation.

IV. STRUCTURE OF THE BOOK

The book is structured as follows.

Part I analyses the main distinctive features of pharmaceutical markets and the rules governing prescription drugs, focusing on three areas of crucial importance: rules regulating access to the market; patents and regulatory exclusivities; and pricing and reimbursement of pharmaceutical products. This part considers regulatory and market pathways in pharmaceutical markets and analyses how the selected jurisdictions have interpreted and implemented their objectives in their policies on prescription drugs.

Firstly, it illustrates the peculiarities of both the supply and demand sides. With regard to the former, it considers the various models of firms and the features and costs of innovative activity through the product life cycle. With regard to the demand side, it explains the persistent information asymmetry characterising markets for medicines and their nature of 'experience' or

[24] On the consideration of welfare model and public finance choices as a fundamental element of the definition of a system, see Zeno-Zencovich, *Comparative Legal Systems*, 58–61.

[25] Among the textbooks, see, eg MM Dabbah, *International and Comparative Competition Law* (Cambridge, Cambridge University Press, 2010); J Duns, A Duke and B Sweeney (eds), *Comparative Competition Law* (Cheltenham, Edward Elgar, 2017); Van den Bergh, *Comparative Competition Law and Economics*. Moreover, a project named 'Comparative Competition Law' has been started by Anu Bradford and Adam Chilton, based on the development of a novel dataset on competition laws and enforcement across time and jurisdiction (http://comparativecompetitionlaw.org/).

[26] See, eg A Bradford, *The Brussels Effect. How the European Union Rules the World* (Oxford, Oxford University Press, 2020), 99.

'credence' goods. Regulatory agency's approval for marketing of pharmaceuticals constitutes one means to address such information asymmetry. The 'price disconnect' between the decision maker (the prescribing doctor) and the payor (insurer/NHS/consumer) is a typical feature of prescription drug markets. Thus, chapter one analyses the current EU and US frameworks regulating access to the market and the different choices made by the existing legislation on the matter. Rules on marketing approvals must be read in conjunction with the provisions providing protection to new pharmaceutical products, namely IP rights and regulatory exclusivities. Chapter two addresses the exclusivity provided by IP rules and drug regulations, so long as both limit entry into the pharmaceutical market, albeit pursuing different purposes. Then chapter three focuses on pricing and reimbursement of pharmaceutical products, explaining the crucial differences between the EU, where different national systems and institutions exist, and the US, where no price regulation for prescription drugs is in place.

The understanding of this framework is essential in order to comprehend the functioning and governance of pharmaceutical markets and the conditions for competition between pharmaceutical firms. The comparative analysis of the EU and US systems is conducted with the aim of highlighting the similarities and differences in their regulatory approaches and of providing the necessary basis for the topics treated in the other parts of the book.

Part II is devoted to the analysis of the role and the main areas of intervention of competition law in the pharmaceutical sector, with particular attention to the most challenging issues at the intersection of antitrust, IP law and sector-specific regulation.

Chapter four provides an essential overview of EU and US competition rules and illustrates the main directions pursued by antitrust enforcement in the pharmaceutical sector. Chapters five and six investigate two practices developed by incumbent originator companies in order to respond to generic entry by preventing and/or delaying it. Among the various anti-competitive behaviours, the chapters focus on reverse payment patent settlements (also known as pay-for-delay settlements) and product hopping as paradigmatic examples of the interface between antitrust law, IP law and sectoral regulation. With regard to the former, in the US, a significant case law has been developed on the matter and the ban of pay-for-delay and similar agreements by rule is under consideration. In the EU, pay-for-delay settlements have been the object of recent landmark judgments (*Generics*, *Lundbeck*), which have clarified the European approach towards these agreements as restrictions by object. With regard to product hopping, due to the controversial assessment before US courts, proposals of specific legislative action have been advocated by some scholars as the best option also to address this anti-competitive conduct. While no similar debate exists in the EU, initiatives advanced in the US appear to question the role of existing legal instruments in tackling effectively anti-competitive behaviours in the pharmaceutical sector.

Chapter seven investigates the recent resurgence of excessive pricing cases in Europe and illustrates the relevant discussion in the US, where some authors have called for antitrust intervention. Although price regulation is often at odds with antitrust policy, the growing concern for high prices and price hikes of prescription drugs drives the thinking on the possible intervention of both regulation and competition policy.

Part III explores the intersection between IP law, antitrust and human rights. Concerns about high prescription drug prices are related to the wider issue of the access to medicines as a fundamental element of the right to health, which poses hard challenges to governments. Firstly, chapter eight analyses the right to health, considering its foundations in international law, and the framework governed by the Agreement on Trade-Related Aspects of Intellectual Property Rights (TRIPS). The chapter then provides an overview of the interlinkage between the human right to health and the right of access to medicines, the relevant international patent protection rules and competition rules. Finally, chapter nine illustrates alternative approaches aimed at reconsidering the role of competition rules in a broader perspective, including health-related issues. Indeed, the pure efficiency-oriented approach to antitrust has recently been questioned in favour of a more aggressive enforcement of its rules. Accordingly, the different view of competition law as a tool to promote non-economic objectives has been advanced.

The conclusion further develops the intersections between the different parts of the work and highlights significant challenges relating to the various areas of law and policy analysed, elaborating on a novel approach to the interactions between the different regimes at stake.

Part I

1

Regulating Entry

I. THE MAIN FEATURES OF PHARMACEUTICAL MARKETS: THE SUPPLY SIDE AND THE DEMAND SIDE

THE GLOBAL SIGNIFICANCE and complexities of the pharmaceutical sector make it an infinite source of interest and research. Pharmaceutical markets most definitely do not function in the same way as ordinary markets. Any analysis of the industry's market structure must necessarily begin with an appropriate consideration of the unique features which characterise it on both the supply side and the demand side.

On the supply side, traditionally a fundamental distinction is drawn between two types of firms: originator companies and generic companies. Such distinction essentially lies in the degree of innovation that their activity involves and in the business models they adopt. Different types of competition between firms may be identified too. Originators are generally large, multinational research and development (R&D)-based companies, whose activity is deemed to play a crucial role in innovating and developing new and more effective products. They typically rely on patent law protection in order to ensure returns on their investments. In addition, they enjoy further protection due to specific regulations intended to grant them other types of exclusivity. Originators primarily compete within themselves 'for the market', trying to be the first to innovate, develop products superior to existing ones and discover new medicines. This type of competition is also known as therapeutic competition.[1] In contrast, manufacturers of generic products develop non-innovative and cheaper versions of originator products that have already been authorised (ie reference medicines), having their same qualitative and quantitative composition, form, safety and performance characteristics, with the aim of marketing them as soon as the branded products lose the exclusivities provided by patent law and regulation. Generic products are intended to be interchangeable with the originator brand products. They may be marketed either under a non-proprietary name (INN)[2] or under a proprietary or brand name, often called 'branded generics'.

[1] L Hancher, 'The EU Pharmaceutical Market: Parameters and Pathways' in E Mossialos, G Permanand, R Baeten and TK Hervey (eds), *Health Systems Governance in Europe: The Role of European Union Law and Policy* (Cambridge, Cambridge University Press, 2010) 640.

[2] The International Non-proprietary Name identifies pharmaceutical substances or active pharmaceutical ingredients. Each INN is a unique name that is globally recognised and is public property.

Generic firms often produce the medicine by sourcing the molecule as bulk material from independent active pharmaceutical ingredient (API) producers. Several other producers are active in the industry, such as manufacturers of intermediate products, contract manufacturers and companies specialising in technology for dosages or forms of administration.[3]

An additional business model is that of smaller firms focused on biotechnology or large-molecule drugs, which may partner with multinationals in the later stages of the process of product launch.[4] This is also linked with the evolution of the range of products developed by pharmaceutical companies in time. Not only chemically synthesised small molecules, which have been the traditional innovative reference drugs present on the market, but also large and complex molecules (ie biologics, or biological drugs) currently constitute an important type of drugs available for medical treatments. In particular, biological drugs represent an increasingly significant option for treatment of chronic and disabling diseases (such as diabetes, autoimmune diseases and cancers).

Nowadays, the traditional dominance of the industry by large multinational firms has suffered from the emergence of biotech and generic companies, and this, in addition to increasing vertical specialisation and horizontal mergers, has led the market structure of the industry to change.[5] In reality, the distinction between the types of firms mentioned above is not so clear-cut anymore. This happens with regard to both the business models adopted – as, for instance, many multinationals own generic subsidiaries and there are companies which operate in the market as owners of both brand and generic drugs[6] – and the products marketed – for example, some biotech firms have also invested in small-molecule products and some generic firms have started making efforts for the development of novel compounds.[7]

Generic entry is generally sustained by governments in the light of the associated reduction of prices and benefit for consumers and governmental health systems. A study prepared for the European Commission in 2018 found that prices of innovator medicinal products drop by 40 per cent on average in the period from six quarters before to five quarters following generic entry.[8] It also showed that when generic medicinal products enter the market, their price is on average 50 per cent lower than the initial price of the corresponding originator product in the first five quarters after the launch of the generic product. Thus, it is

[3] H Mische, E Kamilarova and D Schnichels, 'Pharma' in J Faull and A Nikpay (eds), *The EU Law of Competition*, 3rd edn (Oxford, Oxford University Press, 2014) 1869, 1871.

[4] MK Kyle, 'Economic Analysis of Supplementary Protection Certificates in Europe' (2017) 5, https://ec.europa.eu/docsroom/documents/25621/attachments/1/translations/en/renditions/native.

[5] MK Kyle and F Scott Morton, 'Markets for Pharmaceutical Products' in MV Pauly, TG Mcguire and PP Barros (eds), *Handbook of Health Economics* (Oxford, Elsevier, 2012) vol 2, 763, 764.

[6] See MA Carrier, MA Lemley and SP Miller, 'Playing Both Sides: Branded Sales, Generic Drugs, and Antitrust Policy' (2020) 71 *Hastings Law Journal* 307.

[7] Kyle, 'Economic Analysis' 5.

[8] European Commission, 'Study on the Economic Impact of Supplementary Protection Certificates, Pharmaceutical Incentives and Rewards in Europe: Final Report' (2018) 14, https://data.europa.eu/doi/10.2873/886648.

easy to understand that inter-brand competition between original products and generic ones is the major concern for brand-name drug manufacturers, which depend mainly upon the period of exclusivity provided by patents in order to earn a return on the substantial investment they make in innovative products. States are particularly concerned with market entry, the natural tension between originator and generic companies also being fostered by government action, as testified by practices targeted at prescribing doctors (developing guidelines or imposing doctors to prescribe by INN rather than by brand) and substitution or drug product selection laws (ie legislation allowing pharmacists to substitute a generic drug when presented with a prescription for its branded equivalent, unless a physician directs or the patient requests otherwise).[9] This issue is linked with the ever-present complex matter of the balancing of price benefits with the maintenance of the incentives for R&D in this sector. As originators typically lose significant profits when facing generic competition, unsurprisingly they have developed a toolbox aimed at responding to generic entry. Also, competition between generic manufacturers can be characterised by risks to the market, as they can engage in anti-competitive practices too. These issues will be addressed in Part II of this book.

A tension similar to the competitive dynamics between originator and generic medicines is that concerning biological drugs and biosimilar ones. The former are based on active substances made of proteins deriving from a biological source, such as living cells or organisms. Compared to small-molecule drugs, they are more difficult to produce, and their origin and complexity, involving a high marginal manufacturing cost on a per-patient basis, do not allow their full duplication just by copying the molecular formula as for chemically synthesised medicines. Biologics, which are today often used to cure severe diseases that cannot be treated efficaciously through small-molecule drugs, are very expensive, so that encouraging the use of biosimilar medicines, ie biological drugs similar – but not identical – to a reference biological medicine, may be pursued by regulators with the same goals driving the support for the adoption of generics, in particular introducing competition, thereby leading to savings while not compromising on quality. However, substitution of originator biologics by biosimilars is not as simple as that between originators and generics for small-molecule medicines, so specific rules have been defined in order to ensure the safety and efficacy of biosimilars.[10] This, in turn, means that it is more difficult to achieve cost savings via traditional competition mechanisms.

A further important distinction within types of drugs relevant for this study must be made between: (i) prescription drugs, ie those products prescribed by a doctor and intended to be used by a patient and bought at pharmacies; (ii) non-reimbursed or over-the-counter (OTC) or non-prescription medicines;

[9] See also ch 3.
[10] See s III.

and (iii) pharmaceuticals purchased by hospitals.[11] Typically, the market of non-prescription drugs is not affected by the distortions due to reimbursement and insurance and the full cost of the products is borne by consumers on their own.[12] The case of prescription drugs, which are the subject of this book, differs crucially from other such types of medicine.

With regard to the distribution of medicines, business for prescription drugs is highly sophisticated. Two main channels can be identified: hospitals, which typically procure medicines directly from producers; and pharmacies, which are generally supplied by wholesalers and only occasionally by producers directly. The latter generally deal with chemical drugs, as biologics are typically administered by a healthcare provider in a hospital.[13] Throughout Europe, prescription-only chemical medicines are mainly dispensed to outpatients in community pharmacies rather than by dispensing doctors and hospital pharmacies.

A particular type of intra-brand competition in the EU derives from another category active in distribution chain, ie parallel traders, who gain their profits from price differentials among Member States. Parallel trade is a form of reimportation, occurring when products protected by the intellectual property (IP) system are first placed into circulation on one market, then reimported into a second market without the authorisation of the original owner of the intellectual property rights (IPRs). As will be explained, the European experience has shown several cases of parallel imports of cheaper medicines from low-priced Member States into higher priced markets.[14]

In order to analyse the main features of the demand side, it is crucial to consider that the final users of prescription medicines are patients, but generally they neither decide on their own which drugs to use nor pay their full price. The final consumer (the patient) has a low involvement in therapeutic choices and differs both from the decision-making subject (the doctor – or, in some cases, the pharmacist) and from the subject on which the price of the drug weighs (typically, national health systems or private insurance companies).[15]

[11] In the market for pharmaceuticals purchased by hospitals, typically the latter manage their own budget expenditure.

[12] Moreover, non-prescription drugs, as they are not reimbursed or subsidised, are typically assumed to be not essential and/or that there are alternative products in the market. In the EU, non-prescription drugs are defined in Art 72 of Directive 2001/83/EC of the European Parliament and of the Council on the Community code relating to medicinal products for human use [2011] OJ L311/67. In the USA, they are regulated by the FDA through OTC Drug monographs. In general, they may also include drugs sold with the advice of the pharmacist (so-called 'behind the counter'). See P Danzon, 'Competition and Antitrust Issues in the Pharmaceutical Industry: Final Report' (2014) 9, https://faculty.wharton.upenn.edu/wp-content/uploads/2017/06/Competition-and-Antitrust-Issues-in-the-Pharmaceutical-IndustryFinal7.2.14.pdf.

[13] F Scott Morton, AD Stern and S Stern, 'The Impact of the Entry of Biosimilars: Evidence from Europe' (2018) 53 *Review of Industrial Organization* 173, 179.

[14] Parallel trade refers to trade in genuine products outside official channels of distribution. It should not be confused with trade in products that infringe on an IPR, such as counterfeit goods. See ch 2.

[15] Doctors decide which prescription medicine the patient will use, but may also advise the patient about which OTC drug to use. Pharmacists may influence the demand for medicines too, as in the

Markets for pharmaceuticals are characterised by a persistent information asymmetry as final users are not able to identify the product which best fits their needs and doctors, as professionals, are usually the sole subjects who are assumed to hold the necessary expertise to take an informed choice on the appropriate therapeutic treatment to adopt and verify its efficacy. It follows that the consumption of drugs is influenced by agency problems.[16] Medicines and healthcare products in general are typically considered as 'experience' or 'credence' goods. The former have features that are not observable for the consumer ex ante, but their quality is revealed after their purchase or consumption; therefore, consumers can only evaluate the quality of such products ex post. Credence goods are those products whose quality cannot be assessed by consumers ex ante and it is hard to verify it even after purchase or use. Both situations may occur in the case of medicines with regard to both their efficacy and safety. Approval by the regulatory agency for the marketing of pharmaceuticals constitutes one means to address such information asymmetry.[17]

The existing practice in the consumption of pharmaceutical products on medical prescription is a central factor, where the choice between different medicines is typically guided by their therapeutic appropriateness and effectiveness rather than by their price. In addition, as a large part of the cost of medicines is supported by public or private health schemes, the reimbursement regime for drugs influences prescribers' behaviour. On the one hand, it should be noted that over the years some European countries have introduced measures incentivising doctors to take prices into consideration in their prescribing practice as a part of their general effort to reduce public expenditures.[18] On the other hand, the fact that typically medicines are not paid for by patients or by prescribers determines the inelasticity of demand and a resulting potential moral hazard.[19] It follows that the context in which they operate leads pharmaceutical companies to often compete through tools other than price, including information to doctors and the financing of clinical studies.

Moreover, the relationship between physicians and pharmaceutical companies is the subject of critical opinions. Doctors are subject to various promotional and detailing activities, and it is widely assumed that marketing efforts of pharmaceutical companies include the adoption of strategies aimed at (unduly) influencing their prescribing behaviour.[20] More generally, pharmaceutical firms

case of substitution laws mentioned above. Moreover, they represent the main source of advice for patients on OTC drugs.

[16] The choice underlying a drug prescription resembles the classical principal-agent model, in which the patient is the 'principal' and the doctor acts as an 'agent', making a choice on the former's behalf. This being a fundamental theory in economics, suffice it to cite SA Ross, 'The Economic Theory of Agency. The Principal's Problem' (1973) 63 *American Economic Review* 134.

[17] Kyle and Scott Morton, 'Markets for Pharmaceutical Products', 765.

[18] For details, see European Commission, 'Joint Report on Health Care and Long-Term Care Systems & Fiscal Sustainability' (2019) Institutional Paper 105, https://ec.europa.eu/info/sites/default/files/economy-finance/ip105_en.pdf.

[19] Kyle and Scott Morton, 'Markets for Pharmaceutical Products', 788.

[20] 'Detailing' refers to the practice of sending company representatives to doctors' offices, in addition to other marketing efforts such as giving doctors free samples, trips, consultancy fees, etc.

are considered not to be an unbiased source of information about their own products and their worthiness compared to competitors.[21] Drug product selection laws are typically designed to address the 'price disconnect' between prescribing doctors and paying insurers and consumers once generic manufacturers have entered the market.[22] They carve out a role for pharmacists, who are more price sensitive than physicians and may recommend cheaper drugs to consumers.[23]

Finally, the existence of large buyers such as national health insurers impacts crucially on the structure of the demand. As will be explained in detail in chapter three, unlike in the US, in general in European countries pharmaceutical firms are subject to forms of price control by regulation and are bound to negotiate prices of medicines with national regulators, acting as monopsonists.

II. THE PRODUCT LIFE CYCLE AND THE COSTS OF INNOVATION

Pharmaceutical products typically derive from a long, risky and costly process. The development of medicines requires a pre-clinical stage, including laboratory tests and clinical trials, at the end of which only a small number of molecules succeed in being found safe and effective.[24] The nature of pharmaceutical products implies that the social cost of a low-quality drug is not comparable to that of other products, thus justifying the pervasive regulation established in the sector.[25] Originator firms, but also independent research entities such as universities or laboratories, often supported by governments, play a pre-eminent role in R&D activity. Large fixed and sunk costs are sustained by originator firms in the development stages of a pharmaceutical product. This pre-launch period, the marketing authorisation (MA) process enacted once a new medicine is effective and safe and the following steps, reimbursement and pricing decisions up to the commercialisation of the product constitute the first phase of the life cycle of a new drug.

[21] Kyle and Scott Morton, 'Markets for Pharmaceutical Products', 768.

[22] MA Carrier and S Shadowen, 'Product Hopping: A New Framework' (2016) 92 *Notre Dame Law Review* 167, 179.

[23] See E Mossialos, M Mrazek and T Walley, 'Regulating Pharmaceuticals in Europe: An Overview' in E Mossialos, M Mrazek and T Walley (eds), *Regulating Pharmaceuticals in Europe: Striving for Efficiency, Equity and Quality* (Maidenhead, Open University Press, 2004) 7 (noting that the doctor–patient relationship has changed in time as patients have become more involved in the choice of treatment and can easily access a lot of detailed medical information through books, the media and the internet; furthermore, in an environment oriented towards containing healthcare spending, patients may be encouraged to care for minor diseases with over-the-counter medicines).

[24] See, eg OECD, 'Pharmaceutical Innovation and Access to Medicines' (2018) 4, according to which: successful development of a new medicine takes an average of 10–15 years; the probability of obtaining marketing approval for a drug entering phase I clinical trials ranges from 7% to 45%, depending on the type of drug and approval process; of 466 novel active substances launched in the US between 1991 and 2009, half achieved lifetime sales of less than $1.5 billion, and only approximately 10% had sales exceeding $10 billion. On product life cycle, see also European Commission, 'Pharmaceutical Sector Inquiry: Final Report (2009) (2009 Sector Inquiry) 49ff.

[25] Kyle and Scott Morton, 'Markets for Pharmaceutical Products', 772.

Global pharmaceutical innovation has been dominated by the US over the past decades.[26] In general, the R&D costs of developing a new drug are very high. The debate on costs incurred by innovative firms is also linked to the lack of transparency of data by pharmaceutical companies. Measuring the degree of innovation related to new drugs is also difficult. Costs depend on several factors, including the type of drug and the likelihood of failure. However, the effective amount of such costs is controversial.[27] A recurrent argument adduced against pharmaceutical companies is that the most innovative products are developed by government laboratories and government-backed universities rather than by private undertakings, which are deemed to prefer to focus on slight variations of existing drugs and the development and the marketing side of the business.[28] Important funding for research is in fact undertaken by governments and public entities, and many fundamental discoveries on which new drugs are based have their origin in public-funded research.[29] Data show that public funding is often at the bottom of the main innovative research, and firms are largely recycling and repurposing existing medicines rather than creating new ones. Recent literature has also shown that lower rates of innovation may derive from the tendency of incumbent pharmaceutical firms to engage in so-called 'killer acquisitions', ie strategies of acquiring innovative targets and terminating their projects in order to eliminate future competition.[30]

[26] The US and the EU are the largest markets for pharmaceuticals in the world. According to data, a significant shift of economic and research activity towards the US occurred during the period 1995–2005 and Europe is also now facing increasing competition from emerging economies, especially Brazil and China (see eg European Federation of Pharmaceutical Industries Associations (EFPIA), 'The Pharmaceutical Industry in Figures – Key Data' (2020) 9, https://www.efpia.eu/media/554521/efpia_pharmafigures_2020_web.pdf).

[27] See, eg in the US, the Tufts Center for the Study of Drug Development's study on the R&D costs of new drug development, which has been particularly influential in the policy debate but is also controversial: JA DiMasi, HG Grabowski and RW Hansen, 'Innovation in the Pharmaceutical Industry: New Estimates of R&D Costs' (2016) 47 *Journal of Health Economics* 20, 27 (estimating the cost of developing a new drug to be in the $2.3–2.8 billion range).

[28] See, eg M Mazzucato, *The Entrepreneurial State: Debunking Public vs Private Sector Myths* (London, Anthem Press, 2013), 64. See also M Angell, *The Truth about the Drug Companies: How They Deceive Us and What to Do about It* (New York, Random House, 2004). The decline of productivity in pharmaceutical markets is a subject of discussion in the literature, which has identified several possible reasons justifying this phenomenon. For a detailed analysis, see Kyle and Scott Morton, 'Markets for Pharmaceutical Products', 777ff.

[29] In general, eg in the US, see data on R&D spending reported by the National Science Foundation's Science and Engineering Indicators 2022, https://ncses.nsf.gov/pubs/nsb20221/data. Details on spending by the National Institute of Health can be found at www.nih.gov/about-nih/what-we-do/budget#note. It should be noted that the Bayh-Dole Act encourages patents on federally funded inventions: 35 USC §§ 200–12 (2012). Subsidisation of R&D of patented prescription medicines by the federal government is the subject of the so-called 'paying-twice' (first for the research and second through the above market pricing of resulting products) critique. See RE Wolitz, 'The Pay-Twice Critique, Government Funding, and Reasonable Pricing Clauses' (2019) 39 *Journal of Legal Medicine* 177; DJ Hemel and LL Ouellette, 'Bayh-Dole beyond Borders' (2017) 4 *Journal of Law and the Biosciences* 282 (analysing two lines of criticism, the first taking the perspective of consumers and taxpayers within the US and the second attacking the effect of Bayh-Dole (and university patenting more broadly) on the developing world).

[30] C Cunningham, F Ederer and S Ma, 'Killer Acquisitions' (2021) 129 *Journal of Political Economy* 649.

Despite dealing mainly with radical innovation, aimed at discovering new drugs containing new chemical entities, which is representative of the overall costs of R&D activity in this sector, this section must also consider the development of existing medicinal products as an important side of the activity of pharmaceutical firms. Incremental innovation may lead, for instance, to the novel use of existing products in new therapeutic areas. However, it is debatable whether the therapeutic benefits deriving from follow-on products (also often called 'me-too drugs', though different and more detailed terms can be found in the specialised literature)[31] outweigh the potential negative effects on the incentives to undertake pioneering innovation and the risks of opportunistic and anti-competitive behaviours by firms which may use such products to artificially extend IP protection against generic competition.[32]

Costs and uncertainty are still higher when dealing with the development and commercialisation of new biological entities. This is due to the distinctive features of biologic products, whose effects on patients are variable and difficult to predict, as well as their manufacturing process, where even small changes may have an unforeseeable impact on the clinical attributes of the drugs. Thus, even if it has been argued that biologic drug development costs are likely comparable in magnitude to the cost of developing new chemical drugs, they are different as they include higher discovery and preclinical expenditures, longer average pre-clinical trial development times, higher costs that are associated with process engineering and manufacturing, but shorter subsequent clinical trial times.[33]

Costs also influence the decision of pharmaceutical firms regarding organisational choices, such as the outsourcing of functions. An example is provided by clinical trials, which typically occur after a pre-clinical stage, are aimed at ascertaining toxicity and include specific steps tests have to follow. Trials constitute an important cost element. Specialised firms known as contract research organisations have emerged in this area, and there is a growing tendency to delocalise trials in emerging markets, such as India and Eastern Europe, where the cost of conducting such studies is lower. Outsourcing is increasingly adopted by pharmaceutical firms also in contract manufacturing and in the marketing sales force.[34]

The high costs described above constitute the main justification for IP protection, it being a decisive element for incentivising R&D efforts by pharmaceutical companies. As will be analysed further in the next chapters, benefits of innovation in this market are crucial to enable patients to take advantage of ever more effective treatments and to allow the discovery of new medicines for diseases for which there is no adequate treatment. The need to preserve such kinds of effort

[31] See, eg JK Aronson and AR Green, 'Me-Too Pharmaceutical Products: History, Definitions, Examples, and Relevance to Drug Shortages and Essential Medicines Lists' (2020) 86 *British Journal of Clinical Pharmacology* 2114.

[32] See chs 2 and 6.

[33] See Scott Morton et al, 'The Impact of the Entry of Biosimilars', 179, and the literature cited therein.

[34] Kyle and Scott Morton, 'Markets for Pharmaceutical Products', 776.

is directly linked to the social value of pharmaceutical products and has led to the adoption of different incentives and rewards, including primarily patents, but also regulatory tools. In this overview, a peculiar position is that of the so-called orphan drugs, ie medicinal products addressed at rare, life-threatening or chronically or seriously debilitating diseases, whose conditions occur so infrequently that the development and marketing of a medicinal product would not be profitable for a pharmaceutical company without the incentives provided by regulation.

After R&D and market launch, the second phase of the life cycle of a new drug covers the period between launch and loss of exclusivity, when originator companies aim at recouping the investments sustained and earning a profit through sales. Once generic products can enter the market, ie in the third phase of the life cycle, the sales of the originator companies and average prices are deemed to drop as a result of competitive pressure exercised by generic entry. However, entry by generic producers may have positive effects on innovation too, as depriving originators of the high profits of their market exclusivity grants may motivate them to carry out further R&D activity for future products. Finally, throughout the lifetime of products, pharmaceutical companies are subject to pharmacovigilance requirements, aimed at monitoring adverse reactions and/or new side effects related to the use of the medicine at issue (also referred to as Phase IV studies). This is also the stage in which further R&D activity is typically conducted by originator companies in order to improve the product or find new applications.[35]

III. THE ACCESS TO THE MARKET: REGULATORY APPROACHES

In general, countries control the entry of new drugs onto the market, with the primary objective of ensuring drug safety. The process of obtaining marketing approval can be extremely costly and time consuming. In the following subsections, the relevant provisions of the European and US regulatory frameworks in accessing the pharmaceuticals market will be analysed.

A. The European Regulatory Framework

In the EU, no medicinal product may be placed on the market of a Member State unless an MA has been issued by the competent authority upon request of the pharmaceutical company.[36] The EU regulatory framework, which is based

[35] European Commission, '2009 Sector Inquiry', 55.

[36] For an overview on the EU regulatory framework, see A Mahalatchimy, 'Regulating Medicines in the European Union' in D Orentlicher and TK Hervey (eds), *The Oxford Handbook of Comparative Health Law* (Oxford, Oxford University Press, 2020) 721. For an analysis of the roots and evolution of EU regulation in the pharmaceutical sector, see F Papadopoulou, *Evergreening Patent Exclusivity*

on Directive 2001/83 and Regulation No 726/2004 as amended by subsequent legislations,[37] provides that applicants may apply for a national authorisation to the concerned Member State or for Union authorisation. There are three methods of obtaining such Union authorisation: the centralised procedure (CP), the mutual recognition procedure (MRP) and the decentralised procedure (DCP). The national procedure, ie a country-specific approval scheme, exists at state level. The submission strategy for a given product will depend on the nature of the product, the target indications, the history of the product and the marketing plan.[38]

The CP, which is based on a single application, a single evaluation and a single authorisation, is used to obtain an MA valid in all EU countries and is mandatory for products derived by biotechnological processes, orphan medicinal products and products containing new active substances for the treatment of specific diseases. This procedure is optional for products containing new active substances not yet authorised in the Union at the time of the entry into force of Regulation No 726/2004, products which constitute a significant therapeutic, scientific or technical innovation or products for which the granting of a Union authorisation would be in the interests of patients' health at Union level.[39] The applicant has to request confirmation that the product is eligible for evaluation through the CP (optional scope). The applications are submitted to the European Medicines Agency (EMA) and evaluated by the Committee for Medicinal Products for Human Use (CHMP).[40] Once granted, the MA is valid

in Pharmaceutical Products. Supplementary Protection Certificates, Orphan Drugs, Paediatric Extensions and ATMPs (Oxford, Hart Publishing, 2021) 1ff. Medicinal product is defined by Directive 2001/83/EC, Art 1 as '(a) Any substance or combination of substances presented as having properties for treating or preventing disease in human beings; or (b) Any substance or combination of substances which may be used in or administered to human beings either with a view to restoring, correcting or modifying physiological functions by exerting a pharmacological, immunological or metabolic action, or to making a medical diagnosis'.

[37] See Directive 2001/83/EC and subsequent amending legislation; Regulation (EC) No 726/2004 of the European Parliament and of the Council laying down Community procedures for the authorisation and supervision of medicinal products for human and veterinary use and establishing a European Medicines Agency [2004] OJ L136/1, and subsequent amending legislation. It should be noted that specific rules are set out for Paediatric Use Marketing Authorisation by Regulation (EC) No 1901/2006 of the European Parliament and of the Council on medicinal products for paediatric use and amending Regulation (EEC) No 1768/92, Directive 2001/20/EC, Directive 2001/83/EC and Regulation (EC) No 726/2004 [2004] OJ L378/1.

[38] In addition, Art 6(1), subpara 2 of Directive 2001/83/EC provides that when a medicinal product has been granted an initial MA, any additional strengths, pharmaceutical forms, administration routes, presentations, variations or extensions must also be granted an authorisation or be included in the initial MA: all these MAs are considered as belonging to the same 'global marketing authorisation' in particular for the purpose of the application of Art 10 of the Directive, which lays down rules on data exclusivity and market protection.

[39] Regulation 726/2004, Art 3(1)–(2). See also Article 3(3) concerning generic products.

[40] For further details on the procedure and timing, see Regulation No 726/2004, Arts 5–10. Once a central MA has been issued, the maintenance of existing national MAs or the issuing of new national MAs for the same medicinal product could be envisaged only as long as the therapeutic indications are different in national and central MAs. Indeed, if a product falls under the optional scope of the centralised procedure, the applicant has the choice of using either the centralised or the national (decentralised/mutual recognition) procedure for the same medicinal product.

for five years and may be renewed on the basis of a re-evaluation by the EMA of the risk–benefit balance upon application by the holder at least nine months before the MA expires.[41] It should be noted that the refusal of a Union MA constitutes a prohibition on the placing on the market of the medicinal product concerned throughout the EU.[42]

The other two procedures both concern the applications for MAs in more than one Member State.[43] The applicant must submit an application containing the same information required for the CP to the competent authority of each of the Member States where the MA is sought. Through the MRP, manufacturers which have previously obtained an MA in a Member State – the so-called Reference Member State (RMS) – can apply for its recognition in the other given Concerned Member States (CMSs).[44] The DCP addresses the cases where a product has not been granted an MA at the time of application. The different national applications must be based on identical dossiers in the case of MRP as well as in the case of DCP, which rely on the principle of mutual recognition and thus provide that assessment on the medicinal product for the grant of an MA is only conducted by one Member State (the RMS).[45]

Legislation also provides the possibility of requesting conditional MAs for drugs aimed at the treatment, prevention or medical diagnosis of seriously debilitating or life-threatening diseases, or to be used in emergency situations in response to public health threats, and for orphan drugs. In such cases, conditional MAs can be granted if the applicant has not yet provided all clinical data required to demonstrate the safety and efficacy of the relevant medicinal product, though certain requirements must still be met, eg: the risk–benefit balance of the medicinal product is positive; it is likely that the applicant will be in a position to provide the comprehensive clinical data; unmet medical needs will be fulfilled; and the benefit to public health of the immediate availability on the market of the medicinal product concerned outweighs the risk inherent in the fact that additional data are still required. The holder of a conditional MA is required to provide data and evidence that support the conclusion that the benefits continually outweigh the risks. This kind of MA is valid for one year but may be reviewed annually. Once the applicant has fulfilled the specific obligations requested in the conditional MA, the MA may be granted unconditionally.[46]

If comprehensive data cannot be provided by the applicant and it is not likely that this would become possible in a short time, legislation still allows for the

[41] Regulation 726/2004, Art 14.

[42] Regulation 726/2004, Art 12(2).

[43] National procedures have been harmonised by Directive 2001/83/EC.

[44] The competent authority in each CMS has 90 days to decide whether it agrees with the RMS's marketing approval decision; in case of disagreement, the RMS sends the concerns to the CHMP and, if a consensus is not reached after 60 days, the procedure moves into arbitration. See Directive 2001/83/EC, Arts 28–29.

[45] Directive 2001/83/EC, Arts 28–39.

[46] Commission Regulation (EC) No 507/2006 on the conditional marketing authorisation for medicinal products for human use falling within the scope of Regulation (EC) No 726/2004 of the European Parliament and of the Council [2006] OJ L92/6, Arts 4–7.

granting of MAs under exceptional circumstances.[47] For example, MAs can be granted when the indications for which the product in question is intended are encountered so rarely that the applicant cannot reasonably be expected to provide comprehensive evidence or when, in the present state of scientific knowledge, comprehensive information cannot be provided or it would be contrary to the generally accepted principles of medical ethics to collect such information. The authorisation under exceptional circumstances is subject to a requirement for the applicant to introduce specific procedures, in particular concerning the safety of the medicinal product, notification to the competent authorities of any incident relating to its use and action to be taken. It is valid for five years, but must be reassessed annually.

When an MA is requested for a generic product of a previously authorised drug, it is possible to file a so-called 'abridged' application exempting the applicant from the requirement to prove safety and efficacy. A generic product is defined by Directive 2001/83/EC as 'a medicinal product which has the same qualitative and quantitative composition in active substances and the same pharmaceutical form as the reference medicinal product, and whose bioequivalence with the reference medicinal product has been demonstrated by appropriate bioavailability studies'. In this case, the EMA relies on the tests and trials for the reference product, but only after the expiration of the data exclusivity period of the reference product itself.[48]

An abridged application is also provided in the case of biosimilars. 'Biosimilar' is defined as a biological medicine highly similar to another already approved biological drug.[49] This kind of medicine typically cannot be considered as generic mainly due to manufacturing process characteristics, raw materials used, molecular characteristics and therapeutic modes of action. The rationale behind the establishment of the abridged procedure is to accelerate competitive challenges to the original patented products. However, as clarified above, due to the specific characteristics of biological drugs and the impossibility of fully replicating the reference product, substitution of originator biologics by biosimilar products is not as simple as that between originators and generics for small-molecule medicines. Moreover, the efficacy of biosimilars is also more difficult to prove, in particular when they relate to medicines targeting relatively small patient numbers, so that the possibility for clinical trials is limited. Such peculiarities have led to the adoption of an abridged procedure for biosimilars different from the existing regime valid for generics. The EU pioneered the regulation in this field by introducing a biosimilar pathway in 2004,[50] since when

[47] Regulation 726/2004, Art 14(8) in conjunction with the relevant provisions of Annex I, Part II of Directive 2001/83/EC.

[48] Directive 2001/83/EC, Art 10(1) and (2).

[49] Directive 2001/83/EC, Art 10(3) and (4).

[50] Directive 2004/27/EC of the European Parliament and of the Council of 31 March 2004 amending Directive 2001/83/EC on the Community code relating to medicinal products for human use [2004] OJ L136/34.

it has approved the highest number of biosimilars worldwide.[51] All medicines produced using biotechnology must be approved through the EMA via the centralised procedure, so that nearly all biosimilars approved for use in the EU have been approved centrally. According to the EU rules, additional data, in particular concerning the toxicological and clinical profile, are required in order to demonstrate biosimilarity.[52]

Finally, it should be noted that approval procedures have been challenged with regard to their results in terms of expedited access to new therapeutics. One initiative taken by EMA is Priority Medicines (PRIME), launched in March 2016 to provide supplementary support for certain priority medicines. A medicine is eligible for PRIME if early clinical data show its potential to benefit patients with unmet medical needs, as it thus might offer a major therapeutic advantage over existing treatments or benefit patients without treatment options. Moreover, the EMA has developed an 'adaptive pathways' approach, according to which an applicant may either (i) obtain (conditional) marketing authorisation based on early data using 'surrogate endpoints' (early time points, or a smaller population sample), expanding later with additional clinical data to reduce uncertainty, or (ii) obtain approval in stages, beginning with a narrow patient population and expanding later to a broader patient population. This kind of approach can be also found in proposals advanced in the literature to make the approval of drugs more responsive to scientific development and to foster connections between regulation and innovation. Such ideas are based on the alleged increase in costs and complexity of clinical trials that are not matched with a corresponding increase in the number of new drug approvals.[53] However, the adaptive pathway has attracted strong interest as well as being met with many questions and doubts, as it necessarily involves a trade-off between early access and certainty about the risks and benefits of a drug.[54]

B. The US Regulatory Framework

Despite some similarities, the US regulatory framework is remarkably different from that of the EU. The Federal Food, Drug, and Cosmetic (FD&C) Act is the

[51] EMA and European Commission, 'Biosimilars in the EU' (2019) www.ema.europa.eu/en/documents/leaflet/biosimilars-eu-information-guide-healthcare-professionals_en.pdf.

[52] Directive 2001/83/EC, Annex I, Part II, s 4.

[53] G Rasi and S Bonini, 'Innovative Medicines: New Regulatory Procedures for the Third Millennium' (2015) 15(Suppl 1) *Expert Opinion on Biological Therapy* 5. See also the overview provided by B Dorbeck-Jung, 'Transcending the Myth of Law's Stifling Technological Innovation: How Adaptive Drug Licensing Processes Are Maintaining Legitimate Regulatory Connections' in R Brownsword, E Scotford and K Yeung (eds), *The Oxford Handbook of Law, Regulation and Technology* (Oxford, Oxford University Press, 2016) 929.

[54] Mahalatchimy, 'Regulating Medicines', 9–10. The author explains that adaptive approaches require the involvement of Health Technology Assessment (HTA) bodies in the discussion of individual product development programmes. The involvement of HTA bodies in the new adaptive pathways approach is part of a new European trend of promoting collaboration between regulators and HTA bodies. See also ch 3.

basic food and drug law of the United States. Among the amendments to the FD&C Act, a fundamental point of reference is the Drug Price Competition and Patent Term Restoration Act, commonly known as the Hatch-Waxman Act.[55] Also, US rules provide that a pharmaceutical company must obtain approval from the Food and Drug Administration (FDA) before it may market a new drug product. The FDA is the agency within the US Department of Health and Human Services responsible, inter alia, for protecting the public health by assuring the safety, effectiveness, quality and security of drugs.[56] For a new drug, the approval process requires the submission of a new drug application (NDA), which comprises exhaustive information about the drug, including safety and efficacy studies, the method of producing the drug and any patents issued on drug substance (active ingredient), drug product (composition or formulation) or methods of use.[57] The FDA publishes the patent information submitted in NDAs in 'Approved Drug Products with Therapeutic Equivalence Evaluations', otherwise known as the Orange Book.

A different procedure may be enacted for generic drugs, as a potential manufacturer of a generic version of a patented drug is allowed to file an abbreviated application: with this short-form application, known as an abbreviated new drug application (ANDA), the applicant must demonstrate bioequivalence of the generic drug with the branded one. If it does, the FDA assigns the generic drug an 'AB' rating and allows the applicant to not include safety and efficacy data and to rely on the NDA application of the patented drug, ie it allows it to piggyback on its predecessor's clinical research.[58] To demonstrate bioequivalence, the applicant must acquire substantial quantities of the referenced branded drug and conduct testing comparing the generic version against it. A particular category is that of 'authorised generics', which are created by makers of branded drugs under the same NDA authorisation as the original branded drug, and may be sold before drug patents expire.[59]

With regard to biological products, a biologics licence application (BLA) is required for them under the Public Health Service (PHS) Act. US Congress

[55] The Federal Food, Drug, and Cosmetic (FD&C) Act, PL 75-717, 52 Stat 1040 (1938) is codified into Title 21, ch 9 of the United States Code; Drug Price Competition and Patent Term Restoration Act of 1984 (commonly known as the Hatch-Waxman Act) PL 98-417, 98 Stat 1585 (codified at 21 USC §§ 355, 360 (2012); 35 USC §§ 156, 271 (2012)), amended by Medicare Prescription Drug, Improvement, and Modernization Act of 2003, PL 108-173, 117 Stat 2066.

[56] 'Drug' is defined as an 'article' which is 'intended for use in the diagnosis, cure, mitigation, treatment, or prevention of disease' or 'intended to affect the structure or any function of the body': 21 USC § 321(g).

[57] With regard to NDA, see 21 USC § 355(b)(2). In addition, a further type of application, the Investigational New Drug Application (IND), should be noted. It is a request for authorisation from the FDA to administer an investigational drug or biological product to humans across state lines before marketing application, being the first step in the FDA's review process aimed at starting clinical trials. See 21 USC § 312.

[58] 21 USC §355(j).

[59] For an overview on authorised generics, see JR Thomas, 'Pharmaceutical Patents' in T Takenaka (ed), *Research Handbook on Patent Law and Theory*, 2nd edn (Cheltenham, Edward Elgar, 2019) 353, 362.

only passed the Biologics Price Competition and Innovation (BPCI) Act, which established a specific procedure for biosimilars, in 2010, as part of President Obama's health reform (Affordable Care Act).[60] The BPCI Act has created an abbreviated licensure pathway in section 351(k) of the PHS Act for biological products shown to be biosimilar to or interchangeable with an FDA-licensed reference product. This procedure permits a biosimilar biological product to be licensed based on less than a full complement of product-specific preclinical and clinical data. In particular, a biosimilar is defined as a biological product that is highly similar to and has no clinically meaningful differences from an existing reference product: as to similarity, the manufacturer is required to demonstrate it by extensively analysing the structure and function of both products, being minor differences between clinically inactive components acceptable, although any of them are carefully evaluated by the FDA to ensure the biosimilar meets the FDA's high approval standards; as to the absence of clinically meaningful differences, the manufacturer must demonstrate the safety, purity and potency of the proposed biosimilar product through human pharmacokinetic (exposure) and pharmacodynamic (response) studies, an assessment of clinical immunogenicity and, if needed, additional clinical studies. The PHS Act also identifies a further category: that of interchangeable products. An interchangeable product is a biosimilar product that meets additional requirements outlined by the BPCI Act, including information aimed at showing that such product is expected to produce the same clinical result as the reference product in any given patient. An interchangeable product also differs from a biosimilar in that the former may be substituted for the reference product without the involvement of the prescriber.

The Hatch-Waxman Act is generally defined as a compromise between the conflicting interests of pharmaceutical innovators and generic companies.[61] A peculiar feature of the Hatch-Waxman Act, which cannot be found in other systems such as the EU one, are the rules applicable to incentivise generic entry. According to such rules, when a generic manufacturer files an ANDA, it is also required to file a certification that, in the opinion of the applicant and to the best of its knowledge, the proposed generic drug does not infringe any patent listed with the FDA as covering the patented drug. The generic manufacturer can satisfy this requirement by certifying one of the following four options with respect to the patent for the listed drug: (I) that the patent information has not been filed; (II) that the patent has expired; (III) the date on which the patent will expire; or (IV) that the patent is invalid or will not be infringed by the manufacture,

[60] Biologics Price Competition and Innovation Act of 2009, PL 111-148, 124 Stat 804 (2010) (BPCI Act). The BPCI Act amended the PHS Act and other statutes to create an abbreviated licensure pathway for biological products (see Patient Protection and Affordable Care Act, Pub L No 111-148, 124 Stat 119 (2010), §§ 7001-03). The requirements for the licensure of a proposed biosimilar or proposed interchangeable product are set forth in §351(k) of the PHS Act (42 USC 76 262(k)), added by the BPCI Act.

[61] See E Stotland Weiswasser and SD Danzis, 'The Hatch-Waxman Act: History, Structure, and Legacy' (2003) 71 *Antitrust Law Journal* 585.

use or sale of the new drug for which the application is submitted.[62] These are commonly called paragraph I, II, III and IV certifications, respectively.

When a would-be generic manufacturer attempts to enter the market prior to the expiration of the brand-name's patent by filing a paragraph IV certification, it must consult the Orange Book and provide written notice to each listed patent owner impacted by the ANDA. Technically, a paragraph IV certification constitutes an 'artificial' act of patent infringement.[63] As a consequence, if the patent holder initiates an infringement suit within 45 days after the generic applicant files its ANDA and paragraph IV certification, FDA approval of the generic drug is automatically stayed for 30 months, unless the patent expires before that time or is judicially determined to be invalid or not infringed – in which case, and also if a suit is not filed within that time, the ANDA can be approved immediately.[64]

In order to encourage generic entry and challenges to weak patents, the Hatch-Waxman Act rewards the first generic manufacturer submitting an ANDA and a paragraph IV certification by providing it with a 180-day period of marketing exclusivity starting from the date of the first commercial marketing by the first filer and during which the FDA cannot approve subsequent ANDA applications. During this period, the first filer's product will be the only generic equivalent on the market,[65] as a later filer may only force the first filer to use its reward (ie enter with exclusivity) or else lose it if the later filer wins a patent suit of its own.[66]

[62] 21 USC §355(j)(2)(A)(vii).

[63] R Feldman and E Frondorf, 'Drug Wars: A New Generation of Generic Pharmaceutical Delay' (2016) 53 *Harvard Journal on Legislation* 499, 507.

[64] It should be noted that under the Hatch-Waxman Act an NDA holder could obtain multiple 30-month stays by strategically listing its patents related to a drug product in the Orange Book: in response to the 2002 FTC study on 'Generic Drug Entry Prior to Patent Expiration' (www.ftc.gov/sites/default/files/documents/reports/generic-drug-entry-prior-patent-expiration-ftc-study/genericdrugstudy_0.pdf), showing that brand-name drug companies had been abusing the 30-month stay provision to delay generic entry, the FDA amended its rules to allow only one 30-month stay and Congress codified these rules in the Medicare Prescription Drug, Improvement, and Modernization Act of 2003. An alternative to paragraph IV certification is the 'section viii carve-out' (also known as the 'skinny label'), which is reserved for patents on methods of using a drug (21 USC § 505(j)(2)(A)(viii)): under this option, the generic drug's proposed labelling omits, to the FDA's satisfaction, uses of the drug that would infringe the method-of-use patent. It does not trigger the consequences of paragraph IV. Controversy has arisen in particular after the Federal Circuit decision in *GlaxoSmithKline LLC v Teva Pharmaceuticals USA*, Inc, Nos 2018-1976 and 2018-2023 (5 Aug 2021) (holding FDA-approved language in a generic drug label to be the basis for inducement under 35 USC § 271(b)). Petition for certiorari was filed. See Brief of 42 Professors of Law, Economics, Business, and Medicine as Amici Curiae in Support of the Petition (10 August 2022) https://www.supremecourt.gov/DocketPDF/22/22-37/233146/20220810074700359_brief-teva-gsk-cert.pdf.

[65] However, a first-filer can forfeit its exclusivity under certain conditions (eg due to a failure to market by a specified date, a failure to obtain tentative FDA approval, withdrawal of the ANDA, amendment of the ANDA to non-paragraph IV status, commission of an antitrust violation or expiration of the patent). See 21 USC § 355(j)(5)(D).

[66] According to the Hatch-Waxman Act (21 USC § 355(j)(5)(D)(i)(I)(bb)(AA)), only an appellate win by the later filer triggers the first filer's obligation to enter with exclusivity, which it must do within 75 days or else forfeit the bounty. As clarified by C Scott Hemphill and MA Lemley, 'Earning Exclusivity: Generic Drug Incentives and the Hatch-Waxman Act' (2011) 77 *Antitrust Law Journal* 947, 964, 'The resulting delay from this process – file the ANDA, conduct the district court suit, win the appeal, wait until just before the end of seventy-five days, then wait another 180 days – can easily stretch to several years. Moreover, in some cases, the settlement between the brand-name firm

This exclusivity period is very valuable to generic manufacturers, as they can sell their product at a price significantly higher than they could if multiple generics were on the market, and it creates a de facto duopoly between the brand company and the generic company for the first six months of generic competition.[67] As will be analysed in depth in chapter five, this system has created a peculiar ground for anti-competitive gaming behaviours by pharmaceutical firms.

It should be noted that the BPCI Act provides for the first approved generic biologic a period of exclusivity which depends on a number of conditions, and can range between 12 and 42 months.[68]

Regulations such as the federal Hatch-Waxman Act and state substitution laws foster widespread generic competition. Recently, an important statute has made available a pathway for developers of potential drug and biological products to obtain samples of brand products that they need to support their applications. This law is generally known as the CREATES Act (Creating and Restoring Equal Access to Equivalent Samples Act), and was enacted in December 2019 as part of the Further Consolidated Appropriations Act of 2020 (section 610).[69] This legislation also addresses the concerns relating to the manipulation by originator companies of the FDA safety regulations, such as the Risk Evaluation and Mitigation Strategy (REMS),[70] created by the Food and Drug Administration Amendments Act of 2007 (FDAAA).[71] Section 505-1 FDAAA authorises the FDA to require sponsors of drug applications to submit a proposed REMS if the agency determines that it is necessary to ensure that a drug's benefits outweigh its risks, considering several factors (including the

and the first filer permits the first filer to launch upon FDA approval or launch of the later filer's product, further reducing the incentive to pursue this strategy'. See also MA Carrier, 'Payment after Actavis' (2014) 100 *Iowa Law Review* 7, 15. The Author notes that the 2003 Medicare Amendments 'were largely toothless' as 'they provide for the forfeiture of the first-filer's exclusivity period upon the later of: (i) 75 days after FDA approval; or (ii) 75 days after an appellate court decision finding invalidity or non-infringement. But appellate court decisions typically are not issued until years after a lawsuit challenging settlement is filed. … As a result, the forfeiture provisions do not typically apply.' It should be noted that during the 180-day exclusivity period, the authorised generics mentioned before can be marketed (see ch 5, s B).

[67] Feldman and Frondorf, 'Drug Wars', 508.

[68] BPCI Act, § 351(k)(6). The first generic biologic can have an exclusivity period of one year after commercial product launch. Such period may be delayed to: 18 months after – (i) a final court decision on all patents in suit in an action instituted under subsection (l)(6) against the applicant that submitted the application for the first approved interchangeable biosimilar biological product; or (ii) the dismissal with or without prejudice of an action instituted under subsection (l)(6) against the applicant that submitted the application for the first approved interchangeable biosimilar biological product; or (i) 42 months after approval of the first interchangeable biosimilar biological product if the applicant that submitted such application has been sued under subsection (l)(6) and such litigation is still ongoing within such 42-month period; or (ii) 18 months after approval of the first interchangeable biosimilar biological product if the applicant that submitted such application has not been sued under subsection (l)(6).

[69] Division N, § 610 of the Further Consolidated Appropriations Act, 2020 (Public Law No 116-94).

[70] US Department of Health and Human Services et al, 'REMS: FDA's Application of Statutory Factors in determining When a REMS Is Necessary – Guidance for Industry' (2019) www.fda.gov/media/100307/download.

[71] 21 USC § 355-1 (Supp 2016).

population size likely to use the drug; the seriousness of the disease; the expected benefit of the drug; the expected duration of treatment; the seriousness of adverse effects; and the novelty of the medicine at issue). This may apply to any NDA, ANDA or BLA. Depending on the risks associated with a specific drug, among the several elements that the FDA may require, REMS may comprise, where necessary, elements to assure safe use (ETASU), which are essentially restrictions on the manner in which drugs are provided to patients and may include prescriber experience requirements, certification systems, patient monitoring or registration, or controlled distribution. ETASU may require that the drug: only be prescribed by healthcare providers having particular training or experience, or who are specially certified; be dispensed by certain specially certified pharmacies, practitioners or healthcare settings; be dispensed to patients only in certain healthcare settings, such as hospitals; and be dispensed to patients with evidence or other documentation of safe-use conditions, such as laboratory test results. ETASU may also require that patients using the drug be monitored or enrolled in a registry. Thus, REMS may prohibit the sale by distributors to persons or organisations not approved in the programme. As will be further mentioned in chapter four, experience has shown that REMS may be used by drugmakers in order to restrict generic competition, preventing generic manufacturers from obtaining samples of the brand drug. Section 610 of the Further Consolidated Appropriations Act provides a private right of action allowing developers to sue a licence holder that refuses to sell them product samples on commercially reasonable, market-based terms.

To conclude this overview, it should be noted that the FDA sought to expedite the development and approval of new medicines, as did the EMA, by including: a fast track, designed to facilitate the development and expedite the review of drugs to treat serious conditions and fill an unmet medical need;[72] breakthrough therapy designation, aimed at offering expedited development and review of drugs intended to treat a serious or life-threatening condition and that indicate 'substantial improvement over existing therapies' based on preliminary clinical evidence;[73] accelerated approval, allowing drugs for serious conditions that fill an unmet medical need to be approved based on a surrogate or an intermediate clinical endpoint;[74] and a 'priority review' designation, concerning the evaluation of applications for drugs that, if approved, would be significant improvements in the safety or effectiveness of the treatment, diagnosis or

[72] FD&C Act, § 506(b), as added by § 112 of the Food and Drug Administration Modernization Act of 1997 (FDAMA) and amended by § 901 of the Food and Drug Administration Safety and Innovation Act of 2012 (FDASIA).

[73] FD&C Act, § 506 (a), as added by § 902 FDASIA.

[74] 21 CFR part 314, subpart H; 21 CFR part 601, subpart E; § 506(c) of the FD&C Act, as amended by § 901 FDASIA. A surrogate endpoint is a marker, eg a laboratory measurement, radiographic image or other measure that is thought to predict clinical benefit, but is not itself a measure of clinical benefit. An intermediate clinical endpoint is a measure of a therapeutic effect that is considered reasonably likely to predict the clinical benefit of a drug, such as an effect on irreversible morbidity and mortality.

prevention of serious conditions and providing for the FDA to take action within six months (compared to 10 months under a standard review).[75]

IV. CONCLUDING REMARKS

The analysis of the rules governing access to pharmaceutical markets in the EU and the US shows common features and divergences between these two systems. Both systems rely on the establishment of an authorisation system governed by competent medicines agencies aimed at ensuring safety and quality of the medicinal products.[76] As, in both jurisdictions, the requirement to establish safety applies before product launch, medicinal products must be the subjects of extensive applications presenting the results of studies performed and asking permission to launch from regulatory agencies. To secure product safety, both jurisdictions also impose 'quality' requirements, a prerequisite which generally means that the manufacturer must tightly control the manufacturing process in order to prevent errors and ensure consistency in product characteristics. In line with this, a medical product may be launched only if its benefits outweigh its risks, based on the information available at the time.[77]

Another important common feature is that both EU and US systems facilitate entry of manufacturers of non-innovative products. This is pursued by lowering the requirements for application by those companies, in the case of both generic and biosimilar products, although the abridged procedures are different due to the specific features of large-molecule drugs. This choice is grounded on the idea of encouraging the use of generics and biosimilar medicines in order to expedite competitive challenges to the original patented products and to allow cost savings for buyers. However, a specific feature of the US framework is that rules link regulatory approval of generic applications with the patents held by the corresponding innovator, and the Hatch-Waxman Act provides for a unique system that incentivises and rewards challenges to patented products by would-be generic entrants.

[75] The two-tiered system of review times was created by the FDA under the Prescription Drug User Fee Act (PDUFA), first passed by Congress in 1992.

[76] There can be some slight variations in the terminology adopted. See E Lietzan and PJ Zettler, 'Regulating Medicines in the United States' in Orentlicher and Hervey, *The Oxford Handbook of Comparative Health Law*, 690 (noting that the overall goal of the European medicines framework is usually said to be ensuring the safety, efficacy and quality of medicines – where quality is a broad concept that refers generally to the identity, strength, purity and similar features of a medicine that allows it to reach the required levels of safety and effectiveness – while generally, in the USA, reference is simply made to ensuring the safety and effectiveness of medicines; however, both jurisdictions place the same high emphasis on product quality).

[77] In both jurisdictions the regulatory framework governing medicines at any given time reflects the then-acceptable level of uncertainty about the safety and effectiveness of particular interventions given the cost and delay that would be involved in generating additional evidence. See E Lietzan, A Mahalatchimy and PJ Zettler, 'Introduction to Medical Products Law' in Orentlicher and Hervey, *The Oxford Handbook of Comparative Health Law*, 684, 687.

2

Regulating Exclusivity

I. THE INTERPLAY BETWEEN REGULATORY EXCLUSIVITIES AND INTELLECTUAL PROPERTY RIGHTS

RULES ON MARKETING authorisation, treated in the previous chapter, must be read in conjunction with the provisions providing protection to new pharmaceutical products, which generally benefit from two main forms of protection: intellectual property rights (IPRs) and regulatory exclusivities.

As a necessary premise, it is worth stressing that, generally, IPRs are considered the main (and inevitable) tool to compensate the costs and risks that innovative pharmaceutical research implies. However, it would be misleading to not consider the essential relationship between the patent system and the sector-specific regulation, which work independently from one another but in parallel in the pharmaceutical sector. The traditional idea that 'it is the patent system that makes drug development profitable, and drug regulation that makes it costly' disregards how drug regulation has become an increasingly important source of market exclusivity for innovating firms.[1] In fact, both patent rules and drug regulations limit entry into the pharmaceutical market, albeit pursuing different purposes. In theory, the patent system seeks to promote scientific progress by awarding limited-term monopolies on new inventions; drug regulation aims at protecting consumers from unsafe or ineffective products and controlling prices. But drug regulation also shares with patents the goal of promoting innovation in the pharmaceutical sector by imposing limits on competition and market entry through regulatory exclusivities.

The roles of both types of protection have been debated in the literature, with some scholars claiming that regulatory exclusivity could be better suited than patent law to protecting heavily regulated industries like pharmaceuticals.[2]

[1] RS Eisenberg, 'The Role of the FDA in Innovation Policy' (2007) 13 *Michigan Telecommunications and Technology Law Review* 345, 349 (defining the exclusivities administered by the FDA in the context of pharmaceutical technologies as 'pseudo-patents'). See also Y Heled, 'Regulatory Competitive Shelters' (2015) 76 *Ohio State Law Journal* 299, 305 (using the terminology of regulatory competitive shelters (RCSs), which are the result of non-action by an agency due to a temporary loss of the agency's ability to use its powers to benefit applicants subsequent to the RCS beneficiary; RCSs 'effectuate a competitive advantage in the relevant market or product and, often, even de facto monopoly status with respect to a particular product').

[2] See, eg Eisenberg, 'The Role of the FDA'; JF Cárdena-Navia, 'Thirty Years of Flawed Incentives: An Empirical an Economic Analysis of Hatch-Waxman Patent-Term Restoration' (2014) 29 *Berkeley Technology Law Journal* 1301, 1376–81; JR Thomas, 'The End of "Patent Medicines"? Thoughts on the Rise of Regulatory Exclusivities' (2015) 70 *Food & Drug Law Journal* 39.

In any case, due to the increasing role of drug regulation in fostering innovation, scholars have found a 'shifting functional balance' of patents and drug regulation.[3] In the following sections both IP and regulatory exclusivities will be examined in order to outline their roles and functioning in the pharmaceutical industry.

It should be noted that in some countries, the practice of linking the marketing approval of generic drugs with the originator drug's patent status is established by law ('patent linkage'), so that such marketing approval cannot be provided until a valid patent on the reference product exists. Whereas, as seen in the previous chapter, in the US the concept is statutorily recognised in the Hatch-Waxman Act, the EU forbids any such patent linkage system and regulatory bodies' assessment is confined to quality, safety and efficacy of the product concerned.[4] Patent linkage is controversial for two main reasons: first, it establishes a relationship between the assessment made by the drug regulatory authorities and the patent status, which are two separate issues; and second, it is considered a practice that favours patent holders and disadvantages generic producers in accessing the market.[5]

II. INTELLECTUAL PROPERTY RIGHTS IN THE PHARMACEUTICAL INDUSTRY: AN OVERVIEW ON THE ROLE OF PATENTS

As a general rule, a patent confers on its owner the exclusive right to prevent third parties from making, using, offering for sale, selling, or importing the invention without the owner's consent for a period of 20 years in all TRIPS (Agreement on Trade-Related Aspects of Intellectual Property Rights)-compliant parties, including the EU and the US.[6]

With specific reference to the pharmaceutical sector, as a premise it is worth stressing that marketing authorisations (MAs) are issued on the basis of scientific criteria concerning the quality, safety and efficacy of the medicinal product concerned. For the peculiarities of the pharmaceutical products and their essential function serving the fundamental right to health, patents play a crucial role in this sector compared to others having similar high rates of patenting.

[3] RS Eisenberg, 'The Shifting Functional Balance of Patents and Drug Regulation' (2001) *Health Affairs* 119.

[4] See 21 USC §355(j)(2)(A)(vii); European Commission, 'Pharmaceutical Sector Inquiry: Final Report' (2009) (2009 Sector Inquiry) 315 (clarifying that Article 81 of Regulation (EC) 726/2004 and Article 126 of Directive (EC) 2001/83 outlaw patent linkage and that the Commission may launch infringement proceedings against Member States not complying with these provisions, as reported therein).

[5] FM Abbott, 'Health and Intellectual Property Rights' in GL Burci and B Toebes (eds), *Research Handbook on Global Health Law* (Cheltenham, Edward Elgar, 2018) 135, 143.

[6] Agreement on Trade-Related Aspects of Intellectual Property Rights, 15 April 1994, Marrakesh Agreement Establishing the World Trade Organization, Annex 1C, 1869 UNTS 299, 33 ILM 1197 (1994) (TRIPS Agreement) Art 28.

In industries such as the pharmaceutical one, in which new products usually include relatively few patentable elements, patents are generally used by firms to collect monopoly rents, whether by commercialising the inventions themselves or licensing them to other firms, or to block rivals from developing competing technologies.[7] Whereas formulating an innovative drug requires a huge investment, typically copying it involves less effort and may allow the imitator to sell the copied product at a price significantly lower than the inventor, limiting the first-mover advantage and its incentive to innovate. However, by giving to the innovator absolute protection from competition for a certain period of time, patents create a sort of legal monopoly, which may lead to higher prices of drugs in the short term. The trade-off between such a monopoly and the supposed stronger investment incentives in the longer term recalls the relationship between the economic concepts of allocative efficiency in a static manner and dynamic efficiency.[8] This is a classic topic, and the literature shows both scholars extolling the virtues of patent protection in promoting pharmaceutical innovation and others criticising patents for providing too much protection for drugs.[9]

As already noted, the relationship between IPRs and competition law is a complex one, as the extensive body of literature on the topic reveals. In addition, social feelings are torn about the protection given by patent law in order to ensure profit maximisation to pharmaceutical firms, as this legitimate goal may conflict with the general call to provide affordable medicines to patients. According to

[7] Eisenberg, 'The Shifting Functional Balance', 120.

[8] A Chowdhury and A Gaigl, 'The Economics of Competition Law and of Pharmaceutical Patents' in G Muscolo and G Pitruzzella (eds), *Competition and Patent Law in the Pharmaceutical Sector: An International Perspective* (Alphen aan den Rijn, Kluwer, 2016) 5, 7–9. Two distinct theories of patents, the 'reward theory' and the 'contract theory', are customarily adopted by the courts to justify the patent system. According to the former theory – by far the most prominent approach to the economic analysis of patents – the function of the patent system is to remunerate successful innovators so as to encourage R&D effort. In contrast, the latter emphasises the 'non-rival' nature of innovation and, on the assumption that absent patent protection firms can practice their innovations secretly, it views patents as a 'contract' between innovators and society, whereby a temporary property right is granted in exchange for disclosure. Thus, the contract theory holds that the function of the patent system is to promote the diffusion of innovative knowledge. For an overview on the arguments of the 'incentive to invent' theory and the 'incentive to disclose' theory, see RS Eisenberg, 'Patents and the Progress of Science: Exclusive Rights and Experimental Use' (1989) 56 *University of Chicago Law Review* 1017, 1024ff.

[9] The economic literature emphasises a basic trade-off between the welfare gains deriving from stronger innovation incentives provided by patents and the welfare loss created by the resulting higher prices. See the fundamental work of KJ Arrow, 'Economic Welfare and the Allocation of Resources for Invention' in R Nelson (ed), *The Rate and Direction of Economic Activities: Economic and Social Factors* (Princeton, Princeton University Press, 1962) 609. For an overview, see R Moufang, 'Patentability of Pharmaceutical Innovation: The European Perspective' in J Drexl and N Lee, *Pharmaceutical Innovation, Competition and Patent Law. A Trilateral Perspective* (Cheltenham, Edward Elgar, 2013) 54 (summarising the different theories deriving from Arrow and Schumpeter). The more recent empirical literature increasingly investigates the causal relationship between IPRs and inventive activity. See, eg MK Kyle and AM McGahan, 'Investments in Pharmaceuticals Before and After TRIPS' (2012) 94 *Review of Economics and Statistics* 1157; E Budish, B Roin and H Williams, 'Do Firms Underinvest in Long-Term Research? Evidence from Cancer Clinical Trials' (2015) 105 *American Economic Review* 2044 (2015). For an overview, see HL Williams, 'How Do Patents Affect Research Investments?' (2017) 9 *Annual Review of Economics* 441.

the EU courts, patent rights, like other IPRs, are not absolute; rather, they must be viewed in relation to their social function and must be reconciled with other fundamental rights, so that in the case of the pharmaceutical sector it is necessary to balance the interests of the patent-holding pharmaceutical industry and those of public health.[10] The complex relationship between patents, competition and the fundamental right to health will be analysed and developed further in chapters eight and nine.

It should be noted that in the EU, pending the entry into force of the Unitary Patent system,[11] patents are granted either by the competent national patent office or, centrally, by the European Patent Office (EPO), but are enforced at the national level. Patents are geographically bound, so that the inventor is required to apply for patent protection in all markets concerned. As a consequence, in the EU, European patents are split into a bundle of national patents requiring validation in each Member State. In the US, patent law is a federal competence and patents are granted by the federal agency US Patent and Trademark Office (USPTO).

Patentable subject matters are inventions that fulfil the three essential requirements of novelty, involvement of an inventive step/non-obviousness and industrial applicability/utility.[12] In addition to complying with patentability requirements, the grant of a patent is generally conditional upon sufficient disclosure of the invention.[13] In the case of pharmaceuticals, the claims and description must disclose specific therapeutic effects, even if it is found that the substances have more effects than anticipated once used in practice. Patents may cover different aspects of the pharmaceuticals, ie the product, the production process (process patent), formulations, dosage forms, uses in new therapeutic classes, new combinations and so on. A distinction is usually made between the primary patent covering the molecule and the so-called 'secondary patents' regarding other elements, each with a specific expiration date. Such 'secondary patents' may claim, for instance: formulations of the drug

[10] See, eg Case C-70/10 *Scarlet Extended SA v Société belge des auteurs, compositeurs et éditeurs SCRL (SABAM)* ECLI:EU:C:2011:771, paras 43–44; Case C-577/13 *Actavis Group PTC and Actavis UK* ECLI:EU:C:2015:165, para 36.

[11] The Unitary Patent Package consists of three main sources of law: Regulation (EU) No 1257/2012 of the European Parliament and of the Council implementing enhanced cooperation in the area of the creation of unitary patent protection [2012] OJ L361/1; Regulation (EU) No 1260/2012 of the European Parliament and of the Council implementing enhanced cooperation in the area of the creation of unitary patent protection with regard to the applicable translation arrangements [2012] OJ L361/89; and Agreement on a Unified Patent Court (UPCA) [2013] OJ EPO 287. The new system is intended to start on 1 April 2023.

[12] See TRIPS, Arts 27ff; European Patent Convention (EPC), Arts 52(1)ff; US Patent Act, 35 USC §§ 101ff. The TRIPS Agreement establishes minimum standards for the protection of IPRs by members of the World Trade Organization (WTO), which may adopt different concepts of 'invention', novelty inventive step or non-obviousness, and industrial applicability or utility. It should be noted that, unlike the novelty and non-obviousness standards, the utility/industrial application threshold is generally quite low and, for the vast majority of inventions, poses no significant barrier to patentability. See BN Roin, 'Unpatentable Drugs and the Standards of Patentability' (2009) 87 *Texas Law Review* 503, 516.

[13] In other words, the specifications should provide information to allow a person skilled in the art to make or practise the claimed invention. See, eg EPC, Art 83; 35 USC §112.

or biologic (eg an administrable form or dosage); methods of using the pharmaceutical (eg an indication or use for treating a particular disease); methods of manufacturing or manufacturing technologies used to make the pharmaceutical; methods of administrating or technologies used to administer the pharmaceutical; or other chemicals related to the active ingredient, such as crystalline forms, intermediaries, etc.

From a patent law perspective, both primary and secondary patents grant the same degree of protection, so that the latter are not to be understood as patents of lesser quality, but are just applied for at a later stage than the former. In practice, the widespread use of secondary patents in the pharmaceutical industry has raised many concerns and has led some to the idea that, whereas the importance of primary patents directed at new chemical entities cannot be denied, the inventions covered by secondary patents generally should deserve less protection.[14] Criticism is grounded on the idea that substantive requirements for the protection of a second or further medical indication are applied in a lax manner, as often, in practice, they are based on slight modifications of the patented drug and case law shows how the multiplication of secondary patents may be used strategically by originator companies. The reasons for such concerns is that the existence of several possibilities for secondary patents may lead to the extension of the total IP protection well beyond the 20 years conferred by the primary patent. This may typically happen, for instance, when the secondary patent protects an essential process used to manufacture the product, so that the drug at issue cannot be produced through any other production process: in such a case, the total IP patent protection would in practice be extended until the expiry of the secondary patent. Moreover, such multiple patents may have very different application dates, so that patent protection may change over time and legal uncertainty may arise.

The interpretation of patentability standards for pharmaceutical products has been the subject of considerable debate.[15] One of the subjects particularly discussed is the case of follow-on drugs. On the one hand, scholars have warned how, in practice, pharmaceutical companies often obtain follow-on patents on trivial variants of their basic chemical once the initial patent is about to expire.[16]

[14] See, eg the General Court in the landmark judgment of Case T-321/05 *AstraZeneca v Commission* EU:T:2010:266, [2010] ECR II-02805, which stated, at para 607, that 'the ability of a formulation patent to confer exclusivity on a product is not equivalent, in any event, to that of a substance patent, since an active substance can be incorporated into different formulations'.

[15] As for the novelty and non-obviousness standard, see, eg Roin, 'Unpatentable Drugs', 517–31 (claiming that patents are important not only in promoting inventive activity, but also for the subsequent development and commercialisation of the invention, and that in the current system the novelty and non-obviousness requirements can cause patents to be denied for socially valuable drugs that are unlikely to reach the public without that protection); M Lemley, 'Expecting the Unexpected' (2017) 92 *Notre Dame Law Review* 1369 (criticising the theory of patents as designed to encourage not invention, but commercialisation of existing knowledge and supporting the application of the obvious-to-try rule to exclude unmeritorious products, such as follow-on patents, from patent protection).

[16] Lemley, 'Expecting the Unexpected', 1393.

A more stringent application of high patentability requirements has been also advocated by the Guidelines for Pharmaceutical Patent Examination released by the United Nations Development Programme in 2015, with the proposed aim of incorporating public health perspectives in procedures for granting pharmaceutical patents.[17] On the other hand, other scholars have argued that often the value of a follow-on patent is comparable to, or might even exceed, that of a primary patent and have challenged the idea that follow-on pharmaceutical innovation should be categorically singled out for unfavourable treatment under the patent laws.[18]

Patent expiry represents the major threat for originator companies. Especially from 2010 onwards, several blockbuster drugs have lost patent protection (a phenomenon known as the 'patent cliff'), paving the way for lower-priced generics. As will be analysed in Part II, the ability of originator companies to adopting a series of life-cycle strategies aimed at expanding the exclusivity period of their products is a major concern for competition authorities. So-called patent 'evergreening' refers in general to the already mentioned practices aimed at artificially extending patent exclusivity over the original term.[19] Such concerns must be also read in conjunction with the probabilistic nature of the patent system[20] and the imperfect information between the actors involved, such as the pharmaceutical companies, patent offices and courts. In particular, the patent system has been subjected to a number of criticisms as patent offices typically have limited resources and time, and thus a limited ability to investigate in depth the accuracy of the information they receive. As a result, the system does not ensure that patent protection is granted only to meritorious inventions, thereby allowing a high number of weak patents.[21] This is also reflected

[17] CM Correa, 'Guidelines for Pharmaceutical Patent Examination: Examining Pharmaceutical Patents from a Public Health Perspective' (UNDP, 2015). A previous report was published as a working paper by the International Centre for Trade and Sustainable Development (ICTSD), the United Nations Conference on Trade and Development (UNCTAD) and the World Health Organisation (WHO): CM Correa, 'Guidelines for the Examination of Pharmaceutical Patents: Developing a Public Health Perspective – A Working Paper' (ICTSD, WHO, UNCTAD, 2006).

[18] CM Holman, T Minssen and EM Solovy, 'Patentability Standards for Follow-On Pharmaceutical Innovation' (2018) 37 *Biotechnology Law Report* 131, 134, 137. The authors criticise the UNDP Guidelines and argue that modifications that do not directly improve therapeutic effect can nonetheless provide substantial benefits to patients. Moreover, they challenge the idea that follow-on drugs favour evergreening, pointing out that a follow-on patent directed towards a new use or new formulation cannot extend the term of the original patent as, once the primary patent expires, there is no patent-based restriction on the ability of generic competitors to bring competing versions of the original formulation to market.

[19] See R Feldman, 'May Your Drug Price Be Evergreen' (2018) 5 *Journal of Law and the Biosciences* 590; E Lietzan, 'The "Evergreening" Metaphor in Intellectual Property Scholarship' (2019) 53 *Akron Law Review* 805.

[20] See MA Lemley and C Shapiro, 'Probabilistic Patents' (2005) 19 *Journal of Economic Perspectives* 75 (affirming that patents are not the well-defined property rights that some economic models assume and demonstrating that patents contain a greater level of uncertainty than other property rights).

[21] See, eg MA Lemley, 'Rational Ignorance at the Patent Office' (2001) 95 *Northwestern University Law Review* 1495.

in the uncertainty typical of patent litigation, which is risky for both parties but is particularly dangerous for originator companies, which are exposed to the immediate loss of a large part of the market if the generic wins in suit. This exacerbates the likelihood of opportunistic behaviours, including the recourse to anti-competitive settlements between the firms involved.

A further aspect relates to the ability of an IPR holder to put geographic restrictions on the sale or use of products, which is traditionally subject to the fundamental limitation of the exhaustion (in the EU) or first sale (in the US) doctrine, meaning that once the relevant good is put on sale for the first time by the IPR holder, whether directly or with her consent, she cannot object to subsequent circulation of the product – indeed, her rights are 'exhausted'. At international level, the issue is treated by Article 6 TRIPS, leaving to each nation the discretion to determine the issue of international exhaustion, whereby the patent holder exhausts her right to block importation once she launches the drug in another country. In the EU, Member States recognise regional exhaustion (to be distinguished from the other two types of exhaustion, ie international and national), so that a product first sold in a Member State will exhaust the patent owner's rights in all other Member States and importation (parallel trade) is permitted between EU countries, but not from outside the EU. Thus, a first sale in the EU does not exhaust rights in non-EU countries, and vice versa. In the US, whereas in the past the national exhaustion approach has prevailed in the case of patents, in 2017 the Supreme Court ruled that international exhaustion applies in this area too.[22] This issue will be addressed in section V below.

Pharmaceutical companies may also supplement their patent portfolios with trade secrets. In general, trade secret laws protect commercially valuable information that is not publicly available and is guarded with reasonable security measures by the rightful holder to protect it against misappropriation.[23] While these general standards are set out in Article 39 TRIPS, countries have provided different conditions for trade secret protection.[24] In the case of pharmaceuticals, trade secrets may cover production processes, formulas for chemicals and other valuable information, such as clinical trial data. Whereas the relationship

[22] *Impression Product, Inc v Lexmark International, Inc* 581 US_ (2017).

[23] Patents and trade secrets may be complementary tools. In a nutshell, unlike patents, trade secret protection may last indefinitely (as long as the secret is not disclosed). In addition, advantages to trade secret ownership include the ability to protect innovations that might not qualify for other IP, the lack of a need for registration and for compliance with formalities, and having an immediate effect. Disadvantages of trade secrets, for their owners, include that their protection may be relatively weak and they are vulnerable to misappropriation, independent discovery and reverse engineering. In the pharmaceutical context, see, eg Abbott, 'Health and Intellectual Property Rights', 149 (explaining that a chemical combination leading to a finished product developed over several years might be reverse engineered in considerably less time at a relatively modest cost).

[24] The EU has harmonised trade secrecy protection across Member States with Directive (EU) 2016/943 of the European Parliament and of the Council on the protection of undisclosed know-how and business information (trade secrets) against their unlawful acquisition, use and disclosure (Trade Secrets Directive) [2016] OJ L157/1. In the same year, the US expanded protections with the Defend Trade Secrets Act, embedded in the existing Economic Espionage Act of 1995 (18 USC §§ 1831–39).

between patents and access to medicines has been the subject of extensive inquiry, the role that trade secrecy law plays in the pharmaceutical sector has received far less attention until recently. Increasing attention has been paid to this issue especially in the wake of the COVID-19 pandemic and the controversial problem of granting access to vaccines (in particular, the latest generation of mRNA vaccines) at global level.

III. EU SUPPLEMENTARY PROTECTION CERTIFICATE AND US PATENT TERM RESTORATION

Patent applications are typically made by firms as soon as possible after discovery in order to get the first-mover advantage and avoid the risk of pre-emption by other firms. In the pharmaceutical industry, commercialisation occurs at a later stage after the mandatory marketing authorisation by the competent regulatory authority has been granted, so that effective patent terms, which begin at the time of the patent application, are significantly reduced. Long commercialisation lags (meaning the time between invention and marketability) for R&D-based products may dramatically impact on incentives for private firms to engage in long-term research. For these reasons, further incentive measures have been adopted by governments with the aim of recovering marketing time lost during development and regulatory approval.

In the EU, a supplementary protection certificate (SPC) has been introduced by Regulation (EC) No 1768/92, followed by Regulation (EC) No 469/2009 (hereinafter, SPC Regulation), further amended by Regulation (EU) 2019/933.[25] An SPC grants a further IP protection period of up to five years, depending on the duration of the R&D and testing processes, so that the holder of both a patent and a certificate should be able to enjoy an overall maximum of 15 years of exclusivity from the time the medicinal product in question first obtains authorisation to be placed on the market in the EU. As clarified by the European Court of Justice, the objective of the SPC is

> to re-establish a sufficient period of effective protection of the basic patent by permitting the holder to enjoy an additional period of exclusivity on the expiry of that patent, which is intended to compensate, at least in part, for the delay to the commercial exploitation of his invention by reason of the time which has elapsed between the

[25] Council Regulation (EEC) No 1768/92 of 18 June 1992 concerning the creation of a supplementary protection certificate for medicinal products [1992] OJ L182/1; Regulation (EC) No 469/2009 of the European Parliament and of the Council concerning the supplementary protection certificate for medicinal products [2009] OJ L152/1; Regulation (EU) 2019/933 of the European Parliament and of the Council amending Regulation (EC) No 469/2009 concerning the supplementary protection certificate for medicinal products [2019] OJ L153/1. SPCs are also provided for plant protection products by Regulation (EC) No 1610/96 of the European Parliament and of the Council concerning the creation of a supplementary protection certificate for plant protection products [1996] OJ L198/30.

> date on which the application for the patent was filed and the date on which the first MA in the European Union was granted.[26]

The purpose of this additional period of exclusivity is to encourage research and, to that end, it is designed to ensure that the investments put into such research activity are covered.[27]

SPC protection is not strictly a patent term extension; rather, it confers separate rights, several aspects of which differ from patents, as SPCs have a hybrid nature.[28] Two systems, which have very different aims and approaches, are involved in SPCs: patent protection and marketing authorisation. According to Article 3 of the SPC Regulation, for a certificate to be granted, the following conditions must occur: (i) the product is protected by a basic patent in force; (ii) a valid marketing authorisation has been granted; (iii) the product has not already been the subject of a certificate; and (iv) the marketing authorisation is the first one to place the product on the market as a medicinal product.[29] It should be noted that an SPC is requested by the holder(s) of the patent to be extended, which can sometimes be different from the firm owner of the MA. Moreover, SPCs are granted only on a national basis by national patent offices, so that the application must be presented to each national patent office where the supplementary protection is sought and differences in timing among Member States and in examination outcomes across national patent offices may arise.[30] According to the SPC Regulation, the application for a certificate must be lodged within six months of the date on which the MA was granted. The certificate takes effect at the end of the lawful term of the basic patent and the period of validity may be extended only in specific cases, such as the six-months extension allowed in the case that the inventor undertakes studies in compliance with an agreed paediatric investigation plan (PIP).[31]

The requirements set out by the SPC Regulation have been subject to extensive case law at both national and EU level. The wording of the SPC Regulation has proved to be unclear in some places and the Court of Justice has intervened

[26] Case C-121/17 *Teva UK Ltd and Others v Gilead Sciences Inc* ECLI:EU:C:2018:585, para 39.

[27] Case C-493/12 *Eli Lilly and Company* ECLI:EU:C:2013:835, paras 41–42 and the case law cited therein.

[28] European Commission, R Romandini, P Slowinski, G Wright, et al, 'Study on the Legal Aspects of Supplementary Protection Certificates in the EU: Final Report' (2018) https://data.europa.eu/doi/10.2873/680006 (SPC Report).

[29] See also SPC Regulation, Art 7ff.

[30] M Mejer, '25 Years of SPC Protection for Medicinal Products in Europe: Insights and Challenges' (2017) https://ec.europa.eu/docsroom/documents/26001. The author notes (at 4) that the SPC Regulation provides conditions for obtaining a certificate (Art 3), but the procedural aspects are harmonised to a lesser extent. For example, there is no obligation for the national patent office to examine ex officio whether conditions put forward in Art 3 are satisfied.

[31] SPC Regulation, Art 13; Regulation (EC) No 1901/2006 of the European Parliament and of the Council on medicinal products for paediatric use and amending Regulation (EEC) No 1768/92, Directive 2001/20/EC, Directive 2001/83/EC and Regulation (EC) No 726/2004, [2006] OJ L378/1, Art 36.

in many instances, but has not always provided straightforward guidance.[32] First of all, how the concept of 'active ingredient' should be defined has been questioned for the purposes of the application of the SPC Regulation. Article 1 of the SPC Regulation in fact defines 'product' as 'the active ingredient or combination of active ingredients of a medicinal product', and defines 'medicinal product' as 'any substance or combination of substances presented for treating or preventing disease in human beings or animals and any substance or combination of substances which may be administered to human beings or animals with a view to making a medical diagnosis or to restoring, correcting or modifying physiological functions in humans or in animals.'

However, the term 'active ingredient' is not defined in the SPC Regulation, and its meaning has been the subject of a number of disputes.[33] In line with the original purpose of the SPC Regulation, which was intended to incentivise research on new active ingredients, the Court of Justice has clarified that the term 'active ingredient' is consistent with the concept of active substance under Article 3(a) Directive 2001/83 and covers substances which produce a pharmacological, immunological or metabolic action of their own.[34] Thus, an excipient or an adjuvant cannot be considered new active ingredients and a combination of an adjuvant with an active ingredient is not a new product within the meaning of Article 1(b) of the SPC Regulation.[35]

Further debates regard the other requirements of Article 3 of the SPC Regulation. In particular, a very controversial issue concerns the possibility of obtaining an SPC for new medical uses of an active ingredient already authorised as a medicinal product. The basic patent is defined as 'a patent which protects a product as such, a process to obtain a product or an application of a product, and which is designated by its holder for the purpose of the procedure for grant of a certificate'.[36] However, there is a lack of clarity about the requirement of the

[32] For an extensive treatment of these issues, see European Commission, SPC Report. The Report (at 156–70) also considers the issue of what types of MA could be the basis for granting an SPC, as at the time of the SPC Regulation the regulatory framework for MAs was simpler than the current one.

[33] On this point, see European Commission, SPC Report, 136ff.

[34] Case C-431/04 *Massachusetts Institute of Technology* ECLI:EU:C:2006:291, [2006] ECR I-4089, paras 18–25; Case C-631/13 *Arne Forsgren v Österreichisches Patentamt* ECLI:EU:C:2015:13, para 47.

[35] See also Case C-210/13 *GlaxoSmithKline Biologicals* ECLI:EU:C:2013:762, para 35. Widely on this issue, see European Commission, SPC Report, 134ff. On this basis, the Report affirms (at 155) that an SPC should be admitted for the derivatives of an active substance that was already authorised in the past for medicinal use and even the subject of a previous certificate only when such derivative represents a new active substance under regulatory law and the corresponding authorisation supplied in support of the application for a certificate was based on complete clinical tests.

[36] SPC Regulation, Art 1(c). It should be noted that the requirement that the product must be protected by the patent has been the subject of several requests for preliminary rulings before the Court of Justice about what 'protected' under Art 3(a) of Regulation 469/2009 means. Today, however, it seems that the Court has failed to provide clear guidance in applying Art 3(a) of Regulation 469/2009. On this issue, see European Commission, SPC Report, 180ff.

'basic patent'. All patents that protect either the process for obtaining an active ingredient or the active ingredient thereof or the use of this active ingredient can, in principle, be the basis for an SPC. This principle also applies to patents granted for the first, second or further medical uses of a known substance. In practice, where the product is protected by a number of basic patents in force, any of those patents may be designated for the purpose of the grant of an SPC. In addition, when there is a plurality of holders of patents related to the same product, each patent holder might get an SPC.[37]

Article 3(d) does not appear to give any relevance to the medical indication or to the use for which an active ingredient is authorised, as it only requires that the MA must be the first authorisation granted to place the product on the market as a medicinal product. However, case law has provided unclear interpretations of such provisions. In cases where a second MA concerned the use of the active ingredient on a different species (ie human and veterinary use) but for the same indication as the first MA, or, conversely, a second MA concerned the use of the active ingredient on the same species as the first MA but for a different indication, the principle according to which the decisive factor for the grant of the SPC is not the intended use of the medicinal product but the active ingredient (so that only the very first MA matters) has been affirmed.[38] In contrast, in the case where the second MA concerned the use of the active ingredient on a different species and for a different indication, the Court of Justice has adopted a teleological approach relativising the principle that the issue of an SPC and its duration must be based on the first MA in the Member State and in the EU. In *Neurim*, the Court stated that

> the mere existence of an earlier MA obtained for a veterinary medicinal product does not preclude the grant of an SPC for a different application of the same product for

[37] See, eg Case C-181/95 *Biogen Inc v Smithkline Beecham Biologicals SA* ECLI:EU:C:1997:32, [1997] ECR I-00357; Case C-482/07 *AHP Manufacturing BV v Bureau voor de Industriële Eigendom* ECLI:EU:C:2009:501, [2009] ECR I-07295. See Mejer, '25 Years', 10 (reporting data according to which an SPC was applied for with reference to more than one basic patent in at least one EU Member State for 20% of the products, and noting that the probability increases over time and is higher for biological medicines than for those derived in chemical synthesis). See also MK Kyle, 'Economic Analysis of Supplementary Protection Certificates in Europe' (2017) 5, https://ec.europa.eu/docsroom/documents/25621/attachments/1/translations/en/renditions/native. At 19–20, the author reports that only a single patent is concerned in the SPC application(s) for a drug in more than 80% of cases, whereas in the remaining cases, a single drug has multiple SPC applications associated with different patents in a single country, and notes that when an SPC extends a patent that is not the first one, the result can be an effective extension of protection beyond the maximum of 5 years intended by the policy, assuming that the first patent is the basic one. Kyle also shows (at 18) that, on average, a single drug is associated with more than 20 SPC applications, is granted about 15 of them and is denied an average of 2.58.

[38] Case C-31/03 *Pharmacia Italia* ECLI:EU:C:2004:641, [2004] ECR I-10001; Case C-202/05 *Yissum* ECLI:EU:C:2007:214, [2007] ECR I-2839. See European Commission, SPC Report, 226 (noting that, even if these decisions concerned Arts 1(b) and 19 of Regulation 1768/92, they had a direct impact on Art 3(d) of Regulation 469/2009, because the concepts of active ingredient and MA have the same meaning within the Regulations).

> which an MA has been granted, provided that the application is within the limits of the protection conferred by the basic patent relied upon for the purposes of the SPC application.[39]

This way, the Court accepted the possibility that an SPC may be granted on the basis of a more recent MA for old active ingredients, ie that were already authorised in the past for medicinal use. This has led to criticism by those who stressed that the grant of the SPC should be possible only if the MA on which the SPC application relies is the first granted for the active ingredient and the other requirements set out by the SPC Regulation are met. On that basis, departing from this principle would undermine one of the main purposes of Article 13 of the Regulation, ie to ensure that the duration of an SPC for a product is no more than 15 years from the first application to place it on the market as a medicinal product, as only the first MA required extensive clinical trials, thus entailing the delay that the rules are intended to compensate.[40] The lack of clarity and the potential important effects of *Neurim* on the treatment of follow-on products have led to further preliminary rulings on the issue. In *Abraxis*, the Court of Justice affirmed that

> the legislature intended, in establishing the SPC regime, to protect not all pharmaceutical research giving rise to the grant of a patent and the marketing of a new medicinal product, but to protect research leading to the first placing on the market of an active ingredient or a combination of active ingredients as a medicinal product.[41]

The Court reduced the scope for the application of *Neurim*, referring to it as an 'exception to the narrow interpretation of Article 3(d)' which 'does not, in any event, refer to cases of new formulations of the product'.[42] In *Santen*, the Court further stressed that Article 3(d) of the SPC Regulation must be interpreted as meaning that a marketing authorisation cannot be considered to be the first marketing authorisation, for the purpose of that provision, where it covers a new therapeutic application of an active ingredient or of a combination of active ingredients, and that active ingredient or combination has

[39] Case C-130/11 *Neurim Pharmaceuticals (1991) Ltd v Comptroller-General of Patents* ECLI:EU:C:2012:489. See also the Opinion of AG Trstenjak ECLI:EU:C:2012:268. The AG argued that second medical uses are essentially the new and inventive specific use of known medical active ingredients: as patent protection for second and further uses takes account of legitimate interests because research into therapeutic effects of known substances has considerable health and economic importance, and given that the aim of granting SPCs for medicinal products is essentially to extend the term of patent protection for active ingredients used in such products, the literal interpretation of Art 3(d) of Regulation 1768/92 should be 'supplemented by a schematic-teleological interpretation, according to which a supplementary protection certificate may also be granted under certain conditions on the basis of a second or further authorisation to place a patented active ingredient on the market as a medicinal product in the Member State for which the application is made' (para 52).

[40] See European Commission, SPC Report, 230ff.

[41] Case C-443/17 *Abraxis Bioscience LLC v Comptroller General of Patents* ECLI:EU:C:2019:238, para 37.

[42] ibid para 43.

already been the subject of a marketing authorisation for a different therapeutic application.[43]

The SPC is intended to confer a purpose-bound protection, as – within the limits of the protection conferred by the basic patent – it extends only to the product covered by the authorisation to place the corresponding medicinal product on the market and for any use of the product as a medicine that has been authorised before the expiry of the certificate.[44] As a general principle, the certificate confers the same rights as the basic patent and is subject to the same limitations and the same obligations. Recently, an exception to this principle (known as the manufacturing waiver) was introduced by Regulation (EU) 2019/933. This occurred in the wake of the 2015 Single Market Strategy, when the Commission declared its intention to explore a recalibration of certain aspects of patent and SPC protection with the aim of strengthening EU-based manufacturing and competitiveness in industry sectors whose products are subject to regulated market authorisations.[45] This amendment to the SPC Regulation was originally due to the alleged competitive disadvantage suffered by EU-based manufacturers of generic and biosimilar drugs with respect to companies that are based in non-EU countries where SPC protection does not exist (eg Brazil, Russia, India and China) and that enter markets in which patent protection expired up to five years earlier. The reason for this is that EU-based manufactures are not allowed to produce in EU Member States during the period of the SPC protection of the reference medicine. One of the main risks of this situation is that European manufacturers of generic and biosimilar medicines could be incentivised to move their production outside the EU – either via delocalisation or long-term outsourcing contracts.[46] To avoid this, and with the aim of granting the timely entry of generics and biosimilars, after discussions and criticisms, a limited and targeted SPC manufacturing waiver was introduced in Article 5 of the SPC Regulation so as to allow the making of a product for the purpose of export to third countries or of storing, and any related acts in the Union strictly necessary for that making or for the actual export or the actual storing, where such acts would otherwise require the consent of a certificate holder. This exception is also intended to allow makers to compete effectively in the Union immediately after protection has expired ('EU day-one entry'). According to this provision, the manufacturing for export is allowed throughout the entire

[43] Case C-673/18 *Santen SAS v Directeur général de l'Institut national de la propriété industrielle* ECLI:EU:C:2020:531. According to the Court, a different interpretation might compromise the simplicity and the predictability which the EU legislature intended the system to have in order to guarantee the implementation of a uniform solution at the EU level by the national patent offices (para 59).

[44] SPC Regulation, Art 4.

[45] European Commission, 'Upgrading the Single Market: More Opportunities for People and Business', COM/2015/0550 final, SWD(2015) 202 final, SWD(2015) 203 final.

[46] European Commission, 'A Single Market Strategy for Europe – Analysis and Evidence Accompanying the Document Upgrading the Single Market: More Opportunities for People and Business', Staff Working Document, COM(2015) 550 final, SWD(2015) 203 final, para 3.3.3. See also Recitals 4ff of Regulation 2019/933.

SPC lifetime, whereas the manufacturing and stockpiling for day-1 marketing in the EU is permitted only during the last six months before SPC expiry.[47]

Data demonstrate that SPC protection constitutes a fundamental tool in the European pharmaceutical market and the use of it has significantly increased from its introduction in the 1990s. Similar to what has already been noted with regard to patent policy, the role of SPC protection to maintain pharmaceutical development incentives is in constant tension with its negative impact on drug availability and cost. The main critical issues on the application of SPC protection concern the lack of clarity over the requirements set out by the legislation, as mentioned above, and the inconsistencies among Member States.[48] In fact, the differences in SPCs at the national level, together with the still existing differences in patenting and in litigation, lead to several difficulties. It should be noted that, in addition to the general framework of the Unitary Patent system, the possibility of creating a unitary SPC title with a single granting procedure is under consideration by the Commission.[49]

The EU authorities decided to implement the *sui generis* system of SPCs rather that a patent-extension model, which was adopted in the US, where the Hatch-Waxman Act includes rules providing for patent restoration up to five years in order to compensate development and regulatory delays.[50] The period of restoration depends on the total effective patent life after marketing authorisation and extends from the original expiration date of the patent. Such period is reduced by any portion of the regulatory review period during which the applicant did not act 'with due diligence'.[51] In any case, the total patent term – and thus, the time between the FDA market approval and the expiry of the patent – cannot exceed 14 years. According to US rules, the patent owner is required to apply to the USPTO for the extension within 60 days of FDA approval of the drug at issue. In order to determine the length of the extension, the regulatory review period calculated by the FDA is divided into two phases: the testing phase and the approval phase. The former is the period between the date an Investigational New Drug Application (IND) requested to conduct clinical trials becomes effective and the

[47] See Art 5 of the SPC Regulation for all the requirements set out by the amended provision. For a detailed treatment of this issue, see M Vidal-Quadras, 'Analysis of EU Regulation 2019/933 on the SPC Manufacturing Waiver Exception' (2019) 50 *International Review of Intellectual Property and Competition Law* 971.

[48] A further critical argument points to the absence of a link between SPC protection and therapeutic value. Kyle, 'Economic Analysis', 18 has highlighted that whereas, at the time a patent is granted, the therapeutic effects of a new drug are usually not sufficiently known as this information results from the clinical trials that follow, at the time of product launch, when SPC applications are filed, such information exists, so that, even if SPC policy is designed to address distortions in research incentives caused by differences in development times across products, it would be important to consider whether SPCs in practice benefit relatively more therapeutically important drugs.

[49] See, eg European Parliament, Resolution of 11 November 2021 on an intellectual property action plan to support the EU's recovery and resilience (2021/2007(INI)).

[50] 35 USC §156.

[51] 35 USC §156(c). An interim patent term extension may be granted in specific cases (35 USC §§156(d)(5), 156(e)(2)).

initial submission of the marketing application (NDA or BLA); the latter is the period between the submission and approval of the marketing application. The following conditions are required in order to obtain a patent extension, ie: the applicant must show that the patent has not expired and must establish that the patent has not previously been extended; the patent owner must submit an application for patent term restoration that includes details about the patent and the activities undertaken to secure FDA approval; the applicant must establish the product was subject to a regulatory review period before its commercial marketing or use, and must show that the product either represents the first permitted commercial marketing or use of the product after such regulatory review period or, in the case of a product manufactured under a process patent that primarily uses recombinant deoxyribonucleic acid (DNA) technology, represents the first permitted commercial marketing or use of a product manufactured under the process claimed in the patent.[52]

IV. REGULATORY EXCLUSIVITY

As said above, regulatory exclusivity tools work in parallel with IP protection. At the international level, differences in exclusivity regimes exist among states. Although differences in terminology can be found, two main general categories of regulatory exclusivity may be distinguished: (i) data exclusivity, which precludes applicants from relying on the reference product's clinical data to demonstrate the safety and effectiveness of the follow-on product; and (ii) marketing exclusivity, which precludes the regulatory agency from approving any other application for an identical or biosimilar product for the same use, irrespective of whether the applicant has generated its own data or not.

With regard to the EU, policies on exclusivity varied across Member States until 2005, when new harmonised rules – taking full effect in 2013 – were introduced.[53] The periods of both data and market protection run from the date of granting of the MA. Data protection rules grant originator companies a period of eight years during which generic manufacturers are prohibited from referring to the data produced by the originator company and enclosed in its application for MA. Once this data exclusivity period has elapsed, generic producers may submit valid applications for their products and can obtain an MA based on the data produced by the originator company. In parallel to the eight years of data protection, a generic product authorised on the basis of the abridged application cannot be placed on the market until 10 years have elapsed

[52] 35 USC § 156(a). For details, see MA Bagley, 'Patent Term Restoration and Non-patent Exclusivity in the US' in Muscolo and Pitruzzella, *Competition and Patent Law*, 111, 121–23.

[53] These new rules have been introduced by Directive 2004/27 amending Directive 2001/83, and Regulation (EC) No 726/2004. It is worth clarifying that the terms 'data protection' and 'data exclusivity' are generally used synonymously in this context.

from the initial authorisation of the reference product. This period amounts to the 'market protection', which can be extended by one year if a new therapeutic indication with a significant clinical benefit is approved for the reference product: this means that if a company already has a medicinal product on the market and subsequently obtains an MA for the same product but with a new strength, this does not imply a new period of regulatory exclusivities, but an additional year of protection. This system is known as the 8+2(+1) Formula, and is valid not only for generics, but also for hybrids and biosimilars.[54]

It should be noted that other possible one-year data protection extensions are provided in two cases. Firstly, it may occur when an MA is granted for a new indication for a well-established substance (ie a substance where at least 10 years have elapsed since the granting of the first MA for it), provided that significant pre-clinical or clinical studies were carried out in relation to the new indication: in this case, the protection is non-cumulative and refers exclusively to the data concerning the new indications. This data exclusivity period is an incentive for the development of new indications for which data protection would not otherwise apply.[55] Secondly, an extension is provided in the case that a classification change in the legal status of a medicinal product has been granted on the basis of significant pre-clinical tests or clinical trials.[56]

A peculiar situation concerns orphan drugs. The designation of a medicinal product as an orphan requires: that it is intended for the diagnosis, prevention or treatment of a life-threatening or chronically debilitating condition affecting not more than five in 10,000 persons in the EU when the application is made; that without incentives it is unlikely that the marketing of the medicinal product would generate sufficient return to justify the necessary investment; and that there exists no satisfactory method of diagnosis, prevention or treatment of the condition in question or, if such method exists, that the medicinal product will be of significant benefit to those affected by that condition. The aim of legislation is to stimulate research and development of drugs for rare diseases that would not be pursued under normal market conditions by providing incentives to sponsors. Such kinds of drugs are subject to different provisions. The period of market exclusivity for an orphan designated pharmaceutical product is 10 years (rather than eight years of data exclusivity plus two years' marketing exclusivity for non-orphan new drugs), with the possibility of a further two years

[54] See Directive 2001/83/EC, Art 10; Regulation 726/2004, Art 14(11). For further details, see European Commission, 'Study on the Economic Impact of Supplementary Protection Certificates, Pharmaceutical Incentives and Rewards in Europe: Final Report' (2018) 32, https://data.europa.eu/doi/10.2873/886648. See also European Commission, 'Notice to Applicants, Procedures for marketing authorization' (2019) vol. 2A, ch 1, revision 11.

[55] See Directive 2001/83/EC, Art 10(5). See also the European Commission, 'Notice to Applicants', 47: 'Therefore, the concerned medicinal product could be used as reference medicinal product with the exclusion of the indication(s) which is covered by this data protection if the medicinal product fulfils the general requirements of reference medicinal product. Such data protection period is an incentive for development of new indications whilst data protection would not otherwise apply.'

[56] Directive 2001/83/EC, Art 74(a).

if studies following a PIP are carried out and approved. However, the market exclusivity period can be reduced to six years if, after five years, it is established that the medicinal product no longer lives up to the criteria on which the orphan designation was granted. Moreover, as a derogation to this exclusivity rule, an MA may be granted, for the same therapeutic indication, to a similar medicinal product if the producer of the original orphan medicinal product has given its consent to the second applicant or is unable to supply sufficient quantities of the medicinal product, or if the second applicant can establish in the application that its product, although similar to the orphan medicinal product already authorised, is safer, more effective or otherwise clinically superior.[57]

With regard to the US context, as a consequence of the discovery of new chemical entities, NDA holders receive a five-year exclusivity period (four years in the case of a paragraph IV certification), which is intended as data exclusivity and during which no ANDA may be submitted (new chemical entity exclusivity). New clinical investigation exclusivity, which is granted to drugs containing a previously approved active moiety[58] when new clinical studies have been undertaken and the application is based on results from these, runs for three years. A particular regime applies to orphan drugs, which are subject to seven-year marketing exclusivity. For paediatric drugs an extension of six months of exclusivity is provided to incentivise studies in children. With regard to biologics, no application may be submitted until four years and approved until 12 years after the reference product is originally licensed. These exclusivities must be read together with those awarded to the first generic and first biosimilar producers.[59]

In practice, regulatory exclusivities cause market barriers and may work de facto as a further R&D incentive, which may remedy an insufficient patent protection, but their role is different from that of IPRs and they do not belong to that category.[60] Although patents are generally considered the main tool granting the profits of drug development and regulation is criticised for its costs, in practice these two regimes operate in parallel to limit competition in pharmaceutical markets.[61] As explained before, in order to obtain marketing approval, safety, efficacy and quality requirements must be shown to the drug regulatory authority, which relies on information derived from the data submitted by the

[57] Regulation 141/2000, Art 8.

[58] See 21 CFR § 314.3(b). The active moiety 'is the molecule or ion, excluding those appended portions of the molecule that cause the drug to be an ester, salt (including a salt with hydrogen or coordination bonds), or other noncovalent derivative (such as a complex, chelate, or clathrate) of the molecule, responsible for the physiological or pharmacological action of the drug substance'.

[59] See §§ 505(c)(3)(E), 505(j)(5)(B)(iv), 505(j)(5)(B)(v), 505(j)(5)(F), 505A (21 USC 355a), 505E (21 USC 355f), 506H (21 USC 356h), and 527 (21 USC 360cc) of the FD&C Act; see also 21 CFR §§ 314.108, 316.31, 316.34; § 351(k)(7) of the PHS Act.

[60] CR Fackelmann, 'Clinical Data, Data Exclusivity and Private Investment Protection in Europe' in Muscolo and Pitruzzella, *Competition and Patent Law* 141, 169ff (affirming also, at 159 and 173, that the subject of protection of data exclusivity is not the data itself but the market authorisation-related effect of the know-how contained in the data, eg the evidence of safety and efficacy).

[61] See Eisenberg, 'The Shifting Functional Balance' (claiming, at 132, that regulatory measures are also driven by economic goals rather than only by health and safety issues).

manufacturing company, including the chemical composition of the drug and the results of pre-clinical and clinical drug trials and tests conducted in the manufacturing process. For as long as the data exclusivity lasts, generic producers cannot rely on the originator's data but have to submit their own data to prove safety and efficacy, which would oblige them to repeat the clinical trials and other tests. This does not really constitute a viable alternative. In addition to obliging generic producers to bear the high costs of generating their own test data, there are ethical issues in that option, as a duplication of tests for purely commercial reasons would be onerous and unnecessary from this point of view. Thus, generic producers typically are compelled to delay the launch of their product until the end of the exclusivity period.

As the provisions on regulatory exclusivity are part of the rules governing marketing authorisations, they are separate from patent protection. In other words, data exclusivity can be provided irrespective of the presence of a patent on the basis of the requirements set out in the regulatory framework. In practical terms, as the protection granted by the patent runs from the patent application (which is generally filed upon the discovery of the molecule underlying a potential drug) and the data exclusivity runs from the marketing authorisation, upon marketing approval a new patented drug enjoys concurrent coverage from the remaining IP protection's term and from the regulatory exclusivity. The period of the latter is normally shorter than the patent duration, with the exception of extraordinary cases. As a result, the 'loss of exclusivity' occurs when both forms of protection expire.

A discussion has arisen about the role and the scope of data exclusivity protection. At the international level, an important reference to data protection rules is contained in the TRIPS Agreement, Article 39.3 of which requires governments to protect undisclosed test data requested and submitted for the marketing approval of new chemical entities against unfair commercial use, provided that the origination of such data involves a considerable effort. This provision does not bind member countries to confer exclusivity and leaves flexibility for data protection regimes, only requiring 'protection' of undisclosed data required by a national authority as a condition for obtaining marketing approval for a medicine. This means that data exclusivities, such as those provided by the EU and US rules, derive from the choice of such regimes to provide a stronger form of protection. The opportunity for providing such additional protection to originators is under policy debate, and it has sometimes been criticised as not being beneficial from the perspective of public health and access to medicines.[62] Concerns on data exclusivity provisions are similar to those that occur with patents, as they regard the usual trade-off between the welfare gains arising from incentives to innovate and the additional cost to society in terms of higher

[62] World Health Organization (WHO), 'Data Exclusivity and Other "TRIPS-plus" Measures' (2017) 2–3, https://apps.who.int/iris/handle/10665/272979. It should be noted that least-developed countries are not required to provide the data protection mandated by TRIPS on pharmaceuticals until 2033.

final prices. Nevertheless, while there is a wide literature on the design and impact of IPRs in the pharmaceutical industry, there is little empirical evidence on the effects of the overall duration of market exclusivity – granted by both patents and regulatory exclusivities together – on innovation efforts by originator companies.[63]

V. RESEARCH AND BOLAR EXEMPTIONS

Safe harbours provided by patent law, such as research exemption and the so-called Bolar exemption, are also relevant in the pharmaceutical field. A research exemption, which has a general application, admits certain research activities that would otherwise be qualified as patent infringement, whereas the Bolar exemption, which is provided specifically in the pharmaceutical sector, allows producers of generic or biosimilar drugs to conduct research before the expiry of the IPRs covering a reference medicine. In general, at the international level, a legal basis can be found in Article 30 TRIPS that allows Member States to provide limited exceptions to the exclusive rights conferred by a patent, compatibly with the normal exploitation of the patent and the legitimate interests of the patent owner and of third parties.

With regard to research exemptions, they are widespread all over the world.[64] In the US, the traditional research exemption (known also as 'common law exemption' or 'experimental use' exemption) to patent infringement has its origins in the case law of the early nineteenth century and in Justice Story's remarks in *Whittemore v Cutter*.[65] According to this approach, 'it could never have been the intention of the legislature to punish a man, who constructed such a [patented] machine merely for philosophical experiments, or for the purpose of ascertaining the sufficiency of the machine to produce its described effects'.[66] The scope of this exemption has been the subject of subsequent case law, whereas no statutory provisions have been implemented.[67] However, although courts have consistently recognised the existence of an experimental use exemption in theory, such a defence has almost never succeeded in practice.

[63] F Gaessler and S Wagner, 'Patents, Data Exclusivity, and the Development of New Drugs' (2019) Rationality and Competition Discussion Paper Series 176, https://rationality-and-competition.de/wp-content/uploads/discussion_paper/176.pdf.

[64] For an overview, see World Intellectual Property Organization (WIPO), 'Exceptions and Limitations to Patent Rights: Experimental Use and/or Scientific Research' (2013) SCP/20/4.

[65] *Whittemore v Cutter*, 29 F Cas 1120 (CCD Mass 1813) (No 17, 600). For a detailed overview of US case law on research exemption, see KJ Strandburg, 'The Research Exemption to Patent Infringement: The Delicate Balance between Current and Future Technical Progress' in PK Yu (ed), *Intellectual Property and Information Wealth* (Westport, Praeger, 2007); KJ Strandburg, 'What Does the Public Get? Experimental Use and the Patent Bargain' (2004) 2004 *Wisconsin Law Review* 81.

[66] *Whittemore* 1121. See also *Sawin v Guild*, 29 F Cas 554 (CCD Mass 1813) (No 12,391).

[67] House of Representatives Committee on the Judiciary, 'Proposed Revision and Amendment of the Patent Laws: Preliminary Draft with Notes' (1950). In 1950, the House of Representatives

One particularly relevant case is *Roche Products v Bolar Pharmaceutical*, in which the Court of Appeals for the Federal Circuit concluded that the exception is 'truly narrow' – so much so that it does not allow 'a violation of the patent laws in the guise of "scientific inquiry", when that inquiry has definite, cognisable, and not insubstantial commercial purposes' – and 'unlicensed experiments conducted with a view to the adaption of the patented invention to the experimentor's business' violate the rights of the patent owner.[68] The case regarded a generic firm, Bolar, which, in order to be ready to market the generic equivalent of Dalmane, a sleep disorder medication, as soon as the patent expired, conducted studies during the term of the patent to demonstrate bioequivalence to the FDA. When the originator, Roche, sued for infringement, Bolar defended on the ground that its use was in the public's interest, and therefore should be exempted from infringement liability.[69] The Federal Circuit disagreed, declining to extend the experimental use exception to such conduct. The Congress reacted by including the so-called 'Bolar' provision in the Hatch-Waxman Act, ie providing a safe harbour exempting those who

> make, use, offer to sell, or sell within the United States or import into the United States a patented invention ... solely for uses reasonably related to the development and submission of information under a Federal law which regulates the manufacture, use or sale of drugs or veterinary biological products.[70]

In other words, under this provision (also known as statutory or FDA exemption) it is not an act of patent infringement to engage in otherwise infringing uses reasonably related to preparing an ANDA for FDA approval.

More recently, the experimental use exception has been narrowed further in *Embrex, Inc v Service Engineering Corp* and in *Madey v Duke University*, relating to academic contexts.[71] According to this approach, US patent statutes do not recognise a general experimental use exception, which is extremely narrow, as it 'clearly does not immunize use that is in any way commercial in nature' or 'immunize any conduct that is in keeping with the alleged infringer's legitimate business': this applies also to academic institutions.[72] However, uncertainties

Committee on the Judiciary drafted proposed legislation including a very broad and general exclusion from infringement for experimental uses, excluding from its ambit only commercial sales for such uses. However, a specific experimental use provision was not ultimately adopted.

[68] *Roche Products, Inc v Bolar Pharmaceutical Co, Inc* 733 F 2d 858, 863, 898 (Fed Cir 1984).

[69] ibid 865.

[70] 35 USC § 271(e)(1).

[71] *Embrex, Inc v Serv Engineering Corp* 216 F 3d 1343 (Fed Cir 2000); *Madey v Duke University* 307 F3d 1351 (Fed Cir 2002).

[72] *Madey* 1353, 1361–62. In this case, the Federal Circuit held an academic research institution (Duke University) liable for infringement for using a patented technology during its research. According to this approach, the research projects of major research universities 'unmistakably further the institution's legitimate business objectives' (at 1362). Such business objectives include education and enlightening students, increasing the status of the institution and luring lucrative research grants, students and faculty. Moreover, the profit or non-profit status of the user is not determinative.

remain, in particular with regard to the relevance of the distinction between 'experimenting on' a patented invention (eg to reach a better understanding of the invention or improve it, or to explore unknown effects) and 'experimenting with' it (ie using it as a tool for other research) to the traditional research exemption.[73] The case of *Integra Lifesciences I, Ltd v Merck KGaA*, which arrived at the Supreme Court in 2005, could have provided a good occasion for the courts to give some clarifications on this point. However, the majority of the panel at the Federal Circuit found that the case dealt only with the FDA statutory exemption, so that the issue of the scope of the traditional research exemption was not at stake,[74] and the Supreme Court did not rule on it. In particular, the Supreme Court disagreed with the Federal Circuit, rejecting arguments that the statutory exemption would cover only clinical tests and not pre-clinical ones and arguing that it applies

> [a]t least where a drug-maker has a reasonable basis for believing that a patented compound may work, through a particular biological process, to produce a particular physiological effect, and uses the compound in research that, if successful, would be appropriate to include in a submission to the FDA.[75]

However, no indications on the traditional research exemption and on the relationship between it and the FDA statutory exemption were been provided in this case. Thus, the narrow approach adopted by the US courts towards the experimental use exemption is the subject of debate in the literature, with scholars suggesting a number of different proposals aimed at reconsidering it.[76]

[73] Strandburg, 'The Research Exemption to Patent Infringement' (affirming that whereas 'experimenting on' is an 'easy case', 'experimenting with' a patented invention is using it according to the purpose for which it was originally designed and for which the patentee was granted monopoly rights, so that the invention is used to study something other than the invention itself).

[74] *Integra LifeSciences I, Ltd v Merck KGaA*, 331 F 3d 860 (Fed Cir 2003). It should be noted that Judge Newman in her dissenting Opinion pointed to the common law research exemption (at 866–67) by arguing that 'The majority's prohibition of all research into patented subject matter is as impractical as it is incorrect. The information contained in patents is a major source of scientific as well as technologic knowledge … The subject matter of patents may be studied in order to understand it, or to improve upon it, or to find a new use for it, or to modify or "design around" it … Today's accelerated technological advance is based in large part on knowledge of the details of patented inventions and how they are made and used. Prohibition of research into such knowledge cannot be squared with the framework of the patent law … The better rule is to recognize the exemption for research conducted in order to understand or improve upon or modify the patented subject matter, whatever the ultimate goal. That is how the patent system has always worked: the patent is infringed by and bars activity associated with development and commercialization of infringing subject matter, but the research itself is not prohibited, nor is comparison of the patented subject matter with improved technology or with designs whose purpose is to avoid the patent.'

[75] *Merck KGaA v Integra LifeSciences I Ltd* 545 US 193, 206 (2005), in which the Supreme Court expressly declined to express an opinion on whether § 271(e)(1) 'exempts from infringement the use of 'research tools' in the development of information for the regulatory process': ibid 205, fn 7.

[76] See RS Eisenberg, 'Patents and the Progress of Science: Exclusive Rights and Experimental Use' (1989) 56 *University of Chicago Law Review* 1017, 1023–24; RD Hantman, 'Experimental Use as an Exception to Patent Infringement' (1986) 67 *Journal of the Patent and Trademark Society* 617; DM Gitter, 'International Conflicts over Patenting Human DNA Sequences in the United States and

It is generally agreed that the European approach is less strict than the US one as for the research exemption.[77] Although there is not a common basis in European law, an exception for experimental use was first included in Article 31 of the 1975 Convention for the European Patent for the Common Market (Community Patent Convention, CPC), which was revised and renumbered in 1989 (Article 27 CPC 1989). However, due to a lack of ratification by the necessary number of contracting states, neither ever came into force.[78] It is now prescribed by Article 27 of the Agreement on a Unified Patent Court (UPCA), according to which 'The rights conferred by a patent shall not extend to: (a) acts done privately and for non-commercial purposes; (b) acts done for experimental purposes relating to the subject matter of the patented invention'. The same Article includes at (d) the acts allowed pursuant to Article 10(6) of Directive 2001/83/EC in respect of any patent covering the product within the meaning of such Directive. Thus, (b) refers to the case of experimental use and (d) to that of regulatory exception or Bolar provision.

With regard to experimental use, the wording of the UPCA reflects prior CPC text and experience under European national patent laws that generally avoided treating as infringements uses that did not have significant economic effects (private and non-commercial uses) as well as scientific experiments.[79] As clarified above with regard to the Unitary Patent Package, at the time of writing, the UPCA has not still come into force. However, many European countries have implemented this kind of provision in their national legislation in the past, although differences exist between Member States in the scope of the research exemption.[80]

the European Union: An Argument For Compulsory Licensing and a Fair-Use Exemption' (2001) 76 *New York University Law Review* 1623, 1637; JM Mueller, 'No "Dilettante Affair": Rethinking the Experimental Use Exception to Patent Infringement for Biomedical Research Tools' (2001) 76 *Washington Law Review* 1, 17; MA O'Rourke, 'Toward a Doctrine of Fair Use in Patent Law' (2000) 100 *Columbia Law Review* 1177, 1205; R Dreyfuss, 'Protecting the Public Domain of Science: Has the Time for an Experimental Use Defense Arrived?' (2004) 46 *Arizona Law Review* 457, 462–63; R Dreyfuss, 'Reconsidering Experimental Use' (2017) 50 *Akron Law Review* 699; Strandburg, 'The Research Exemption to Patent Infringement'; SM O'Connor, 'Enabling Research or Unfair Competition? De Jure and De Facto Research Use Exceptions in Major Technology Countries' in T Takenaka (ed), *Patent Law & Theory: A Handbook of Contemporary Research* (Cheltenham, Edward Elgar, 2009) ch 19.

[77] N Siebrasse and K Culver, 'The Experimental Use Defence to Patent Infringement: A Comparative Assessment' (2006) 56 *University of Toronto Law Journal* 333. See also H Holzapfel and JD Sarnoff, 'A Cross-Atlantic Dialog on Experimental Use and Research Tools' (2008) 48 *IDEA Intellectual Property Law Review* 123.

[78] Convention for the European Patent for the Common Market (Community Patent Convention), 76/76/EEC, [1976] OJ L17/1; Agreement relating to Community patents 89/695/EEC (Luxembourg, 15 December 1989) [1989] OJ L401/1.

[79] Holzapfel and Sarnoff, 'A Cross-Atlantic Dialog', 151, fn 126 (arguing that by authorising private and non-commercial uses separately from experimental uses, the CPC formulation creates exceptions that are closer to the 'fair use' exception to copyright infringement in US law; see 17 USC § 107).

[80] For a detailed overview, see A Kupecz et al, 'Safe Harbors in Europe: An Update on the Research and Bolar Exemptions to Patent Infringement' (2015) 33 *Nature Biotechnology* 710; H-R Jaenichen

In *Monsanto v Stauffer*, the UK Court of Appeal defined the meaning of 'experimental purposes' in Article 31(b) CPC 1975 and section 60(5)(b) UK Patents Act 1977, respectively.[81] According to the Court, acts carried out in order to discover something unknown or to test a hypothesis, or even in order to find out whether something which is known to work in specific conditions will work in different conditions, can fairly be regarded as experiments. This does not apply to trials carried out in order to demonstrate to a third party that a product works or in order to amass information to satisfy a third party, whether a customer or a regulatory body, that the product works as its maker claims, which cannot be regarded as done for 'experimental purposes'.

In Germany, the Bundesgerichtshof (Federal Court of Justice) stated in its *Clinical Trials I* decision[82] that any systematic procedure aimed at obtaining new information is considered an experiment, irrespective of the purpose which the information gained is eventually intended to serve. In particular, the Federal Court of Justice affirmed the applicability of section 11 no 2 of the German Patent Act, containing the exemption for acts done for experimental purposes relating to the subject matter of the patented invention, also for experiments on humans which are conducted with the intention of finding out whether a patented drug is suitable for curing or alleviating other diseases. The exemption provision is even applicable if the nature of experiments goes beyond pure research and economic interests are also pursued.[83] In a second ruling in 1997 (*Clinical Trials II*), the Federal Court of Justice confirmed this broad interpretation, declaring the national patent rule at issue also applicable if the trials

and J Pitz, 'Research Exemption/Experimental Use in the European Union: Patents Do Not Block the Progress of Science' (2015) 5 *Cold Spring Harbor Perspectives in Medicine* 1.

[81] *Monsanto Co v Stauffer Chemical Co* [1985] RPC 515.

[82] Federal Court of Justice (Bundesgerichtshof – BGH) judgment of 11 July 1995 – X ZR 99/92 – *Klinische Versuche I* (*Clinical Trials I*). For details, see T Cook, 'A European Perspective as to the Extent to Which Experimental Use, and Certain Other, Defences to Patent Infringement, Apply to Differing Types of Research' (Intellectual Property Institute, 2006) 28ff. According to *Clinical Trials I*, an action for experimental purposes, which is related to the subject matter of the invention and therefore legitimate, can exist if a patented pharmaceutically active substance is used in clinical trials with the aim of finding whether and, where appropriate, in what form the active substance is suitable for curing or alleviating certain other human diseases. The wording of the national law in principle exempts all experimental acts as long as they serve to gain information and thus to carry out scientific research into the subject matter of the invention, including its use (comprising, eg, utilisation acts for experimental purposes undertaken with the subject matter of the invention in order to discover the effects of a substance or possible new uses hitherto unknown). Since the provision makes no limit, either qualitative or quantitative, on the experimental acts, it cannot matter whether the experiments are used only to check the statements made in the patent or else to obtain further research results, and whether they are employed for wider purposes, such as commercial interests.

[83] German patent law contains an exception for experimental or research purposes (research exception) in s 11, No 2 of the Patent Act (Patentgesetz), which stipulates that those acts done for experimental purposes which relate to the subject matter of a patented invention are exempt from patent protection. The BGH dealt with s 11, No 2 of the Patent Act in particular in the decisions *Clinical Trials I and II*, and shaped the interpretation of the provision. The interpretation of the *Clinical Trials I* proceedings was indirectly confirmed by the Federal Constitutional Court (Bundesverfassungsgericht, BVerfG). BGH, judgment of 17 April 1997 – X ZR 68/94 – *Klinische Versuche II*; BVerfG, ruling of 10 May 2000 – 1 BvR 1864/95.

served the purpose of obtaining data for gaining authorisation to put medicinal products on the market in respect of a pharmaceutical composition, provided that such activities were indeed experimental and related to the subject matter. In this context, the Federal Court of Justice confirmed its view that economic interests, as a rule, did not conflict with the application of section 11 no 2 of the Patent Act, but it specified that the exemption provision did not apply to experiments which only served to clarify commercial factors, such as market needs, price acceptability and distribution options.

These rulings are generally quoted in the European debate over the scope of the research exemption. The German cases mentioned above – having established that, in line with the objective of promoting technological progress, a commercial aim does not prevent true experimentation from being subject to the defence of use for experimental purposes relating to the subject matter of the invention – show the liberal interpretation given by the German Federal Court of Justice.[84] However, variations between the approaches adopted by national systems throughout the EU occur on the matter and narrower views can also be found. Furthermore, whereas the applicability of the safe harbour for research 'on' patented inventions is generally accepted, specific exemptions for research 'with' patented inventions have been provided in very few instances.[85]

With specific regard to the pharmaceutical context, the most important issue concerns the possibility for generic producers of conducting the necessary bioequivalence studies or trials with a view to preparing the application to obtain marketing authorisation without committing patent infringement. Greater clarity has resulted as a safe harbour, similar to the US one mentioned before, ie the so-called Bolar provision, has been introduced also in the European context and included in the relevant regulatory framework. The central idea of the Bolar exemption is to allow competitors to test inventions covered by a patent prior to the expiry of protection in order to instigate the procedures to achieve marketing authorisation for a generic or biosimilar product. Particularly in the pharmaceutical sector, the conduct of R&D and clinical trials needed even for a generic product to get a marketing approval may take several years. Thus, if a competing generic or biosimilar producer were not allowed to start this work before the patent protection for the original product had elapsed, the de facto IP protection would further extend the period formally granted by the patent. Through the Bolar exemption the period between the

[84] See, eg also the French case before the Tribunal de Grande Instance Paris, *Wellcome Foundation v Parexel International & Flamel* 20 February 2001.

[85] For an overview, see R Gold and Y Joly, 'The Patent System and Research Freedom: A Comparative Study', prepared for WIPO, 2 August 2010, SCP/15/3; A Kupecz et al, 'Safe Harbors in Europe' 710–712 (reporting, eg, the adoption of a broad approach in Belgium and a narrow interpretation in the Netherlands).

expiry of the patent protection and the market entry of generic products can be shortened to the advantage of the public at large.

In the US, this safe harbour provision, originating from *Roche Products v Bolar Pharmaceutical*, has been interpreted broadly by the Supreme Court and covers not only drugs, but also medical devices.[86] However, the exact boundaries of the exemption are not fixed and any inquiry into its applicability remains highly fact-specific.[87] In the EU, before the introduction of the Bolar exemption in 2004,[88] pre-patent-expiry development was regulated not at the EU level but at national one, and legal uncertainty existed with regard to testing activities, as noted above. As generic manufacturers could not enjoy this provision at EU level, they had to move their studies and development activities in countries where patent protection had expired or was not provided or where such an exception already existed.[89] The inclusion of the Bolar provision in the EU regulatory framework has allowed generic producers to conduct the necessary studies and trials within the EU with a view to obtaining MA for their products. The provision refers to both patent rights and SPCs. However, Article 10(6) of Directive 2001/83/EC has been implemented in different ways by Member States, some adopting a wide approach, extending the scope of the exception to innovative drugs, and other relying on a narrower one, limiting the exception to activities relating to marketing approval of generic medicines. Moreover, national laws also differ as to whether the exception applies to tests aimed at applying for MA outside the EU.[90] As already mentioned above, such exemption is also included in Article 27 of the UPCA.

[86] *Eli Lilly & Co v Medtronic, Inc* 496 US 661 (1990). As seen before, the Supreme Court held that the exemption applies also to any pre-clinical testing of patented compounds that is reasonably related to the submission of information to a regulatory agency: *Merck KgaA v Integra Lifesciences I, Ltd*. With regard to biologics, see *Amgen, Inc v International Trade Commission* 565 F 3d 846, 852, 853 (Fed Cir 2009).

[87] Post-approval testing has been the subject of controversy. See *Classen Immunotherapies, Inc v Biogen IDEC* 659 F 3d 1057 (Fed Cir 2011), where the Federal Circuit adopted a narrow approach, excluding post-approval testing from the safe harbour provision, and, later, *Momenta Pharmaceuticals, Inc v Amphastar Pharmaceuticals, Inc* 686 F 3d 1348 (Fed Cir 2012), where the Federal Circuit adopted a broader stance (holding that if testing is carried out to satisfy the FDA's requirements, it falls within the scope of the exception, even though the activity is carried out after approval and the information collected is not submitted to a regulatory agency). The Supreme Court declined to review both cases.

[88] Art 10(6) of Directive 2001/83/EC as amended by Directive 2004/27/EC.

[89] See EU Commission, 2009 Sector Inquiry, 122–23: generic manufacturers had to carry out their product development and related testing in countries where the basic patent had already expired or where such protection did not exist, outside the EU or in European countries where a Bolar-type provision existed or in EU Member States where experimental work was permitted in certain cases; the Bolar provision creates a safe harbour for conducting such activities so as to enable the generic producer to apply for MA once the data exclusivity period has elapsed.

[90] For details on the application of Bolar exemptions all over the world, see A Tridico, J Jacobstein and L Wall, 'Facilitating Generic Drug Manufacturing: Bolar Exemptions Worldwide' (*WIPO Magazine*, 2014) www.wipo.int/wipo_magazine/en/2014/03/article_0004.html. See also WIPO, Standing Committee on the Laws of Patents, 'Reference Document on Exception Regarding Acts for Obtaining Regulatory Approval from Authorities' (second draft) (2018) SCP 28/3, 8ff. See also ch 8.

Whereas in the US the law specifies the type of action covered by the exception (ie making, using, offering for sale or selling within the US, or importing into the US a patented invention for the purposes stipulated by law), in several European national legislations the specific acts permitted are specified (such as studies, trials, tests) with some degree of variation.[91] A question has arisen about the applicability of the regulatory exception to third-party suppliers in cases such as those where the third party produces and/or supplies a patented active pharmaceutical ingredient (API) to another party, for example the generic company that conducts studies and tests on that ingredient in order to obtain an MA. In the US, according to the decision issued by the Court of Appeals for the Federal Circuit in *Shire LLC v Amneal Pharmaceuticals, LLC*, third-party suppliers are to be considered immunised from patent infringement insofar as their activity is limited to supplying materials for use related to seeking FDA approval.[92] In the EU, there is uncertainty over the issue. In the German case *Astellas Pharma Inc v Polpharma SA Pharmaceutical Works*,[93] after the Düsseldorf District Court held that a third-party supplier could be protected by the regulatory exception only when it is a co-organiser of the studies carried out by its customer, the Court of Appeal asked the Court of Justice to give an indication on the matter, but it did not issue any interpretation as the case was withdrawn.[94]

VI. EXHAUSTION DOCTRINE AND PARALLEL TRADE

As anticipated in the previous section, the exhaustion doctrine typically limits the right to exclude granted to the IP holder, by providing that her control over the protected good or service ends once it has been placed on the market. Thus, first sale rules are aimed at balancing the exclusive rights granted to businesses and inventors in their products and works against the rights of retailers, consumers and second-hand dealers to freely resell or dispose of these products after having lawfully acquired them in the market.[95] At international level, a laissez-faire approach by individual countries is included in Article 6 of the

[91] See, eg, s 11, No 2b of German Patent Act; Art 68(1)(b) of the Italian Industrial Property Code. For more details, see WIPO, 'Reference Document', 18ff.

[92] *Shire LLC v Amneal Pharmaceuticals, LLC* 802 F 3d 1301 (Fed Cir 2015), reversing the district court's decision No 11-3781 (DNJ, 12 May 2014).

[93] The case has been under consideration in Poland too. The Polish Supreme Court held that the sale of an API is not covered by the regulatory exception, irrespective of its purpose, and constitutes patent infringement, as the third-party supplier cannot control the subsequent use of it by the customer (CSK 92/13). See WIPO, 'Reference Document', 22.

[94] Decision of 26 July 2012, 4a O 282/10; Case C-661/13 *Astellas Pharma Inc v Polpharma SA Pharmaceutical Works*, request for a preliminary ruling from the Oberlandesgericht Düsseldorf (Germany) lodged on 13 December 2013.

[95] I Calboli, 'Corporate Strategies, First Sale Rules, and Copyright Misuse: Waiting for Answers from Kirstsaeng v Wiley and Omega v Costco (II)' (2013) 11 *Northwestern Journal of Technology and Intellectual Property* 221, 223.

TRIPS Agreement, stating that 'nothing in this Agreement shall be used to address the issue of the exhaustion of intellectual property rights'.[96] Opponents to parallel imports have relied on Article 28 TRIPS, granting patent holders the right to 'prevent third parties from making, using, offering for sale, selling or importing' a product as a limit to the application of Article 6. However, this argument was rebuked, as confirmed by a footnote in Article 28 stating explicitly that the provision of Article 28 is subject to Article 6 and by the 2001 Doha Declaration.[97]

The doctrine of exhaustion of rights provides the legal basis for 'parallel importation', which is permitted under 'regional' and 'international' exhaustion policies. In contrast, under national exhaustion, according to which the IP holder's right to exclude is only extinguished when the good or service is put onto the market in the national territory, a patent holder can price discriminate across countries and block parallel importation of a patented product, preventing price arbitrage by unlicensed third-party importers. Regional exhaustion, where the IP holder's right is extinguished when a good or service is put onto the market within any country of a defined region – so that parallel trade is admitted within a particular group of countries – is applied in the EU.[98] In the US, the application of international exhaustion to patents was affirmed in 2017 by the US Supreme Court ruling in *Impression Products*, according to which a US patent holder's rights are exhausted by an authorised foreign sale and the importation of such goods does not constitute infringement (whereas previously exhaustion applied to domestic but not international sales).[99] Even though the case at issue

[96] In general, see S Ghosh and I Calboli, *Exhausting Intellectual Property Rights: A Comparative Law and Policy Analysis* (Cambridge, Cambridge University Press, 2019).

[97] World Trade Organization, Ministerial Declaration of 14 November 2001, WTO Doc WT/MIN(01)/DEC/1, 41 ILM 746 (2002) (Doha Declaration). In particular, para 5(d) of the Doha Declaration clarified that: 'the effect of the provisions in the TRIPS Agreement that are relevant to the exhaustion of intellectual property rights is to leave each member free to establish its own regime for such exhaustion without challenge, subject to the MFN and national treatment provisions of Articles 3 and 4'. See FM Abbott, 'The Doha Declaration on the TRIPS Agreement and Public Health: Lighting a Dark Corner at the WTO' (2002) 5 *Journal of International Economic Law* 469.

[98] The EU rules on exhaustion are largely the result of the jurisprudence of the Court of Justice interpreting Art 34 TFEU on measures having equivalent effect to quantitative restrictions between Member States. The Court of Justice has always interpreted the Treaty as meaning that rights conferred by IPRs are exhausted within the single market by virtue of putting the relevant goods on the market (by the right holder or with his/her consent) in the EU. See, eg Case C-15/74 *Centrafarm and Adriaan de Peijper v Sterling Drug Inc* ECLI:EU:C:1974:114, [1974] ECR 01147; Case C-187/80, *Merck and Co Inc v Stephar BV and Petrus Stephanus Exler* ECLI:EU:C:1981:180, [1981] ECR 02063. EU secondary law in relation to patents (including rules on supplementary protection certificates extending the protection of patents for pharmaceutical and plant protection products) do not include specific rules on exhaustion of intellectual property rights, but the general principles affirmed by the jurisprudence of the Court of Justice apply.

[99] Prior to this case, the majoritarian position was that sale of a product in a foreign country did not exhaust the US patent – see *Fuji Photo Film Co, Ltd v Jazz Photo Corp* 394 F 3d 1368, 1370 (Fed Cir 2005). The Federal Circuit took the same position in *Lexmark International, Inc v Impression Products, Inc* 816 F 3d 721 (Fed Cir 2016), then the Supreme Court reversed it. However, the

related to toner cartridges, this ruling has provoked a debate on its implications to pharmaceutical markets and its full applicability to medicines.[100]

Controversy exists about the effects of parallel trade, and its implications for social welfare are not unanimous in most economic models.[101] The significance of the exhaustion doctrine depends on several factors, including national decisions, the size of the markets involved and the extent to which private contractual means can intervene in restricting parallel imports.[102] In fact, in general, strong disputes have occurred regarding the application of first sale rules in the context of international trade, as IP owners generally oppose the international arbitrage of their products by grey marketers.[103]

In the pharmaceutical sector, a policy of open parallel importation with respect to patented medicines is considered to improve the accessibility for consumers to the lowest-priced versions of the same authorised products available on the world market. Considering that parallel import medicines are not counterfeit products, benefits would derive in terms of providing consumers with lower prices for the same products and making patented drugs more accessible to lower-income individuals, while reducing strain on public health budgets. On the contrary, arguments against parallel importation include the claimed benefits of price discrimination, which, according to originator companies, would allow them to earn more revenues to be subsequently invested in R&D and without which those firms would have to raise prices and reduce supply in lower income regions to avoid undermining their profitability in wealthier regions. In addition, other arguments sustained by originator companies affirm that parallel importation may represent a threat to public safety, because imported pharmaceutical products are first sold to wholesalers, which may not be as reliable as the

Court did not exclude that contractual restrictions could not prevent parallel imports. On this point, see I Calboli, 'Intellectual Property Exhaustion and Parallel Imports of Pharmaceuticals: A Comparative and Critical Review' in CM Correa and R Hilty (eds), *Intellectual Property, Access to Medicines, and Innovation* (Cham, Springer, 2022).

[100] See FM Abbott, Brief of Amicus Curiae (Frederick M Abbott) in Support of Petitioner in Impression Products v Lexmark International, US Supreme Court, No 15-1189, filed 20 January 2017. Amicus Brief to US Supreme Court (2017), FSU College of Law, Public Law Research Paper No 827, https://ssrn.com/abstract=2906967. See also comments made by L Ouellette and D Hemel, 'Licensing in the Shadow of Impression Products' (2017) https://law.stanford.edu/2017/05/31/licensing-in-the-shadow-of-impression-products/.

[101] It should be noted that two categories of parallel importation may be identified: (i) passive parallel imports, which is the most common category and relates to the situation in which third-party importers purchase products in one country and sell them in another; and (ii) active parallel imports, occurring when a foreign licensee, or authorised distributor abroad, sells into the national market of the IP holders without her consent (this latter case is less frequent and is often prohibited through specific clauses in licensing agreements). See C Fink, 'Entering the Jungle of Intellectual Property Rights Exhaustion and Parallel Imports' in KE Maskus and C Fink (eds), *Intellectual Property and Development: Lessons from Recent Economic Research* (Washington, World Bank and Oxford University Press, 2005) 171, 172.

[102] ibid.

[103] On the application of exhaustion on IPRs in the pharmaceutical sector in several jurisdictions, see Calboli, 'Intellectual Property Exhaustion'.

originator companies themselves, and that it is inherently unfair as most countries impose price controls on medicines, with the important exception of the US, where drug prices are particularly high. Against those arguments, supporters of international exhaustion of patent rights aver that it would not have any effect on ordinary strict regulatory controls, such as on the safety of products, made by competent agencies and that the industry has not presented compelling evidence it would suffer severe losses which would affect reinvestment in R&D; rather, it is likely to exert downward pressure on pharmaceutical prices in countries such as the US.[104] Clearly, especially in states where drug price control does not operate, an international exhaustion regime may constitute a tremendous threat to patent-holding companies facing competition from imports originating in countries where such measures are in place.

For the purposes of this overview, it should be noted that at the EU level, parallel trade is a classical topic of competition policy in the European pharmaceutical market, where national pricing policies result in price differentials among Member States, thereby creating the opportunity for traders to buy drugs in lower-priced Member States and resell them in those where the price is higher.[105] Here, the role of competition policy is twofold: it governs the extent to which the IP holder may exploit her monopoly power, in particular in pricing decisions; and it determines the legality of possible reactions of IP owners to parallel trade.[106] While leading to intra-brand competition, originator companies may elaborate strategies to prevent parallel trade, such as reducing supply in countries affected or use restrictive clauses in distribution contracts with wholesalers. Parallel trade here is to be contextualised in the peculiar features of the EU Internal Market, which is a paramount objective of the construction of the Union itself, and is strictly linked to the fundamental principle of the free movement of goods. Such principles, coupled with the regional exhaustion, imply that pharmaceutical companies cannot oppose parallel imports of their drugs in other Member States on the ground of a violation of IP rules (trademark or patent provisions) unless the conditions of the product have been somehow impaired (which is relevant in the case of relabelling or repackaging of a drug).[107] But also, importantly, traditional restrictions to parallel trade, in the

[104] Widely on the topic, see FM Abbott, 'Parallel Importation: Economic and Social Welfare Dimensions' (International Institute for Sustainable Development, 2007) www.iisd.org/system/files/publications/parallel_importation.pdf; FM Abbott, 'Parallel Trade in Pharmaceuticals: Trade Therapy for Market Distortions' in I Calboli and E Lee (ed), *Research Handbook on Intellectual Property Exhaustion and Parallel Imports* (Cheltenham, Edward Elgar, 2016) 145.

[105] On this topic, see C Stothers, *Parallel Trade in Europe: Intellectual Property, Competition and Regulatory Law* (Oxford, Hart Publishing, 2007). Arts 34 and 36 TFEU are the rules applicable to exhaustion of patented products within the EU.

[106] See MK Kyle, 'Parallel Trade in Pharmaceuticals: Firm Responses and Competition Policy' in B Hawk (ed), *International Antitrust Law & Policy: Fordham Competition Law 2009* (Huntington, Juris Publishing, 2009).

[107] On quality verification, labelling and repackaging of pharmaceutical products, see P Caro De Sousa, 'Free Movement and Competition in the European Market for Pharmaceuticals' in

form of agreements between a manufacturer and authorised dealers introducing a prohibition on exports or in the form of abusive practices by dominant undertakings, such as through supply quotas (limiting the volumes of medicines available for sale)[108] and dual pricing (imposing different prices on the basis of the destination of the medicine),[109] have been considered as serious breaches of competition rules.

VII. CONCLUDING REMARKS

Intellectual property and regulation are both fundamental sources of exclusivity in the pharmaceutical sector. Understanding this framework, together with rules governing entry into the market, is essential in order to investigate the interface between sector-specific regulation, IP and competition law in this context.

The established set-up considered as a whole balances various objectives. On the one side, patents have been complemented with specific instruments aimed at recovering long commercialisation lags, despite there being some differences between the tools adopted (supplementary protection certificates and patent term restoration, in the EU and US respectively). Regulatory exclusivities work in parallel with IP rules. On the other side, the provision of the Bolar exemption responds to the goal of facilitating the timely market entry of generics. While, in the US, the patent extension system, marketing authorisation rules and the Bolar exemption are all included in the Hatch-Waxman Act, in the EU there is no unique set of rules to which one may refer.[110]

The variety of tools, provisions and safe harbours implemented mirror the complexity of the various interests pursued in this area. As will be further explored in this book, such an intricate institutional architecture inevitably contains gaps and loopholes that create the conditions for strategic behaviours by market players.

P Figueroa and A Guerrero (eds), *EU Law of Competition and Trade in the Pharmaceutical Sector* (Cheltenham, Edward Elgar, 2019) 431.

[108] See Joined Cases C-2/01 P and C-3/01 P *Bundesverband der Arzneimittel-Importeure eV and Commission v Bayer AG* ECLI:EU:C:2004:2, [2004] ECR I-00023; Case C-277/87 *Sandoz prodotti farmaceutici SpA v Commission* ECLI:EU:C:1990:6, [1990] ECR *I-00045*; Joined Cases C-468/06 to C-478/06 *Sot Lélos kai Sia EE and Others v GlaxoSmithKline AEVE Farmakeftikon Proïonton, formerly Glaxowellcome AEVE* ECLI:EU:C:2008:504, [2008] ECR I-07139.

[109] See Joined Cases C-501/06 P, C-513/06 P, C-515/06 P and C-519/06 P *GlaxoSmithKline Services Unlimited v Commission of the European Communities* ECLI:EU:C:2009:610, [2009] ECR I-09291.

[110] See F Papadopoulou, *Evergreening Patent Exclusivity in Pharmaceutical Products. Supplementary Protection Certificates, Orphan Drugs, Paediatric Extensions and ATMPs* (Oxford, Hart Publishing, 2021) 134 (arguing that the Unitary Patent Package could provide a more holistic approach, closer to the US alternative).

3

Regulating Prices

I. PHARMACEUTICAL PRICING AND REIMBURSEMENT SYSTEMS IN EUROPE

THE PHARMACEUTICAL INDUSTRY has unique and distinctive features with regard to pricing of medicinal products too, where again the roles of regulation and public bodies crucially matter.

Governments may decide to directly set the sale prices, may negotiate them with manufacturers or fix a reimbursement price of a new drug at an artificially low level, or can leave companies free to set the price of their products. There are a variety of strategies used by states to control prices of pharmaceuticals (including direct and indirect price controls, profit controls, reference pricing, etc). Where national or social health insurance systems are put in place – which is the case in most industrialised countries – price regulation is a way to discipline moral hazard by suppliers, which tend to respond to the inelasticity of the demand by charging higher prices than would occur in the absence of insurance.[1] Universal national health insurance schemes or systems of mandatory social insurance funds control reimbursed prices for drugs – and typically also for physician and hospital services – and price regulation in most countries applies only to drugs that are reimbursed under the national public health plan. Insurance also has important effects on promotion efforts, as doctors and patients may be inclined to use a higher number or unnecessarily costly drugs disregarding their price. Therefore, as mentioned in chapter one, many countries have implemented controls on pharmaceutical expenditure too, aimed at constraining utilisation volume and penalising above-target manufacturer promotion or above-target physician prescribing.[2]

Summarising the process of setting prices across different countries is difficult because of the differences among the relevant institutions and policies adopted.[3] With regard to the EU, it is worth stressing that pricing and

[1] PM Danzon, 'Regulation of Price and Reimbursement for Pharmaceuticals' in PM Danzon and S Nicholson (eds), *The Oxford Handbook of the Economics of the Biopharmaceutical Industry* (Oxford, Oxford University Press, 2012) 266–67.

[2] ibid 270.

[3] A useful database is provided by Pharmaceutical Pricing and Reimbursement Information (PPRI), a network including largely European countries as well as international and European institutions, on which data this section is based. PPRI is the name of one flagship project of GÖG Pharmacoeconomics. Data used in this section are contained in: S Vogler, N Zimmermann and

reimbursement of pharmaceutical products are not harmonised. While the EU has carved out a significant role in the 'regulatory pathway' for authorising the access of new products to the market in accordance with strict criteria on safety, quality and efficacy, it has less control on the 'market pathway', including the pricing of pharmaceuticals, as it lacks competence in this area.[4] A certain degree of harmonisation exists only with regard to the transparency of measures regulating the pricing and reimbursement of pharmaceuticals through the Transparency Directive, which defines a series of procedural requirements designed to verify that national pricing and reimbursement decisions do not create obstacles to the pharmaceutical trade within the EU's internal market.[5] Thus, pricing and reimbursement of pharmaceutical products fall under the exclusive competence of the individual Member States. As a result, there are different national health system schemes and rules. Moreover, although the objectives are similar, and Member States respect the same criteria for marketing approval, each country may evaluate the importance of a specific drug in a different manner or have different priorities in treating diseases. This can lead to divergences across countries in the decisions on reimbursement and on the price level of drugs. Other factors leading to price differences are the approaches adopted to regulate wholesale and retail distribution and the taxation of pharmaceuticals, in particular value-added tax (VAT).

In most EU Member States, reimbursable medicines and prescription-only medicines (and not non-reimbursable ones – and thus frequently over-the-counter drugs) are typically subject to a form of price control, with the exception of a small number of European countries applying such control to all medicines,[6] so that there is a close link between pricing and reimbursement. In general, national health systems are funded by taxpayers and act as the main or sole payor (monopsonist) for prescription drugs (for example, the dispensing pharmacies are reimbursed by the NHS when fulfilling prescriptions covered

MA Haasis, 'PPRI Report 2018 – Pharmaceutical Pricing and Reimbursement Policies in 47 PPRI Network Member Countries' (Vienna, Gesundheit Österreich, 2019) (PPRI Report 2018) 24–25, https://ppri.goeg.at/sites/ppri.goeg.at/files/inline-files/PPRI%20Report2018_2nd_edition_final.pdf. As a general premise, different pricing policies may be applied for different price types, ie prices at different stages, such as the ex-factory price (manufacturer price), pharmacy purchasing price (wholesale price) and pharmacy retail price (consumer price). The latter usually includes distribution remuneration (eg mark-ups, fee-for-service), whose extent can be regulated by government authorities, and taxes, mainly VAT. Many countries have mechanisms in place to set medicine prices at the ex-factory or wholesale price level, mostly in case of reimbursable or prescription-only medicines. Price-setting mechanisms governing the distribution of medicines through retail pharmacies differ from those regarding the supply to hospitals, which may negotiate directly with manufacturers, eg through tendering or risk-sharing procedures.

[4] L Hancher, 'The EU Pharmaceutical Market: Parameters and Pathways' in E Mossialos, G Permanand, R Baeten and TK Hervey (eds), *Health Systems Governance in Europe: The Role of European Union Law and Policy* (Cambridge, Cambridge University Press, 2010) 635.

[5] Council Directive 89/105/EEC relating to the transparency of measures regulating the prices of medicinal products for human use and their inclusion in the scope of national health insurance systems [1989] OJ L40/8.

[6] For details, see PPRI Report 2018, 25.

by national reimbursement scheme). In some countries, patients or their insurers may be required to pay fixed charges or co-payments for a prescription. Moreover, as pricing policies can be focused on specific groups of medicines (eg on-patent or off-patent medicines) or can be targeted at a specific sector or setting (eg hospital or outpatient) and may be applied as a sole, dominant or supplementary policy for defined medicines, several pricing policies can be used in parallel within a country.

In general, the two main criteria used to regulate prices are internal referencing, or benchmarking, and external price referencing (EPR) or international reference pricing, while other criteria include, for example, regulation of prices based on cost and regulation of profit or return on capital.[7] Internal benchmarking is based on the comparison of the price of the new drug to that of one or more established medicines in the same class, including consideration of further relevant factors, such as potential mark-ups for improved outcomes or superior value of the new product. A particular case of internal benchmarking is reference price reimbursement (also called reference pricing, RP), according to which products are clustered for reimbursement based on either the same compound (generic RP) or different compounds with a similar mode of action or the same indication (therapeutic RP): all products in a group are reimbursed at the same price per daily dose and the reference price is set at the price of the lowest or a relatively low-priced product in the group. This model limits reimbursement but not the ability of the manufacturers to charge prices above the reference price, in which case patients must pay any excess. In contrast, external referencing caps the price of a specific new drug in a specific country to an average, median or minimum price of the same drug in selected other countries, thereby limiting the ability of manufacturers to price discriminate across countries.[8]

In the case of originator pharmaceuticals, most Member States adopt EPR.[9] The reference price is the lowest price – or an average of the lowest prices – in a basket comprising the selected countries and EPR is used as a means to set a maximum price for a pharmaceutical product. EPR may be applied either at the launch of new medicines, where an average price rule is followed, or on an ongoing basis, where the use of a lowest price rule can result in price reductions over time. Even if EPR is a common cost-containment tool, it has received several critiques claiming that it is an arbitrary price-targeting measure that does not take into consideration other aspects of the market and the health priorities of each country concerned, which also creates uncertainty for the industry, especially due to the impact of exchange rate fluctuations on reference prices.[10]

[7] Danzon, 'Regulation of Price and Reimbursement', 276.
[8] ibid 283ff.
[9] PPRI Report 2018, 28.
[10] P Kanavos, S Vandoros, R Irwin, E Nicod and M Casson, 'Differences in Costs of and Access to Pharmaceutical Products in the EU' (European Parliament, 2011) IP/A/ENVI/ST/2010-12, 36, www.europarl.europa.eu/document/activities/cont/201201/20120130ATT36575/20120130ATT36575EN.pdf. EPR is also debated in the economic literature. Among the most recent papers, see L Maini and

In several European countries, regulation provides for statutory pricing, ie setting the price on a regulatory basis, accompanied by negotiations between the healthcare bodies of Member States and manufacturers, which are particularly relevant with regard to reimbursement and possible discounts.[11] Differences among Member States also exist with regard to pricing of generic products. The main pricing policy approach is based on linking generic prices to the originator price. This is a form of internal price referencing, but it is not applied in a consistent way across the EU (for example, in the range of price reductions required for first generic and subsequent ones). Such a price-linking policy is also applied to biosimilars, but less frequently.[12]

With regard to reimbursement, different criteria may guide decision-making on pharmaceutical reimbursement, including the therapeutic benefit of a medicine, medical need and financial considerations such as budget impact and cost-effectiveness.[13] Among the various tools complementary to the pricing mechanisms discussed above, the following must be mentioned: (i) positive/negative formulary, ie a list of all pharmaceuticals that health insurance will or will not reimburse and, if so, by how much; (ii) internal reference pricing, frequently used to regulate off-patent drug prices, by which health insurance uses generic prices within a product market – usually the lower-priced generics – to set a maximum reimbursement level for a particular product that has generic alternatives, the maximum reimbursement level being called the reference price (products whose price exceeds the reference price are either not reimbursed or the patient has to pay the difference between the reference price and the actual price of the product out of pocket); (iii) health technology assessment (HTA), introduced by an increasing number of Member States in pricing and reimbursement settings, whereby the costs and benefits of a new drug are weighed against those of an existing therapeutic alternative;[14] and (iv) performance-based and risk-sharing agreements, including different approaches to setting the reimbursement price, especially for new and expensive medicines, with the aim of protecting

F Pammolli, 'Reference Pricing as a Deterrent to Entry: Evidence from the European Pharmaceutical Market' (2020) https://ssrn.com/abstract=3694471.

[11] S Vogler and JE Martikainen, 'Pharmaceutical Pricing in Europe' in Z-U-D Babar (ed), *Pharmaceutical Prices in the 21st Century* (Cham, Springer, 2015) 343, 352.

[12] Other policies are available, including cost-plus pricing, which is not frequently used anymore, value-based pricing in outpatient sector and tendering in hospital sector. For details, see PPRI Report 2018, 33ff.

[13] In many countries, the MA holder is required to submit an application dossier if it intends its medicine to be considered for reimbursement and scientific evidence on the medicine's benefit is commonly appraised by an independent expert committee tasked with advising decision-makers on reimbursement.

[14] HTA is an evidence-based process that independently and objectively assesses a new or existing technology and compares it with other health technologies and/or the current standard of care. It may include medicinal products, a medical device or medical and surgical procedures, as well as measures for disease prevention, diagnosis or treatment used in healthcare. HTA is primarily used to inform decision-making in Member States by providing a scientific evidence base for decisions on the pricing and reimbursement of health technologies.

insurers while enabling patients to have access to innovative medicines under certain circumstances. It should be noted that HTA is used by many states to guide both their reimbursement decisions and their pricing decisions, and that at the EU level, where there has been joint work within the European network for health technology assessment (EUnetHTA), a Regulation has recently been implemented.[15]

In addition to the supply-side practices treated above, pricing policies generally also include demand-side practices with the aim of enhancing the uptake of generics, off-patent and in general lower-priced medicines. Such practices are typically directed at: doctors, requiring prescribing by the non-proprietary name (INN) rather than by brand; dispensing pharmacists, such as through substitution laws, which entitle them to substitute a medicine with an equivalent generic cheaper version; and patients, as many states provide for co-payments of outpatient medicines or other forms of cost sharing.[16]

National decisions on pricing and reimbursement levels have strong consequences as they influence not only the accessibility and affordability of drugs, but also decisions by pharmaceutical companies on whether to market their products in a given country. As Member States often set pricing and reimbursement levels on the basis of those present in other Member States, it could be profitable for companies to commercialise their product first in a Member State that can afford the highest price or reimbursement level. This allows companies to influence prices in several states by putting forward the higher price already approved in those first countries, but it can also lead to differences in market access across the EU, as apparently high-income Member States, such as Germany, gain access earlier than smaller states.

Of the various national systems, the German and French ones deserve particular attention as they are subjects of study in the US. With regard to the former, health insurance is mandatory in Germany, with the vast majority of the population getting coverage through statutory health insurance (SHI) and only a small minority being covered by private insurance or special schemes.[17] Statutory health insurance is provided by more than 110 competing, not-for-profit, self-governing

[15] Regulation (EU) 2021/2282 of the European Parliament and of the Council on health technology assessment and amending Directive 2011/24/EU [2021] OJ L458/1.

[16] PPRI Report 2018, 48–53: among the three types of co-payments, the most commonly used is percentage co-payment, followed by prescription fees charged on reimbursable medicines and finally deductibles. Combinations of different types of co-payments for outpatient medicines are also possible, being a mixture of percentage co-payments, with the prescription fee the most commonly applied one. States also have mechanisms in place to exempt and charge lower co-payments for some medicines and defined population groups.

[17] For details, see MA Rodwin, 'Common Pharmaceutical Price and Cost Controls in the United Kingdom, France, and Germany: Lessons for the United States' (2021) *International Journal of Health Services* 1; AD Stern, F Pietrulla, A Herr, AS Kesselheim and A Sarpatwari, 'The Impact of Price Regulation on the Availability of New Drugs in Germany' (2019) 38 *Health Affairs* 1182; M Wenzl and V Paris, 'Pharmaceutical Reimbursement Pricing in Germany' (Paris, OECD, 2018);

sickness funds, based on premiums paid by employers and employees, with governmental subsidies for the unemployed and retired. The basket of goods and services covered by SHI is defined at the national level by law, in terms of general principles, and the Joint Federal Committee (Gemeinsamer Bundesausschuss, G-BA), through decisions on individual products or services that should be excluded from or included in the basket. Private health insurers generally cover more or less similar baskets, though they are allowed to extend or restrict benefits. Unlike medicines used in inpatient care, which are fully covered by health insurance, compulsory health insurance covers more than the 80 per cent of the expenditure for outpatient medicines and patients pay the remainder through co-insurance payments.[18] German law, in particular the Arzneimittelmark t-Neuordnungsgesetz (AMNOG), which entered into force in 2011, provides for free pricing at product launch but requires an HTA to be conducted by the G-BA – a college of representatives from the umbrella associations of physicians, dentists, hospitals and health insurance funds – aimed at verifying the 'added therapeutic benefit' of the new medicine.[19] Positive assessments are followed by reimbursement price negotiations between the Association of Statutory Health Insurance Funds (GKV-SV) and the pharmaceutical company, and the negotiated reimbursement price applies as of the thirteenth month after the initial product launch. The negotiations are based on the additional benefit as assessed by the G-BA and must take into account the annual cost of therapy of other comparable pharmaceuticals and prices paid in other European countries as reported by the company. If parties cannot reach an agreement, the reimbursement price is set by arbitration. In the case of negative assessment, the new drug is included in a reference price cluster (*Festbetrag*) where possible; otherwise, a price is negotiated that should not be higher than the price of the appropriate comparator. If the manufacturer is not satisfied with the outcome of the assessment or of the arbitration procedure mentioned above, it can decide to opt out and withdraw its drug from Germany. Then, it should be noted that there are

R Busse, M Blümel, F Knieps and T Bärnighausen, 'Statutory Health Insurance in Germany: A Health System Shaped by 135 Years of Solidarity, Self-Governance, and Competition' (2017) 390 *Lancet* 882.

[18] Wenzl and Paris, 'Pharmaceutical Reimbursement', 5. Patients are generally required to contribute to the costs of pharmaceuticals through a 10% co-insurance rate. When products are included in reference price clusters, subject to a unique maximum reimbursement amount, patients have to pay any difference between the market price and the maximum reimbursement amount.

[19] The G-BA can conduct such an assessment directly or can request it from the Institute for Quality and Efficiency in Health Care (Institut für Qualität und Wirtschaftlichkeit im Gesundheitswesen), an independent body in charge of evaluating the quality and efficiency of health services and health products, as is often the case, or from a third party. This process applies to all new patented medicines introduced onto the German market, except those with annual SHI expenditure below €1 million. For orphan drugs, additional therapeutic benefit is assumed by virtue of marketing authorisation without reference to an appropriate comparator in Germany for as long as the annual SHI expenditure for the entire population treated with the drug remains below €50 million. See Wenzl and Paris, 'Pharmaceutical Reimbursement', 6.

various price regulation mechanisms provided by the German system, ranging from price-freezing to compulsory rebates.[20]

With regard to France, both compulsory insurance schemes (national health insurance programmes) and supplementary ones (offered, for example, by private insurance companies) are employed.[21] Prescription drugs are covered either entirely or partially by the health insurance system and coverage for medications authorised by the Ministry of Health typically follows the recommendations of the Transparency Commission (TC), which assesses each drug's therapeutic value. In particular, the TC assigns each drug a score, corresponding to its value, referred to as the 'medical service rendered' (*service medical rendu*), considering the gravity of the problem, the medication's effects and its public health impact, and the classification determines the share of the drug's cost that the national insurance will cover. The prices of reimbursed drugs are regulated through conventions negotiated between the manufacturers and the Economic Committee for Health Products (Comité économique des produits de santé), which includes representatives from the health and economic ministries, the national health insurer and private complementary insurers. Such negotiation is framed by a national agreement and the price of a specific drug takes into account the product's added medical benefit (*amelioration du service médical rendu* (ASMR)), indicating the benefit of the drug in comparison with the available alternatives. The TC ranks each drug on the basis of its ASMR on a five-point scale,[22] with those belonging to the first three classes having list prices no lower that those applied in the reference countries.[23]

II. THE US SYSTEM

In order to examine the US system, a necessary premise is that it is very complex and pharmaceutical pricing constitutes an extremely controversial topic, as

[20] ibid. Mandatory rebates that pharmaceutical companies must grant include: a general 7% discount of ex-factory price to sickness funds and other health insurers on patented pharmaceuticals that are not clustered in reference price groups; a 6% discount plus an additional discount not exceeding 10% for generics that are not clustered in reference price groups; and price-freezing until the end of 2022 for all pharmaceuticals launched before 1 August 2009. In fact, legislation prohibits price increases, as it requires manufacturers to grant a rebate equalling any price increase over prices on 1 August 2009. This 'price moratorium' was extended to the end of 2022, subject to an adjustment for inflation as of 2018, in the 2017 law strengthening the pharmaceutical supply (*Gesetz zur Stärkung der Arzneimittelversorgung*). However, the prize freeze does not apply to medicines that have been subject to internal price referencing, nor is it relevant for medicines that have a negotiated price after the AMNOG procedure. See European Commission, 'Joint Report on Health Care and Long-Term Care Systems and Fiscal Sustainability – Country Documents' (2019) 104, https://ec.europa.eu/info/sites/default/files/economy-finance/ip105_en.pdf.

[21] Public programmes provide for compulsory participation based on income and access to care defined according to need, whereas supplementary ones are eg based on employment or chosen by individuals separately and conditions vary on the basis of the contract.

[22] ASMR (I), important (II), moderate (III), mild (IV) or absent (V).

[23] In France a basket of four reference countries has been generally used (UK, Germany, Spain and Italy). For further details, see Rodwin, 'Common Pharmaceutical Price'.

prescription drug prices in the US are particularly high in comparison to other countries and drug spending has increased at a faster rate than any other component of the healthcare industry.[24] The US pharmaceutical market is the largest in the world, driving innovation in the whole sector at the global level. Price increases derive mainly by rising prices in branded medicines. The combined effect of the Hatch-Waxman Act and the rules incentivising pharmacy substitution have contributed to the high generic volume share and competition in this market, where prices have been traditionally lower than in major European countries, despite recent experience testifying to significant price increases for these drugs in some circumstances.[25] Very high prices ordinarily affect strongly branded medicines and 'specialty drugs',[26] which jeopardise the savings derived from generic competition to some extent.[27]

The main distinctive feature of the US system is that no price regulation for pharmaceutical products is in place. One of the main features of the system can be found in the traditional predominance in the US of competing private health plans, which have influenced the sector more than have public insurance programmes, such as Medicare and Medicaid.[28] Health insurance plans determine which drugs are covered and at what price for each payer, private plans normally being more flexible in this regard. Plans typically include various cost containment measures which may influence the access of beneficiaries to certain drugs. The formulary system, establishing which drugs are covered by reimbursement, is a mechanism apt to contain drug spending. Formularies are generally based on the definition of tiers that determine the level of payment drugs require. Whereas in theory tiering should reflect the cost of a drug, in practice private and public payers impact on prices set by pharmaceutical companies essentially through the use of such tiered formularies, offering preferred formulary

[24] See D Goldman and D Lakdawalla, 'The Global Burden of Medical Innovation' (2018) https://healthpolicy.usc.edu/wp-content/uploads/2018/01/01.2018_Global20Burden20of20Medical20Innovation.pdf. The RAND Corporation found in 2021 that the price of brand-name prescription drugs in the US was 256% of the prices in 32 OECD countries combined (AW Mulcahy, MW Christopher, G Mahlet, D Schwam, N Edenfield and AU Becerra-Ornelas, 'International Prescription Drug Price Comparisons: Current Empirical Estimates and Comparisons with Previous Studies' (RAND Corporation, 2021) www.rand.org/pubs/research_reports/RR2956.html. For updated data on health and pharmaceutical spending, see OECD, Health Spending (Indicator) https://data.oecd.org/healthres/health-spending.htm#indicator-chart; OECD, Pharmaceutical Spending (Indicator) https://data.oecd.org/healthres/pharmaceutical-spending.htm#indicator-chart.

[25] See ch 7.

[26] Although no consistent definition can be found, they are typically considered to include those drugs which are novel therapies with ongoing clinical assessment, are used to treat rare conditions or require special handling, monitoring or administration.

[27] R Feldman, *Drugs, Money, and Secret Handshakes. The Unstoppable Growth of Prescription Drug Prices* (Cambridge, Cambridge University Press, 2019) 8.

[28] In 2021, private health insurance coverage was more prevalent than public coverage, covering respectively 66.0% and 35.7% of insured people (91.7%), considering that some people may have more than one coverage type during the calendar year. See K Keisler-Starkey and LN Bunch, 'Health Insurance Coverage in the United States: 2021' (US Census Bureau, 2022) Current Population Report P60-278, 2, www.census.gov/content/dam/Census/library/publications/2022/demo/p60-278.pdf. A number of public safety net or private assistance programmes may be available for Americans who either do not have insurance or have inadequate coverage.

positions to drugs that are advantageously priced in comparison to other drugs with similar therapeutic features.

In the absence of price regulation, the supply chain plays a crucial role in determining the level of drug prices. The US price and distribution system is based on manufacturers' list price, combined with discounts mechanisms. Pharmaceutical manufacturers typically sell drugs at a list price (the wholesale acquisition cost (WAC)) to wholesalers, which in turn distribute medicines to retail and hospital pharmacies, adding a mark-up to cover their distribution costs. Although there are list prices such as the average wholesale price which can be used by payers as a basis for their reimbursement to pharmacies, usually significant discounts occur between the payer and the pharmacy. Private payers may also negotiate discounts from manufacturers of patented drugs directly, thereby bypassing the intermediate retailing system and preventing price arbitrage: in this case, the average manufacturer price (AMP) received by producers include these discounts, whose availability and amount depend on the payer's ability to influence drug use through its formulary design, whereas mandatory rebates are provided to some public payers by statute.[29] In the case of generic drugs, the negotiated discounts are given by the manufacturers directly to dispensing pharmacies, which are often the final decision-makers over off-patent products.[30]

In practice, drug manufacturers rarely receive the WAC or list price due to the discounts negotiated throughout the distribution system. Thus, the net price paid to the drug company, which is typically secret, is usually less than the list price. But the amounts paid by patients to insurance plans may be based on schemes referring to the list price rather than the net price, so that at the end consumers may be deprived of the benefit of the rebates bargained along the drug chain. Practice shows the trend is for the list prices of branded drugs to rise sharply.[31]

A peculiar role in the drug supply chain is played by pharmacy benefit managers (PBMs), middle players between drug companies and health insurers whose task is to establish the drug formularies and negotiate discounts from manufacturers on behalf of private insurance plans. The power such intermediaries have on prices is related to their ability to design formularies with a number of tiers for different types of drugs with corresponding co-payments, step edits (sometimes referred to as 'fail-first policies', requiring patients to try

[29] AMP is defined as the average price paid to drug manufacturers by wholesalers and retail pharmacies.

[30] PM Danzon, 'Pricing and Reimbursement of Biopharmaceuticals and Medical Devices in the USA' in AJ Culyer (ed), *Encyclopedia of Health Economics* (Cheltenham, Edward Elgar, 2014) vol 3, 127.

[31] Feldman, *Drugs, Money, and Secret Handshakes*, 9–10. On the critical issues deriving from formulary system, see R Feldman, 'The Devil in the Tiers' (2021) 8 *Journal of Law and the Biosciences* 1.

drugs in a particular order in order to get reimbursement)[32] and prior authorisation (according to which the physician may be required to obtain prior approval from the insurer before reimbursement). Such mechanisms allow intermediaries to negotiate discounts in exchange for preferred formulary placement (or even to prevent a competing drug in the same class from being reimbursed at all).[33] In other words, PBMs may exercise significant leverage over manufacturer prices. The opacity of PBMs' activity and their formulary and rebate games are particularly controversial for their effects on prices.

With regard to federal healthcare plans, Medicare Part D is a voluntary outpatient prescription drug benefit provided through private plans approved by the federal government and concerning medicines that beneficiaries obtain from bricks-and-mortar and mail-order pharmacies.[34] Beneficiaries can choose to enrol in either a stand-alone prescription drug plan (PDP) to supplement traditional Medicare or a Medicare Advantage prescription drug plan that covers all Medicare benefits including drugs. Private PBMs and PDPs act in a similar way to manage drug costs, negotiating price concessions and rebates with manufacturers in exchange for market share through the formulary design.[35]

A different system is applied in the case of the other public health plan, the Medicaid programme, which provides coverage for millions of Americans, including low-income beneficiaries.[36] The Medicaid programme is based on mandatory rebates, according to which a manufacturer is required to enter into an agreement with the Department of Health and Human Services (HHS) stating that it will rebate a specified portion of the Medicaid payment for the drug to the states, which in turn share the rebates with the federal government. In exchange, Medicaid programmes cover nearly all of the manufacturer's FDA-approved drugs, and the drugs are eligible for federal matching funds. The Medicaid rebate amount is set by statute and ensures that the programme gets the 'best price' (meaning the lowest price available to any wholesaler, retailer or provider, excluding certain government programmes, such as the health

[32] Step edits are a mechanism designed by health insurers to control cost and provide for the rejection of reimbursement of a drug unless the patient meets certain conditions, such as prior failure on a generic alternative.

[33] Feldman, *Drugs, Money, and Secret Handshakes*, 20.

[34] The Medicare programme primarily covers individuals 65 years old and over. It is divided into four parts: Part A provides hospital insurance, covering inpatient hospital services and a series of post-hospital and home health services; Part B covers a range of outpatient services, including physician-administered drugs; Part C, also called Medicare Advantage Plans, includes plans offered by private companies approved by Medicare, which may provide the benefits of Parts A and B combined and offer extra coverage on the basis of specific rules; Part D concerns prescription drug coverage. The Centers for Medicare & Medicaid Services reviews formularies to endure their consistency with federal requirements.

[35] Danzon, 'Pricing and Reimbursement', 129.

[36] The Medicaid Prescription Drug Rebate Program (MDRP) was created in 1990 by the Omnibus Reconciliation Act. Subsequently, the Affordable Care Act of 2010 made significant changes to the MDRP, increasing, inter alia, the rebate amount for both brand drugs and generic drugs.

programme for veterans).[37] Under the Affordable Care Act of 2010, the rebate formula has provided for a discount of 23.1 per cent of the AMP or the difference between the AMP and the 'best price', whichever is greater, for branded drugs.[38] For generic drugs, the rebate amount has been fixed at 13 per cent of the AMP, and there is no best price provision. Moreover, an additional inflation-adjusted rebate is provided, which effectively anchors the Medicaid price of any drug to its inflation-adjusted launch price. In addition to federal statutory rebates, several states negotiate with manufacturers for supplemental rebates, using placement on a preferred drug list as leverage. A significant role is played by managed care organisations, which provide services and support to Medicaid beneficiaries and receive a monthly fee by states on the basis of risk-based contracts. Many states also use PBMs in their Medicaid prescription drug programmes. The Medicaid system has been the subject of criticism, in particular with regard to its best price clause. According to empirical studies, the Medicaid best price has led private sector rebates to decline:[39] in fact, the policy has reduced manufacturers' willingness to grant discounts to private payers in excess of the mandatory minimum Medicaid rebate, in particular with regard to drugs relatively heavily used by Medicaid patients. This, in turn, has led drugs with a high Medicaid share to experience larger increases in price to private payers.

As noted above, the debate over drug pricing is particularly heated in the US. In this context, lawmakers are considering strategies to reduce spending on prescription drugs. Bearing in mind that drug benefit assessments are not routinely used in Medicare and Medicaid drug coverage decisions, recent proposals in the literature have suggested that US lawmakers evaluate the adoption of approaches taken in other countries. In particular, while the negative impact of price controls on innovation has long been debated, some scholars have supported the introduction in the US of a system similar to the German benefit assessment model, which is considered to provide a formal and transparent comparative effectiveness analysis with beneficial effects in terms of satisfactory price negotiations and no evidence of decreased access to the types of novel therapies that provide important clinical value.[40] Also, the French system has

[37] The Medicaid statute defines best price as 'the lowest price available from the manufacturer during the rebate period to any wholesaler, retailer, provider, health maintenance organization, nonprofit entity, or government entity within the United States'. Exclusions concern the Department of Veterans Affairs, the 340B Drug Pricing Program, the Department of Defense, the Public Health Service and the Indian Health Service. The best price includes rebates in general, but not Medicaid supplemental rebates or rebates provided through the MDRP [42 USC § 1396r-8 (c)(1)(C)].

[38] Certain pediatric and clotting drugs have a lower rebate amount of 17.1%. It should be noted that, as a condition of participation in the MDRP, manufacturers are also required to participate in the federal 340B Program (42 USC § 1396r-8 (a) (5)), which offers discounted drugs to certain safety net providers that serve vulnerable or underserved populations, including Medicaid beneficiaries.

[39] M Duggan and FM Scott Morton, 'The Distortionary Effects of Government Procurement: Evidence From Medicaid Prescription Drug Purchasing' (2006) 121 *Quarterly Journal of Economics* 1 (also finding empirical evidence that firms producing newer drugs with larger sales to Medicaid are more likely to introduce new versions and concluding that government procurement rules can alter both equilibrium price and product proliferation in the private sector).

[40] See Stern et al, 'The Impact of Price Regulation'.

been indicated by scholars as a point of reference that could inform discussions of US prescription drug policy and potential Medicare price negotiations.[41]

At the time of writing, the debate is still ongoing. It should be noted that, due to the increasing number of cases of excessively priced prescription drugs, which will be more extensively treated in Part II of the book, several bills addressing the issue have been proposed in Federal Congress and relevant efforts have been taken at state level in the last years. The current Biden–Harris administration has expressed concerns and the need for an intervention on drug pricing at federal level, and is supporting initiatives aimed at improving affordability and access to prescription drugs through increased government regulations. In particular, the US President (POTUS) has released a wide-ranging Executive Order on Promoting Competition in the American Economy,[42] which, among numerous points, includes a specific reference to high prescription drug prices.[43] In this Executive Order, POTUS has mentioned several objectives in this area, including improving access to prescription drugs and biologics and urging, inter alia, the Secretary of the HHS to submit a plan 'to combat excessive pricing of prescription drugs and enhance domestic pharmaceutical supply chains, to reduce the prices paid by the Federal Government for such drugs, and to address the recurrent problem of price gouging'.[44] Such a plan was released in September 2021 by the HHS, which has called for 'bold legislative action' from Congress and has identified three 'guiding principles' for drug pricing reform: (i) making drug prices 'more affordable and equitable', in particular through Medicare direct price negotiations with drug manufacturers and limits on price increases; (ii) improving competition through market changes that promote biosimilars and generics and increase transparency; and (iii) fostering innovation through research and aligning incentives to promote discovery of new treatments, and not 'market gaming'.

Recent measures directed at addressing high drug prices have been adopted in the Inflation Reduction Act of 2022, including several provisions aimed at lowering prescription drug costs for people with Medicare and reducing drug spending by the federal government.[45] Among those provisions, the Act requires the Secretary of the HHS to negotiate prices for certain drugs covered under Medicare Parts B (physician-administered drugs) and D (retail prescription

[41] VC Raimond, WB Feldman, BN Rome and AS Kesselheim, 'Why France Spends Less Than the United States on Drugs: A Comparative Study of Drug Pricing and Pricing Regulation' (2021) 99 *Milbank Quarterly* 240.

[42] Executive Order No 14036 on Promoting Competition in the American Economy, 86 Fed Reg 36,987 (9 July 2021). For a first comment, see H Hovenkamp, 'President Biden's Executive Order on Promoting Competition: An Antitrust Analysis' (2021) https://ssrn.com/abstract=3887776.

[43] For details, see KA Gavulic and SB Dusetzina, 'Prescription Drug Priorities under the Biden Administration' (2021) 46 *Journal of Health Politics, Policy and Law* 599.

[44] Other measures include the mandate for the FDA to work with states and tribes to safely import prescription drugs from Canada and the encouragement of the FTC to ban pay-for-delay and similar agreements by rule. See ch 5.

[45] HR 5376 – Inflation Reduction Act of 2022, PL 117-169 (16 August 2022).

drugs). It also requires drug manufacturers to pay rebates for price increases above inflation for drugs covered and introduces provisions directed at capping out-of-pocket drug spending under Medicare Part D, in addition to a cap on monthly cost sharing for insulin products.[46]

III. CONCLUDING REMARKS

Pricing and reimbursement of prescription drugs are the area where the most striking difference between EU and US systems can be observed.

The EU lacks competence in this area, which is exclusively the responsibility of the individual Member States. In general, national policies have put in place various systems of pricing and reimbursement for prescription drugs. There is an increasing confidence in the implementation of value-based pricing systems and HTA-based benefit evaluations in pricing decision-making.

The US has embraced a completely different approach, and the supply and distribution chain has ended up playing a prominent role in dictating price level. However, the traditional reluctance to resort to price regulation has to a certain extent been challenged by the exponential rise in prescription drug costs. Increasing pressure is on the federal government to take measures to address drug prices. This constitutes a complex and controversial issue, obviously subject to strong opposition from pharmaceutical companies, that has been a hard battleground in the American political context. In the literature, reference is made to the experience of some European Member States as possible models for reform. Recent legislative initiatives are of limited scope, although relevant to the system, and, while their impact remains to be seen, arguably there is still room for further thoughts and action on the issue.

[46] The Inflation Reduction Act introduces an exception to the so-called non-interference clause, according to which the HHS Secretary was forbidden to interfere with the negotiations between drug manufacturers, pharmacies and PDP sponsors or to require a particular formulary or institute a price structure for the reimbursement of covered drugs. The Act adds an exception that requires the Secretary to negotiate prices for certain drugs, starting with 10 high-cost, single-source drugs for 2026 and increasing to 20 by 2029. The initial negotiations will begin in 2023. See also §§ 1101–02 (regarding prescription drug inflation rebates), 11201 (regarding out-of-pocket cap for Medicare beneficiaries) and 11406 (regarding a $35 cap on monthly cost sharing for insulin products).

Part II

4

Competition Law Enforcement in Pharmaceutical Markets: An Introduction

I. EU AND US ANTITRUST RULES: AN ESSENTIAL OVERVIEW

HAVING PREVIOUSLY DEFINED the unique nature of the drug industry and having provided a survey of the relevant legal frameworks and issues under sector-specific and intellectual property (IP) rules, this chapter contains an essential overview of competition rules and trends in antitrust enforcement in the pharmaceutical sector. The aim is to provide, as has already been done with the other disciplines relevant for this study, the background to examine the relationship of such rules with health-related issues and introduce the following chapters dedicated to the analysis of specific anti-competitive practices. For consistency in the analysis, with regard to the EU, only cases decided at the EU level (and not merely at the national level) are examined.

As a general premise, there is a global consensus on the desirability of competition and a free market economy as leading to the best and most efficient outcomes for society, as grounded in the neoclassical economic theory.[1] Competitive markets are generally deemed to promote allocative and productive

[1] The term 'classical school' generally refers to the first school of economic thought, which flourished in the 18th and 19th centuries and elaborated on economic growth, theory of value and the idea of free markets (basically from William Petty to Karl Marx, including, among the most relevant scholars, Adam Smith, David Ricardo, Thomas Malthus and John Stuart Mill). The term 'neoclassical school' (also named 'mainstream economics') arose in the 1870s and developed the two fundamental theorems of welfare economics. For the sake of brevity, neoclassical economic theory relies on a set of assumptions, including: scarcity (ie availability of resources only in limited quantities) and the *Homo oeconomicus* paradigm, postulating the rationality of economic agents as self-interested individuals with complete information and making their choices in a consistent manner. The analysis of competition in the neoclassical theory is contained in the model of perfect competition, which describes the ideal conditions that must occur in a market in which efficiency is maximised (a large number of buyers and sellers; homogeneity of the product; perfect information; no barriers to entry or exit; no transaction costs; no externalities). According to this model, a perfectly competitive market maximises society's wealth overall as it guarantees the achievement of allocative and productive efficiency. As a related benefit, dynamic efficiency may be improved, even though the relation of dynamic efficiency to the concept of perfect competition is complex (as also shown by the Schumpeterian idea according to which the motivation to innovate lies in the prospects of monopoly profits and that competition is a dynamic process of 'creative disruption',

efficiency while stimulating innovation in a dynamic perspective, and to provide consumers with lower prices, higher quality and a greater degree of choice than non-competitive ones. However, which goals competition law should pursue has long been and still is a controversial issue both in the EU and in the US.[2]

Competition law in the EU constitutes one of the most important policy areas, and its fundamental role in shaping the EU's internal market has been set out since the beginning, being embedded in the Treaty of Rome as part of the instruments oriented towards the objective of European economic integration. This distinguishes EU law from any other system of competition law – whether in the US or elsewhere – and is based on the 'single market imperative', aimed at dismantling internal barriers to trade within the EU and allowing complete freedom of movement. Such a role has been reaffirmed and strengthened in the practice of both the EU courts and the Commission, and has been the subject of a substantial body of academic literature.[3]

The substantive antitrust provisions, in particular Articles 101 and 102 TFEU, addressing anti-competitive agreements and abuse of dominant position respectively, do not contain an explicit reference to a particular policy and, similarly to other substantive Treaty provisions, are worded in broad terms. However, they contain concepts which are relevant in delineating the objectives of the rules (for example, the reference to fairness and consumers in the exemption provision in Article 101(3)).[4] The choice of an open-ended approach in the drafting of the provisions has the clear advantage of rendering them adaptable to changes in policy in time and of including a wide range of practices that are potentially subject to EU competition law, including new ones. Among several cases, pay-for-delay agreements occurring in the pharmaceutical sector (treated in chapter five of this book) provide an illustrative example of new practices attracting antitrust scrutiny. At the same time, challenges arise in the concrete application of the rules to factual scenarios.[5]

where short-term positions of market power stimulate others to further innovate). Therefore, the more a market moves away from perfect competition towards monopoly (ie the higher market power that a firm holds), the higher are the social costs that the market produces.

[2] The term 'competition law' is used as a synonym for 'antitrust law', commonly used in the US. This Chapter analyses the rules dealing with anti-competitive agreements and unilateral conduct, ie Arts 101 and 102 of the Treaty on the Functioning of the European Union (TFEU) and ss 1 and 2 of the Sherman Act (15 USC §§1-2). Among other relevant provisions, with regard to the application of s 5 of the FTC Act (15 USC §45), see ch 7.

[3] See, eg C-D Ehlermann, 'The Contribution of EC Competition Policy to the Single Market' (1992) 29 *CML Rev* 257; J Baquero Cruz, *Between Competition and Free Movement: The Economic Constitutional Law of the European Community* (Oxford, Hart Publishing, 2002); K Klaus Patel and Heike Schweitzer (eds), *The Historical Foundations of EU Competition Law* (Oxford, Oxford University Press, 2013). For a recent analysis of the evolution of EU competition law, see P Ibáñez Colomo, *The Shaping of EU Competition Law* (Cambridge, Cambridge University Press, 2018).

[4] For a wide analysis, see A Jones, B Sufrin and N Dunne, *Jones and Sufrin's EU Competition Law*, 7th edn (Oxford, Oxford University Press, 2019) 43ff.

[5] Ibáñez Colomo, *The Shaping of EU Competition Law*, 24–25 (discussing the risks of inconsistencies in interpretation and enforcement that may arise).

Article 101 TFEU applies to a broad range of collusive arrangements between undertakings which appreciably affect trade between Member States and has a bifurcated structure. The prohibition rule contained in Article 101(1) is aimed at catching different forms of coordination and collusion, establishing the fundamental distinction between agreements that restrict competition 'by object' and 'by effect': the former are prohibited as anti-competitive 'by their very nature', while the latter are subject to the prohibition insofar as they have restrictive effects. The wording of Article 101(1) contains a non-exhaustive list of the most common manifestations of cartel conduct, including price-fixing, market-sharing and output restriction. Such prohibition may be declared inapplicable to agreements that fulfil the cumulative conditions set out in Article 101(3) (ie whether they provide specified benefits – by improving the production or distribution of goods or services or promoting technical or economic progress – allowing consumers a fair share of the benefit, do not contain any indispensable restrictions and do not eliminate competition in a substantial part of the product in question). While the burden of proving an infringement of Article 101(1) is on the Commission, as the competition law enforcer at the EU level, the burden of showing that Article 101(3) is satisfied is on the undertakings making that claim. Even if it is very difficult to run convincing arguments and provide evidence of such a claim, a feature of EU law is that in principle there are no agreements that are irredeemably illegal.[6]

Article 102 TFEU is concerned with unilateral behaviour by undertakings holding a 'dominant position': this is a legal term that determines the point at which the conduct becomes subject to scrutiny under the Article, which can be equated to the economic concept of substantial market power.[7] Notably, it prohibits the abuse of the dominant position, covering both conduct that exploits its customers directly (exploitative abuses, such as imposing unfair prices) and exclusionary conduct through which the dominant undertaking seeks to harm the competitive position of its actual or potential competitors or to exclude them from the market. In addition to these fundamental categories of abuse, others have been identified, such as discriminatory abuses covered by Article 102(c) and market integration-oriented abuses.[8] Also, in the case of unilateral abuses, although Article 102 provides no textual basis similar to

[6] It should be noted that block exemptions provided for specific types of agreements may be particularly relevant in the pharmaceutical sector, such as those applying to horizontal cooperation agreements, which may be beneficial by enabling firms to bring new products to the market, sharing risks, pooling know-how, etc. See European Commission, 'Guidelines on the Applicability of Article 101 of the Treaty on the Functioning of the European Union to Horizontal Co-operation Agreements' [2011] OJ C11/1 (at the time of writing, under revision). See ch 9. In the US, see Federal Trade Commission and US Department of Justice, 'Antitrust Guidelines for Collaborations Among Competitors' (2000).

[7] R Whish and D Bailey, *Competition Law*, 10th edn (Oxford, Oxford University Press, 2021) 183. See European Commission, 'Guidance on the Commission's Enforcement Priorities in Applying Article 82 of the EC Treaty to Abusive Exclusionary Conduct by Dominant Undertakings' (Guidance Paper) [2009] OJ C45/7, para 10.

[8] On this point, see in general Jones et al, *EU Competition Law*, 361–62.

Article 101(3), the prohibition has been interpreted as incorporating the possibility of 'objective justification', which requires a demonstration either of countervailing efficiencies stemming from the alleged restraint or its objective necessity.[9] Understandably, the burden of proof is on the defendant.

The substantive scope of Articles 101 and 102 TFEU has been clarified by the EU courts over the years. With regard to Article 101, the notion of restriction of competition, as well as other elements of the provision, has been shaped by the principles laid down in the case law. Nevertheless, some uncertainty around the boundaries of the category of 'by object' infringements still exists and it is a matter of debate. The essential criterion for ascertaining whether coordination between undertakings constitutes a restriction by object is the finding that it 'reveals in itself a sufficient degree of harm to competition'.[10] Restrictions by object are assumed to be a threat to the attainment of the Treaty's objectives and to restrict competition appreciably irrespective of their actual effects. The practice of the Commission and courts in the past has led to criticism for the alleged expansion of the category of object restrictions over its boundaries.[11] Recent judgments have stressed the narrow nature of the category of object restraints and the importance of the context of the agreement in their identification.[12] It should be noted that cases occurring in the pharmaceutical sector have recently led to the identification of novel types of object restrictions[13] – namely, pay for delay[14] and dissemination of misleading information relating to adverse reactions resulting from the use of a competing medicinal product.[15]

With regard to Article 102, case law has consistently defined dominance in terms of an undertaking's economic strength and its ability to behave independently on the market,[16] and has held that dominant firms have a 'special responsibility' not to impair genuine competition.[17] The concept of abuse is an objective one based on the notion of 'recourse to methods different from those which condition normal competition',[18] such condition generally being

[9] See, eg European Commission, Guidance Paper, paras 28–31.

[10] Case C-67/13 *Groupement des cartes bancaires (CB) v European Commission* ECLI:EU:C:2014:2204, para 57.

[11] Among the various judgments, one of the most representative of this tendency can be found in Case C-8/08 *T-Mobile Netherlands BV, KPN Mobile NV, Orange Nederland NV and Vodafone Libertel NV v Raad van bestuur van de Nederlandse Mededingingsautoriteit (T-Mobile)* ECLI:EU:C:2009:343.

[12] See Case C-67/13 *Groupement des cartes bancaires*.

[13] In general, on this point see Whish and Bailey, *Competition Law*, 128ff.

[14] Pay-for-delay cases will be addressed in ch 5.

[15] See n 63.

[16] With regard to these fundamental principles, which are routinely repeated in the subsequent cases, suffice it to recall the following landmark rulings: Case C-27/76 *United Brands Company and United Brands Continentaal BV v Commission* ECLI:EU:C:1978:22, paras 65–66; and Case 85/76 *Hoffmann-La Roche & Co AG v Commission of the European Communities* ECLI:EU:C:1979:36, [1979] ECR 00461, paras 38–39.

[17] Case 322/81 *NV Nederlandsche Banden Industrie Michelin v Commission of the European Communities* ECLI:EU:C:1983:313, [1983] ECR 313, para 57.

[18] Case C-85/76 *Hoffmann-La Roche*, para 91.

called 'competition on the merits'.[19] Drawing the line between anti-competitive behaviour and competition on the merits is a difficult and controversial matter, which has been discussed widely in the literature too.[20] Similarly to what happens with object restrictions in Article 101 TFEU, a contentious aspect in the application of Article 102 – and the related dichotomy between over- and under-enforcement risks – is whether certain unilateral conducts could or should be characterised as intrinsically anti-competitive or whether an effect-based analysis should be applied.[21]

The US equivalent of Articles 101 and 102 TFEU are sections 1 and 2 of the Sherman Act. US courts have interpreted the wording of section 1 as meaning that agreements must not restrain trade unreasonably and have traditionally adopted two categories of analysis: the per se rule and the rule of reason.[22] The former applies to those agreements that lack any redeeming virtue so are presumed to be unreasonable and thus illegal, whereas the latter provides that agreements must be assessed in their legal and economic context to balance their pro- and anti-competitive effects. Unlike Article 101 TFEU, no exception to the prohibition is provided.

Section 2 of the Sherman Act represents the most striking difference with the EU system, as it forbids 'monopolization' and 'attempts to monopolize'. While Article 102 TFEU only applies to undertakings which already hold a dominant position, US antitrust rules prosecute conduct by which market power is acquired unlawfully. At its core, section 2 makes it illegal to acquire or maintain monopoly power through improper means. Moreover, US rules address single-firm exclusionary conduct but do not include exploitative behaviour. Section 2 of the Sherman Act and Article 102 TFEU have been compared widely in the antitrust literature.[23] According to the mainstream reconstruction of the

[19] Case C-280/08 P *Deutsche Telekom AG v European Commission* ECLI:EU:C:2010:603, [2010] ECR I-09555, para 177; European Commission, Guidance Paper, paras 1 and 6.

[20] For a recent analysis, see P Ibáñez Colomo, 'What Is an Abuse of a Dominant Position? Deconstructing the Prohibition and Categorizing Practices' in P Akman, O Brook and K Stylianou (eds), *Research Handbook on Abuse of Dominance and Monopolization* (Cheltenham, Edward Elgar, forthcoming).

[21] *Ex multis*, for a detailed treatment of the issue, see P Akman, *The Concept of Abuse in EU Competition Law* (Oxford, Hart Publishing, 2012) 130–43. See also L Peeperkorn, 'Coherence in the Application of Articles 101 and 102: A Realistic Prospect or an Elusive Goal?' (2016) 39 *World Competition* 389; P Ibáñez Colomo, 'Beyond the "More Economics-Based Approach": A Legal Perspective on Article 102 TFEU Case Law' (2016) 53 *CML Rev* 709.

[22] *Standard Oil Co v United States* 221 US 1 (1911); *United States v Socony-Vacuum Oil Co*, 310 US 150 (1940).

[23] See, eg R Joliet, *Monopolization and Abuse of Dominant Position. A Comparative Study of the American and European Approaches to the Control of Economic Power* (Leiden, Martinus Nijhoff, 1970); EM Fox, 'Monopolization and Dominance in the United States and the European Community: Efficiency, Opportunity, and Fairness' (1986) 61 *Notre Dame Law Review* 981, 1017–18; WE Kovacic, 'The Intellectual DNA of Modern US Competition Law for Dominant Firm Conduct: The Chicago/Harvard Double Helix' (2007) 2007 *Columbia Business Law Review* 1; M Gal, 'Monopoly Pricing as an Antitrust Offense in the US and the EC: Two Systems of Belief about Monopoly?' (2004) 49 *Antitrust Bulletin* 343, 363ff.

differences between the two systems, whereas section 2 of the Sherman Act has been revolutionised under the influence of the Chicago School and brought into line with economic theory, Article 102 TFEU has for a long time been considered as being interpreted by courts with a view to protecting competitors and not competition, and of pursuing fairness goals instead of efficiency ones. This reading is based on a recurring criticism of the law and practice of Article 102 as shaped by ordoliberal legacies[24] and recalls the attacks on the 'old' section 2 jurisprudence.[25] However, this 'standard story' has been criticised as it does not reflect the reality, which is more nuanced than that, and some authors have suggested a different reading.[26] Being aware of this criticism, both the Commission and the EU courts have stressed the importance of efficient competition as the key objective of Article 102.[27] It is true that Article 102 TFEU has been applied in a more interventionist way than section 2 of the Sherman Act. However, distinguishing between competitive and exclusionary conduct and determining which means of acquiring and maintaining monopoly power should be prohibited as improper are difficult tasks that US courts and commentators have long recognised. In fact, both US and EU law have struggled to formulate an adequate test for distinguishing between meritorious competition and anti-competitive conduct.[28]

As the wording of the antitrust statutes does not provide detailed guidance, in the US, too, the role of the courts is fundamental in the interpretation and the

[24] See, eg P Beherens, 'The Ordoliberal Concept of "Abuse" of a Dominant Position and Its Impact on Article 102 TFEU' in F Di Porto and R Podszun (eds), *Abusive Practices in Competition* Law (Cheltenham, Edward Elgar, 2018) 5; C Ahlborn and J Padilla, 'From Fairness To Welfare: Implications for the Assessment of Unilateral Conduct under EC Competition Law' in CD Ehlermann and M Marquis, *European Competition Law Annual 2007: A Reformed Approach to Article 82 EC* (Oxford, Hart Publishing, 2008) 55.

[25] The reference is to the attack made by Robert Bork on antitrust enforcement in the US in the 1960s and 1970s. See generally RH Bork, *The Antitrust Paradox: A Policy at War with Itself* (New York, Basic Books, 1978).

[26] H Schweitzer, 'The History, Interpretation and Underlying Principles of Section 2 Sherman Act and Article 82 EC' in D Ehlermann and Marquis, *European Competition Law Annual 2007*, 119, 120 (explaining that the reasons for the European approach are rooted in the pro-regulatory philosophy that underestimates the ability of the market to self-correct and in the legacies of the ordoliberal thinking). See also P Akman, 'Searching for the Long-Lost Soul of Articles 82 EC' (2009) 29 *OJLS* 267 (examining the *travaux préparatoires* of Art 102 and challenging the idea that its drafters were not concerned with economic efficiency); Whish and Bailey, *Competition Law*, 201. In general, for a comprehensive analysis of Art 102 and its application, see R Nazzini, *The Foundations of European Union Competition Law: The Objective and Principles of Article 102* (Oxford, Oxford University Press, 2011).

[27] See Whish and Bailey, *Competition Law*, 201–02, and the case law cited therein. See European Commission, Guidance Paper, paras 5, 6 and 23. The EU Courts have made reference to the protection of the process of competition and to the protection only of 'as-efficient' competitors as opposed to inefficient ones in various judgments, eg Case C-280/08 P *Deutsche Telekom*, paras 176–77; Case C-52/09 *Konkurrensverket v TeliaSonera Sverige AB* ECLI:EU:C:2011:83, [2011] ECR I-00527, paras 24, 31–33 and 39–40; Case C-413/14 P *Intel Corp v European Commission* ECLI:EU:C:2017:632 para 133.

[28] Schweitzer, 'The History', 161.

development of competition rules. This also concerns the application of the rule of reason, which has become the prevailing standard since the late 1970s.[29] There are different means of implementing the rule-of-reason appraisal. However, in general, courts tend to apply a burden-shifting structured version (first, the plaintiff must show a significant anti-competitive effect; second, the burden shifts to the defendant to demonstrate a legitimate pro-competitive justification; third, the plaintiff can overcome the defendant's showing, and establish liability, if it can prove that a viable and substantially less restrictive, yet equally effective, alternative to the conduct exists; if no such alternative is available, then courts will weigh the anti-competitive effects against the pro-competitive benefits to determine if the conduct is an 'unreasonable' restraint of trade).[30] It should be noted that the EU courts have consistently affirmed that EU competition law does not recognise the rule of reason as in the US model.[31]

With regard to public enforcement, at the EU level, this is a task of the Commission, which takes decisions that are binding on firms and that may be challenged before the General Court and the European Court of Justice; at the national level, national competition authorities and national judges can enforce EU competition law. In contrast, in the US, there are two main competition agencies, the Department of Justice Antitrust Division and the Federal Trade Commission (FTC), which are primarily prosecutors rather than decision-makers and enforce antitrust laws by bringing action before the ordinary federal courts.[32]

[29] The rule of reason was born in the 1911 case *Standard Oil Co v United States* and is famously traced to *Chicago Board of Trade v United States* 246 US 231, 238 (1918). While, by the 1960s, several restraints had been considered as illegal per se, towards the end of the 1970s the Supreme Court started changing its approach as it embraced a consumer welfare objective. Difficulties had arisen in the practical application of the rule-of-reason analysis and criticism pointed out that it can result in being imprecise and unpredictable. Among the many critiques of the Chicago Board formulation, see H Hovenkamp, *Federal Antitrust Policy: The Law of Competition and Its Practice*, 5th edn (St Paul, West Academic Publishing, 2016) § 5.6b; RA Posner, 'The Rule of Reason and the Economic Approach: Reflections on the Sylvania Decision' (1977) 45 *University of Chicago Law Review* 1, 15; ME Stucke, 'Does the Rule of Reason Violate the Rule of Law?' (2009) *UC Davis Law Review* 1375, 1489; AI Gavil, 'Moving beyond Caricature and Characterization: The Modern Rule of Reason in Practice' (2012) 85 *Southern California Law Review* 733, 743–44; JW Markham Jr, 'Sailing a Sea of Doubt: A Critique of the Rule of Reason in US Antitrust Law' (2012) 17 *Fordham Journal of Corporate & Financial Law* 591, 655. For a recent overview, see HJ Hovenkamp, 'The Rule of Reason' (2018) 70 *Florida Law Review* 81.

[30] The Supreme Court argued that the rule of reason involves a 'three-step, burden-shifting framework' in *Ohio v American Express Co* 138 S Ct 2274, 2284 (2018). For a critical analysis against the omission of the fourth step concerning the balancing, see, eg MA Carrier, 'The Four-Step Rule of Reason' (2019) 33 *Antitrust* 50.

[31] See Case T-112/99 *Métropole télévision (M6), Suez-Lyonnaise des eaux, France Télécom and Télévision française 1 SA (TF1) v Commission* ECLI:EU:T:2001:215, [2001] ECR II-02459, paras 73–76. See also Joined Cases 56/64 and 58/64 *Consten and Grundig v Commission* ECLI:EU:C:1966:41, [1966] ECR 00429, para 343; Case C-307/18 *Generics (UK) Ltd and Others v Competition and Markets Authority* ECLI:EU:C:2020:52, para 104.

[32] For a comparative analysis of the governance in competition policy, see F Cengiz, *Antitrust Federalism in the EU and the US* (London, Routledge, 2012).

The main standard on which antitrust enforcement has relied in several systems is the consumer welfare one.[33] In the EU, this standard is meant to ensure that competition rules are applied to deliver low prices, greater output and choice, higher quality and more innovation; in the US, consumer welfare is mainly focused on output and low prices.[34] The adherence to the welfarist approach narrows the elements that competition enforcement must take into account, namely welfare and efficiency. Under the consumer welfare principle, as it is generally understood today, antitrust policy encourages markets to produce output as high as is consistent with sustainable competition, with prices that are accordingly low.[35] There are various reasons behind this choice. In addition to being an easier test to apply than any general welfare test, it represents 'a politically acceptable way of arguing for an economic approach to competition law'[36] and implies less tolerance of ever increasing amounts of market power in the economy.[37]

The roots of the argument that competition law should be concerned only with efficiency are commonly traced to the principles supported by the Chicago School. These principles, which have had a huge impact on the development of US antitrust and have crucially influenced thinking in scholarship in this field, are challenged both from the 'right', ie those advocating a move towards a total welfare standard, and from the 'left', especially by the rise of the so-called 'neo-Brandeisian School'.[38] Advocates of this latter approach consider the

[33] The reference to the 'consumer welfare' is generally traced to Bork, *The Antitrust Paradox*, 66, 90 and 97. However, for Bork, 'consumer welfare' referred to the sum of the welfare, or surplus, enjoyed by both consumers and producers, and he referred to consumer welfare as 'merely another term for the wealth of the nation'. In conventional economics, the combined producer and consumer surplus is called 'total welfare' or 'social welfare'. On this point and on the confusion in terminology, see, eg BY Orbach, 'The Antitrust Consumer Welfare Paradox' (2010) 7 *Journal of Competition Law & Economics* 133, 148. On the influence of the Chicago School and the claims of the neo-Brandeis approach, see HJ Hovenkamp, 'Is Antitrust's Consumer Welfare Principle Imperiled?' (2019) 45 *Journal of Corporation Law* 101. In economics, 'consumer welfare' refers to the buyer's well-being in the form of the benefits derived from consuming goods and services; in competition law, it refers to consumer surplus (the aggregate measure of the surplus of all consumers). The maximisation of consumer welfare is achieved when market prices are equal to the marginal cost of production, a situation that occurs under the ideal model of perfect competition. With regard to the notion of consumer welfare, see also R Van den Bergh, *Comparative Competition Law and Economics* (Cheltenham, Edward Elgar, 2017), 86, 95ff (distinguishing between two potential interpretations, ie: (i) consumer welfare as the result of maximising consumer surplus; and (ii) consumer welfare resulting from improving consumer choice as the ultimate expression on consumers); K Cseres, 'The Controversies of the Consumer Welfare Standard' (2007) 3 *Competition Law Review* 121.

[34] See Sufrin et al, *EU Competition Law*, 39 and 48. The authors recall that sometimes it is argued that the consumer welfare standard in the US also takes into account quality, choice and innovation (quoting JD Wright, E Dorsey, J Klick and JM Rybnicek, 'Requiem for a Paradox: The Dubious Rise and Inevitable Fall of Hipster Antitrust' (2019) 51 *Arizona State Law Journal* 292, 306).

[35] Hovenkamp, 'Is Antitrust's Consumer Welfare', 102.

[36] Nazzini, *The Foundations*, 44–45.

[37] Hovenkamp, 'Is Antitrust's Consumer Welfare', 109, 128.

[38] For an overview, see ibid.

simple pursuit of an economically oriented understanding of consumer welfare as being both ill-conceived and inappropriate, and call for a rejection of the commitment to the economic methodology and evidence-based policy that lies at the heart of modern antitrust enforcement.[39] This view, in the wake of the increasing concentration of markets in recent times (in particular with regard to the rise of powerful digital platforms), is understood to argue that antitrust law should take into account political and social values.[40]

Analysing such wide discussion and the different approaches taken to identify competition law's possible objectives is outside the scope of this book. The principal distinction this book will consider is between the pursuit of purely economic goals and that of a wider range of policy objectives that are relevant for the application of competition law in the pharmaceutical sector; this will be treated in Part III of this book.

II. ANTITRUST ENFORCEMENT IN THE PHARMACEUTICAL SECTOR

The pharmaceutical sector is permanently on the agenda of antitrust agencies in both the EU and the US. While many practices dangerous for competition occur in both regions, others may be specific to each system, depending on its regulatory framework and its specific features.

In the EU, one of the first areas on which antitrust enforcement focused was the removal of private intra-brand obstacles to competition in the internal market in the form of parallel trade.[41] Parallel trade has generated a significant body of case law under the EU free movement rules in the past.[42] Then, antitrust

[39] The Neo-Brandeisian School is also called, mostly with a pejorative connotation, 'hipster antitrust'. See, eg T Wu, 'After Consumer Welfare, Now What? The "Protection of Competition" Standard in Practice' [2018] *Competition Policy International*; L Khan, 'The Ideological Roots of America's Market Power Problem' (2018) 127 *Yale Law Journal Forum* 960; L Khan, 'The New Brandeis Movement: America's Antimonopoly Debate' (2018) 9 *Journal of European Competition Law and Practice* 131. For a critical comment, see, eg Hovenkamp, 'Is Antitrust's Consumer Welfare', 103.

[40] Z Teachout and L Khan, 'Market Structure and Political Law: A Taxonomy of Power' (2014) 9 *Duke Journal of Constitutional Law & Public Policy* 37, 72 (arguing that antitrust law and other de-concentration rules should be understood not solely as part of corporate law, but also as part of political law).

[41] See, inter alia, E Navarro Varona and C Caballero Candelairo, 'The Pharmaceutical Sector and Parallel Trade' in P Figueroa and A Guerriero (eds), *EU Law of Competition and Trade in the Pharmaceutical Sector* (Cheltenham, Edward Elgar, 2019) 405. See ch 2.

[42] See, eg Case C-277/87 *Sandoz prodotti farmaceutici SpA v Commission* ECLI:EU:C:1990:6 [1990] ECR I-45; Case T-41/96 *Bayer AG v Commission* (*Adalat*) ECLI:EU:T:2000:242, [2000] ECR II-3383; Joined Cases C-2/01 P and C-3/01 P *Bundesverband der Arzneimittel-Importeure eV and Commission v Bayer AG* ECLI:EU:C:2004:2, [2004] ECR I-23; Joined Cases C-501/06 P, C-513/06 P, C-515/06 P and C-519/06 P *GlaxoSmithKline Services Unlimited v Commission of the European Communities and Commission of the European Communities v GlaxoSmithKline*

enforcement relating to pharmaceuticals has involved a broader range of issues, in particular concerning inter-brand competition from generic substitutes.[43] It has been argued that the trend in enforcement priorities of antitrust agencies reveals a focus on IP-intensive and high technology industries, in which competition between firms is guided by the research and development of new goods and services rather than by the price.[44]

The first abuse of dominance decision adopted by the Commission in the pharmaceutical sector in 2005, *AstraZeneca*, which was concluded with the landmark ruling issued by the Court of Justice in 2012, remains a unique application of Article 102 TFEU and is a fundamental case for various reasons, as it includes different types of violation of competition rules and has guided subsequent case law.[45] For this reason, some further details on the case are provided here.

In brief, the case concerned two abuses of the Swedish company's dominant position during the marketing of the omeprazole-based drug Losec, used in the treatment of gastrointestinal diseases and falling within the category of proton pump inhibitors. Two behaviours, aimed at preventing the launch of generic versions of the active drug ingredient in a number of markets in Europe, had been sanctioned: (i) the misrepresentation by the originator company to patent offices in Belgium, Denmark, Germany, the Netherlands, Norway and the UK, as well as to national courts in Germany and Norway, in order to obtain or maintain supplementary protection certificates (SPCs) for omeprazole, to which it was not entitled or to which it was entitled for a more limited period, thereby excluding generic manufacturers from the market; and (ii) the filing of applications for the revocation of marketing authorisations for Losec capsules in Denmark, Norway and Sweden, along with the simultaneous withdrawal of Losec capsules from the market and then the launch of a new tablet formulation of the drug in those countries.[46]

With regard to the first abuse, according to the Commission and the European courts, the dominant firm knowingly and deliberately tried to mislead the patent offices and the judicial authorities of several Member States to

Services Unlimited and European Association of Euro Pharmaceutical Companies (EAEPC) v Commission of the European Communities and Asociación de exportadores españoles de productos farmacéuticos (Aseprofar) v Commission of the European Communities ECLI:EU:C:2009:610, [2009] ECR I-09291; Joined Cases C-468/06 to C-478/06 *Sot Lélos kai Sia EE and Others v GlaxoSmithKline AEVE Farmakeftikon Proïonton, formerly Glaxowellcome AEVE* ECLI:EU:C:2008:504, [2008] ECR I-7139.

[43] For an overview, see L Hancher and W Sauter, 'A Dose of Competition: EU Antitrust Law in the Pharmaceuticals Sector' (2016) 4 *Journal of Antitrust Enforcement* 381.

[44] P Ibáñez Colomo, 'Restrictions on Innovation in EU Competition Law' (2016) 41 *EL Rev* 201.

[45] *Generics/Astra Zeneca* (Case COMP/37507) [2005] Commission Decision, upheld on appeal in Cases T-321/05 *AstraZeneca AB and AstraZeneca plc v European Commission* ECLI:EU:T:2010:266, [2010] ECR II-02805 and Case C-457/10 P *AstraZeneca AB and AstraZeneca plc v European Commission* ECLI:EU:C:2012:770.

[46] In addition, AstraZeneca introduced a new-generation product called esomeprazole, which was supposed to have significant clinical benefits compared to omeprazole, the active pharmaceutical ingredient in Losec. However, this has no relevance to the finding of the abuse.

artificially prolong the IP coverage of its product and maintain its monopoly on the markets concerned for as long as possible. Accordingly, by delivering misleading representations in order to obtain the required SPCs, it could not be said that AstraZeneca competed on its merits and its conduct amounted to a violation of Article 102 TFEU.[47] It is worth stressing that the assessment of whether the conduct of the dominant firm in the market could induce public authorities to raise undue regulatory barriers to competition (in this case, by fraudulently inducing the granting of exclusive rights) is decisive. In particular, the public authorities' limited margin of appreciation or the absence of an obligation on them to check the accuracy or veracity of the information communicated (a condition which existed in this specific case given the limited degree of discretion on the part of the patent offices when assessing the information submitted by the SPC applicants) are important factors.[48]

AstraZeneca represents a significant example of cases in which companies deliberately disseminate false or misleading information to regulators with the aim of excluding competitors from the market. This resembles a behaviour that is recurrent also in other sectors, ie that of dominant companies which seek to defraud agencies such as the Patent and Trade Office[49] or the Food and Drug Administration[50] with the goal of unduly acquiring or exercising a right

[47] Case T-321/05 *AstraZeneca*, para 355. The relevance given to subjective intention in this case has been matter of debate. The General Court (para 59) answered to applicants' argument in that regard by asserting that although proof of the deliberate nature of conduct liable to deceive the public authorities is not necessary for the purposes of identifying an abuse of a dominant position, intention nonetheless also constitutes a relevant factor which may be taken into consideration by the Commission. On this issue, see, eg M Maggiolino and ML Montagnani, 'Astrazeneca's Abuse of IPR-Related Procedures: A Hypothesis of Antitrust Offence, Abuse of Rights, and IPR Misuse' (2011) 34 *World Competition* 245, 251.

[48] Case T-321/05 *AstraZeneca*, paras 357 and 360.

[49] In the US context, the main point of reference is the decision *Walker Process Equipment, Inc v Food Machinery & Chemical Corp* 382 US 172, 173 (1965); see also *Therasense, Inc v Becton, Dickinson and Co* 649 F 3d 1276, 1276 (Fed Cir 2011); HJ Hovenkamp, 'Patent Exclusions and Antitrust after Therasense' (2013) Faculty Scholarship at Penn Law 1870, https://scholarship.law.upenn.edu/faculty_scholarship/1870 (clarifying that in *Walker Process* the Supreme Court held that one who obtained a patent by defrauding the Patent and Trademark Office and subsequently filed an infringement suit in order to exclude a rival, could violate the antitrust laws; in addition to the impropriety in obtaining the patent, the usual structural requirements for a monopolisation or attempt to monopolise offence obtained as well).

[50] See, eg *Xechem, Inc v Bristol-Myers Squibb Co* 372 F 3d 899, 902 (7th Cir 2004); *In re Remeron* 335 F Supp 2d 522, 522 (DNJ 2004); *Organon Inc v Mylan Pharmaceuticals* 293 F Supp 2d 453, 456 (DNJ 2003); *In re Buspirone*, 185 F Supp 2d 363, 366 (SDNY 2002); *In the Matter of Biovail Corporation* 011 0094, 2002 WL 727033 (FTC 2002). The US FTC published a study including so-called 'Orange Book' practices by certain pharmaceutical enterprises, finding that patents had been abused at the FDA to prevent the entry of generic drugs. See US Federal Trade Commission, 'Generic Drug Entry Prior to Patent Expiration: An FTC Study' (2002) www.ftc.gov/sites/default/files/documents/reports/generic-drug-entry-prior-patent-expiration-ftc-study/genericdrugstudy_0.pdf. With regard to the antitrust relevance of the conduct of pharmaceutical companies which wrongly list patents in FDA's Orange Book, see, eg *In re Lantus Direct Purchaser Antitrust Litigation* Case No 18-2086 (1st Cir 13 February 2020), where the US Court of Appeals for the First Circuit held that in such case firms must prove they acted in good faith to avoid antitrust liability.

to exclude competitors through legal barriers. The *AstraZeneca* case has thus become an important precedent quoted in the debated issue of whether the strategic use of patent filings and procedures before the patent offices can be considered a violation of competition law.[51]

The second abuse – dealing with the selective deregistration of the marketing authorisations of a blockbuster drug, in combination with the withdrawal of the original form of the drug from the market and the launch of a reformulated version – will be further examined in chapter six. Here, it is sufficient to say that *AstraZeneca* is also representative of another type of behaviour recurrent in the pharmaceutical sector: regulatory gaming. Regulatory gaming can be defined as private behaviour that abuses a neutral or pro-competitive regulatory structure and uses it as a tool to accomplish anti-competitive results.[52] As will be seen in the next chapters of this Part, regulatory gaming typically involves conduct that is plausibly within the letter of the formal rules, but targets results that are at odds with the aim of the underlying legal framework.[53]

In 2009, the Commission released its first Sector Inquiry, covering the period from January 2000 to June 2008, which found that originator companies had employed a number of instruments composing a 'toolbox' aimed at blocking or delaying generic entry, including, for example: patent strategies, involving multiple patent applications for the same international non-proprietary name ('patent clusters' or 'patent thickets') and divisional applications; patent litigation; patent settlements; strategies aimed at national regulatory bodies, stakeholders, distributors and active pharmaceutical ingredient producers; and life cycle strategies for follow-on products.[54] Moreover, defensive patent strategies by originators aimed at blocking other competing originator companies have been reported.[55] More recently, in 2019, the Commission released a new report, upon the request of the Council and the Parliament, expressing concerns that access to affordable and innovative essential medicines could be endangered

[51] The fraudulent nature of the first procedure and the misused application of the second procedure constituted the 'further elements' that, together with anti-competitive foreclosure, created antitrust liability for AstraZeneca. For comments and diverging opinions on the case, see Maggiolino and Montagnani, 'Astrazeneca's Abuse'; L Kjølbye, 'Article 82 EC as Remedy to Patent System Imperfections: Fighting Fire with Fire?' (2009) 32 *World Competition* 163; J Drexl, 'Astra-Zeneca and the EU Sector Inquiry: When Do Patent Filings Violate Competition Law?' (2012) Max Planck Institute for Intellectual Property & Competition Law Research Paper No 2; D Hull, 'The AstraZeneca Judgment: Implications for IP and Regulatory Strategies' (2010) 1 *Journal of European Competition Law & Practice* 500.

[52] SL Dogan and MA Lemley, 'Antitrust Law and Regulatory Gaming' (2009) 87 *Texas Law Review* 685, 708.

[53] N Dunne, 'The Role of Regulation in EU Competition Law Assessment' (2021) 44 *World Competition* 287, 301.

[54] European Commission, 'Pharmaceutical Sector Inquiry: Final Report' (2009) 182.

[55] ibid 385ff.

by a combination of very high and unsustainable price levels, market withdrawals or other business strategies by pharmaceutical companies, and the limited bargaining power of national governments against those firms.[56] This report, covering the period 2009–17, also treats practices that hinder or delay the entry of generic medicines, including patent settlement agreements and misuse of regulatory procedures, in addition to other practices that either directly or indirectly lead to higher prices of medicines, eg various types of coordination between competitors and excessive pricing.[57]

As already mentioned, generic entry is one of the main concerns for antitrust agencies on both sides of the Atlantic, as generics are typically sold at a fraction of the price of the branded equivalent drug and exert strong competitive pressure on the latter. The effects of generic entry on other on-patent potential substitutes are less clear, as some scholars in the economic literature argue that the price of such drugs is barely affected.[58] However, it is a recurrent idea that pharmaceutical companies are subject to antitrust scrutiny with regard to practices developed by incumbent originator companies to prevent or delay the entry of generics, often artificially extending patent protection to unduly preserve their market power. In fact, such practices are widespread in the pharmaceutical sector and, while they may not be illegitimate per se, they may well be subject to antitrust rules under certain conditions.[59]

[56] European Commission, 'Competition Enforcement in the Pharmaceutical Sector (2009–2017): European Competition Authorities Working Together for Affordable and Innovative Medicines' (2019) https://data.europa.eu/doi/10.2763/218954. Council conclusions on strengthening the balance in the pharmaceutical systems in the EU and its Member States, 17 June 2016, para 48; European Parliament resolution of 2 March 2017 on EU options for improving access to medicines (2016/2057(INI)).

[57] The antitrust treatment of excessive drug pricing, which represents an issue in which US and EU rules and policies considerably diverge, will be explored in ch 7. In addition, the European competition authorities have also addressed a number of other anti-competitive practices (eg bid rigging in hospital tenders, market sharing between pharmacies, restrictions of parallel trade).

[58] M Castanheira, C Ornaghi and G Siotis, 'The Unexpected Consequences of Generic Entry' (2019) 68 *Journal of Health Economics* 22 (according to whom, despite price drops as high as 45% for the drug experiencing generic entry, the average effect is to boost the market share of competing molecules). See also D Neven and G Siotis, 'Dominance and Market Definition in the Pharmaceutical Industry following the ECJ Paroxetine Judgment' (2020) 11 *Journal of European Competition Law & Practice* 194, 195 (claiming that the effect of the generic entry on consumers is a priori unclear, as it: (i) leads to intense price competition for one molecule (ii) but reduces non-price competition between the genericised molecule and other drugs still benefiting from exclusivity and (iii) softens competition among these other drugs).

[59] The issue has been subject to wide analysis in the literature. In general, it should be noted that in the US, IP doctrines, such as patent and copyright misuse, have always played a significant role in the definition of the interface between IPRs and antitrust. Patent misuse doctrine, which has arisen as a defence in patent infringement cases in order to prevent patentees obtaining relief, has always been conceived with the view of deeming illegal those patentee practices that improperly extend patents' scope. Patent misuse doctrine requires the alleged infringer to prove that the IPR holder has wrongfully broadened the physical and temporal scope of the IPR, producing anti-competitive effects. US scholars and courts have debated on the boundaries of this doctrine and

Patent strategies are not, in principle, unique to the pharmaceutical sector, as they may occur, more or less frequently, in other sectors where the role of IPRs in protecting innovation is crucial. Practices occurring in the pharmaceutical markets represent adaptations of this kind of strategy to the specific features of the industry.[60] The common element is their underlying motivation, which generally includes not only protecting the innovation of the product of the applicant, but also blocking substitute innovations by competitors. A distinction is typically drawn between defensive and aggressive blocking patents, depending on whether such patents are applied to broaden the field of activity of the applicant or to limit the scope of action of competing firms. The role and way in which these objectives are pursued, together with protection against imitation and other objectives such as increasing reputation and signalling technological capacity, depends on the competitive strategy of each firm.[61]

Concern about the anti-competitive effects of patent strategies is shared by both EU and US agencies. Within the toolbox developed by originator companies in order to prepare for and respond to generic entry, prominent positions must be given to two types of practices, which are relevant examples of joint and unilateral conducts respectively: reverse payment patent settlement agreements and so-called product hopping. They will be the subjects of specific treatment in chapters five and six respectively.

Moreover, experience shows that there are several recurrent practices that are not necessarily related to IP protection but lead to a significant number and variety of antitrust infringements resulting from the most diverse

its overlapping with those of the antitrust offences. The first application of this doctrine dates back to *Motion Picture Patents Co v Universal Film Manufacturing Corp* 243 US 502 (1917). It should be mentioned that the misuse doctrine is the subject of criticism, in particular for the overlap it creates between antitrust law and intellectual property law. On this issue, suffice it to mention: M Lemley, 'The Economic Irrationality of the Patent Misuse Doctrine' (1990) 78 *California Law Review* 1599; RJ Hoerner, 'The Decline (and Fall?) of the Patent Misuse Doctrine in the Federal Circuit' (2001) 69 *Antitrust Law Journal* 669; CJ Laser, 'Continuing the Conversation of "The Economic Irrationality of the Patent Misuse Doctrine"' (2012) 11 *Chicago-Kent Journal of Intellectual Property* 104. In the EU, although a European judge-made misuse doctrine does not exist, the concept of misuse is well known both to the national courts that apply their national IP law and to the Commission and the Court of Justice, which has held that although a patent conferred on its holder a special protection at the national level, it could only infringe Art 102 'if the use of the patents were to degenerate into an abuse of the abovementioned protection' (see Case 24/67 *Parke, Davis and Co v Probel, Reese, Beintema-Interpharm and Centrafarm* ECLI:EU:C:1968:11, [1968] ECR 81, para 72). On this point and for a comprehensive comparative analysis, see M Maggiolino, *Intellectual Property and Antitrust. A Comparative Economic Analysis of US and EU Law* (Cheltenham, Edward Elgar, 2011) 38, 174ff.

[60] H Ullrich, 'Strategic Patenting by the Pharmaceutical Industry: Towards a Concept of Abusive Practices of Protection' in J Drexl and N Lee (eds), *Pharmaceutical Innovation, Competition and Patent Law* (Cheltenham, Edward Elgar, 2013) 241, 248.

[61] ibid 249.

conducts, including vexatious/sham litigation,[62] dissemination of misleading information[63] and disparagement.[64]

In addition to these practices, in the US particular attention is being devoted to some peculiar types of anti-competitive strategies, which are strictly related to the existing regulatory framework. One of these is the use of a risk

[62] 'Sham litigation' (in the US) or 'vexatious litigation' (in the EU) refers to the distorted use of the adjudicatory system by the plaintiff with the aim of achieving a goal different from that for which the procedure was created (eg preventing or delaying the entry of competing products in the market). With regard to its antitrust treatment and use in pharmaceutical markets, see V Guimarães de Lima e Silva, 'Sham Litigation in the Pharmaceutical Sector' (2011) 7 *European Competition Journal* 455.

[63] Case C-179/16 *F. Hoffmann-La Roche Ltd & Others v Autorità Garante della Concorrenza e del Mercato* ECLI:EU:C:2018:25. This case originated from the request for a preliminary ruling submitted by the Italian Supreme Administrative Court, the Council of State, as part of national proceedings regarding the controversial decision adopted by the Italian Competition Authority concerning the medicines Avastin and Lucentis: Roche and Novartis were sanctioned as they were found to have colluded in disseminating information that was likely to raise public concern about the safety of the intravitreal use of Avastin in order to prevent its off-label application from intruding into the market for the on-label application of Lucentis, thus artificially boosting demand for the latter. On appeal, the Council of State referred several questions to the Court of Justice for a preliminary ruling. The crucial issue of the misleading nature of the information disseminated by the firms was treated by the Court as follows: such information is 'to be regarded as misleading if the purpose of that information, which is a matter for the referring court to determine, was (i) to confuse the EMA and the Commission and have the adverse reaction mentioned in the summary of product characteristics so as to enable the MA holder to launch a communication campaign aimed at healthcare professionals, patients and other persons concerned with a view to exaggerating that perception artificially, and (ii) to emphasise, in a context of scientific uncertainty, the public perception of the risks associated with the off-label use of Avastin' (para 92). Given the characteristics of the market for medicinal products, it is likely that the dissemination of such information would encourage doctors to refrain from prescribing that product, thus resulting in a lower demand for that usage, and also constitutes an infringement of the EU pharmaceutical rules (paras 84–87 and 93). For these reasons, such an arrangement was considered by the Court to be sufficiently harmful to competition to render any examination of its effects superfluous (para 94). Among the comments in English on this case, see M Colangelo, 'The Dissemination of Misleading Information in the Pharmaceutical Market: The Italian Experience' in W Sauter, M Canoy and J Mulder (eds), *EU Competition Law and Pharmaceuticals* (Cheltenham, Edward Elgar, 2022) 197; M Todino and N Colombo, 'Case C-179/16 Hoffmann-La Roche: By Object Restrictions Still Bitter Pills to Swallow? A Close Watch on the Pharmaceutical Sector' (2018) 9 *Journal of European Competition Law & Practice* 376; T Klimenta and W Sauter, 'An Eye for an Eye: Off-label Use and Misleading Information: Hoffmann-La Roche v AGCM' (2018) 2 *European Pharmaceutical Law Review* 100; P Actis Perinetto, 'A Formalistic Approach to Competition Law and Its Risks: The Curious Case of Roche/Novartis' (2020) 43 *World Competition* 319.

[64] In the US, disparagement of competitors and/or competing products is under attention mainly because of its use to block biosimilars. See MA Carrier, 'Don't Die! How Biosimilar Disparagement Violates Antitrust Law' (2020) 115 *Northwestern University Law Review* 119. In the EU, a series of investigations has been conducted, mainly at the national level, addressing the disparaging practices of incumbents to curb the uptake of generic products. Several cases have been prosecuted in France. For details, see A Giraud, J Raffaitin and C Dobelmann, 'Disparagement: The European Union and France' in Sauter et al, *EU Competition Law*, 173. At EU level, in March 2021, the EU Commission started an investigation into Teva (case number AT.40588) and sent a Statement of Objections in October 2022, also targeting exclusionary disparagement of competing products, in addition to misuse of patent procedures. Another investigation was commenced in June 2022 into Vifor Pharma for allegedly disparaging the safety of a competitor's drug (case number AT.40577).

evaluation and mitigation strategy (REMS) for anti-competitive purposes.[65] As mentioned in chapter one, drug manufacturers have started exploiting REMS as a tool to deter generic entry. Potential generic and biosimilar entrants require samples of a reference drug in order to perform testing, prove bioequivalence of their product and proceed with an abbreviated new drug application or a follow-on biologics licence application. Practice shows that originator companies claim that when their products are subject to REMS, it would be dangerous to sell to any person or entity who is not a patient with a prescription, thus effectively preventing generic entry. There have been various lawsuits between generic manufacturers and brands over sample withholding.[66] Other antitrust concerns derive from the specific features of the US distribution system, where the role of pharmacy benefit managers (PBMs) has been progressively questioned, in particular after increased consolidation in the sector, as the largest PBMs are now vertically integrated with the biggest health insurance companies and wholly owned mail order and speciality pharmacies. The FTC has recently launched an inquiry into the prescription drug middleman industry, where PBMs – as already seen in chapter three – are hired to negotiate rebates and fees with drug manufacturers, create drug formularies and surrounding policies, and reimburse pharmacies for patients' prescriptions.[67] Due also to the opacity of contractual relationships set up by them, the behaviour of PBMs has been criticised in the literature, which has shown that complex payment structures may provide incentives for PBMs to keep list prices high in order to increase their net gain.[68]

[65] There are other concerns regarding citizen petitions filed with the FDA, which are intended to serve the public interest by bringing safety concerns to the agency's attention. However, data show that most petitions that target generic drugs are denied and have become a tool by which brand firms may delay generic entry. See MA Carrier and C Minniti, 'Citizen Petitions: Long, Late-Filed, and At-Last Denied' (2016) 66 *American University Law Review* 305; MA Carrier, 'Five Actions to Stop Citizen Petition Abuse' (2018) 118 *Columbia Law Review Online* 81.

[66] For a detailed analysis, see MA Carrier, 'Sharing, Samples, and Generics: an Antitrust Framework' (2017) 103 *Cornell Law Review* 1. See also DS Tucker, GF Wells and ME Sheer, 'REMS: The Next Pharmaceutical Enforcement Priority?' (2014) 28 *Antitrust Magazine*; A Sarpatwari, J Avorn and AS Kesselheim, 'Using a Drug-Safety Tool to Prevent Competition' (2014) 370 *New England Journal of Medicine* 1476.

[67] See FTC Press Release, 'FTC Launches Inquiry into Prescription Drug Middlemen Industry' (7 July 2022) www.ftc.gov/news-events/news/press-releases/2022/06/ftc-launches-inquiry-prescription-drug-middlemen-industry. The inquiry intends to scrutinise the impact of vertically integrated PBMs on the accessibility to and affordability of prescription drugs. The declared aim of the inquiry is to shed light on several practices that have drawn scrutiny in recent years, including: fees and clawbacks charged to unaffiliated pharmacies; methods to steer patients towards PBM-owned pharmacies; potentially unfair audits of independent pharmacies; complicated and opaque methods to determine pharmacy reimbursement; the prevalence of prior authorisations and other administrative restrictions; the use of specialty drug lists and surrounding specialty drug policies; the impact of rebates and fees from drug manufacturers on formulary design; and the costs of prescription drugs to payers and patients.

[68] R Feldman, *Drugs, Money and Secret Handshakes. The Unstoppable Growth of Prescription Drug Prices* (Cambridge, Cambridge University Press, 2019) 19 (explaining how the system works: insurers pay their PBMs based on the extent of the discount that the PBM can negotiate with

Finally, to conclude this brief overview, it should be noted that an area where there is considerable attention – but is not treated in this book – is that of pharmaceutical mergers, on which the European Commission's Directorate General for Competition, the FTC, the Canadian Competition Bureau, the UK Competition and Markets Authority, the US Department of Justice and three Offices of Attorneys General have together created a multilateral working group with the aim of analysing their effects in the sector.[69]

III. MARKET DEFINITION

The peculiarities of the pharmaceutical sector are also represented in the definition of the 'relevant market' in this context. The definition of the relevant market is the first step in assessing a firm's market power and is aimed at identifying which products are close enough substitutes for one another that they exert competitive pressure on the behaviour of the suppliers of those products. It is a complex operation, which implies an in-depth analysis of the context in which the conduct under investigation takes place. This task can be particularly complicated in those sectors where firms compete through non-price elements and/or where other forms of public intervention impact on prices. As already seen in chapter one, the combination of extensive research and development, high promotion intensity, regulation and information asymmetries – which are all elements present in the pharmaceutical markets – generate complex competition dynamics, so that the typical main indicators of market power (ie market shares and competitors' price reaction) are less informative than usual.[70]

In general, demand-side substitutability, which is the primary criterion in market definition, must be assessed with express reference to the specific allegations of the anti-competitive effects in question. With regard to the relevant product market, the criterion of functional interchangeability constitutes an important parameter and is aimed at identifying all products that are considered substitutable by the consumer due to their characteristics, price and intended

individual drug companies; thus, 'the greater the distance between the list price and the final price, the more money a PBM makes'). See also F Scott Morton and LT Boller, 'Enabling Competition in Pharmaceutical Markets' (2017) Hutchins Center Working Paper #30, 21–23 (affirming, at 22, that 'complex payment structures may provide incentives for PBMs to keep list prices high, despite rebates, because the PBM has the ability to make the rebate increase smaller than the price increase, and keep the net gain').

[69] See European Commission Press Release, 'The European Commission Forms a Multilateral Working Group with Leading Competition Authorities to Exchange Best Practices on Pharmaceutical Mergers' (16 March 2021) https://ec.europa.eu/commission/presscorner/detail/en/ip_21_1203. The working group was initiated by the FTC and is in line with close cooperation between national competition authorities.

[70] G Siotis, C Ornaghi and M Castanheira De Moura, 'Market Definition and Competition Policy Enforcement in the Pharmaceutical Industry' (Université Libre de Bruxelles, 2020) Working Papers ECARES 2020-49, 6.

use, though other factors may be relevant.[71] Such general indications are not sufficient when the antitrust investigation concerns medicines. In fact, the definition of the relevant product market in the pharmaceutical sector necessarily requires the overall consideration of factors and conditions of competition in that industry.

In the US, courts have recognised the possibility that broad and narrow definitions for relevant markets for pharmaceuticals may coexist, and that the relevant product market may vary considerably depending on the anti-competitive effects at stake in each case.[72] In this section, the most relevant issues in this area are treated mainly through the European practice and case law as indicative.

As a first point, the existing practice in the consumption of prescription drugs constitutes a central factor, where the choice between different medicines is typically done by physicians and is guided by their therapeutic appropriateness and efficacy rather than by price. The criterion of functional interchangeability applied to the pharmaceutical market requires that special consideration should be given to therapeutic substitution – including specialist literature, product information and expert witness statements – and to the established medical prescribing practice over the years.[73] In contrast, the price analyses typically used in market definition are hardly informative. Therapeutic substitutability

[71] See European Commission, 'Notice on the Definition of the Relevant Market for the Purposes of Community Competition Law' [1997] OJ C372/5, para 7. The definition of the relevant market involves defining, first, the product market and then, secondly, the geographical market. For the purposes of this chapter, the relevant product market is taken into consideration.

[72] See Federal Trade Commission, Amicus Brief in Staley v Gilead Sciences Inc, case pending before the US District Court for the Northern District of California (2019) (Case No 3:19-cv-02573-EMC). The FTC explained that the relevant market might consist of an entire therapeutic class of drugs when the anti-competitive effects are likely to manifest among that entire class, such as in a merger between two branded manufacturers (eg *In re Novartis AG & GlaxoSmithKline*, Dkt No C-4510 (FTC 8 April 2015)); in other circumstances, the relevant market might be limited to only a subset of a therapeutic class (see *Safeway Inc v Abbott Laboratories*, 761 F Supp 2d 874, 884–85 (ND Cal 2011), where the Third Circuit limited the relevant market to cephalosporin antibiotics because they were sufficiently differentiated from other antibiotics). Where anti-competitive effects are alleged to result from conduct excluding lower-cost generic versions of a given drug, the relevant market is frequently more limited, consisting of only the brand and generic versions of that product (see, eg *In re Impax Labs* Dkt No 9373 (FTC 7 June 2019) 26 (defining the relevant antitrust product market as branded and generic oxymorphone ER, noting that 'in most cases arising in the [pharmaceutical reverse payment] context, a brand and its generics will constitute the relevant market'). The FTC also affirms, with regard to the Gilead case at issue, that if there are multiple theories of harm in the same case, the case may implicate multiple relevant markets. See A Vaishnav, 'Product Market Definition in Pharmaceutical Antitrust Cases: Evaluating Cross-Price Elasticity of Demand' (2012) 2011 *Columbia Business Law Review* 586, 595 (arguing that there is a relative scarcity of judicial decisions addressing product market definition in the pharmaceutical industry in non-merger cases in the US case law and that consent decrees provide a major source for understanding the FTC's market definition methodology); MH Morse, 'Product Market Definition in the Pharmaceutical Industry' (2003) 71 *Antitrust Law Journal* 633, 642 (claiming that the FTC's approach to product market definition in its pharmaceutical cases has not been transparent).

[73] See A Coscelli and A Overd, 'Market Definition in the Pharmaceutical Sector' (2007) 28 *European Competition Law Review* 294, 295. Therapeutic substitutability is a necessary precondition for another medicine to be potentially capable of exercising significant competitive constraints

must, therefore, be seen as pre-eminent over economic substitutability. In other words, where different products are considered non-substitutable from a clinical–therapeutic point of view, the analysis of economic substitutability between those products loses its significance.

The definition of the relevant market is based on the World Health Organization (WHO)'s Anatomical Therapeutical Chemical (ATC) classification system, whereby medicines are grouped according to the organ or anatomical system on which they act as well as their chemical, pharmacological and therapeutic properties. Among the five therapeutic classes in the WHO classification, ATC level 3 allows medicines to be grouped according to the specific therapeutic indication, ie their intended use, and thus contains potential substitute products for a given customer to address a medical condition. This is the starting point generally used by the Commission for the assessment of the relevant market. However, this level is not always sufficient and appropriate per se to properly define the market, so the analysis must also be conducted on other levels where it appears that the strongest competitive constraints take place and factors militating against a more far-reaching market definition include the active principle, tolerance, toxicity, and side effects: specifically, ATC level 4 considers the modes of action of the product,[74] while the narrowest classes are identified at ATC level 5 according to the active ingredient (chemical substance).[75] The practice of antitrust enforcement reveals an increasing tendency to consider these more specific levels.

However, controversy exists as to the best approach to be adopted.[76] It is clear from European case law concerning the finding of a dominant position that the concept of the relevant market implies that there can be effective competition

on a given product. The Commission has considered that in the majority of cases drugs available without prescription (over-the-counter) belong to a different product market than only-prescription drugs, as medical indications (including possible side-effects), legal framework, marketing and distribution all differ between the two categories of medicines, even when the active ingredients are identical. See, eg *Sanofi-Aventis/Zentiva* (Case COMP/M.5253) [2009] Commission Decision, point 21.

[74] See, eg *Ciba-Geigy/Sandoz* (Case No IV/M.737) [1996] Commission Decision, point 21; *Pfizer/Pharmacia* (Case COMP/M.2922) [2003] Commission Decision, points 37, 61; *AstraZeneca* (Case COMP/A.37.507/F3) [2005] Commission Decision, point 371. Substitutability may be limited by the fact that medicines are differentiated not only by their active ingredient(s), but also by their dosage, pharmaceutical form and route of administration. See *Sanofi-Aventis/Zentiva,* point 20; *Teva/Ratiopharm* (Case COMP/M.5865) [2010] Commission Decision, point 16; *Sanofi Aventis/Genzyme* (Case COMP/M.5999) [2011] Commission Decision, point 13; *Pfizer/Hospira* (Case COMP/M.7559) [2015] Commission Decision, point 85.

[75] See *Perindopril (Servier)* (Case AT.39612) [2014] Commission Decision.

[76] See European Commission, 'Notice on Market Definition', 15–19. In *AstraZeneca*, the General Court acknowledged the use of the SSNIP test, according to which the Commission assesses demand substitutability in the light of a theoretical approach which presupposes a small (in the range of 5–10%) but permanent relative price increase in the product on the basis of which the relevant market is defined, and evaluates whether that hypothetical increase could be applied profitably by the hypothetical monopolist of the relevant product (see paras 89–107). However, the use of SSNIP test in pharmaceutical markets is controversial. See, eg RL Smith and A Duke, 'Pharmaceuticals and Market Definition: A Cautionary Tale' (2021) 17 *European Competition Journal* 593 (arguing

between the products which form part of it, which presupposes that there is a sufficient degree of interchangeability between all the products or services forming part of the same market insofar as the specific use of such products or services is concerned. That interchangeability or substitutability is assessed in relation not only to the objective characteristics of the products, but also to the conditions of competition and the structure of supply and demand on the market.[77]

Recent case law in the EU has further confirmed the relevance of qualitative and non-price constraints, in addition to the usual mechanisms of price pressure that may exist in relation to therapeutic substitution as operated by prescribing doctors and also in relation to the superior therapeutic value of one product over that of other drugs treating the same condition where such available drugs are perceived or recognised as equivalent by prescribers. In *Servier*, the General Court clarified that where, for the treatment of the same condition, prescribers have a choice between medicinal products of which none is recognised or perceived as superior to the others (because their mode of action is the same or because their therapeutic benefits or their adverse or side effects do not make it possible to distinguish between them), the analysis of the competition between those medicinal products also relies, in large part, on a qualitative comparison. In the case of medicinal products recognised or perceived as fully equivalent, the variable of price may be important[78] and

> the market analysis must pay particular attention to the factors making it possible to identify qualitative or non-price competitive constraints, reflected, inter alia, in efforts to make a medicinal product the initial choice of treatment for new prescribers, in switching by continued-use patients to other competing medicinal products and in the intensity of promotional activities carried out for a medicinal product where equivalent or less expensive alternatives exist.[79]

If it is not possible to find evidence indicating such non-price competitive pressure, in particular due to a high level of inertia among doctors in their

that in the case of drugs that are functional alternatives, the next step is to consider whether the prescribing practices of doctors provides a basis for modifying the Hypothetical Monopolist Test; instead of assessing the response to a SSNIP, the response to a small but significant non-transitory decrease in quality could be investigated); Siotis et al, 'Market Definition' (supporting the approach of defining relevant markets contingent on theory of harm); Vaishnav, 'Product Market Definition' (supporting the approach to pharmaceutical market definition that focuses on non-price elements of competition rather than cross elasticity of demand).

[77] Case C-179/16 *Hoffmann-La Roche*, para 51 and the case law cited therein.

[78] Case T-691/14 *Servier SAS and Others v European Commission* ECLI:EU:T:2018:922, paras 1397–1398: 'A significant decrease in the price of a medicinal product, in particular through the introduction of its generic version on the market, may justify that medicinal product being favoured by doctors and the prescription of its generic version being encouraged by those managing the social security system and the regulatory authorities.'

[79] ibid para 1402.

prescribing patterns, which can be a result of loyalty effects leading to market foreclosure, the drug concerned may be shielded from effective competitive pressure as long as its generic version does not enter the market, a fortiori because the regulatory framework mitigates the role of competition factors based on pricing. In such a case, the definition of the relevant market at the level of the compound of that medicinal product, in both its originator and generic versions, can be justified.[80] However, in the case at issue, where the Commission restricted the relevant market to the perindopril compound alone, the Court stated that it made a series of errors in the analysis of the definition of the relevant market, as it failed to consider significant non-price competitive pressure to which the compound itself was subject from other medicinal products.[81] At the time of writing, the appeal to the European Court of Justice brought by the Commission is pending.[82]

In *Generics*, the Court of Justice was asked by the UK Competition Appeal Tribunal to provide guidance on a fundamental question, ie whether, if a patented drug is therapeutically substitutable with a number of other drugs in a class and the alleged abuse is a conduct by the patent holder that effectively excludes generic versions of that drug from the market, those generic products should be taken into account for the purpose of defining the relevant product market, although they could not lawfully enter the market before expiry of the patent if (which is uncertain) the patent is valid.

In its preliminary ruling, the Court of Justice answered that the competitive constraint from generics should be taken into account

> if the manufacturers concerned of generic medicines are in a position to present themselves within a short period on the market concerned with sufficient strength to constitute a serious counterbalance to the manufacturer of the originator medicine already on the market.[83]

[80] ibid para 1403.

[81] ibid para 1589: 'The Commission: – wrongly considered, with regard to therapeutic use, that ACE inhibitors were a class of heterogeneous medicinal products and that perindopril had particular characteristics within that class of medicinal products; – wrongly concluded that a mechanism of doctors' 'inertia' had significantly restricted the competitive pressure exerted on perindopril by the other ACE inhibitors with respect to new patients; – underestimated the propensity of patients treated with perindopril to switch treatment; – failed to give due consideration to the companies' promotional activities and their significance in the analysis of competitive relationships; – disregarded the particular characteristics of competition in the pharmaceutical sector, erroneously inferring from an analysis of natural events based primarily on price changes that perindopril was not subject to significant competitive pressures from other ACE inhibitors.' On the role of inertia, see also Case C-457/10 P *AstraZeneca*, paras 47 and 50.

[82] Cases C-176/19 P *Commission v Servier and Others* and C-201/19 P *Servier and Others v Commission*.

[83] Case C-307/18 *Generics (UK) Ltd and Others v Competition and Markets Authority* ECLI:EU:C:2020:52, para 133.

In the case at issue, the fact that the originator holds a presumptively valid patent covering a process (as opposed to the active ingredient) does not exclude a finding of substitutability. This issue will be further examined in chapter five.

The assessment of the conditions of therapeutic substitutability involves an analysis covering all medicinal products as possible substitutes, whether approved for a specific use (on-label) or off-label, having regard to the effective interchangeability. The issue has been clarified in *Hoffmann-La Roche*, where the Court of Justice stated that

> the fact that pharmaceutical products are manufactured or sold illegally prevents them, in principle, from being regarded as substitutable or interchangeable products, both on the supply side, because of the legal, economic and technical risks, as well as the risks of reputational damage, to which they expose the manufacturers and distributors of those products, and on the demand side, in particular due to the risk to public health that they cause among healthcare professionals and patients.[84]

However, this does not apply when – as in the case at issue – the drug under consideration is covered by a marketing authorisation that had been issued in a valid manner, as EU rules do not prohibit either the off-label prescription of a medicinal product or its repackaging for such use.[85] This issue is also related to the value of the marketing authorisation in this respect: in fact, the content of the marketing authorisation in principle affects the substitutability between products and is suitable for guiding doctors towards the most appropriate treatment for their patients, but it does not exclude the possibility that they may decide to use the drug for a purpose other than that envisaged by the marketing authorisation itself. In the case of the proven wide use of an off-label medicinal product, it could not be excluded that this medicinal product belongs to the same market as the medicinal products authorised for these indications.[86]

IV. CONCLUDING REMARKS

The pharmaceutical sector has traditionally required close competition law scrutiny. Its peculiar features and the role of IP and sectoral rules are mirrored in the existing antitrust investigations and case law, which are numerous with regard to both joint and unilateral actions. In fact, in addition to 'traditional' anti-competitive behaviours, a number of cases in this sector are strictly linked to the complex legal architecture governing it.

[84] Case C-179/16 *Hoffmann-La Roche*, para 52.

[85] This point is further clarified in the related Case C-29/17 *Novartis Farma SpA v AIFA and Others* ECLI:EU:C:2018:931.

[86] *Hoffmann-La Roche*, AG Opinion, points 75ff, 86–87. With regard to the US context, see G Dolin, 'Non-Price Competition in "Substitute" Drugs: The FTC's Blind Spot' (2014) 59 *Antitrust Bulletin* 579.

Although a variety of practices may be found, some cases revolving around attempts to block generic entry in various ways are emblematic examples of behaviours found at the intersection between IP, regulation and competition law, including sophisticated plans to game the regulatory scheme or misuse of the patent system. In fact, the existing frameworks frequently expose pharmaceutical markets to patent strategies and regulatory gaming behaviours by private players. While antitrust enforcement has usually targeted a number of exclusionary practices, recently attention to exploitative actions has gained ground. These issues will be further examined in the next chapters, which analyse reverse payment patent settlements, product hopping and excessive pricing.

5

Reverse Payment Patent Settlements

I. THE RECURRENCE OF REVERSE PAYMENT PATENT SETTLEMENTS IN PHARMACEUTICAL MARKETS

In general, a patent settlement agreement can be defined as any formal or informal agreement that settles an actual or potential patent-related issue. One such category is known as 'reverse payment' patent settlement agreements (also called pay-for-delay settlements), because they provide for the patentee to pay the alleged infringer, rather than the opposite (considering the standard expectation that a defendant would pay a plaintiff to settle), with the aim of delaying its market entry. In other words, in its typical scheme, the brand-name drug pharmaceutical company enters into an agreement with the generic competitor to settle the dispute and to limit its market entry in return for a transfer of value.[1] Such transfer can take different forms, including either a direct monetary payment or another form of valuable agreement (eg an authorised licensed entry at a specific date, distribution agreements, favourable terms in a side deal in which the originator company grants a commercial benefit to the generic company), or both.

In the EU, a first indication on the topic was provided by the Commission in the 2009 Sector Inquiry, in which a categorisation of patent settlement agreements was proposed as follows: (a) A-type, ie agreements that do not restrict the generic company's ability to market its own product; and (b) B-type, ie agreements limiting generic entry. There are two groups in the latter: (i) B.I settlements, comprising those settlements where no value transfer from the originator to the generic company took place; and (ii) B.II settlements, which foresee a value transfer from the originator to the generic.[2] This categorisation was made on the basis of two main criteria: first, according to whether the agreements limited the generic company's ability to market its

[1] A generic company's ability to enter the market can be limited in several ways. The most straightforward limitation is a clause explicitly stating that the generic company will refrain from challenging the validity of the originator company's patent ('non-challenge clause') and/or refrains from entering the market until the patent has expired ('non-compete clause').

[2] European Commission, 'Pharmaceutical Sector Inquiry: Final Report' (2009) 269 (2009 Sector Inquiry).

own product; and second, according to whether they involved a value transfer from the originator to the generic company. As can be easily understood, whereas category A and B.I settlements are generally unproblematic from a competition law perspective, category B.II settlements give rise to more antitrust concern and need to be assessed on a case-by-case basis.[3] Among the examples of category B.II settlements, the Inquiry reported those in combination with licensing agreements between the parties (royalty-bearing or royalty-free), allowing the generic to sell or produce certain quantities of its product in a limited territory, and those in combination with a supply or distribution agreement making the generic company a distributor of limited quantities of the originator company's product in certain geographic areas.[4]

In the same period, in its 2010 report, the Federal Trade Commission (FTC) estimated that pay-for-delay agreements would cost consumers $35 billion over the next 10 years and, given the alleged permissive treatment adopted by courts regarding these settlements, urged a legislative solution to the matter.[5] Competition agencies on both sides of the Atlantic have conducted, and still conduct, a close monitoring on such agreements, despite the low numbers reported for those that might be problematic from a competition law perspective. Recently, an updated EU report concerning the monitoring exercise covering the entire year 2016 cites B.II agreements accounting for 11 per cent (12 out of 107) of all agreements.[6] According to the FTC report released in December 2020 and concerning the year 2017, following the *Actavis* decision and subsequent case law, while the total number of settlements has increased, a continued decline in the use of anti-competitive reverse payment agreements has been observed.[7]

[3] See European Union submission to OECD, 'Generic Pharmaceuticals' (2014) DAF/COMP/WD(2014)62. With regard to B.I settlements, it should be noted that in reality some settlement agreements in this category may attract competition law scrutiny: this may be the case for settlements concluded outside the exclusionary zone of the patent and/or settlement agreements on a patent for which the patent holder knows that it does not meet the patentability criteria, eg where the patent was granted following the provision of incorrect, misleading or incomplete information. It is also worth mentioning that the guidelines on technology transfer agreements contain specific provisions on settlement agreements. See European Commission, 'Guidelines on the Application of Article 101 of the Treaty on the Functioning of the European Union to Technology Transfer Agreements' [2014] OJ C89/3, s 4.3.

[4] European Commission, 2009 Sector Inquiry 281–82.

[5] FTC, 'Pay-for-Delay: How Drug Company Pay-offs cost Consumer Billions' (2010) 2.

[6] European Commission, '8th Report on the Monitoring of Patent Settlements' (January–December 2016) 13. It should be noted that in general the highest number of patent settlements take place in Portugal, apparently due to the implementation of Portuguese Law 62/201, according to which an originator must initiate arbitration proceedings within 30 days of the publication of a marketing authorisation (MA) application by a generic company; if they do not comply with this provision, the originators will lose the ability to assert their IPRs. Hence, since 2012, originators in Portugal are obliged to systematically bring arbitration proceedings against all generics applying for an MA: according to the Commission (at 8), many of these proceedings, where there is no issue on the validity of the underlying rights, are settled very rapidly.

[7] See FTC, 'FY 2017 Report on Branded Drug Firms' Patent Settlements with Generic Competitors' (2020) www.ftc.gov/news-events/news/press-releases/2020/12/ftc-staff-issues-fy-2017-report-branded-drug-firms-patent-settlements-generic-competitors.

Reverse payment settlement agreements are subject to mandatory reporting both in the US and in the EU. They arise mainly in the pharmaceutical industry.[8] As a necessary premise, it is worth stressing that patent litigation is considered to all intents and purposes a form of competition in the pharmaceutical sector, being, on the one side, an expression of the independent efforts of generic undertakings to enter the market and, on the other side, an expression of the defence by the originator undertakings of their market position.[9]

The recourse to settlements during patent disputes originates from the probabilistic nature of the patent system[10] – which does not ensure that patent protection is granted only to meritorious inventions and produces a high number of weak patents – and the imperfect information between the actors involved, ie the patent bodies, originators, generic companies and courts. In fact, all of them are afflicted by some degree of uncertainty as to the strength and validity of originators' patents. Under perfect information, patent bodies would not grant invalid patents to originators that might be successfully challenged in court and generic competitors would neither infringe upon nor legally challenge originators' patents because courts would rule against them.[11]

In this context, for the parties concerned, the reverse payment may result in being economically rational for both the brand and the generic manufacturer.[12] This is because the profit that the generic entering the market anticipates selling at a significant discount to the price of the brand-name product will be much less than the profit the brand-name drug company loses from the same sales applying the monopolistic price: by settling the dispute and thereby eliminating the potential for competition, the parties can share the savings that would result if they were to compete. In addition, settlements remove for both parties the risks deriving from the uncertainty typical of patent litigation, which is particularly dangerous for originator companies exposed to the immediate loss of a large part of the market if the generic wins the suit in court. At the same time, reverse

[8] See generally A Athanassiadou, *Patent Settlements in the Pharmaceutical Industry under US Antitrust and EU Competition Law* (Alphen aan den Rijn, Kluwer, 2018).

[9] On the nature of patent litigation, see S Yelderman, 'Do Patent Challenges Increase Competition?' (2016) 83 *University of Chicago Law Review* 1943 (analysing theories which support patent litigation being considered different from other disputes, in particular because it would offer the opportunity to increase competition by freeing the public from the burdens of the monopoly established by the patent).

[10] MA Lemley and C Shapiro, 'Probabilistic Patents' (2005) 19 *Journal of Economic Perspectives* 75. See also I Ayres and P Klemperer, 'Limiting Patentees' Market Power Without Reducing Innovation Incentives: The Perverse Benefits of Uncertainty and Non-injunctive Remedies' (1999) 97 *Michigan Law Review* 985.

[11] F Maier-Rigaud, N Blalock and O Gannon, 'Reverse Payments: An EU and US Perspective' in P Figueroa and A Guerrero (eds), *EU Law of Competition and Trade in the Pharmaceutical Sector* (Cheltenham, Edward Elgar, 2019) 35, 42.

[12] R Feldman, 'The Price Tag of "Pay-for-Delay"' (2022) 23 *Columbia Science and Technology Law Review* 1, 10 (affirming that 'with pay-for delay settlements, brand-name companies can extend their monopoly by taking advantage of shared interests with generic companies').

payment patent settlements, which can in principle be legitimate and allow courts and competent authorities to save time and effort, in addition to cost savings for the private parties involved in the litigation, are nevertheless controversial under antitrust scrutiny because of their impact on the market entry of generic drugs and thus on prices, and consequently on consumer welfare and public healthcare budgets.

Pay-for-delay cases are interesting for several reasons. Firstly, there is still some controversy around the analytical framework to evaluate whether an agreement is by its very nature anti-competitive. Secondly, they typically show how the antitrust assessment is further complicated by the presence of intellectual property rights (IPRs) in the legal and economic context of the practice under scrutiny, considering the uncertainty typical of patent infringement claims. Thirdly, they represent an area where a reconciliation between antitrust and IP might be improved.

II. REVERSE PAYMENT PATENT SETTLEMENTS IN THE UNITED STATES

A. Earlier Case Law and the *Actavis* Ruling

In the US, patent settlement agreements have been the subject of much antitrust scrutiny in the last 20 years. In fact, pay-for-delay settlements have been strongly challenged by the antitrust enforcement agencies, in particular by the FTC, which has made them a top enforcement priority.[13] US courts have adopted heterogeneous approaches to reverse payment settlements in pharmaceutical patent litigation. Moreover, the landmark decision taken by the Supreme Court in *Actavis* has not erased all uncertainties about their correct antitrust evaluation.[14]

The earliest case law shows controversy between courts, which have taken different stances on the application of antitrust law to these agreements.[15] While, in *Cardizem*, the Sixth Circuit considered reverse payment settlements

[13] The first cases on patent settlements under the attention of the FTC: *In the Matter of Bristol-Myers Squibb Co*, Docket No C-4076 (18 April 2003); *In the Matter of Schering-Plough Corp*, Docket No 9297, Opinion of the Commission (18 December 2003), vacated, 402 F 3d 1056 (11th Cir 2005), cert denied, 126 S Ct 2929 (2006). See also FTC, 'Generic Drug Entry Prior to Patent Expiration: An FTC Study' (2002). This study included several recommendations regarding the Hatch-Waxman framework, including one that called for brand and generic companies entering into settlements to report them to the FTC. As a consequence, Congress included a requirement that all such settlements be filed with the FTC and the Department of Justice as part of the Medicare Prescription Drug, Improvement, and Modernization Act of 2003 (MMA).

[14] *Federal Trade Commission v Actavis, Inc* 570 US 136 S Ct 2223 (2013).

[15] A detailed analysis on earliest case law may be found in C Scott Hemphill, 'Drug Patent Settlements between Rivals: A Survey' (2007) http://ssrn.com/abstract=969492; C Scott Hemphill, 'An Aggregate Approach to Antitrust: Using New Data and Rulemaking to Preserve Drug Competition' (2009) 109 *Columbia Law Review* 629.

to be a classic example of a per se illegal restraint of trade,[16] other decisions rejected this approach, holding that such arrangements were lawful as long as they did not exceed the exclusionary scope of the patent in suit. In *Valley Drug*, the Eleventh Circuit, having recognised both the patent exception to antitrust liability and that the exception is limited by the terms of the patent and the statutory rights granted to the patentee, applied the 'scope of the patent' test.[17] According to this approach, patent settlement agreements require consideration of (i) the scope of the exclusionary potential of the patent, (ii) the extent to which the provisions of the settlements exceed that scope and (iii) the resulting anti-competitive effects.[18] The Eleventh Circuit also applied this test in *Schering-Plough*.[19] The Second Circuit followed this approach in *Tamoxifen*,[20] as did the Federal Circuit in *Ciprofloxacin*.[21] In the cases mentioned, the antitrust claims advanced by the FTC proved unsuccessful in the courts. With the exception of the Sixth Circuit in the early *Cardizem* case, the established approach followed by the above courts has been to consider the settlements at issue permitted as long as: (i) they do not exceed the patent's exclusionary scope; (ii) the patent litigation is neither a sham nor otherwise baseless; and (iii) the patent is not obtained by fraud. The scope of the patent test has since been confirmed by the Eleventh Circuit in *Watson*.[22]

However, the Third Circuit overturned this test in *K-Dur*, considering it necessary to apply a 'quick-look rule-of-reason analysis' based on the economic realities of the reverse payment settlement and to treat any payment from a patent holder to a generic patent challenger who agrees to delay entry into the market as prima facie evidence of an unreasonable restraint of trade, which could be rebutted by showing that the payment (i) was for a purpose other than delayed entry or (ii) offers some pro-competitive benefit.[23]

In light of the split between circuits, the Supreme Court granted the FTC's petition for certiorari agreeing to review the Eleventh Circuit's ruling in *Watson* and finally reversed it, releasing a decision (known as *Actavis*, referring to the generic manufacturer that acquired Watson) which has been welcomed

[16] *In re Cardizem CD Antitrust Litigation* 332 F 3d 896 (6th Cir 2003).

[17] See H Hovenkamp, 'The Rule of Reason and the Scope of the Patent' (2015) 52 *San Diego Law Review* 515; MA Carrier, 'Why the "Scope of the Patent" Test Cannot Solve the Drug Patent Settlement Problem' (2012) 16 *Stanford Technology Law Review* 1.

[18] *Valley Drug v Geneva Pharmaceuticals* 344 F 3d 1294 (11th Cir 2003).

[19] *Schering-Plough v FTC* 402 F 3d 1056, 1066 (11th Cir 2005).

[20] *In re Tamoxifen Citrate Antitrust Litigation* 466 F 3d 187 (2nd Cir 2006). It should be noted that, citing *Schering-Plough* and Judge Posner in *Asahi Glass v Pentech Pharms* 289 F Supp 2d 986, 991 (N D Ill 2003), the court in this case underlined private and social benefits of the settlements (as opposed to the inveterate and costly effects of litigation), recalling that the general policy of the law is to favour the settlement of litigation and that the policy extends to the settlement of patent infringement suits.

[21] *In re Ciprofloxacin Hydrochloride Antitrust Litigation* 544 F 3d 1323 (Fed Cir 2008) 1336.

[22] *FTC v Watson Pharmaceuticals* 677 F 3d 1298 (11th Cir 2012).

[23] *In re K-Dur Antitrust Litigation* 686 F 3d 197 (3rd Cir 2012) 218.

by the FTC as a significant victory.[24] The case involved settlements between Solvay, the new drug application (NDA) holder for AndroGel (a prescription testosterone cream), Watson and Paddock, which partnered with Par, each filing abbreviated new drug applications (ANDAs) to market generic versions of the drug in May 2003 and making paragraph IV certifications.

In 1999, Solvay Pharmaceuticals filed an NDA for AndroGel and, after approval by the Food and Drug Administration (FDA) in 2000, obtained a patent in 2003, with an expiration date of 2020. Both Actavis and Paddock certified under paragraph IV that Solvay's listed patent was invalid and their drugs did not infringe it. Solvay initiated paragraph IV patent litigation against Actavis and Paddock and 30 months later the FDA approved Actavis's first-to-file generic product, but in 2006 all the parties involved settled. Under the terms of the settlement, Actavis and Paddock agreed not to market generic versions of AndroGel until the end of August 2015, ie several years before patent expiration. Solvay also contemporaneously agreed to make payments to each of the generic companies, purportedly for product promotion and manufacturing services the generics agreed to perform. The FTC found that those services had little independent value and that the payments were intended to secure the generics' agreement to stay out of the market, so were therefore unlawful. Thus, in 2009, the FTC filed a lawsuit alleging that Solvay paid Watson and Par a share of its AndroGel profits to abandon their patent challenges and agreed to delay generic entry, thereby violating section 5 of the FTC Act. The FTC being the losing party in both first instance and appeal, it sought certiorari and the claim was finally decided by the Supreme Court.

The Supreme Court rejected both the view that any settlement within the scope of the patent is legal and the view that any settlement which involves a payment from a patent holder to a generic patent challenger is presumptively illegal, stating that such settlements can sometimes bring with them the risk of significant anti-competitive effects and violate the antitrust laws, and that they therefore must be judged under a rule-of-reason analysis. Specifically, according to the majority opinion authored by Justice Breyer, it would be incongruous to determine antitrust legality by measuring the anti-competitive effects of the settlement solely against patent law policy and not against pro-competitive antitrust policies as well, as both are relevant in determining the scope of monopoly and antitrust immunity conferred by a patent. As a consequence, the legality of an agreement not to compete between a patent holder and a would-be rival is to be assessed using traditional antitrust factors, such as likely anti-competitive effects, redeeming virtues and market power, and potentially offsetting any legal considerations present in the circumstances, such as, in the case at issue, those related to patents.[25]

[24] *Actavis* 570 US 136.
[25] *Actavis* 570 US 149.

The Court identified five sets of important considerations, leading it to conclude that the FTC should have the opportunity to prove the antitrust claim, including the following: (i) the restraint has the potential for genuine adverse effects; (ii) the anti-competitive consequences will sometimes prove unjustified; (iii) the patent holder likely has the power to bring about that anti-competitive harm in practice; (iv) an antitrust action is feasible administratively; and (v) other settlement options are available.[26] This, in turn, means that:

> [A] reverse payment, where large and unjustified, can bring with it the risk of significative anticompetitive effects; one who makes such a payment may be unable to explain and to justify it; such a firm or individual may well possess market power derived from the patent; a court, by examining the size of the payment, may well be able to assess its likely anticompetitive effects along with its potential justifications without litigating the validity of the patent; and parties may well find ways to settle patent disputes without the use of reverse payments.[27]

Thus, the Court remanded the case to the federal District Court for the Northern District of Georgia, stating that the size of the payment, its scale in relation to the payer's anticipated future litigation costs or fair value for other services and the lack of any other convincing justification are the parameters which courts must look at: 'a large, unexplained reverse payment can provide a workable surrogate for a patent's weakness, all without forcing a court to conduct a detailed exploration of the validity of the patent itself'.[28]

This reasoning has been not free of conflicts. The dissenting opinion written by Chief Justice Roberts and concurred in by Justices Scalia and Thomas vigorously criticises the decision of the majority. Roberts, underlining the separation between patent and antitrust laws and the need to safeguard their respective areas of application, questioned the stance of the majority, according to which litigating patent validity is not necessary in order to answer the antitrust questions ('The patent here may or may not be valid, and may or may not be infringed').[29] In the words of the dissenting opinion, 'The majority seems to think that *even if* the patent is valid, a patent holder violates the antitrust laws merely because the settlement took away some chance that his patent would be declared invalid by a court', so that it would impose antitrust liability based on the parties' subjective uncertainty about the legal conclusion on the patent validity.[30] Moreover, according to the minority, a large payment does not necessarily mean that the patent is weak; therefore, offering a large sum should not be considered reliable evidence of the patent's weakness: what is actually motivating a patent holder

[26] ibid 152–57.
[27] ibid 158.
[28] ibid.
[29] ibid 147.
[30] ibid 171.

(ie uncertainty about its patent or other legitimate factors like risk aversion) is a question district courts should resolve on a case-by-case basis.[31]

Finally, the case was terminated by the settlement of the last of the drug companies, accepting a stipulated injunction not to engage in similar reverse payment agreements, which occurred in February 2019.[32]

B. Critical Issues after *Actavis*

Much debate has arisen from the Supreme Court's ruling in *Actavis*, in particular with regard to its likely effects on the assessment of reverse payment settlements to be made by lower courts, which are called to dissipate the uncertainties hidden in the application of the rule of reason to pay-for-delay settlements.[33] In fact, little guidance has been provided by the Supreme Court on how effectively to 'activate *Actavis*'.[34]

One question concerned whether the label of reverse payment should be limited to cash-only payments or whether it should also cover other forms of valuable agreements. Some companies have elaborated highly complex forms of agreements in which reverse payment settlements go together with other side

[31] For a critique of Roberts's opinion, see MA Carrier, 'A Response to Chief Justice Roberts: Why Antitrust Must Play a Role in the Analysis of Drug Patent Settlements' (2014) 15 *Minnesota Journal of Law, Science & Technology* 31 (arguing that Roberts ignored the patent law policy of challenging and eliminating invalid patents; that he downplayed the role of antitrust law; and that he neglected the importance of the Hatch-Waxman Act, Congress's resolution of the patent–antitrust trade-off in the pharmaceutical industry). See also R Feldman, 'Ending Patent Exceptionalism and Structuring the Rule of Reason: The Supreme Court Opens the Door for Both' (2014) 5 *Minnesota Journal of Law, Science & Technology* 61, 67 (arguing that this approach fails to distinguish between deploying the right and deploying the system); S Ghosh, 'Convergence?' (2014) 15 *Minnesota Journal of Law, Science & Technology* 95, 100 (arguing that 'the three dissenting judges ignore the Hatch-Waxman Act itself, which accords no immunity to patent holders and whose passage supports placing limitations on patent rights based on principles of competition policy'). For an in-depth analysis of *Actavis*, see also MS Gal and A Miller, 'Patent Challenge Clauses: A New Antitrust Offense?' (2017) 102 *Iowa Law Review* 1477 (extending the *Actavis* ruling to patent challenge clauses).

[32] FTC Press Release, 'Last Remaining Defendant Settles FTC Suit that Led to Landmark Supreme Court Ruling on Drug Company "Reverse Payments"' (28 February 2019) www.ftc.gov/news-events/news/press-releases/2019/02/last-remaining-defendant-settles-ftc-suit-led-landmark-supreme-court-ruling-drug-company-reverse.

[33] Among the several comments on the judgment at issue, see TF Cotter, 'FTC v Actavis, Inc: When Is the Rule of Reason Not the Rule of Reason?' (2014) 15 *Minnesota Journal of Law, Science & Technology* 41; DA Crane, 'Actavis, the Reverse Payment Fallacy, and the Continuing Need for Regulatory Solutions' (2014) 15 *Minnesota Journal of Law, Science & Technology* 51, 52 (according to which 'the opinion failed to grapple with the most challenging issues of regulatory policy raised by pharmaceutical patent settlements').

[34] See A Edlin, C Scott Hemphill, H Hovenkamp and C Shapiro, 'Activating Actavis' [2013] *Antitrust* 16 (clarifying also that, although brought under s 5 of the FTC Act, Sherman Act standards are applied); A Edlin, C Scott Hemphill, H Hovenkamp and C Shapiro, 'Actavis and Error Costs: A Reply to Critics' [2014] (October) *Antitrust Source* 1; A Edlin, C Scott Hemphill, H Hovenkamp and C Shapiro, 'The Actavis Inference: Theory and Practice' (2015) 67 *Rutgers University Law Review* 1.

deals, such as: promises on the part of the generic to promote or market the brand-name drug (co-promotion deals); licensing deals allowing the originator company or the generic to manufacture the other party's drug; agreements to share research and development duties on a future project; or deals to supply the brand-name company with raw materials for manufacturing.[35] Among these deals, particular attention must be paid to contractual clauses such as the acceleration or coordination clauses and no-authorised-generic (no-AG) agreements.

Acceleration clauses are very common in settlements and stipulate that the generic, which has agreed to delay entry, may immediately enter the market should another generic enter the market at an earlier time, thus successfully circumventing the 180-day exclusivity period granted to the first-filer that begins when the generic commercially markets the drug.[36] As clarified in chapter one, the 180-day exclusivity period granted to the first generic to file a paragraph IV certification plays a vital role in reverse payment patent settlements, as by paying the generic to delay entering the market, the brand-drug manufacturer can prevent entry by not only that generic, but also all other generics. Such period is potentially worth hundreds of millions of dollars.[37] Acceleration clauses have been defined as 'poison pills', as they provide that a settling first filer can accelerate its entry upon a later filer's victory, giving itself 180 days of exclusivity.[38] This, in turn, offers the settling generic significant benefits within and after the period and reduces incentives for later filers to pursue litigation challenging the brand's patent.

Through no-AG agreements, the originator agrees not to launch a generic version of its own drug during the first-filer's 180-day exclusivity period. As there is no provision in the Hatch-Waxman Act prohibiting the originator company from marketing its own generic version during that exclusivity period,[39] this possibility allows the originator company to enjoy a portion of the profits that would otherwise go to the first generic filer, while continuing to sell the branded product.[40] The use of no-AG provisions in return for the delayed entry of the generic company has significantly increased in recent years and courts have been called upon to determine whether they constitute payment

[35] R Feldman and E Frondorf, *Drug Wars. How Big Pharma Raises Prices and Keeps Generics Off the Market* (Cambridge, Cambridge University Press, 2017), 49 (arguing that *Actavis* came years too late, when a second generation of pay-for-delay had already been implemented).

[36] Feldman and Fordorf, *Drug Wars*, 57.

[37] Carrier, 'Payment After Actavis', 41.

[38] ibid 37ff, 41. Carrier adds that poison-pill clauses are often accompanied by 'no-licence' clauses by which a brand agrees not to grant a licence to any other generic to enter within 180 days of the first-filer's entry. See also Feldman and Fordorf, *Drug Wars*, 57 (explaining that after an acceleration clause is put in place, any generic willing to enter the market does so knowing that, in case of success, it will immediately face generic competition from the first filer).

[39] Courts have uniformly stated in this direction. On this issue, see M Carrier, 'Eight Reasons Why "No-Authorized-Generic" Promises Constitute Payment' (2015) 67 *Rutgers University Law Review* 697, 701–02.

[40] Feldman and Fordorf, *Drug Wars*, 59.

consistent with the *Actavis* ruling. After the first courts' decisions confining the *Actavis* principle to cash-only payments, it is now generally accepted that the form of the reverse payment does not matter for the purposes of the application of the *Actavis* ruling.[41] The first cases have aroused the opposition of scholars, claiming that no-AG clauses are market-division promises that prove to be more anti-competitive than cash payments for delayed entry. In fact, the generic's delayed-entry pledge transforms a period of two-seller rivalry for the drug into an extended monopoly period for the brand; and the no-AG promise transforms the six-month exclusivity from a three-way rivalry to a two-way rivalry, with a monopoly for the first-filer in the generic market.[42] A no-AG commitment can be extremely valuable to the first-filer generic, because it ensures that this company will capture all generic sales and be able to charge higher prices during the exclusivity period. In brief, the final result is a loss for consumers in terms of a longer period of higher prices.

Another controversial issue concerns how to assess whether the reverse payment is 'large and unjustified'. The wording of the Supreme Court in *Actavis* has been meticulously analysed by commentators trying to clarify the criteria on which the size of the payment should be practically calculated. Eminent scholars have elaborated on this point, claiming that *Actavis* does not require evidence of a payment of a particular size, but only a payment in excess of the patentee's reasonably anticipated avoided litigation costs plus the value to the originator of goods and services provided by the generic manufacturer.[43] The underlying idea is that the size of the payment for delay can be relevant in several ways, as it may signal the degree of doubt about the underlying patent dispute and would vary inversely with the patent's perceived quality. On these grounds, where the payment involves a form other than a simple cash transfer from the patentee to the claimed infringer, consideration should be valued from the perspective of

[41] See, eg *In re Lamictal Direct Purchaser Antitrust Litigation* 18 F Supp 3d 560, 567 (DNJ 2014) (where the New Jersey District Court affirmed that 'nothing in *Actavis* says that a settlement contains a reverse payment when it confers substantial benefits or that a no-AG agreement is a "payment"'). However, the district court's ruling was then overturned by the Appellate Court: *King Drug Co of Florence Inc v SmithKline Beecham Corp* 791 F 3d 388, 394 (3d Cir 2015) (affirming that 'this no-AG agreement falls under *Actavis*'s rule because it may represent an unusual, unexplained reverse transfer of considerable value from the patentee to the alleged infringer and may therefore give rise to the inference that it is a payment to eliminate the risk of competition'). See also *Rochester Drug Co-Operative, Inc v Warner Chilcott Co (In re Loestrin 24 FE Antitrust Litigation)* 814 F 3d 538, 550 (1st Cir 2016) (vacating and remanding a district court's decision that non-cash payments did not fall under the scope of *Actavis*, on the grounds that it would 'give drug manufacturers carte blanche to negotiate anticompetitive settlements so long as they involve non-cash reverse payments').

[42] See M Carrier, 'How Not To Apply Actavis' (2014) 109 *Northwestern University Law Review Online* 113; Carrier, 'Eight Reasons', 699 (arguing that the danger deriving from these agreements is similar to that connected to market division, but, instead of allocating geographic space, they allocate time); Edlin et al, 'The Actavis Inference', 597 (affirming that a no-AG provision operates as an additional anti-competitive market division).

[43] Edlin et al, 'The Actavis Inference', 16–17.

the patentee.[44] However, this view, which can be found in the scholarship before *Actavis* too, is not free from criticism from those who consider it to be downplaying any possible alternative explanation of a large payment, such as the risk aversion of the parties.[45]

This issue is strictly related to the particular rule of reason established in *Actavis*. The rule-of-reason test is the normal standard used for antitrust assessment; however, it is generally considered complex and burdensome. While rebutting the quick-look approach under which reverse payment settlement agreements are presumptively unlawful and which would have shifted the burden onto the defence to show pro-competitive effects, the Court in *Actavis* opened the door to a more streamlined version of the rule-of-reason test, leaving the lower courts to structure it. Scholars have clarified that, according to the narrowly focused inquiry required in *Actavis*, both an anti-competitive effect and market power may be inferred from large reverse payments themselves. Using the *Actavis* language, plaintiffs are required to establish that the claimed infringer (the generic company) has agreed to abstain in some respect from competing using the patented innovation (the drug) for a period and that the former is receiving an unexplained payment from the patent holder (the brand-name company).[46] The payment prong includes the following steps: (i) valuing any consideration flowing from the patentee to the claimed infringer, which may be made over time and may take forms other than cash; (ii) deducting from that payment the patent holder's avoided litigation costs; and (iii) deducting from that payment the value of goods, services or other consideration provided by the claimed infringer to the patent holder as part of the same transaction or linked transactions. The resulting net payment is 'otherwise unexplained' and, if it is a positive quantity, may be understood to be payment for delaying entry.[47] It has been argued that, as the burden falls on those who want to challenge, it is no surprise that defendants are incentivised to 'muddy' the settlement with various elements and services that make it more difficult to determine both the direction and the magnitude of payments.[48]

[44] Edlin et al, 'Activating Actavis', 18.

[45] On the relevance of risk aversion, see MG Baumann, JP Bigelow, BC Harris, KM Murphy, JA Ordover, RD Willig and MB Wright, 'Activating *Actavis* with a More Complete Model' (2014) 28 *Antitrust* 83, 85.

[46] Edlin et al, 'Activating Actavis', 17–18. Then, should the evidence required in this step be satisfied, the following stages require the defendants to justify the agreement alleging its pro-competitive effects and finally the plaintiff to eventually rebut these justifications. See also MA Carrier, 'Why a "Large and Unjustified" Payment Threshold is Not Consistent with Actavis' (2016) 91 *Washington Law Review* 109 (arguing that requiring the plaintiff to demonstrate a large and unjustified payment before reaching the rule of reason large analysis – and thus attributing him a separate threshold burden – is inconsistent with *Actavis* and the Court's shortcuts for plaintiffs and burdens for defendants).

[47] Edlin et al, 'Activating Actavis', 18.

[48] R Feldman and P Misra, 'The Fatal Attraction of Pay-for-Delay' (2019) 18 *Chicago-Kent Journal of Intellectual Property* 249, 260.

C. Further Developments

Lower courts and the FTC have dealt with the application of rule-of-reason inquiry deriving from *Actavis* to specific cases. In this regard, a recent and interesting case derives from Opana antitrust litigation.[49] The facts are rather complex. In 2006, the brand manufacturer Endo received FDA approval for and launched Opana ER, an opioid with extended-release formulation of oxymorphone. One year later, Impax filed an ANDA to market a generic version of Opana ER through a paragraph IV certification. Being the first generic manufacturer to do so, Impax was entitled to 180 days of exclusivity from competition with other generic producers. Endo timely sued Impax in January 2008, claiming that Impax's ANDA infringed two of its patents, expiring in September 2013. The suit triggered the Hatch-Waxman Act's 30-month stay, precluding the FDA from finally approving Impax's ANDA until 2010 or until the patent dispute was resolved in Impax's favour. Endo and Impax first discussed settlement in the autumn of 2009, but Endo rejected Impax's proposals for a generic entry date in 2011 or 2012. Endo reopened settlement talks in 2010, approximately three days after learning that the FDA tentatively approved Impax's ANDA, three weeks before the patent trial was scheduled to begin and one month before the 30-month stay would have expired. The trial in the Endo/Impax patent litigation commenced in June 2010 and, just a few days later, the parties settled. Finally, Endo sought a commitment from Impax that it would refrain from launching its generic until 2013. In January 2017, the FTC filed an administrative complaint alleging that Endo had entered an illegal reverse payment agreement with Impax to delay entering the market with a generic version of Opana ER.

The FTC alleged that the reverse payment settlement involved an unlawful transfer of value in several forms: (i) a no-AG commitment, involving the freedom from generic competition during Impax's first 180 days on the market by virtue of Endo's agreement to refrain from offering an authorised generic version of Opana ER; (ii) a contingent payment – ultimately worth $102 million – designed to ensure that Impax would recoup the value of the no-AG commitment in the event that Endo undermined the generic oxymorphone market through its product hopping strategy, ie transitioning consumers to a reformulated Opana ER;[50] and (iii) a payment to Impax of $10–40 million,

[49] *In the Matter of Impax Labs, Inc* FTC Dkt No 9373, 42 (Opinion of the Commission, 28 March 2019) and 85 (Initial Decision, 11 May 2018).

[50] *Impax Labs, Inc v FTC* 994 F 3d 484, 488 (5th Cir 2021). The strategy of Endo included the removal of the original Opana ER from the market, its replacement with a crush-resistant version of the drug and the obtainment of new patents to protect the reformulated drug. The success of this 'product hop' depended on the reformulated Opana ER reaching the market sufficiently in advance of Impax's generic entry to allow patients to move away from the original drug before pharmacists started substituting the generic version. This transition period to the reformulated drug would take roughly six to nine months. The company projected that the reformulated Opana ER would

purportedly for an independent development and co-promotion deal. The 2010 patent settlement agreement also included a patent licence from Endo to Impax, providing the latter with a licence to all the then-issued patents and any Endo-owned or -controlled patents that could cover the manufacture, sale or marketing of Impax's generic version of Opana ER. This patent licence ensured that Impax could sell an oxymorphone ER product as soon as January 2013, even if Endo were later to obtain additional patents that covered Opana ER. According to the FTC, Impax's conduct denied patients the opportunity to purchase lower-cost generic versions of Opana ER until at least January 2013. The FTC brought separate actions against Endo and Impax alleging that the settlement was an unfair method of competition under the FTC Act and an unreasonable restraint on trade under the Sherman Act. While Endo settled, Impax successfully argued that the case should proceed in an administrative proceeding rather than in a federal district court, where the Commission had first filed. After a 12-day trial, the Chief Administrative Law Judge found that complaint counsel had failed to prove a violation of section 5 of the FTC Act and dismissed the complaint. Complaint counsel appealed, and the Commission reversed the initial decision. Impax appealed to the US Court of Appeals for the Fifth Circuit, which confirmed the Commission's decision.

The Court of Appeals first clarified that the rule-of-reason inquiry deriving from *Actavis* uses a burden-shifting framework, where the initial burden is on the FTC as plaintiff to show anti-competitive effects and then, if it succeeds in doing so, the burden shifts to the defendant, which would be required to demonstrate that the restraint produced pro-competitive benefits. If the defendant does so, then the burden shifts back to the plaintiff to demonstrate that the pro-competitive efficiencies could reasonably be achieved through less anti-competitive means. If the plaintiff carries this burden, it prevails; if the plaintiff does not, the court must weigh the harms and benefits – and if the anti-competitive harms outweigh the pro-competitive benefits, then the agreement is illegal.[51]

generate about $200 million in annual sales by 2016 if the market transitioned to the new drug before the generic entered. However, if the generic launched first, then 2016 sales of the new formulation would fall to $10 million. Afterwards, in 2012, Endo introduced its reformulated drug and withdrew the original drug, publicly stating that the original drug was unsafe (though the FDA later disagreed that safety concerns motivated the withdrawal). As a consequence, the market for the original Opana ER shriveled and Endo had to pay Impax $102 million in credits. Endo subsequently succeeded in securing additional patents, and in 2015 and 2016 secured injunctions that prevented all manufacturers, including Impax, from marketing generic versions of the reformulated drug. However, in 2017, the FDA asked Endo to voluntarily withdraw the reformulated Opana ER from the market due to safety concerns. For its part, Impax began marketing an original formulation generic oxymorphone in January 2013, despite the damaged market Endo had left behind. Because of the injunctions Endo secured against other generics and because Endo eventually withdrew the reformulated Opana ER from the market, Impax's generic was the only extended-release oxymorphone available to consumers at the time of the judgment of the Court of Appeals for the Fifth Circuit.

[51] *Ohio v American Express* 138 S Ct 2274, 2284 (2018).

Thus, initially the Court explained that, according to *Actavis*, 'in contrast to the typical horizontal agreement to divvy up markets, reverse payment settlements might produce both anti- and procompetitive effects'. On the one hand, the payment by a brand manufacturer to a generic to delay entry

> in effect amounts to a purchase by the patentee of the exclusive right to sell its product, a right it already claims but would lose if the patent litigation were to continue and the patent were held invalid or not infringed by the generic product.[52]

Accordingly, reverse payment settlements may restrict competition even more than typical market allocation agreements because delaying entry of the first generic does not just eliminate one competitor – it prolongs the 'bottleneck' that delays the entry of other generic competitors.[53] However, if the patent is valid, then a settlement that allows generic entry after the FDA's approval of the drug but still before the patent expiration date may result in more competition than would have existed without the settlement.[54]

The Court considered that a large reverse payment might be justified if it represents avoided litigation costs or fair value for services, and concluded that it was not the case. The Court also emphasised that no inquiry into the validity of the patent is required: 'the fact that generic competition was possible, and that Endo was willing to pay a large amount to prevent that risk, is enough to infer anticompetitive effect'.[55]

In its opinion, the FTC clarified that the restraint to be justified is not the entire agreement but the commitment not to enter the market made in exchange for a large and unjustified payment. The link between this restraint and a possible pro-competitive justification must be demonstrated by the plaintiff.[56] Then, on the basis of the less-restrictive-alternative standard as applied by the FTC,[57]

[52] *Actavis* 570 US 153–54.

[53] *Impax Labs, Inc v FTC* 493 (citing *In re Nexium (Esomeprazole) Antitrust Litigation* 842 F 3d 34, 41 (1st Cir 2016)).

[54] *Actavis* 570 US 154.

[55] *Impax Labs, Inc v FTC* 498. The Court affirmed that 'This large and unjustified payment generated anticompetitive effects'. The Commission explained that there 'was a real threat of competition from Impax' being snuffed out by Endo's agreement to make the reverse payments. The FDA had just approved Impax's generic, allowing it to sell the drug. Impax had taken steps to do so, even though its market entry would be 'at risk' of infringement liability. Endo's known product hopping plans increased Impax's incentive to quickly enter the market. The Commission thus had substantial evidence to conclude that the reverse payments replaced the 'possibility of competition with the certainty of none'. The FTC, in its Opinion (at 24, fn 26), explained that it did not mean 'that Impax *would* have entered earlier but for the agreement … The relevant question is whether it was plausible Impax *could* enter earlier, which tells us whether a risk of entry – the harm *Actavis* instructs us to guard against – was eliminated'.

[56] FTC Opinion, *Impax*, 33–36 and fn 40 (explaining that 'A contrary rule would allow parties to skirt liability for anticompetitive behavior by inserting unrelated provisions into their contracts and claiming that those provisions benefited competition').

[57] This standard is based on the assumption that a restraint is unreasonable when any procompetitive benefits it produces 'could be reasonably achieved through less anticompetitive means'. *Am Express* 138 S Ct 2284. See C Scott Hemphill, 'Less Restrictive Alternatives in Antitrust Law'

the Court upheld the finding of the Commission – based on three evidentiary legs, ie industry practice, credibility determinations about settlement negotiations and economic analysis – that Impax could have achieved an entry date even earlier than 2013 by entering into a settlement without reverse payments that would have resulted in greater generic competition. The Court clarified that the question to be answered was whether there was evidence that would allow a reasonable factfinder to conclude that a no-payment settlement was feasible, and this was exactly the case. It followed that Impax agreed to an unreasonable restraint of trade.[58] Finally, the Supreme Court denied certiorari in December 2021.

This case is particularly relevant for a number of reasons. Firstly, it covers several issues that needed further guidance and consolidation after *Actavis*, including those relating to large and unjustified payments, the transfer of value through various types of arrangements, pro-competitive justifications and their connection with the restraint, the less restrictive alternative of a no-payment settlement. Moreover, it has clearly shown how reverse payment settlements may include several types of arrangements, including product hopping.

For the sake of completeness, it should be noted that the Opana saga includes other lawsuits and class actions. In March 2022, a judgment dismissed the suit arising from a new complaint filed by the FTC in 2021 against Endo and Impax, alleging that a 2017 agreement between them violated the antitrust laws. At the centre of this suit is the provision in the former agreement between the two companies according to which, in exchange for not launching its product before 2013, Impax received from Endo a licence to any then-issued and future patents that could cover oxymorphone. Such agreement provided that Impax could sell its oxymorphone ER product even if Endo later obtained additional patents covering the drug (which, in fact, Endo enforced against all other generics).[59] The DC District Court found that *Actavis* does not apply to the 2017 agreement, which provides for a valid exclusive licence.[60]

(2016) 116 *Columbia Law Review* 927, 937–42. The Court explained that 'When a less restrictive alternative exists, a party's decision to nonetheless engage in conduct "that harms consumers" likely results from a desire "to gain from the resulting consumer harm" … The question, in short, is whether "the good [could] have been achieved equally well with less bad"' (citing Scott Hemphill, 'Less Restrictive', 929). On its part, Impax argued that the FTC only recognised what it considers an equally restrictive alternative – the possibility of a settlement with the same entry date but no reverse payments. But the Commission recognised the feasibility of no-payment settlements with both the same or an earlier entry date.

[58] *Impax Labs, Inc v FTC*, 500. The Court affirmed that 'the reverse payment settlement was an agreement to preserve and split monopoly profits that was not necessary to allow generic competition before the expiration of Endo's patent. As a result, Impax agreed to an unreasonable restraint of trade.'

[59] The US Patent and Trademark Office issued Endo additional patents covering Opana ER. Through these newly issued patents, Endo prevented all producers of generic Opana ER from launching until 2029.

[60] 2022 WL 951640 (DDC 30 March 2022). To stay in the oxymorphone ER market, Endo prepared to relaunch Opana ER with an approved ANDA (the 'Watson ANDA') for generic oxymorphone ER.

Looking at the US landscape, as already mentioned, according to the last FTC report released in December 2020, following the *Actavis* decision and subsequent case law, while the total number of settlements has increased, a continued decline in the use of anti-competitive reverse payment agreements has been seen.[61] However, some authors have warned that this finding should not lead to the conclusion that there is no more cause of concern. Rather, pay-for-delay agreements have taken more nuanced forms and may have found 'better ways to camouflage [themselves]'.[62] In particular, four categories of patent settlements are identified by the FTC report: (i) settlements containing explicit compensation to the generic company and a restriction on selling a generic product for a period of time; (ii) agreements with 'possible compensation' to the generic company, ie cases in which it is not immediately obvious whether the generic patent challenger received compensation – that would require an inquiry into the specific marketplace circumstances – thus constituting a worrisome category as such an inquiry is considered by the FTC to be beyond the scope of its summary report;[63] (iii) agreements restricting the generic manufacturer's ability to market its product but containing no explicit or possible compensation; and (iv) settlements containing no restrictions on generic entry.

A further consideration must be given to the fact that up to now pay-for-delay cases have typically regarded traditional small-molecule drugs. Whether this kind of agreement will spread to biologics remains to be seen. On this

Endo took significant strides in early 2017 to relaunch Opana ER using the Watson ANDA. In 2015, while it prepared its potential relaunch, Endo asked Impax to pay it an 85% royalty fee for the licence to the later-issued patents. When Impax refused, Endo sued Impax for breach of the 2010 Agreement in the District Court for the District of New Jersey. In a May 2016 filing, Endo alleged that Impax had breached the 2010 Agreement's requirement to negotiate an amendment in good faith. After that court had denied Impax's motion to dismiss, Endo and Impax settled the breach-of-contract and patent-infringement lawsuit on August 2017 (the '2017 Agreement'), clarifying that Impax's licence in the previous agreement includes any Opana ER patents owned by Endo and obtained after it entered the Agreement. The decision has been criticised by MA Carrier, 'Pharmaceutical Settlements and Judicial Error' [2022] (May) *Competition Policy International Antitrust Chronicle* 5 (noting that the case involved a generic monopoly, and the generic's sharing monopoly profits with the brand).

[61] FTC, 'FY 2017 Report on Branded Drug Firms'. According to this report, the total number of patent settlements entered by pharmaceutical companies in FY 2017 was close to the record high in the previous year; however, settlements including the types of reverse payments that are likely to be anti-competitive remain very low. In addition, for the first time since FY 2004, no settlement agreement in FY 2017 contained a no-AG commitment.

[62] Feldman and Misra, 'The Fatal Attraction', 253.

[63] ibid 263 (defining this kind of settlement as 'the darkest corner of the pay-for-delay universe'). According to the FTC report (at 2), common forms of possible compensation include: (i) a commitment from the brand manufacturer not to use a third party to distribute an authorised generic for a period of time, such as during first-filer exclusivity; (ii) a declining royalty structure, in which the generic's obligation to pay royalties is reduced or eliminated if a brand launches an authorised generic product; and (iii) an agreement that provides AG supply to a non-first-filer ANDA holder during the first-filer's exclusivity period, thereby permitting the non-first filer ANDA holder to sell an authorised generic during the exclusivity period.

point, some authors have stressed that the features of the biologics market – in particular, the modest price erosion from biosimilar entry, the lasting first-mover advantage available to biologics and the frequent use of the IPR process to challenge biologic patents – may suggest that reverse payment patent settlements are less likely in this context.[64] However, others have warned about agreements appearing in the biologics arena, such as that of Humira, a top-selling biologic drug used to treat rheumatoid arthritis and other inflammatory conditions, which was covered by a patent thicket of more than 130 patents and is the subject of a contentious lawsuit, where antitrust claims concerning settlements between the drug's producer (AbbVie) and other companies have been dismissed by the District Court for the Northern District of Illinois and the Seventh Circuit.[65]

Besides the case law, legislation addressing pay-for-delay is under consideration in the US. The US President Executive Order of July 2021 explicitly encourages the FTC to ban pay-for-delay and similar agreements by rule.[66] Meanwhile, among the initiatives at state level, California enacted the first-in-the-nation state law (AB 824) to combat pay-for-delay deals between brand-name and generic pharmaceutical drug manufacturers in 2019, though its implementation has been challenged.[67] Moreover, in April 2021, a Bill

[64] MA Carrier and CJ Minniti, 'Biologics: The New Antitrust Frontier' (2018) 2 *University of Illinois Law Review* 3, 19ff.

[65] Feldman and Misra, 'The Fatal Attraction', 266 and 272. See also L Karas, R Sachs and G Anderson, 'Legal Obstacles to Biosimilar Market Entry' [2021] *Harvard Public Health Review* 28. With regard to Humira case, see M Carrier, 'The US District Court for the Northern District of Illinois Dismisses Antitrust Case Challenging Patent Thicket (Humira)' [2020] *e-Competitions* No 96364. See *In re Humira (Adalimumab) Antitrust Litigation* 2020 WL 3051309 (ND Ill 8 June 2020); *Mayor and City Council of Baltimore, et al v AbbVie Inc, et al* Case No 20-2402 (7th Cir 1 August 2022). The basic US patent for Humira expired at the end of 2016, but AbbVie, its owner, obtained 132 additional patents related to the medicine for details such as manufacturing or administering the drug. The last of these expires in 2034. All of AbbVie's patent suits were sealed on terms that permit biosimilar drugs to enter the US market during 2023 (the dates for different entrants range from January to December). The Seventh Circuit held in August 2022 that the settlements were compromises as many of the 132 patents last beyond 2023. The Court noted that Actavis referred to the Hatch-Waxman Act, and particularly the 180-day period of exclusivity, which does not apply to biologics. AbbVie and affiliated firms have patents for Humira throughout the EU too, where potential competition from biosimilar drugs led to litigation that was sealed with an October 2018 entry date. According to the plaintiffs, AbbVie gifted the biosimilar makers with 4+ years of profits in Europe, in exchange for their agreement not to enter the US market until 2023. However, the Seventh Circuit confirmed the findings of the district court, stating that settlements in the EU and US were traditional resolutions of patent litigation. See also Amicus brief to the US Court of Appeals for the Seventh Circuit (Oct 2020).

[66] Executive Order No 14036 on Promoting Competition in the American Economy, 86 Fed Reg 36,987 (9 July 2021).

[67] In *Association for Accessible Medicines v Becerra*, the district court denied the Association for Accessible Medicines' (AAM) request for a preliminary injunction, finding no imminent threat of harm. The AAM then appealed, seeking to enjoin the law on theories of a violation of the dormant Commerce Clause, violation of due process and federal pre-emption. The Ninth Circuit rejected the case (*Association for Accessible Medicines v Becerra* Case No 20-15014 (9th Cir 2020)). In December 2021, the US District Court of the Eastern District of California ruled in favour of AAM, and in February 2022, it reassessed the scope of the injunction on the request of California AG Rob Bonta and amended it to only apply to settlements that were negotiated,

addressing the issue was proposed in Congress (HR 2891, Preserve Access to Affordable Generics and Biosimilars Act), which sets out a presumption of illegality.[68]

III. EU CASE LAW ON REVERSE PAYMENT PATENT SETTLEMENTS

Since 2013, the EU practice on pay-for-delay settlements has included some decisions issued by the European Commission, finding the agreements at issue anti-competitive (*Lundbeck*,[69] *Fentanyl*,[70] *Perindopril* (*Servier*)[71]

completed or entered into within California's borders (*Association for Accessible Medicines v Bonta* No 2:20-CV-01708-TLN-DB, 2022 WL 463313 (ED Cal 14 February 2022)). However, the court denied the specific request of the AG to allow the enforcement of AB 824 any time an agreement is made relating to in-state pharmaceutical sales that artificially distorts the pharmaceutical market in the state.

[68] In April 2021, some House Representatives presented this new Bill, the Preserve Access to Affordable Generics and Biosimilars Act, www.congress.gov/bill/117th-congress/house-bill/2891/text. According to this Bill, the FTC Act (15 USC 44ff) is amended by inserting § 27, providing that 'an agreement shall be presumed to have anticompetitive effects and shall be a violation of this section if – (i) an ANDA filer or a biosimilar biological product application filer receives anything of value, including an exclusive license; and (ii) the ANDA filer or biosimilar biological product application filer agrees to limit or forgo research, development, manufacturing, marketing, or sales of the ANDA product or biosimilar biological product, as applicable, for any period of time'. Such a presumption shall not apply if the parties of the settlement demonstrate by clear and convincing evidence that either the value transferred is compensation solely for other goods or services with which the ANDA filer or biosimilar biological product application filer has provided the brand-name drug manufacturer or the pro-competitive benefits of the agreement outweigh the anti-competitive effects of the agreement. In more detail, the proposal provides that, in determining whether the settling parties have met their burden, the fact-finder shall not presume that entry would not have occurred until the expiration of the relevant patent or statutory exclusivity; or that the agreement's provision for entry of the ANDA product or biosimilar biological product prior to the expiration of the relevant patent or statutory exclusivity means that the agreement is pro-competitive. Section 27(c)(2) also identifies the amount of litigation expenses that a fact-finder should consider reasonable. In particular, the section does not prohibit a resolution or settlement of a patent infringement claim in which the consideration that the ANDA filer or biosimilar biological product application filer receives as part of the resolution or settlement includes only one or more of the following: '(1) The right to market and secure final regulatory approval for the ANDA product or biosimilar biological product at a date, whether certain or contingent, in the United States prior to the expiration of – (A) any patent that is the basis for the patent infringement claim; or (B) any patent right or other statutory exclusivity that would prevent the marketing of such ANDA product or biosimilar biological product. (2) A payment for reasonable litigation expenses not to exceed – (A) for calendar year 2019, $7,500,000; and (B) for calendar year 2020 and each calendar year thereafter, the amount determined for the preceding calendar year adjusted to reflect the percentage increase (if any) in the Producer Price Index for Legal Services published by the Bureau of Labor Statistics of the Department of Labor for the then most recent 12-month period ending December 31. (3) A covenant not to sue on any claim that the ANDA product or biosimilar biological product infringes a United States patent.'

[69] *Lundbeck*, Case AT.39226, Commission Decision [2013].

[70] *Fentanyl*, Case AT.39685, Commission Decision [2013].

[71] *Servier*, Case AT.39612, Commission Decision [2014]. In July 2014, the Commission imposed fines totalling €427.7 million on the French pharmaceutical company Servier and five producers of generic medicines for concluding a series of deals all aimed at protecting Servier's blockbuster blood pressure medicine from price competition by generics in the EU. The originator's patent for the perindopril molecule expired in 2003, leaving only secondary patents relating to processes

and *Cephalon*[72]), and some rulings of the General Court, one of them, *Lundbeck*, being definitively decided by the Court of Justice.[73] Moreover, the Court of Justice has given a preliminary ruling, *Generics (Paroxetine)*, in which it has provided guidance on the principles and legal reasoning underpinning the current European stance about pay-for-delay settlements.[74] The following subsections analyse these two latter cases, being at the time of writing those decided by the Court of Justice and representing the European approach on the application of competition rules to these agreements.

A. *Lundbeck*

The first famous case of pay-for-delay in the EU concerned citalopram, which is an antidepressant drug and the Danish originator Lundbeck's best-selling branded product. In June 2013 – thus in the same period as *Actavis* – the Commission adopted a decision concerning six agreements which operated in the years 2002 and 2003 between Lundbeck on the one hand and each of four generic pharmaceutical undertakings on the other (namely, Alpharma (now part of Zoetis), Merck KGaA/Generics UK (Generics UK is now part of Mylan), Arrow (now part of Actavis) and Ranbaxy) that were found to be 'designed to replace the uncertainties of the competitive process for the certainty of an agreement between undertakings, in exchange for a payment'.[75] At the time

and form, so generic producers were starting the process of 'getting-ready-for-generic-entry'. Servier has been found responsible for a complex exclusionary strategy, including a technology acquisition and a series of patent settlements with generic rivals pursuant to which the generic companies agreed to abstain from competing in exchange for a share of Servier's rent, resulting in cash payments of several tens of millions of euros from the originator to generics. According to the Commission, Servier misused legitimate tools provided by patent law by shutting out a competing technology and buying out a number of competitors that had developed cheaper medicines to avoid competing on their own merits, thereby violating both Arts 101 (for the anti-competitive agreements with competitors) and 102 TFEU (for the abuse of its dominant position deriving from its significant market power in the market for the perindopril molecule). With regard to the violation of Art 101, the settlements were to be considered restrictions by object. Unusually, the Commission analysed the likely restrictive effects of the agreements on competition too. ibid para 1213ff. See also Case T-691/14 *Servier SAS and others v Commission* ECLI:EU:T:2018:922, the General Court upholding the Commission's findings of the restriction of competition by object under Art 101 TFEU for the settlements between Servier and some companies. However, the Court annulled the Commission's decision for the part concerning the settlement between Servier and Krka and did not uphold the EU Commission's finding of an abuse of dominant position under Art 102 TFEU on the basis of errors in the definition of the relevant product market. Cases C-176/19 P and C-201/19 P are pending.

[72] *Cephalon*, Case AT.39686, Commission Decision [2020]. Case T-74/21 *Teva Pharmaceutical Industries and Cephalon v Commission* is pending.

[73] Case C-591/16 P *H Lundbeck A/S and Lundbeck Ltd v European Commission* ECLI:EU:C:2021:243.

[74] Case C-307/18 *Generics (UK) Ltd and Others v Competition and Markets Authority* ECLI:EU:C:2020:52.

[75] *Lundbeck*, Commission Decision, para 633.

the agreements were concluded, Lundbeck's basic patent for the citalopram molecule had expired but it still held a number of related process patents which granted Lundbeck exclusivity rights on certain, though not all, new ways of producing citalopram (including in particular a crystallisation patent), which provided more limited protection. However, producers of generic versions of citalopram had the possibility of entering the market and several companies were making preparations to this end. Prior to the agreements under investigation, Lundbeck had usually claimed infringement of one or more of its process patents and the generic undertaking concerned had usually claimed non-infringement of the patent(s) concerned or invalidity of the patent(s) Lundbeck invoked. Each of the agreements had been concluded before a court ruling on these issues between the parties involved was given, even by way of an interim measure, and all except one (Lundbeck's agreement with Alpharma regarding the European Economic Area) were concluded before any litigation had started. According to the Commission, settlements provided for Lundbeck's significant payments and other inducements to the generic companies (including the purchase of generics' stock for the sole purpose of destroying it and the offer of guaranteed profit in a distribution agreement) with the aim of preventing them from marketing citalopram products.[76] The Commission concluded that the agreements at issue were anti-competitive by object and imposed a €93.8 million fine on Lundbeck and a total fine of €52.2 million on the generic undertakings.

In 2016, the General Court confirmed the decision of the Commission, releasing the first ruling on reverse payment patent settlements in the EU.[77] Both the Commission and the General Court argued that where a reverse payment is combined with an exclusion of a potential competitor from the market or a limitation of the incentives to seek market entry, such a limitation may not arise exclusively from the parties' assessments of the strength of the patents, but rather can be obtained by means of that transfer of value, therefore constituting a buying-off of competition.[78] In these cases, the size of the reverse payment constituted, according to the Court and the Commission, an indicator of the strength or weakness of the patent, as perceived by the parties to the agreements at the time they were concluded, and of the fact that the

[76] It is worth noting that the patent settlement agreements at issue are assumed to constitute only a part of the originator's strategy aimed at delaying the entry of generic companies into the citalopram market in order to allow a good market penetration of escitalopram (Cipralex, Lundbeck's active enantiomer of citalopram). The investigation, whose evidence is strongly based on the internal documents of the undertakings involved, contains a symbolic assertion made by Lundbeck's representatives, describing the strategy aimed at delaying entry of generics as a poker game: 'We have been dealt a mediocre hand – no aces, a couple of queens and some small uneven cards. But we have a large pile of $$$ at our side. We call it – "the art of playing a losing hand slowly"'. See *Lundbeck*, Commission Decision, para 131.

[77] Case T-472/13 *H Lundbeck A/S and Lundbeck Ltd v European Commission* ECLI:EU:T:2016:449.

[78] ibid paras 638–40.

originator undertaking was not initially convinced of its chances of succeeding in the event of litigation.[79] The disproportionate nature of such payments, combined with several other factors – such as the fact that the amounts of those payments seemed to correspond at least to the profit anticipated by the generic undertakings if they had entered the market, the absence of provisions allowing the generic undertakings to launch their product on the market upon the expiry of the agreement without having to fear infringement actions brought by Lundbeck or the presence, in those agreements, of restrictions going beyond the scope of Lundbeck's patents – led the Commission and the Court to conclude that the agreements at issue, in not resolving the underlying patent dispute but rather incentivising generic undertakings to discontinue their independent efforts to enter the market, had as their object the restriction of competition, within the meaning of Article 101(1) of the Treaty on the Functioning of the European Union (TFEU).[80]

Then, specifically on settlements, the approach taken stressed that not all patent settlements are necessarily problematic from a competition law perspective, and that the existence of a reverse payment in the context of a patent settlement is not problematic when: (i) that payment is linked to the strength of the patent, as perceived by each of the parties; (ii) it is necessary in order to find an acceptable and legitimate solution in the eyes of the two parties; and (iii) it is not accompanied by restrictions intended to delay the market entry of generics.[81] In contrast, in *Lundbeck*, the amounts provided for in the agreements broadly corresponded to the profits expected by the generic undertakings if they had entered the market or to the damages that they would have obtained if they had succeeded in litigation against Lundbeck: by so doing, the parties to the agreements were able to share a part of the profits that Lundbeck continued to enjoy, to the detriment of consumers, who continued to pay higher prices than they would have if the generics had entered the market. In other words, the agreements at issue are comparable to market exclusion agreements, which are among the most serious restrictions of competition, the exclusion of competitors from the market being an extreme form of market sharing and of limitation of production.[82]

The Court of Justice finally delivered its judgment, after *Generics*, in March 2021, dismissing the appeals and substantially reaffirming the principles already established in this case, so that the evolution of the European approach may be analysed through such ruling.

[79] ibid para 353.
[80] ibid para 354.
[81] ibid para 350; *Lundbeck*, Commission Decision, paras 638–39.
[82] Case T-472/13 *Lundbeck*, para 341 (referring to Case C-209/07 *Competition Authority v Beef Industry Development Society Ltd and Barry Brothers (Carrigmore) Meats Ltd* ECLI:EU:C:2008:643 [2008] ECR I-08637).

B. *Generics*

Paroxetine is a prescription-only anti-depressant medicine, belonging to the group of medicines known as selective serotonin re-uptake inhibitors. It was marketed in the UK by the originator company GSK under the brand name Seroxat, and both the patent on the active ingredient and the period of data exclusivity expired between 1999 and 2000. The originator also held a number of secondary patents covering four polymorphs of the active ingredient in question and the process to produce them. In this context, GSK was faced with the possibility that generic companies would enter the market. GSK entered into three agreements with the manufacturers of the generic medicines concerned (IVAX, GUK and Alpharma): the GSK/IVAX agreement (3 October 2001–29 June 2004) appointed IVAX as the sole distributor in the UK of 20 mg paroxetine hydrochloride to be sold as an authorised generic medicine; and the GSK/GUK agreement (13 March 2002–1 July 2004) and the GSK/Alpharma agreement (12 November 2002–13 February 2004) were concluded to bring an end to litigation and provided the commitment of the generic companies not to make, import or supply paroxetine hydrochloride, while GSK agreed to a series of value transfers – including the acquisition of the generic producers' stock, to award them a 'marketing allowance' and to cover a substantial part of their litigation costs.

Against this background, the Competition and Market Authority (CMA) adopted on 12 February 2016 a decision in which it found that GSK had abused its dominant position in the market for paroxetine and that the latter two agreements amounted to a breach of Article 101 TFEU and its national equivalent.[83] The companies on which penalties had been imposed brought an appeal against that decision before the Competition Appeal Tribunal, which, considering that in order to evaluate the legality of the CMA's action it was necessary to interpret Articles 101 and 102 TFEU, submitted a reference to the Court of Justice. As this chapter deals mainly with Article 101 TFEU, the following issues referring to the Court are relevant: (i) with regard to the notion of potential competition, whether an originator and a generic producer can be deemed potential competitors where there is a bona fide dispute between them concerning the validity of the patents and/or whether they have been infringed; (ii) whether the answer to the first question varies depending on a number of factors (ie whether there are pending court proceedings; whether the patent holder has obtained an interim injunction against a generic producer; and whether the former regards the latter as a potential competitor); (iii) with regard to the notion of restriction of competition by object ex Article 101(1) TFEU, whether an agreement whereby a generic producer agrees not to enter

[83] CMA, Case CE-9531/11 (2016).

the market and not to challenge the validity of the patent, on the one hand, and whereby the originator agrees to make a payment 'substantially greater' than the avoided litigation costs and which does not constitute a payment for any good or service, on the other hand, amounts to a 'by object' infringement; (iv) whether the answer to the previous question varies depending on whether the agreement does not exceed the scope of the patent and/or whether the value transfer is less than the profit the generic producer would have made; (v) whether the answer changes where the agreement involves the supply of 'significant but limited' volumes of an authorised generic product which would have benefited consumers had the originator succeeded in the litigation or whether this is relevant only to assessment under Article 101(3) TFEU; and (vi) with regard to the notion of restriction by effects, whether the analysis must consider, in the absence of the settlement, the probability of the generic producer succeeding in litigation (and in particular whether the probability of the patent being declared invalid and/or not infringed would have been above 50 per cent) or whether the parties could have achieved the same aims by virtue of a less restrictive agreement (ie that the chance of a less restrictive settlement was above 50 per cent).

As can be inferred by the questions submitted, the ruling of the Court of Justice is particularly important as it is called on to give guidance on the overall principles that must inform the assessment of reverse payment patent settlements according to EU competition law.[84]

With regard to the notion of potential competition, the reasoning of the Court starts from the consideration that it is necessary to determine whether there are real and concrete possibilities for an undertaking that is not present in the market to join it and compete with one or more undertakings already active in that market.[85] Considering the features of the pharmaceutical sector, relevance must be given to the regulatory framework (in particular, the rules on marketing authorisation) and the intellectual property system. Moreover, according to the Court, subjective considerations may be relevant too; for example, the fact that an incumbent perceives a threat of entry may be sufficient to exercises competitive pressure on it.

Thus, it is necessary to determine, first, whether, at the time the agreement was concluded, the generic producer had taken sufficient preparatory steps

[84] The same approach was previously taken by AG Kokott in the Opinion delivered on the case (EU:C:2020:28).

[85] Case C-307/18 *Generics*, para 36 (citing Case C-234/89 *Stergios Delimitis v Henninger Bräu AG* ECLI:EU:C:1991:91, [1991] ECR I-00935, para 21). Thus, in order to consider a generic undertaking as a potential competitor, it must be determined whether there would have existed, in the absence of the settlement, real and concrete possibilities for it to enter that market: on the one hand, the purely hypothetical possibility of such an entry or even the mere wish of the firm to enter the market is not enough; on the other hand, it is not necessary to demonstrate with certainty that the manufacturer will in fact enter the market concerned and, a fortiori, that it will be capable, thereafter, of retaining its place there.

to enable it to enter the market concerned, which would demonstrate its firm intention and inherent ability to operate such entry (for example, measures taken to be in a position to have, at the requisite time, the required administrative authorisations for the marketing of a generic version of the medicine concerned and an adequate stock of that generic medicine either through its own production or through supply contracts concluded with third parties; legal steps undertaken in order to challenge the process patents held by the originator; and marketing initiatives).[86] Second, the market entry of such a generic producer should not meet insurmountable barriers to entry. Importantly, to this end, the Court affirmed that the existence of a patent on the manufacturing process of an active ingredient that is in the public domain cannot, as such, be regarded as an insurmountable barrier and that such a finding is not undermined by any of the following arguments: (i) the presumption of validity attached to a process patent held by the manufacturer of originator medicines; (ii) the uncertain outcome of the dispute as to the validity of that patent; and (iii) the existence of injunctions granted by a national court, whereby a generic firm is prohibited, on an interim basis, from selling the generic version of the originator medicine at issue.[87]

Therefore, on the crucial issue of the relevance of the patent, the Court affirmed the following arguments: the uncertainty as to the validity of patents covering medicines is a fundamental characteristic of the pharmaceutical sector; the presumption of validity of a patent for an originator medicine (which applies automatically to patents when granted) does not amount to a presumption that a generic version of that medicine properly placed on the market is illegal; a patent does not guarantee protection against actions seeking to contest its validity; such actions, and, in particular, the 'at risk' launch of a generic medicine and the consequent court proceedings, commonly take place in the period before or immediately after the market entry of such a generic medicine; to obtain a marketing authorisation for a generic medicine, there is no requirement to prove that that marketing does not infringe any originator medicine patent rights; and, in the pharmaceutical sector, potential competition may be exerted before the expiry of a compound patent protecting an originator medicine, since the manufacturers of generic medicines want to be ready to enter the market as soon as that patent expires.[88]

[86] Case C-307/18 *Generics*, para 44.
[87] ibid para 46–47.
[88] ibid para 51. The finding of potential competition may derive from several indicia, such as the conclusion of an agreement between the type of undertakings at issue and the intention, made known by an originator company, to make transfers of value to a manufacturer of generic medicines in exchange for the postponement of the latter's market entry, even though the former claims that the latter is infringing one or more of its process patents ('the greater the transfer of value, the stronger the indication'). See paras 55–56 and para 57: 'That intention discloses the perception of the manufacturer of originator medicines of the risk that the manufacturer concerned of generic medicines presents to its commercial interests, that perception being relevant to the assessment of

The second important issue concerns the finding of a restriction by object. The Court confirmed the established case law, according to which the concept of restriction of competition 'by object' must be interpreted strictly and can be applied only to some forms of coordination between undertakings that can be considered in themselves, and having regard to the content of their provisions, their objectives, and the economic and legal context of which they form part, as being harmful to the proper functioning of normal competition. In such cases, as usual, it is not necessary to assess their effects.[89] From the reasoning of the Court, it is clearly affirmed that there is no room for a presumption of illegality for reverse payment patent settlements. The Court provided some examples of transfers of value that can be appropriate and necessary to the attainment of legitimate objectives by the parties: where the generic producer receives from the originator of the medicine sums that correspond to compensation for the costs of or disruption caused by the litigation between them; or that correspond to remuneration for the actual supply, immediate or subsequent, of goods or services to the originator itself; or, when the generic producer discharges undertakings, particularly financial, given to him by the patent holder, such as a cross-undertaking in damages.[90]

A 'restriction by object' must be found when it is plain from the analysis of the settlement agreement that the transfers of value (either pecuniary or non-pecuniary) provided for by it cannot have any explanation other than the commercial interest of both the holder of the patent and the party allegedly infringing the patent not to engage in competition on the merits.[91] In order to assess whether this is the case, it is important: (i) to take into consideration all the transfers of value made between the parties, whether pecuniary or non-pecuniary; (ii) to assess whether the net gain arising from the transfers of value by the originator medicines in favour of the generic firm may be justified by the existence of any quid pro quo or waivers by the generic firm that are proven and legitimate; and if that is not the case (iii) to determine whether that net gain is sufficiently large to actually act as an incentive to the manufacturer of the generic medicines concerned to refrain from entering the market.[92] With regard to the last point, the transfers of value should not necessarily be greater than the profits which the generic firm would have made if it had been successful in the patent proceedings. Rather, the transfers of value must be shown to be sufficiently beneficial to encourage the generic firm to refrain from competition.[93]

the existence of potential competition … where that perception affects the conduct on the market of the manufacturer of originator medicines.' See also Case C-591/16 P *Lundbeck*, paras 76, 84–86, 88.

[89] Case C-307/18 *Generics* para 67 (citing Case C-345/14 *Maxima Latvija* ECLI:EU:C:2015:784, para 20 and Case C-179/16 *F. Hoffmann-La Roche and Others* ECLI:EU:C:2018:25, paras 78–79).

[90] Case C-307/18 *Generics*, para 86.

[91] ibid paras 84–87.

[92] ibid paras 90–93.

[93] ibid para 94. See also Case C-591/16 P *Lundbeck*, paras 114–115.

Then, the Court clarifies that this does not undermine the possibility for the parties to engage in providing proof of the pro-competitive effects of the settlement agreement, which must be capable of giving rise to a reasonable doubt that it causes a sufficient degree of harm to competition. In the words of AG Kokott, if, taking into account the benefits afforded by the agreement, those benefits give rise to doubts or it is unclear whether an agreement providing such benefits may have an anti-competitive object, then it is still not possible to conclude that it has an anti-competitive object.[94]

With regard to the analysis of the effects, the fundamental point that the Court had to address concerned whether the uncertainty about the validity and/or infringement of intellectual property rights must be considered and, if so, how. In this regard, in accordance with the preceding case law, the Court affirmed that the establishment of the counter-factual – which has the sole purpose of establishing the realistic possibilities of the generic producer's conduct in the absence of the agreement – does not involve, on the part of the referring court, any definitive finding in relation to the chances of success of the generic producer in the patent proceedings or the probability of concluding a less restrictive agreement.[95]

Finally, *Generics* also contains important indications about the application of Article 102 in the context of pay-for-delay settlements. Coherently with the previous argument and the case law, the Court held that the exercise of an intellectual property right may amount to an abuse of a dominant position, in particular when the strategy of a patent holder seeks to strengthen its dominant position by denying its potential competitors access to the market.[96]

IV. COMPARATIVE ANALYSIS

A. Legal Frameworks

The comparative analysis of the practice of reverse payment patent settlements in the US and in the EU shows, firstly, that the difference between the two regulatory environments is crucial.[97] Pay-for-delay may concern both primary and

[94] AG Kokott Opinion in Case C-307/18 *Generics* para 165.

[95] Case C-307/18 *Generics*, para 119.

[96] The Court also addressed the issue of the definition of the relevant market, affirming that for the purposes of definition of the product market concerned, it is necessary to take into account not only the originator version of that medicine, but also its generic versions – even if the latter would not be able to enter the market legally before the expiry of that process patent – if the manufacturers of the generic medicines concerned are in a position to present themselves on the market concerned within a short period with sufficient strength to constitute a serious counterbalance to the manufacturer of the originator medicines already on that market (ibid para 140).

[97] For a comparative analysis of EU and US case law and regulatory frameworks, see D Geradin, DH Ginsburg and G Safty, 'Reverse Settlements in the European Union and the United States'

secondary patents, but the latter are the most frequent ones in such cases.[98] When the compound patent had expired, in practice, secondary process patents grant limited protection to the holder: in other words, the originator companies have already benefited from the protection provided by patent law on their invention and settlements can serve as one of a number of strategies aimed at artificially extending this protection still further.

Incentives to generic companies to be the first challenger of a patent-protected product, such as those present in the US, do not exist in the European context. In fact, US rules allow generic entry before patent expiry through paragraph IV certification filing, so that competition may also be anticipated in the initial period of IP protection, when the compound patent is still in force, impacting heavily on the incentives of the companies involved. This is essentially due to the Hatch-Waxman Act system, which has created the basis for strategic behaviour by pharmaceutical companies. In particular, the US rules regarding ANDA applications and the related 180-day exclusivity period constitute a fundamental incentive for the generic manufacturer to challenge the originator's patent and attempt to enter the market before its expiry. The effects of such provision have been analysed in depth by scholars, among whom Lemley and Hemphill proposed an amendment to the Hatch-Waxman Act that would limit the strategic manipulation of the 180-day rule, on the basis of the reported relatively modest price reductions that occur when the first generic enters and the much more substantial price reductions that occur when there are two or more generics in the market. Under this proposal, if a generic manufacturer settles the litigation with an agreed entry date in the future, whether or not that date includes a reverse payment, the generic would forfeit any exclusivity period, whereas it being awarded would be restricted to one of three scenarios: (i) the generic successfully defeated the patent owner by invalidating the patent or proving that the patent was not infringed; (ii) the generic filed a paragraph IV certification but the patent owner did not sue for infringement; or (3) a generic settlement was reached that 'permits entry without delay'.[99]

in G Pitruzzella and G Muscolo (eds), *Competition and Patent Law in the Pharmaceutical Sector. An International Perspective* (Alphen aan den Rijn, Kluwer Law International, 2016) 125; M Colangelo, 'Reverse Payment Patent Settlements in the Pharmaceutical Sector under EU and US Competition Laws: A Comparative Analysis' (2017) 40 *World Competition* 471; Maier-Rigaud et al, 'Reverse Payments'.

[98] C Scott Hemphill and BN Sampat, 'Drug Patents at the Supreme Court' (2013) 339 *Science* 1386 (finding that 89% of patents in pay-for-delay settlements are secondary patents and reporting, for a dataset of completed patent litigation on all drugs that first became eligible for challenges between 2000 and 2008, a 92% branded success rate for active ingredient patents and a 32% success rate for secondary patents).

[99] C Scott Hemphill and MA Lemley, 'Earning Exclusivity: Generic Drug Incentives and the Hatch-Waxman Act' (2011) 77 *Antitrust Law Journal* 947, 949. Against this proposal, see BM Dickey and DL Rubinfeld, 'Would the Per Se Illegal Treatment of Reverse Payment Settlements Inhibit Generic Drug Investment?' (2012) 8 *Journal of Competition Law & Economics* 615 (arguing that outlawing settlements without reverse payments unless exclusivity is relinquished would

But other proposals of reform have also been put forward, supporting the idea that exclusivity should be awarded based on effective entry and not on the time of filing an ANDA.[100]

In the EU, there is no provision of a statutory period for the first generic challenger during which it is protected against market entry by other generic companies. Moreover, it has been argued that originators in the EU may have more incentives to make reverse payments to generics even if their patent position is strong. In fact, in addition to the uncertainty typical of patent litigation, the European patent system, waiting for the entry into force of the unitary patent, turns into a bundle of national patent rights which must be challenged in court at the national level, thus leading to possible diverging national decisions. This situation proves to be costly and time-consuming for originators willing to effectively enforce their patents, who are obliged to act in all countries where their rights are infringed, and in general for all operators concerned, including generic companies, which are, in turn, required to defend themselves before several courts. In this context, the differences between national enforcement regimes do not ensure that the originator ex ante obtains an effective preliminary injunction preventing the sale of infringing products, nor that it is fully compensated ex post for the harm caused by an infringing entry if it ultimately wins in litigation against the generic on infringement or validity of its patents.[101]

B. The Antitrust Assessment

The antitrust treatment of pay-for-delay agreements as restrictive by object/prohibited per se or not is a controversial issue which has been widely discussed in both the legal and economic literature. In order to identify the approach to be applied to patent settlements, the main alternatives range from a per se illegality rule, a rebuttable presumption of illegality to a rebuttable presumption of legality.[102]

substantially decrease the expected benefits of settlement and fearing that this proposal may reduce the incentive of generics to invest in new potential drugs and that the resulting reduction in the generic pipeline will lead to higher pharmaceutical prices in the long run).

[100] R Boscheck, 'Constraining Drug Supply: Product Positioning, Patent Protection and Regulatory Standards' (2008) 31 *World Competition* 485, 496.

[101] R Subiotto, 'The Implications of the Imperfect European Patent System on the Assessment of Reverse Payment Settlemets', Expert Paper, in OECD, 'Generic Pharmaceuticals', DAF/COMP/WD(2014)75.

[102] For a summary of the discussion on the difficulty of agreeing on an appropriate antitrust approach to pay-for-delay settlements before *Actavis* and *Lundbeck*, see S de Margerie, '"Pay-for-Delay" Settlements: In Search of the Right Standard' (2013) 36 *World Competition* 85. In general on settlements of intellectual property disputes, see C Shapiro, 'Antitrust Limits to Patent Settlement' (2003) 34 *RAND Journal of Economics* 391 (proposing a general rule for antitrust evaluation of settlements, aimed at respecting IPRs while encouraging efficient settlements, ie that a settlement must leave consumers at least as well off as they would have been from ongoing

The choice between these alternatives is strictly linked to the identification of the appropriate benchmarks for the assessment and to two main issues: the size of the payment/transfer of value and the significance of the validity of the patent.

The criterion of the size of the payment was adopted by the Supreme Court in *Actavis*, though there was the strong dissenting opinion released in the judgment, which, although criticised by many scholars, also alleged that considering the status of the patent to be immaterial would lead to some absurd results.[103] Different views on this criterion can be found in the literature too. On the one side, before the *Actavis* ruling, some authors had already considered it as an indicator of the weakness of the patent (as 'the less likely the patentee is to win, the more it is willing to pay a generic to stay out of the market'),[104] while, on the other side, others claimed that the mere existence and size of reverse payments should not automatically incline courts to find illegality.[105] In any case, assessing

patent litigation; however, the author clarified that introducing factors such as asymmetric information between the parties and risk aversion may, importantly, affect the settlement). Among the various positions on the antitrust treatment of reverse payment settlements, see eg Dickey and Rubinfeld, 'Would the Per Se Illegal Treatment' (arguing against the application of a per se rule to reverse payment patent settlements, which could reduce the incentives for generic investment by increasing the cost and uncertainty of patent litigation and could deprive consumers of benefits from lower-cost generic drugs); E Elhauge and A Krueger, 'Solving the Patent Settlement Puzzle' (2012) 91 *Texas Law Review* 283 (proposing a model alleging that all pay-for-delay agreements involving a reverse payment greater than the patent holder's anticipated litigation costs are always anticompetitive); against, see V Meunier and J Padilla, 'Should Reverse Payment Patent Settlements Be Prohibited Per Se?' (2016) 3 *Concurrences* (agreeing with the dissenting opinion in *Actavis* and supporting the idea that reverse payment patent settlements should not be treated as restrictions by object and prohibited per se even when the reverse payment is substantial and exceeds the originator's expected litigation costs).

[103] *Actavis* 570 US 172–73: 'Let's say in 2005, a patent holder sues a competitor for infringement and faces a counterclaim that its patent is invalid. The patent holder determines that the risk of losing on the question of validity is low, but after a year of litigating, grows increasingly risk averse, tired of litigation, and concerned about the company's image, so it pays the competitor a "large" payment … in exchange for having the competitor honor its patent. Then let's say in 2006, a different competitor, inspired by the first competitor's success, sues the patent holder and seeks a similar payment. The patent holder, recognizing that this dynamic is unsustainable, litigates this suit to conclusion, all the way to the Supreme Court, which unanimously decides the patent was valid. According to the majority, the first settlement would violate the antitrust laws even though the patent was ultimately declared valid, because that first settlement took away some chance that the patent would be invalidated in the first go around. Under this approach, a patent holder may be found liable under antitrust law for doing what its perfectly valid patent allowed it to do in the first place; its sin was to settle, rather than prove the correctness of its position by litigating until the bitter end.'

[104] See H Hovenkamp, M Janis and MA Lemley, 'Anticompetitive Settlement of Intellectual Property Disputes' (2003) 87 *Minnesota Law Review* 1719, 1759 (suggesting that in an antitrust challenge, a payment from a patentee to an infringement defendant for the latter's exit from the market is presumptively unlawful, shifting the burden of proof to the infringement plaintiff; the latter can defend by showing both (i) that the ex ante likelihood of prevailing in its infringement lawsuit is significant and (ii) that the size of the payment is no more than the expected value of litigation and collateral costs attending the lawsuit).

[105] T Cotter, 'Refining the "Presumptive Illegality" Approach to Settlements of Patent Disputes Involving Reverse Payments: A Commentary on Hovenkamp, Janis & Lemley' (2003) 87 *Minnesota Law Review* 1789.

when a 'large and unjustified' payment limiting the generic's incentives to enter the market occurs is not an easy task (especially in the presence of complex arrangements, including side deals). On the other hand, automatically associating a large payment with a weak patent disregards other possible justifications for the undertakings choosing to settle (such as the risk aversion and high costs associated with litigation). Other benchmarks, based, for example, on the expected date of entry under the agreement compared to the expected date of entry without the agreement, have also been proposed, though without reaching a consensus.[106]

In the EU, whereas the first ruling of the General Court in *Lundbeck* explicitly recalled *Actavis* and the idea that the size of a reverse payment might constitute an indicator of the strength or weakness of a patent, no such reference can be found in the rulings of the Court of Justice. Importantly, the Court of Justice has affirmed that the transfers of value must be shown to be sufficiently beneficial to encourage the generic firm to refrain from competition and should not necessarily be greater than the profits which the generic firm would have made if it had been successful in the patent proceedings.[107] Rather, the main criterion is that the net gain from the transfers of value can have no explanation other than the commercial interest of the parties to the agreement not to engage in competition on the merits.[108]

With regard to the second issue, ie the relevance to be given to the existing patent, the scope of the patent test has been rejected in both the US and the EU, and the assessment of the patent's validity has been separated from the antitrust evaluation of reverse payment agreements, giving no relevance to it. In the US, there is no discussion of the notion of potential competition as in the EU,

[106] RD Willig and JP Bigelow, 'Antitrust Policy towards Agreements That Settle Patent Litigation' (2004) *Antitrust Bulletin* 655 (arguing against a per se rule and that antitrust policy should be configured to encourage a settlement agreement if its date of entry is socially advantageous relative to the expected date of entry under the litigation alternative, taking into account the benefits of avoiding the costs and risks of the litigation). Among the proposals for other benchmarks, see also L Karas, GF Anderson and R Feldman, 'Pharmaceutical "Pay-for-Delay" Reexamined: A Dwindling Practice or a Persistent Problem?' (2020) 71 *Hastings Law Journal* 959, 968 (proposing a change in the current antitrust approach and claiming that the key criterion in determining an unlawful agreement should be the existence of a restriction on generic entry – not the size or presence of a value transfer – considered in light of the strength of the category of patent in question.)

[107] The EU Commission, in *Lundbeck*, applied the category of the restriction by object under Art 101(1) TFEU to payments exceeding the profits that the generic company would have obtained from successfully entering the market which can be rebutted by the defendant proving the existence of the four cumulative conditions provided by Art 101(3), as always granted by EU competition rules: this means that the defendant is required to give the difficult proof that the agreement is efficiency-enhancing, beneficial for consumers and does not entail unnecessary restrictions. The Commission did not refer to the litigation costs, as in the US approach, but to the profits that the generic company would have obtained from successfully entering the market; this difference might also be justified by the differences in the patent systems: it would be extremely difficult and uncertain in the absence of a unitary system in the EU calculating litigation costs before several national courts.

[108] Case C-307/18 *Generics*, para 92.

where it has been the subject of wide treatment in the rulings and debate in the literature.[109] *Generics* requires the following factors for the finding of potential competition. First, the inherent ability of the prospective rival to enter the market is required, considering whether 'insurmountable' barriers to entry exist and preparatory steps 'in administrative, judicial and commercial terms' have been taken:[110] patent infringement litigation is not considered to be an insurmountable barrier, as it is common in the pharmaceutical sector and consistent with competition on the merits;[111] evidence of actual preparatory steps confirms the feasibility of entry. Second, the firm intention of the potential competitor to enter the market and the perception of this risk by the incumbent undertaking must be proved.[112] However, the stance according to which potential competition can exist even where it might or would involve a violation of valid IPRs may appear difficult to reconcile with the idea that only lawful competition would count as competition for the purposes of Article 101(1) TFEU.[113]

Thus, turning back to the choice made by the courts, the approach implemented in *Actavis* may appear a sort of compromise solution. As the Supreme Court intended to adhere to the opinion that the settlements involving a large payment from a patentee to an infringer should be evaluated regardless of the legitimacy of the underlying IP right, this would imply that these settlements would be anti-competitive even if that IP right were valid; thus, again, one might have expected the Court not to adopt the rule of reason, but to formulate a presumption of illegality, which could be rebutted by the plaintiff with a limited number of reasonings, rather than providing a shifting of burden. In fact, a presumption of illegality would generally attempt to resolve antitrust challenges to patent settlement without inquiring into patent validity or infringement, resting on the premise that a very high payment itself is a strong indicator of patent invalidity.[114] By contrast, a rule of reason is more costly

[109] See S Marco Colino, N Dunne, K Fournier, S Pais and D Ritzmann, 'The Lundbeck Case and the Concept of Potential Competition' (2017) 2 *Concurrences*; N Dunne, 'Potential Competition in EU Law' (2021) 42 *European Competition Law Review* 638.

[110] AG Kokott Opinion in Case C-591/16 P *Lundbeck*, para 78.

[111] ibid para 127.

[112] It is interesting to note that in *In the Matter of Impax Labs*, 24, the FTC took into consideration the fact that there 'was a real threat of competition' from the generic producer, which had taken steps to enter the market, even though its entry would be 'at risk' of infringement liability. See also Maier-Rigaud et al, 'Reverse Payments', 71–72 (arguing that the relevance given to the views of both generic companies and originator companies may not necessarily lead to an accurate assessment of the strength of the patent in question upon which a settlement was agreed).

[113] Maier-Rigaud et al, 'Reverse Payments', 71 (arguing that it is unclear as to whether a patent settlement restricting the entry of a generic, where the patent(s) in question had either a 1%, 50% or 80% chance of invalidation, where the generic company had a very different risk profile to the originator (ie aggressive risk-taking) and where the agreement brought about earlier market entry than would have been the case under litigation, would still be considered anti-competitive).

[114] M Carrier, 'Unsettling Drug Patent Settlements: A Framework for Presumptive Illegality' (2009) 108 *Michigan Law Review* 37 (arguing that, given the inability of antitrust courts to directly determine patent validity, the proxy of unjustified settlements provides the best available evidence of invalidity and that courts should treat reverse payment settlements as presumptively

and typically requires a wider inquiry also into validity and infringement.[115] For these reasons, the *Actavis* approach, which has been welcomed by the FTC and many scholars,[116] has nevertheless been read by other authors as a de facto rule of presumptive illegality.[117]

From this perspective, the final outcome would be very similar to that reached by the European approach, based on the existence of a restriction of competition by object. In principle, the *Actavis* ruling could be seen as less restrictive than the European stance as it would require the courts to balance the pro- and anti-competitive effects of the reverse payment patent settlements under scrutiny, whereas in the EU the defendant typically can rebut the application of Article 101(1) by adducing the difficult proof of the existence of the four cumulative conditions of Article 101(3). In fact, some authors have proposed that the US should move closer to a presumptive standard in evaluating pay-for-delay settlements, similar to the European approach.[118] The Court of Justice in *Generics* explicitly recalled that the evaluation of the positive effects resulting from the agreement does not imply engaging in a US-style rule of reason.[119] However, the Court in *Generics* set out that the object restriction is ruled out when the settlement agreement is accompanied by proven pro-competitive effects capable of giving rise to a reasonable doubt that it causes a sufficient degree of harm to competition. Such proof must be 'not only demonstrated and relevant, but also specifically related to the agreement concerned'.[120] This approach would be in line with the recent case law and the restrictive interpretation of the category of the object restrictions, but its implementation in practice in future cases remains to be seen.[121]

Despite the majoritarian approach rejecting the consideration of the validity of the patent as relevant, one may question whether the absence of a direct engagement with the strength of the patent infringement claim is appropriate. In principle, antitrust should not intervene in solving IP and sector-specific

anti-competitive). See also Hovenkamp, 'Antitrust and Patent Law Analysis', 9 (affirming that if the patent is valid and infringed, then even a large payment for the full remaining life of the patent represents a wealth transfer but causes consumer harm only if the payment increases the pioneer's costs and thus may increase its drug price, whereas if the patent is invalid or not infringed, there should be immediate generic entry and the delay imposed by the reverse payment settlement represents competitive harm equivalent to that of any naked market division agreement).

[115] MD Janis and MA Lemley, 'Balancing Ease and Accuracy in Assessing Pharmaceutical Exclusion Payments' (2004) 88 *Minnesota Law Review* 712 (arguing that presumption of liability is less costly than case-specific analysis).

[116] However, see Brief Amici Curiae of 118 Law, Economics, and Business Professors and the American Antitrust Institute in Support of Petitioners, *FTC v Actavis, Inc* 133 S Ct 2233 (2013) (No 12-416) (supporting a 'quick-look' analysis).

[117] TF Cotter, 'FTC v Actavis, Inc: When Is the Rule of Reason Not the Rule of Reason?' (2014) 15 *Minnesota Journal of Law, Science & Technology* 41.

[118] Karas et al, 'Pharmaceutical "Pay-for-Delay" Reexamined', 969.

[119] Case C-307/18 *Generics*, para 104.

[120] ibid para 105.

[121] P Ibáñez Colomo, 'The Legal Status of Pay-for-Delay Agreements in EU Competition Law: Generics (Paroxetine)' (2020) 57 *CML Rev* 1933, 1948.

regulation issues; nevertheless, when required, it should operate on a case-by-case basis in observance of all the relevant counterfactuals. This, in turn, means that evaluating the antitrust relevance of reverse payment patent settlements without any assessment of the validity of the underlying patent substantially rejects the idea that, even under the general assumption that patent settlements are, in principle, legitimate, these agreements are detrimental to consumers only if the generic challenger would have prevailed in litigation.[122] Should one consider an alternative to the sort of inquiry into the patent merits (which the settlement is supposed to avoid), requiring courts to conduct a summary inquiry of the patent or imagining a range of regulatory actors (patent offices and medicines agencies) providing information relevant to the antitrust analysis could be an option to be considered.[123] This would lead a pay-for-delay settlement to be deemed anti-competitive only when it is highly likely that the patent would be considered invalid or not infringed – as, of course, in that case the generic company would be able to enter before the expiry of the patent.

V. CONCLUDING REMARKS

Reverse payment patent settlements in the pharmaceutical sector are a complex issue at the intersection of patent law, competition law and health policy. They have been the subject of important antitrust scrutiny both in the US and in the EU. Whereas the *Actavis* ruling has applied a modified version of the rule-of-reason standard, in the EU pay-for-delay agreements are typically considered restrictive by object. While the direction taken in the EU seems to be clear so far, in the US the application of *Actavis* by lower courts has not always been coherent and univocal. The recent proposals for legislative action at both federal and state level in the US may be considered as a means for reducing such inconsistencies. However, it is questionable whether introducing specific legislations containing a restrictive ban by rule is both appropriate and proportionate, given the decrease in the number of anti-competitive settlements documented by the FTC. Such efforts must also be framed in the broader policy initiatives aimed at increasing legislative involvement against high prescription drug prices.

[122] G Dolin, 'Reverse Settlements as Patent Invalidity Signals' (2011) 4 *Harvard Journal of Law & Technology* 281, 284 (proposing to police these agreements not by subjecting them to an antitrust analysis, but by ordering a re-examination of any patent involved in a reverse settlement).

[123] See G Bruzzone and S Capozzi, 'The Procompetitive and Anticompetitive Impact of Patent Settlements' in Pitruzzella and Muscolo, *Competition and Patent Law*, 15, 27 (referring to Case 193/83 *Windsurfing International Inc v Commission of the European Communities* ECLI:EU:C:1986:75, [1986] ECR 00611; and, arguing that a serious assessment of the patent history is all the more important since it is highly undesirable, from a legal, economic and policy perspective, that a prohibition decision under competition rules is later contradicted by IP judgments and affirming that if competition authorities intervene, they have to clearly identify cases which minimise the risk of clash with the IP system).

In both EU and US cases, pay-for-delay agreements are considered extremely risky from an antitrust perspective regardless of the underlying IP dispute. Despite this, assuming that such patent settlements are detrimental to consumers only if a generic challenger would have prevailed in litigation, this chapter questions whether the absence of any evaluation of the strength of the patent infringement claim is appropriate and argues that further solutions might be explored.

6

Product Hopping

I. PHARMACEUTICAL PRODUCT REFORMULATIONS

THE STRATEGIES ADOPTED by a brand manufacturer to prolong its monopoly protection by making slight variations to an existing drug with the view of patenting 'post-approval' or 'secondary changes' to previously approved drugs, thereby searching for additional exclusivity, are generally named as 'evergreening'. Such term is typically used to indicate a variety of techniques aimed at keeping 'a dying patent alive by refreshing it as long as possible'.[1] As already mentioned before in this book, this constitutes a widespread phenomenon in the pharmaceutical industry.[2]

Commentators – in particular in the US – use the terms 'evergreening', 'line extension' and 'product hopping' in different ways.[3] Product hopping has been defined as a form of evergreening that occurs when pharmaceutical companies faced with the possibility of generic competition once a patent expires or is held invalid make a trivial alteration to their approved drugs, get regulatory approval for those changes and then replace the old product with the new one.[4]

[1] R Feldman, *Rethinking Patent Law* (Cambridge, MA, Harvard University Press, 2012) 170.

[2] See R Feldman, 'May Your Price Be Evergreen' (2018) *Journal of Law and the Biosciences* 1, 12. In this study, the author analysed the patents filed with the US Patent and Trademark Office between 2005 and 2015 for all brand-name, small-molecule drugs on the market and found that 78% of the drugs associated with new patents were not new drugs but existing ones, and extending protection is particularly pronounced among blockbuster drugs. The author also set up the Evergreen Drug Patent Database (https://sites.uchastings.edu/evergreensearch/about/#.Yno9eRNBz0o). See also R Gupta, CJ Morten, AY Zhu, R Ramachandran, ND Shah and JS Ross, 'Approvals and Timing of New Formulations of Novel Drugs Approved by the US Food and Drug Administration Between 1995 and 2010 and Followed Through 2021' (2022) 3 *JAMA Health Forum* e221096 (in this cross-sectional study of 206 brand-name drugs approved in tablet or capsule form by the US FDA between 1995 and 2010, approval of new formulations was four times more likely among blockbuster drugs and 5.5 times more likely among drugs granted accelerated approval; moreover, first new formulation approval was statistically significantly lower after approval of generic competition).

[3] R Feldman and E Frondorf, *Drug Wars. How Big Pharma Raises Prices and Keeps Generics Off the Market* (Cambridge, Cambridge University Press, 2017) 69; MA Carrier, 'A Real-World Analysis of Pharmaceutical Settlements: The Missing Dimension of Product Hopping' (2010) 62 *Florida Law Review* 1009, 1016; SD Shadowen, KB Leffler and JT Lukens, 'Anticompetitive Product Changes in the Pharmaceutical Industry' (2009–10) 41 *Rutgers Law Journal* 1. See also UY Hacohen, 'Evergreening at Risk' (2020) 33 *Harvard Journal of Law & Technology* 480, 488.

[4] H Hovenkamp, MD Janis, MA Lemley and CR Leslie, *IP and Antitrust: An Analysis of Antitrust Principles Applied to Intellectual Property*, 2 edn (New York, Wolter Kluwers, 2013) §§ 12.5 and 15.3c1. See also AJ Devlin, 'Exclusionary Strategies in the Hatch-Waxman Context'

Some authors use a more detailed notion, according to which product hopping refers to the conduct through which a branded drug manufacturer releases new versions or reformulations of its patent-protected drug in a way that makes a generic version of the original product not substitutable, and encourages doctors to prescribe the reformulated rather than the original product.[5] The steps of a product hop have been summarised as follows: first, the brand-name drug company makes a small change to its existing drug just as its regulatory or patent exclusivities are about to expire and introduces a new formulation as an entirely new drug, which is, in turn, protected by new exclusivities corresponding to those minor changes.[6] This redesign may involve the introduction of new forms (ie reformulations from capsules, tablets or solutions to other forms, as well as extended or delayed release versions, etc) or changing molecule parts (known as moieties) by adding or removing compounds, or combining two or more drug compositions that had previously been marketed separately. In any case, typically the originator company facing the prospective expiry of the patent covering its product submits a new application for a modified version of the drug, switching the market to the new product before generic or biosimilar competition on the previously approved product is set to commence. The brand-name manufacturer may adopt different types of measures to grant the market shift to the new drug, including promotion and advertising activities aimed at 'detailing' and pushing doctors to prescribe the new drug.[7]

Incremental innovations can generate pro-competitive benefits: even a seemingly modest change, such as a dosage variation, can substantially improve the effectiveness of medication through increased compliance, reduced adverse effects and the ability to treat new patient populations. Moreover, incremental innovation can help to reduce the overall risk portfolio of a manufacturer's research and development (R&D) projects, which may well include more innovative products and can help to fund overall R&D activities.[8] Nevertheless, this must be balanced against the benefits of price competition from generic drug manufacturers.

Focusing on incremental innovation is a rational strategy for a profit-maximising company. In other industries, there can be cases where, for instance,

(2007) 2007 *Michigan State Law Review* 631 (affirming, at 658, that Professor Hovenkamp coined the term 'product hop'). See also JM Shepherd, 'Deterring Innovation: New York v Actavis and the Duty to Subsidize Competitors' Market Theory' (2016) 17 *Minnesota Journal of Law, Science & Technology* 663 (arguing, at 666, that the term 'product hopping' is derogatory so that she prefers to use 'product replacement').

[5] MA Carrier and S Shadowen, 'Product Hopping: A New Framework' (2016) 92 *Notre Dame Law Review* 167; MA Carrier, 'Product Hopping: The US Approach' in P Figueroa and A Guerriero, *EU Law of Competition and Trade in the Pharmaceutical Sector* (Cheltenham, Edward Elgar, 2019) 716.

[6] R Feldman and E Frondorf, *Drug Wars. How Big Pharma Raises Prices and Keeps Generics Off the Market* (Cambridge, Cambridge University Press, 2017), 69–70.

[7] ibid 70–71.

[8] B Dickey, K Huang and DL Rubinfeld, 'Pharmaceutical Product Hopping: Is There a Role for Antitrust Scrutiny?' (2019) 82 *Antitrust Law Journal* 679, 685.

a new product or design renders products manufactured by other firms less attractive alternatives in the marketplace, if not altogether obsolete.[9] With regard to the pharmaceutical sector, on the one side, patent law provides the same term of protection to drugs without distinguishing between those implying an important clinical breakthrough or those that are just an incremental innovation of little therapeutic importance.[10] On the other side, one of the benefits of competition is the development of new, improved products. Thus, whereas the introduction of a new and superior product raises no antitrust concerns, the problem with product hopping arises as the innovation presented by the new product is negligible or constitutes a pretext for forcing a market shift away from the old one and its only purpose is to eliminate rivals. In this perspective, product hopping cases have been deemed similar to those alleging predatory innovation of one kind or another.[11]

Of course, the competitive significance of such conduct is strictly related to the regulatory process, in particular the approval by medicines agencies[12] and substitution laws.[13] The brand manufacturer, by making reformulations or minor changes to the original product, prevents the generic from obtaining the status of therapeutic equivalence that renders its product substitutable for the new branded one. Product switching strategies are roughly divided in two types: 'hard' switches, where the brand-name manufacturer introduces a new pharmaceutical product and in parallel withdraws the original product from the market; and 'soft' switches, where the brand-name manufacturer leaves the original product on the market, but shifts all of its promotion and marketing efforts to the new product.[14]

The topic has been the subject of much interest in the US. Before 2004, firms could extend their exclusivity for a product almost indefinitely, by adding new patents to their Orange Book filings and taking advantage of consecutive 30-month stays. After new rules corrected this problem, so that only a single 30-month stay could be granted to a patentee on a given drug (regardless of how many patents it may list in the Orange Book), firms started making trivial changes to

[9] eg cases involving the design of interfaces that defeat interoperability and the supply of integrated products, reducing demand for one or more of the integrated components. See RJ Gilbert, 'Not Another Drug: Antitrust for Drug and Other Innovations' (2015) 30 *Antitrust* 38, 39 and the cases cited therein.

[10] CM Ho, 'Should All Drugs Be Patentable?: A Comparative Perspective' (2015) 17 *Vanderbilt Journal of Entertainment and Technology Law* 295, 312.

[11] S Addanki, 'Antitrust and IP: Developments in Pharmaceuticals' in RD Blair and DD Sokol (eds), *The Cambridge Handbook of Antitrust, Intellectual Property, and High Tech* (Cambridge, Cambridge University Press, 2017) 21, 28.

[12] Devlin, 'Exclusionary Strategies', 660.

[13] Carrier, 'Product Hopping', 720.

[14] Shepherd, 'Deterring Innovation', 671 (explaining that such distinction may be not always clear: eg 'a company increasing the price of the old drug to a prohibitive level but leaving it on the market would generally be considered to have made a soft switch. But in reality, making a drug unaffordable is practically equivalent to removing it from the market').

their product and pulling the old drug from the market: 'rather than stacking patents, they stacked products'.[15] The timing is crucial. As noted by Carrier and Shadowen, 'introducing the reformulated product before generic entry ensures that not only will there be almost no competition on price but also that there will be almost no competition on quality'.[16] The issue is familiar to the EU too. In its 2009 Sector Inquiry, the European Commission analysed the case of follow-on products as part of 'life cycle strategies' that go beyond the pure patent strategies to include marketing and promotion strategies.[17] In its analysis, the Commission noted that the timing of the patenting of the originator's incremental innovation is important in ensuring that the exclusivity of the follow-on product will extend beyond the protection of the first product – and the timing of its launch is crucial too, as if cheaper generic versions of the original product come on the market before or simultaneously with the follow-on product, the originator may incur valuable losses.[18] Such 'cannibalisation' of the older product largely occurs when doctors lack a price-related reason to prescribe the original rather than the reformulated product because the generic is not yet available.[19] In any case, if the originator is able to shift the market to the reformulated version and persuade doctors to prescribe it, the fact that a generic can substitute the old version of the drug turns out to be of little significance.[20] Very often, originators take appropriate measures to facilitate the switch, aiming to channel the demand from the first product to the new one.[21]

Pharmaceutical markets constitute the ideal environment for product hopping. In a market in which consumers make rational decisions based on quality and prices, they would not switch to a modified drug with no substantial advantage justifying its high price but would opt for the generic version of the original drug, saving substantial money.[22] From an antitrust point of view, the essential problem with product hopping is that consumer welfare gains associated with shifting consumer demand to the newer product is outweighed by the consumer harm associated with delaying generic entry until the patent protection of that product elapses.[23] When a product withdrawal also occurs,

[15] Hovenkamp et al, *IP and Antitrust*, § 15.3. See ch 1.

[16] Shadowen and Carrier, 'Product Hopping'.

[17] European Commission, 'Pharmaceutical Sector Inquiry: Final Report' (2009) 351 et seq (2009 Sector Inquiry).

[18] ibid 356.

[19] SD Shadowen, KB Leffler and JT Lukens, 'Bringing Market Discipline to Pharmaceutical Product Reformulations' (2011) 42 *International Review of Intellectual Property and Competition Law* 698, 703–04.

[20] Carrier, 'Product Hopping', 722.

[21] European Commission, 2009 Sector Inquiry, 356.

[22] Hacohen, 'Evergreening', 512–13 (claiming that 'The idiosyncrasies of the pharmaceutical market, however, make a product hopping strategy scandalously effective').

[23] DH Ginsburg, K Wong-Ervin and JD Wright, 'Product Hopping and the Limits of Antitrust: The Danger of Micromanaging Innovation' [2015] (December) *Competition Policy International Antitrust Chronicle* 1 (explaining that 'application of the antitrust laws to govern product hopping

it intensifies the harm by marginally increasing the percentage of prescriptions switched from the original to the branded product before generic entry, in addition to the impairment of generic competition.[24]

Quoting eminent scholars, 'innovation necessarily disadvantages rivals who do not keep up'.[25] While dominant undertakings have no duty to aid their competitors, they do have an obligation to refrain from acts that have no purpose or effect except to exclude competition.[26] As the attempts to develop superior products constitute an essential element of lawful competition, the error costs of punishing technological change are rather high. Product hopping certainly constitutes a difficult issue for antitrust courts, as it requires them to inquire into product-design choices and may also raise concerns about second-guessing evaluations made by agencies and legislators regarding how best to balance competition and innovation in regulated markets.[27] Case law in this area is emblematic of such difficulties. In the following sections, the main representative cases will be considered.

II. PRODUCT HOPPING BEFORE US COURTS

A number of antitrust challenges to product hopping have been decided by US courts.[28] A recent example of product hopping combined with other practices, including pay-for-delay, can be found in *Impax*, already treated in chapter five.[29]

An early case addressing product hopping under US antitrust law is *Abbott Labs v Teva Pharms* (*TriCor*).[30] The pharmaceutical company Abbott

requires antitrust agencies or courts to weigh the consumer welfare gain from a change in product design – in this case, a new drug formulation – against the consumer welfare loss from forgone price competition'). See also C Scott Hemphill, 'Unjustified Delays in Generic Competition' (2014) OECD Expert Paper DAF/COMP/WD(2014)7 (explaining, at 8, that from an antitrust point of view it is relevant to consider whether the new product is better than the old and whether customers were forced to make a switch, eg because the product has been withdrawn before the approval of the generic version so that no choice about continuing the existing therapy is left to patients; in addition, some patients might be harmed by such a switch if the new therapy ends up being of lower quality for them in terms of side effects or tolerability).

[24] Shadowen et al, 'Bringing Market Discipline', 704.

[25] Hovenkamp et al, *IP and Antitrust* § 12.2, 5.

[26] *LePage's Inc v 3M* 324 F 3d 141, 151–52 (3d Cir 2003): 'there is no market constraint on a monopolist's behavior' (citing *Aspen Skiing Co v Aspen Highlands Skiing Corp* 472 US 585, 601–04 (1985)). See also *Verizon Communications Inc v Law Offices of Curtis V Trinko, LLP* 540 US 398, 411, 124 S Ct 872 (2004); *United States v Microsoft Corp* 253 F 3d 34, 58 (DC Circ 2001).

[27] SL Dogan and MA Lemley, 'Antitrust Law and Regulatory Gaming' (2009) 87 *Texas Law Review* 685, 687.

[28] Carrier, 'Product Hopping', 731 (noting that some courts have taken into consideration the regulatory regime and/or the 'price disconnect' typical of the pharmaceutical markets in their assessment, while others did not).

[29] *Impax Labs, Inc v FTC* 994 F 3d 484, 488 (5th Cir 2021). See ch 5, n 50.

[30] *Abbott Laboratories v Teva Pharmaceuticals USA, Inc* 432 F Supp 2d 408 (D Del 2006) (*TriCor*).

implemented a series of changes to its blockbuster cholesterol and triglycerides drug TriCor, firstly changing from capsules to tablets and subsequently from those tablets to new ones. Such changes included minor modifications, such as marginally lowering the drug's strength, while the company stopped selling the previous formulations, buying back existing supplies of capsules from pharmacies and changing the code both for the capsules and the first tablets in the National Drug Data File (NDDF) to 'obsolete'.[31]

Relying on relevant literature and case law, the Delaware District Court clarified that 'because, speaking generally, innovation inflicts a natural and lawful harm on competitors, a court faces a difficult task when trying to distinguish harm that results from anticompetitive conduct from harm that results from innovative competition'.[32] The Court applied the rule of reason under section 2 of the Sherman Act, which was deemed justified because the defendants allegedly prevented consumers' choice by removing the old formulations from the market while introducing the new formulations. In doing so, the plaintiffs were not required to prove that the new formulations were no better than the prior version or that the only purpose of the innovation was to eliminate the product of a rival. Rather, if anti-competitive harm from formulation changes were shown by the plaintiffs, then such harm should be weighed against any benefits presented by the defendants.[33] Furthermore, the Court considered whether exclusionary conduct barred competitors only from the cost-efficient means of distribution, not from all of them.[34] The Court found that the plaintiffs had plausibly alleged that the generic substitution system was their cost-efficient means of competition, this being a restriction sufficient to support the antitrust claim. In other words, the Court found it immaterial whether the reformulations did not completely bar the generic manufacturers from entering the market but only prevented automatic substitution at the pharmacies.[35] Accordingly, the Court denied the motion to dismiss the plaintiffs' product hop claim.

Such an approach has typically been applied to 'hard switches', while subsequent case law on other types of switches has taken a different course.

Another famous product hopping case is *Walgreen v AstraZeneca Pharmaceuticals*, concerning the switch made by AstraZeneca from its original drug Prilosec, a proton pump inhibitor used for ulcer and heartburn treatment,

[31] ibid 416–18. The NDDF is a private database that provides information about FDA-approved drugs. Changing the code to 'obsolete' implied removing the TriCor capsule drug formulation from the NDDF, thereby preventing pharmacies from filling TriCor prescriptions with a generic capsule formulation.

[32] ibid 421.

[33] ibid 422.

[34] ibid 423.

[35] Carrier, 'Product Hopping', 725 (affirming that the Court in this case 'offered a thoughtful approach that considered the realities of pharmaceutical markets').

to Nexium.[36] The plaintiffs alleged that AstraZeneca deliberately switched the market from Prilosec, just as its patent was about to expire, to both its newly Food and Drug Administration (FDA)-approved equivalent Nexium, which was 'virtually identical to and no more effective than Prilosec' and had a patent that would not expire for several years, and its newly FDA-approved over-the-counter drug (OTC) Prilosec. According to the plaintiffs, there was virtually no difference between Nexium and Prilosec, and there was no pharmacodynamic reason why a dose of Nexium would interact with the stomach's parietal cells any differently than would an equal dose of Prilosec. Thus, they contended that this switching was exclusionary and violated section 2 of the Sherman Act. Moreover, they alleged that AstraZeneca used distortion and misdirection in the marketing, promoting and detailing of Nexium, and engaged in prohibited exclusionary conduct when it introduced OTC Prilosec, obtaining a grant of exclusivity for three years from the FDA.

However, the District Court of Columbia established that there was no allegation that AstraZeneca eliminated any consumer choices: 'Rather, AstraZeneca added choices. It introduced a new drug to compete with already-established drugs – both its own and others' – and with the generic substitutes for at least one of the established drugs.'[37] Moreover, antitrust law does not require a product new on the market to be superior to existing products and determining which product among several is superior is not a task of courts but is left to the marketplace. Still, the plaintiffs had not identified any antitrust law that prohibits market switching through sales persuasion short of false representations or fraud: 'advertising that emphasizes a producer's strengths and minimizes its weaknesses does not, at least unless it amounts to deception, constitute anticompetitive conduct violative of § 2'.[38] Finally, the Court found that the plaintiffs had not pled facts supporting a reasonable inference that

[36] *Walgreen Co et al v AstraZeneca Pharmaceuticals et al* 534 F Supp 2d 146 (DDC 2008). Prilosec contained the drug substance omeprazole, composed of equal parts of two mirror-image molecular structures, (S)-omeprazole and (R)-omeprazole, which are transformed into an active drug in the parietal cells of the stomach of a person who ingests the substance. AstraZeneca obtained a patent for Prilosec in 1981, and began marketing 20 mg Prilosec capsules in September 1989 after obtaining approval from the FDA. By 1999, prescription Prilosec was producing $4 billion in revenue to AstraZeneca. The Prilosec patent expired in October 2001, and a company not involved in this case first marketed a generic equivalent of Prilosec in December 2002. At the time of the judgment, AstraZeneca still manufactured and marketed its prescription Prilosec capsules. In June 2003, the FDA approved an OTC version of prescription Prilosec, and granted AstraZeneca exclusivity in that market to June 2006 after AstraZeneca conducted and submitted safety studies to the FDA. Nexium contains the drug substance esomeprazole, or (S)-omeprazole. The FDA approved Nexium for sale in February 2001, just eight months before the Prilosec patent expired. The Nexium patent was supposed to not expire until 2014, and Nexium was not subject to generic substitutions before that time. Upon the introduction of Nexium, AstraZeneca very aggressively promoted and 'detailed' Nexium to doctors, and at the same time ceased promoting and detailing Prilosec.

[37] ibid 151.

[38] ibid.

they had been damaged by an antitrust injury or showing that AstraZeneca 'interfere[d] with the[ir] freedom to compete'.[39] This approach towards soft switches has been criticised by some scholars who claim that it did not take into proper consideration the 'price-disconnect' typical of drug markets.[40]

A case combining elements of both hard and soft switches is *In re Suboxone*, concerning a drug used to treat opioid addiction, where Reckitt switched from tablets to sublingual film.[41] Suboxone was the only pharmaceutical product on the market providing maintenance treatment for patients suffering from opioid addiction that could also be prescribed in an office setting for the patient's home use. It is worth noting that the FDA approved Reckitt's NDA for Suboxone tablets in 2002 and, although Reckitt did not have a patent for Suboxone tablets, it was able to obtain a seven-year period of exclusivity because the medicine at issue was found to be an orphan drug. According to the plaintiffs, Reckitt, knowing its period of exclusivity would be over in October 2009, began developing Suboxone film and obtaining patent protection for this new product, which would expire in 2023. Generic Suboxone tablets could not be AB-rated to branded Suboxone film due to the differences in dosage form. As in other cases, the plaintiffs alleged that there were few differences between Suboxone film and Suboxone tablets, and that the former were not superior to the latter.[42] As noted by the Eastern District of Pennsylvania Court, the conduct alleged in the case 'seems to fall somewhere between that alleged in *Walgreen* and *TriCor*'.[43] The behaviour was more concerning than that in *Walgreen*, but less worrying than that in *TriCor*.[44] In fact, unlike in *Walgreen*, Reckitt announced that it was removing Suboxone tablets from the market several months prior to generic approval, and actually did remove the tablets from the market within a few weeks of generic entry. Unlike in *TriCor*, it was not alleged that Reckitt bought back existing Suboxone tablets or labelled the product 'obsolete'.

The Court clarified that:

> Although the issue of product hopping is relatively novel, what is clear from the case law is that simply introducing a new product on the market, whether it is a superior product or not, does not, by itself, constitute exclusionary conduct. The key question is whether the defendant combined the introduction of a new product with some other wrongful conduct, such that the comprehensive effect is likely to stymie

[39] *Prilosec*, 151–52.

[40] Carrier, 'Product Hopping', 726–27. The harm deriving from soft switches has not been recognised in other cases, including *In re Solodyn Antitrust Litigation*, 2015 WL 5458570 (D Mass 16 September 2015); *In re Asacol Antitrust Litigation* 14 233 F Supp 3d 247 (D Mass 2017).

[41] *In re Suboxone (Buprenorphine Hydrochloride and Naxolone) Antitrust Litigation* 64 F Supp 3d 665 (ED Pa 2014).

[42] Reckitt allegedly engaged in a complex strategy, as it, for example, promoted new Suboxone film to physicians, disparaged Suboxone tablets, warned of false safety concerns, filed a sham Citizen Petition and fraudulently delayed the filing of the Citizen Petition.

[43] *Suboxone*, 681.

[44] See Carrier, 'Product Hopping', 728.

> competition, prevent consumer choice and reduce the market's ambit. This analysis must be undertaken with the somewhat unique characteristics of the pharmaceutical market in mind.[45]

Finding that the plaintiffs had sufficiently alleged that the disparagement of the original drug and false safety concerns took place alongside coercive measures, thereby plausibly forcing patients and doctors to switch from tablet to film, the Court denied the motion to dismiss.[46] Importantly, the Court, accepting the view that various market forces unique to the pharmaceutical industry make generic substitution the cost-efficient means of competing for companies selling generic pharmaceuticals, took into account the disconnect existing between the person paying for the prescription and the person selecting the appropriate treatment: due to this, 'the ordinary market forces that would allow consumers to consider price when selecting a product are derailed'.[47]

In *Mylan Pharmaceuticals, Inc v Warner Chilcott Public Ltd Co* (*Doryx*), Mylan and other generic manufacturers claimed that brand drug company Warner Chilcott and its co-defendants engaged in a deliberate strategy to prevent or delay generic competition for Doryx, a branded oral antibiotic used to treat severe acne brought to market in 1985 without patent protection and subject to several product switches (first from a capsule to a tablet, then from 75 mg and 100 mg tablets to a single-scored 150 mg dosage strength, and finally from the single-scored version of the 150 mg tablet to a dual-scored version).[48] Each of these changes would have required generic manufacturers to file, and await approval of, a new ANDA demonstrating the similarities between their product and the reformulated Doryx product in order to continue selling generics that were AB-rated to the newest Doryx product.

The crux of the plaintiffs' complaint was, as usual, that these product changes had little or no therapeutic benefit and served no purpose other than preventing generics from obtaining the benefit of automatic substitution under the Hatch-Waxman Act and substitution laws. After several plaintiffs settled their cases, Mylan was the only plaintiff remaining. Mylan alleged that it was a case of 'hard switch' and, more precisely, that defendants: (i) stopped selling the capsules to wholesalers; (ii) removed Doryx capsules from the Warner Chilcott website; (iii) worked with retailers to 'auto-reference' the Doryx tablet whenever a doctor filed a Doryx prescription; (iv) informed wholesalers, retailers, and doctors that capsules had been replaced by tablets; (v) destroyed some of their remaining capsule inventory; and (vi) bought back some portion of the remaining capsule inventory.[49]

[45] *Suboxone*, 682.
[46] ibid 683.
[47] ibid 684.
[48] *Mylan Pharmaceuticals, Inc v Warner Chilcott Pub Ltd Co* No 12-3824, 2015 WL 1736957 (ED Pa Apr 16, 2015) (*Doryx*).
[49] ibid *3.

On summary judgment, the District Court for the Eastern District of Pennsylvania stated that Warner Chilcott lacked monopoly power and the defendants did not exclude competition when they made each of the above-mentioned changes to Doryx. Moreover, the Court concluded that conduct that prevents generics from taking advantage of automatic substitution laws is not anti-competitive.[50]

On appeal, the Third Circuit agreed with the District Court's analysis, affirming that:

> While product hopping under certain circumstances may be viewed as anticompetitive conduct, this is not one of those cases ... Mylan was not foreclosed from the market. Doryx capsules were available for more than twenty years, and generic companies were free to engineer their own versions during that time. At least one did, but not Mylan. Moreover, the record demonstrates that Mylan received 180 days of exclusive rights to market and sell its 75mg and 100mg tablets once approved, giving Mylan a significant leg up on generic competitors. And the undisputed evidence shows that Mylan set its tablet prices higher than the price of branded Doryx for at least some period of time. Finally, it is clear that Mylan reaped generous profits from its sale of the generic tablet, in the amount of $146.9 million. Thus, far from being harmed by defendants' product changes, Mylan was advantaged in the generic market by its 180-day exclusivity period and ability to profit generously while raising prices.[51]

Moreover, even assuming that the plaintiff had proved the anti-competitive nature of the defendants' conduct, the latter offered strong evidence of non-pretextual purposes for their various product changes, including safety concerns.

Notably, the Third Circuit distinguished this case from *New York ex rel Schneiderman v Actavis PLC* (*Namenda*), another product hopping case decided by the Second Circuit.[52] In this case, New York alleged that, as Namenda IR, a twice-daily drug designed to treat moderate-to-severe Alzheimer's disease, neared the end of its patent protection in 2015, Forest Labs, a subsidiary of Actavis, introduced a new once-daily version of the drug, called Namenda XR, patented until 2029. The defendants decided to withdraw virtually all Namenda IR from the market in order to force the Alzheimer's patients who depended on

[50] ibid *12–14. For a critical analysis of this decision, see Carrier, 'Product Hopping', 729 (claiming that 'like the *Walgreen* court, the *Doryx* court ignored the price disconnect and the regulatory framework regime').

[51] *Mylan Pharmaceuticals, Inc v Warner Chilcott Pub Ltd Co* No 15-2236 (3rd Cir 28 September 2016) *36–37. Moreover, the Court recalled that, as the district court noted, Mylan is one of the largest generic pharmaceutical companies in the world, recording nearly $6.13 billion in revenue in 2011. It is therefore difficult to perceive Mylan as a 'David' and the defendants as 'Goliath' in these circumstances. It should be noted that the Court undertook a wide definition of the relevant market, finding Doryx to be interchangeable with oral tetracyclines other than the equivalent generic drug.

[52] 787 F 3d 638, 645 (2nd Cir 2015).

it to switch to the new drug before the IR generic became available. According to the Court,

> neither product withdrawal nor product improvement alone is anticompetitive. But … when a monopolist *combines* product withdrawal with some other conduct, the overall effect of which is to coerce consumers rather than persuade them on the merits … and to impede competition … its actions are anticompetitive under the Sherman Act.[53]

Moreover, this 'hard switch crosses the line from persuasion to coercion', as the free choice of consumers (doctors and patients in this case) is impeded and competition is hampered without a legitimate business justification, thereby violating section 2 of the Sherman Act.[54]

III. THE EU EXPERIENCE

The terminology of product hopping is not widespread in the EU, where 'evergreening' is more generally used to refer to life cycle strategies leading to second generation products. While product reformulation strategies are not, of course, exclusive to the US, there have not been many enforcement decisions of the European Commission and cases before EU Courts addressing them.

Drug product reformulation occurred in the landmark case *AstraZeneca*, whose facts resemble the *Walgreen* case and which, as already mentioned, concerned two abuses of the Swedish company's dominant position during the marketing of the omeprazole-based drug Losec, used in the treatment of gastrointestinal diseases and falling within the category of proton pump inhibitors.[55] However, there are some remarkable differences with the cases seen in the previous section. As already seen in chapter four, AstraZeneca attempted to prevent the launch of generic versions of the active drug ingredient of its branded blockbuster drug Losec in a number of markets in the European Economic Area through two types of conduct: (i) the misrepresentation by the originator company to patent offices in several Member States, as well as to the national courts in some of them, in order to obtain or maintain supplementary protection certificates for omeprazole to which it was not entitled, or to which it was entitled for a more limited period, thereby excluding generic manufacturers from

[53] ibid 654 (quoting *Berkey Photo, Inc v Eastman Kodak Co* 603 F 2d 263 (2nd Cir 1979)).

[54] ibid 654–55 and 659.

[55] See ch 4. Case C-457/10 P *AstraZeneca AB and AstraZeneca plc v European Commission* EU:C:2012:770 (confirming the ruling of the General Court in Case T-321/05 *AstraZeneca AB and AstraZeneca plc v European Commission* ECLI:EU:T:2010:266, [2010] ECR II-2805). It should be noted that another famous case of product hopping was decided after the General Court's decision in AstraZeneca by the UK NCA, at that time the Office of Fair Trade (now Competition and Markets Authority, CMA), with the *Reckitt Benckiser (Gaviscon)* decision (case CE/8931/08, 12 April 2011).

the market;[56] and (ii) the filing of applications for the revocation of marketing authorisations for Losec capsules in Denmark, Norway and Sweden, along with the simultaneous withdrawal of Losec capsules from the market and then the launch of a new tablet formulation of the drug in those countries.

The second abuse is of interest for this chapter as it relates to the misuse by the originator company of marketing authorisation procedures by switching the original drug to a different pharmaceutical form (from capsules to tablets). More precisely, according to the Commission, the selective deregistration of the marketing authorisations of Losec capsules in some states, in combination with the withdrawal of the original form of the drug from the market and the launch of the reformulated version, blocked or delayed generic versions of the drug entering the market and hindered parallel imports. Importantly, in this respect, the General Court clarified that, although the Commission defined the abuse of a dominant position as the combination of those elements, the central feature of the abuse consisted in the deregistration of the Losec capsule marketing authorisations, the conversion of sales of Losec capsules to Losec MUPS being the context in which such deregistration was carried out. The conversion of sales of Losec capsules to Losec MUPS, namely the withdrawal from the market of Losec capsules and the introduction on the market of Losec MUPS, was not capable, in itself, of producing the anti-competitive effects alleged by the Commission, namely the creation of regulatory obstacles to the market entry of generic omeprazole and to parallel imports of Losec capsules.[57]

The rules at issue in the case were contained in Directive 65/65, which provided for an abbreviated procedure for granting marketing authorisations for generic drug products. At that time, in order for a generic company to use the abridged procedure, rules required that the reference drug should have been authorised in the EU for 6–10 years, and that the reference product was still on the market (or at least its marketing authorisation was still upheld).[58] It is worth noting that such rules have been subsequently amended: under current rules, marketing authorisation survives the discontinuation of the originator product for three years, so that this timing is presumably enough to allow generic companies to file an abridged application.[59] In other words, the strategy of

[56] As already mentioned in ch 4, the first abuse relates to the unlawful acquisition of an exclusive right, namely extra IP protection, through the provision of misleading information to national patent offices and courts, implementing a practice falling outside the scope of competition on the merits.

[57] Case T-321/05 *AstraZeneca*, paras 806–12.

[58] Council Directive 65/65/EEC on the approximation of provisions laid down by Law, Regulation or Administrative Action relating to proprietary medicinal products [1965] OJ 022/369; Directive 2001/83 on the Community code relation to medicinal products for human use [2001] OJ L311/67.

[59] See Directive 2001/83, Art 10 as amended by Directive 2004/27/EC (according to which an applicant for marketing authorisation shall not be required to provide the results of pre-clinical tests and of clinical trials if the applicant can demonstrate that the medicinal product is a generic of a reference medicinal product which is or has been authorised for not less than eight years in a Member

abandoning a marketing authorisation currently does not have the same relevance in a switching scheme, as it has been made ineffective by amendments to EU legislation.[60]

The Court of Justice concurred with the General Court in affirming that the preparation by an undertaking, even in a dominant position, of a strategy whose object it is to minimise the erosion of its sales and to enable it to deal with competition from generic products may be legitimate and be part of the normal competitive process. However, the deregistration, without objective justification and after the expiry of the exclusive right to make use of the results of the pharmacological and toxicological tests and clinical trials granted by Directive 65/65, of the marketing authorisations for Losec capsules in the case at issue did not come within the scope of competition on the merits.[61] This means that the fact that under Directive 65/65 AstraZeneca was entitled to request the withdrawal of its marketing authorisations in no way causes that conduct to escape the prohibition laid down in Article 102 TFEU. On the objective justification, AstraZeneca argued that maintaining a marketing authorisation would have imposed onerous pharmacovigilance obligations on it. According to the Courts, such obligations may in fact constitute an objective justification for the deregistration of a marketing authorisation. However, that argument was raised for the first time at the stage of the proceedings before the General Court and the burden arising from those obligations was never mentioned in AstraZeneca's internal documents relating to its commercial strategy, which casted doubt on the fact that the deregistration of the marketing authorisations was due in this case to those obligations. Moreover, as the company had not requested the deregistration of its marketing authorisations in Germany, Spain, France, Italy, the Netherlands and Austria, it had failed to demonstrate the additional burden on itself.[62]

As stated by the Court of Justice,

> the illegality of abusive conduct under Article [102 TFEU] is unrelated to its compliance or non-compliance with other legal rules and, in the majority of cases, abuses of dominant positions consist of behaviour which is otherwise lawful under branches of law other than competition law.[63]

State or in the Community). See Directive 2004/27/EC of 31 March 2004 amending Directive 2001/83/EC on the Community code relating to medicinal products for human use [2004] OJ L136/34, Art 24, paras 4–5.

[60] B Domeij, 'Anticompetitive Marketing in the Context of Pharmaceutical Switching in Europe' in J Drexl and N Lee (eds), *Pharmaceutical Innovation, Competition and Patent Law: A Trilateral Perspective* (Cheltenham, Edward Elgar, 2013) 273, 274.

[61] Case C-457/10 P *AstraZeneca*, paras 129–30.

[62] See Case T-321/05 *AstraZeneca*, paras 686 and 688–89; Case C-457/10 P *AstraZeneca*, paras 135–37.

[63] Case C-457/10 P *AstraZeneca*, para 132.

The possibility provided for in the Directive of deregistering a marketing authorisation is not equivalent to a property right. In the words of the Court:

> Consequently, the fact that, in the light of its special responsibility, an undertaking in a dominant position cannot make use of such a possibility in such a way as to prevent or render more difficult the entry of competitors on the market, unless it can, as an undertaking engaged in competition on the merits, rely on grounds relating to the defence of its legitimate interests or on objective justifications, does not constitute either an 'effective expropriation' of such a right or an obligation to grant a licence, but a straightforward restriction of the options available under European Union law. The fact that the exercise of such options by an undertaking in a dominant position is limited or made subject to conditions in order to ensure that competition already weakened by the presence of that undertaking is not subsequently undermined is in no way an exceptional case and does not justify a derogation from Article [102 TFEU], unlike a situation in which the unfettered exercise of an exclusive right awarded for the realisation of an investment or creation is limited.[64]

Moreover, the assertion of the appellants that its competitors would have been able to obtain marketing authorisations by means of alternative procedures, albeit being longer and more costly, did not suffice to render the deregistration non-abusive since that deregistration had the sole aim of excluding from the market, at least temporarily, competing manufacturers of generic products.[65]

Finally, it should be noted that the General Court confirmed the objective nature of the concept of abuse, so that it does not require a 'malevolent' or 'intentional' foreclosure strategy. However, it affirmed that there was evidence that AstraZeneca was aware of the utility that the deregistration of the Losec capsule marketing authorisations might have for the purposes of raising barriers to entry of a regulatory nature.[66]

[64] ibid paras 149–50. See also para 151: 'As regards the appellants' argument that AZ still held exclusive rights over the clinical data in the file which were still confidential, that argument fails to have regard to the fact that … Directive 65/65 in any event created a limitation to those alleged rights by establishing, in point 8(a)(iii) of the third paragraph of Article 4 thereof, an abridged procedure which, after the expiry of a period of exclusivity of six or ten years, allows the national authorities to rely on that data and the manufacturers of essentially similar medicinal products to benefit from its existence for the purposes of being granted an MA. The General Court was therefore fully entitled to find, at paragraphs 670, 674, 680 and 830 of the judgment under appeal, that Directive 65/65 no longer gave AZ the exclusive right to make use of the results of the pharmacological and toxicological tests and clinical trials included in the file.'

[65] Case C-457/10 P *AstraZeneca*, para 123.

[66] Case T-321/05 *AstraZeneca*, paras 359, 813–14. On this point, see N Dunne, 'The Role of Regulation in EU Competition Law Assessment' (2021) *World Competition* 44, 287, 300–01 (noting that 'The case … turned, somewhat unusually under the EU competition rules, on significant evidence of anticompetitive intention on the part of the defendant, which functioned to separate deliberately restrictive from otherwise innocuous conduct'). For a comment on the various elements on which the Court characterised the conduct as abusive, see J Drexl, 'AstraZeneca and the EU Sector Inquiry: When Do Patent Filings Violate Competition Law?' (2012) Max Planck Institute for Intellectual Property & Competition Law Research Paper No 2. Drexl notes at 11 that, contrary to US antitrust law, a showing of consumer harm is not required, and cites as a point of reference another

Another case to be mentioned concerns a hard switch that has been put in place by Servier as part of a complex strategy – including a series of pay-for-delay agreements with five generic companies – aimed at protecting its bestselling blood pressure medicine (perindopril) from generic competition.[67] In this context, Servier developed a second generation product, based on a new salt, which was sold in different dosages and 'was considered as the principal weapon with which to fight generic entry'.[68] This new product generated new patent protection for Servier until 2023. Servier's strategy was to switch patients to the second generation product and withdraw its first generation product before generic versions could enter the market, so, depending on the national regulatory regime, generic substitution was made impossible or limited. It is also undisputed that the second generation product had no therapeutic advantages for patients over the first generation product.[69] Relying on the internal documents of the company, the Commission found that the decision to launch perindopril arginine salt at new dosages in the different Member States appeared to be linked to the regulatory framework for generic substitution, with Servier explicitly listing as one advantage of the salt switch that 'Pharmacist's substitution of one salt by another one is currently not permitted in a certain number of countries'.[70] The timing of the switch replacing perindopril erbumine with arginine (between 2006 and 2008) and the withdrawal of the former have often been described as crucial in the action plan to prolong the life cycle of perindopril, complemented by aggressive detailing.[71] According to the Commission, the launch of perindopril arginine was considered by many generic competitors as the most important non-patent barrier for the introduction of generic perindopril. The crucial role of timing is demonstrated by the fact that generic substitution was not possible in cases where Servier launched the arginine product before generic entry (such as in Denmark, Ireland and Belgium), whereas

important ruling in the pharmaceutical sector (Joined Cases C-501/06 P, C-513/06 P, C-515/06 P and C-519/06 P *GlaxoSmithKline v Commission* [2009] ECR II-9291, para 63). This requirement has been discussed as an element of anti-competitive foreclosure in the Guidance Paper on Article 102 TFEU. In general on this issue, see J Drexl, 'Real Knowledge Is to Know the Extent of One's Own Ignorance: On the Consumer Harm Approach in Innovation-Related Competition Cases' (2010) 76 *Antitrust Law Journal* 677; P Marsden, 'Some Outstanding Issues from the European Commission's Guidance on Article 102 TFEU: Not-So-Faint Echoes of Ordoliberalism' in F Etro and I Kokkoris (eds), *Competition Law and the Enforcement of Article 102* (Oxford, Oxford University Press, 2010) ch 3.

[67] EU Commission, Case AT.39612 *Perindopril (Servier)*, Decision of 9 July 2014, C(2014) 4955 final; Case T-691/14 *Servier SAS and Others v European Commission* EU:T:2018:922. See ch 5.

[68] European Commission, *Servier*, para 220.

[69] ibid para 8.

[70] ibid paras 233–34: 'More specifically, Servier explains that generic substitution at the pharmacy level is hindered due to the new dosages (rather than the salt switch in itself): "*... However we are not completely protected from generics. The launch of Coversyl arginine will protect us against the potential generics of Coversyl because pharmacists cannot substitute medicines with different dosages".'

[71] ibid para 325.

Teva reported that it was really possible to gain significant shares of sales only where it was able to launch a generic perindopril product before Servier switched to arginine (such as in the UK and Spain).[72] No final ruling, however, is currently available in this case. The General Court did not address this issue as, as mentioned in chapter four, it annulled that part of the Commission's decision finding an abuse of a dominant position, in particular with regard to market definition, without examining the questions relating to the 'abuse' itself, and at the time of writing, the appeal before the Court of Justice is still pending.

IV. THE ANTITRUST ASSESSMENT OF PRODUCT REFORMULATION

Despite the importance and frequency of the phenomenon, the antitrust and welfare implications of product hopping remain unclear.

As said above, an essential element of product hopping is that its competitive relevance as exclusionary conduct is strictly linked to the regulatory process. In contrast to other practices based on the extension of the reach of the initial patent or on the accumulation of several patents, product hopping is independent of the patent protection and may also occur when a new patent is not in place. Even without a new patent, the generic firm is required to start a new application as its drug is not considered 'therapeutically equivalent' to the new product.[73] However, the presence of patent protection is frequent as it crucially impacts on the relevance of the strategy: product hopping entails risks and costs IP protection could cover, whereas in the absence of a patent effective exclusion may have a shorter term – namely, until the generic manufacturer gets its version of the reformulated product approved as well.[74]

Some scholars have argued that product hopping represents the predictable legal response to the incentives created by patent law and state substitution laws, and frustrates generic companies as they can no longer rely on the marketing efforts of the brand-name drug manufacturer.[75] Indeed, it is clear that product hopping constitutes a paradigmatic example of regulatory gaming behaviour.[76] In fact, in pharmaceutical product hopping, the gaming party uses product reformulation to convert neutral product-approval rules into tools to exclude entry. It is worth recalling that the issue of added value of drugs in the approval process by medicines agencies has been the subject of discussion. As mentioned before in this book, there have been concerns that a weakness of this process is the lack of evaluation of the comparative

[72] ibid para 240–41.
[73] Dogan and Lemley, 'Antitrust Law', 712.
[74] Hacohen, 'Evergreening', 512.
[75] Ginsburg et al, 'Product Hopping', 2–3; Shepherd, 'Deterring Innovation', 671.
[76] Dogan and Lemley, 'Antitrust Law', 714.

therapeutic value of new medicines.[77] Comparative efficacy and safety data are often lacking at the time of new drug approval for market entry, and the regulatory agencies in the US and the EU – the FDA and the European Medicines Agency (EMA), respectively – frequently evaluate each new drug on their own (often in placebo-controlled trials), and without comparative assessments against other available drugs.[78] As a result, drugs that may not have much added clinical benefit will often be approved.[79] Further, the granting of a patent by the competent patent office only requires the product to be novel and non-obvious, rather than to be an improvement. Thus, neither patent law nor the marketing authorisation process requires the reformulated product to be superior to existing products.[80] In addition, the 'price disconnect' prevents the market from determining whether the product effectively constitutes an improvement worth the cost of lost savings from generic competition.[81]

In this context, whether antitrust scrutiny is needed or not is debatable. On the one side, some scholars have argued that it is questionable whether product hopping can ever amount to exclusionary conduct under the antitrust laws, given that the generic company is still free to compete but cannot just free-ride through state substitution laws: according to this view, product hopping should be per se lawful absent objective evidence that the new product is a sham innovation with zero or negative consumer welfare effect.[82] Critics of the antitrust intervention claim that product hopping may at best be considered

[77] See, eg E Mossialos, M Mrazek and T Walley, 'Regulating Pharmaceuticals in Europe: An Overview' in E Mossialos, M Mrazek and T Walley (eds), *Regulating Pharmaceuticals in Europe: Striving for Efficiency, Equity and Quality* (Maidenhead, Open University Press, 2004) 7.

[78] See, eg H Naci and AB O'Connor, 'Assessing Comparative Effectiveness of New Drugs before Approval Using Prospective Network Meta-analyses' (2013) 66 *Journal of Clinical Epidemiology* 812.

[79] Shadowen et al, 'Bringing Market Discipline', 707–08. In the EU, the role of the EMA for market approval was limited from the outset to risk–benefit assessments of efficacy and safety, with no evaluation of the added therapeutic value of a new drug, which is then entirely devolved to each EU Member State's regulatory authority. On this point, see A Padula and L Garattini, 'Health Technology Assessment for Pharmaceutical Regulation in the European Union: Do We Need Another Body?' (2019) 113 *Journal of the Royal Society of Medicine* 12 (according to the authors, this limit has been stretched further by the EMA tendency now to fast-track drugs through 'adaptive licensing': once preliminary efficacy and safety have been assessed for market approval, the EMA passes the buck to national authorities for relative effectiveness analysis, with too weak evidence for reimbursement decisions; moreover, the authors claim that, despite almost 30 years of official endorsement, health technology assessment regulation in the EU has still not taken off in practice; they reference the case of cancer drugs, whose added benefits vary widely and often rely on weak clinical evidence and surrogate endpoints, leading to different decisions in different countries mainly on account of the high level of clinical uncertainty). On this point, see ch 1.

[80] Shadowen et al, 'Anticompetitive Product Changes', 5; Carrier and Shadowen, 'Product Hopping', 181.

[81] Carrier and Shadowen, 'Product Hopping', 221, fn 271.

[82] Ginsburg et al, 'Product Hopping', 5. See also JD Wright and DH Ginsburg, 'Comment on the Canadian Competition Bureau's Draft Updated Intellectual Property Enforcement Guidelines' (2015) George Mason University Law & Economics Research Paper Series Paper No 15–31, 1–5.

a regulatory problem.[83] On the other side, others have stressed that antitrust scrutiny of prescription drug product hops is needed, because high prices and profits might be the result not of valued innovations, but of the exploitation of market failures.[84] It is true that, given the complexity and sophistication of drug product reformulation strategies, finding the proper balance between antitrust scrutiny while preserving essential innovation incentives is not an easy task. Nevertheless, this cannot immunise patently anti-competitive behaviour: in the words of Dogan and Lemley, 'The proper standard requires deference to innovation, but not complete abdication'.[85]

Looking at the US case law, several proposals have been put forward by scholars. Carrier and Shadowen have proposed applying time-based safe harbours and a 'no-economic-sense' test to evaluate product hopping under antitrust rules. According to this view, the following can be immunised from antitrust liability: (i) reformulations made long enough before generic approval that they typically are not intended to impair generic competition;[86] and (ii) reformulations that are not likely to thwart generic competition because they are introduced after the generic version of the original drug has entered the market.[87] Then, the no-economic-sense analysis would offer an economic test to determine whether the monopolist's sole motive was to impair competition. Such a test would ask whether conduct allegedly maintaining a monopoly by excluding new competitors likely would have been profitable if the nascent competition flourished and the monopoly was not retained. Thus, a comparison

[83] DW Carlton, F Flyer and Y Shefi, 'Does the FTC's Theory of Product Hopping Promote Competition?' (2016) 12 *Journal of Competition Law & Economics* 495, 506 (arguing that the FTC's approach reported in its investigations is a misguided use of antitrust law and will likely lead to litigation nightmares in which courts attempt to figure out whether the benefits of a new drug are sufficiently high that the innovating firm can escape antitrust liability). The authors explain, at 501, that 'Instead of foreclosure of the competitive process, the FTC's theory hinges on branded drug manufacturers interfering with the ability of generic producers to free-ride off their detailing and other marketing efforts, and this interference with generic producers free-riding is the purported cause of harm. For this reason, it is simply illogical to use the antitrust laws to attack this behavior. Product hopping does not interfere with the ability of generic producers to use the same marketing resources as those used by the brand name firms, but only interferes with the generic producers' ability to free-ride on the brand name producers' investments in these resources.'

[84] Carrier and Shadowen, 'Product Hopping', 181.

[85] Dogan and Lemley, 'Antitrust Law', 716.

[86] Carrier and Shadowen, 'Product Hopping', 207. The authors propose immunity for the introduction of reformulations outside a four-year window, as they are less likely to have the purpose and effect of undermining generic competition: such a window would begin 18 months before the first generic ANDA is filed seeking approval to market a generic version of the original brand product; the rationale is that 18 months would constitute sufficient time for the generic firm to reformulate the generic product to match the new brand product and file an ANDA on the reformulated version. Thus, a reformulation implemented earlier than 18 months before the first ANDA is filed is unlikely to alter the competitive landscape. The rationale for denying a safe harbour once the ANDA is filed lies in the fact that the brand can get an automatic 30-month stay on approval.

[87] ibid 209. The rationale of this safe harbour is that 'reformulations introduced after generic entry are far less effective in impairing generic competition. Generics make three to ten times more sales if the reformulation is introduced after (compared to before) generic entry.'

of the gains deriving from the conduct (not including those from eliminating competition) and costs to the monopolist is required, with conduct yielding a net negative pay-off to the monopolist failing the test.[88] This approach is, in Carrier and Shadowen's opinion, far superior to the hard switch/soft switch criterion applied by courts, as the fundamental action that impairs generic competition is the reformulation of the brand product and 'cannibalisation' of its sales, whereas the 'choice' theory that underlies the dichotomy between hard and soft switches in US case law is not deemed to be satisfactory.[89]

The relevance of the distinction between hard and soft switches has been criticised by other scholars too, claiming that it ignores the importance of automatic substitution in generating the competitive benefits from generic entry: namely, regardless of whether the switch is hard or soft, it prevents generic producers from taking full advantage of the competition on whose basis their development of the product lies.[90] Dickey, Huang and Rubinfeld argue that when a full rule-of-reason analysis is not feasible, some form of no-economic-sense test can usefully serve as a screen to identify situations in which product hopping is unlikely to harm competition. Such a test is more conservative than a full balancing one: the former requires the plaintiff to show that the product hop should not be profitable without the effect of impairing generic entry; the latter would also take into account the negative effects of product hops on consumer welfare resulting from the impairment of competition. For this reason, the authors warn that applying a no-economic-sense test would deal with the risk of false positives, though 'the costs of having no antitrust rule to address product hopping could be dangerously high'.[91] Another proposal promotes a variation of the rule-of-reason analysis, which would permit an evaluation of both the costs of anti-competitive conduct and the benefits for innovation that such conduct may facilitate, requiring as additional 'weight' evidentiary requirements to demonstrate innovative benefits versus anti-competitive harms.[92]

It is interesting to note how such discussions are very widespread in the US context in comparison to what occurs in the EU. An important difference has been traced by some authors in the regulatory structure that is in place in

[88] ibid 211 (explaining that the test focuses on the conduct's 'reasonably anticipated impact' – according to 'objective economic considerations for a reasonable person' – when undertaken, rather than its actual impact).

[89] For a critical comment, see A Athanasiadou, 'Rethinking Pharmaceutical Product Reformulations' [2020] (May) *Competition Policy International Antitrust Chronicle* 6. It should be noted that a debate has arisen on this topic. See JE Pace and KC Adam, 'Doryx, Namenda, and Coercion: Understanding and Un-tying Product Hopping Litigation' (2018) 32 *Antitrust*; MA Carrier and SD Shadowen, 'A Non-coercive Economic Approach to Product Hopping' (2018) 33 *Antitrust* 102; JE Pace and KC Adam, 'Understanding and Un-tying Product Hopping Litigation, Part II: A Reply to Carrier and Shadowen' (2019) 33 *Antitrust* 68; MA Carrier and SD Shadowen, 'Don't Ditch Antitrust's Role in Product Hopping: A Response to Pace and Adam' (2019) 33 *Antitrust* 72.

[90] Dickey et al, 'Pharmaceutical Product Hopping', 694–97.

[91] ibid 699.

[92] Gilbert, 'Not Another Drug', 41 (proposing a 'weighted' rule of reason as a variation of that described in *United States v Microsoft Corp* 253 F 3d 34, 95–97 (DC Cir 2001)).

European Member States, which comprises forms of price controls and would allow the price disconnect to be mitigated so that competition law would only have the complementary role of ensuring that generic entry is not impaired by unlawful behaviour.[93] However, it should be noted that, in the EU too, the price disconnect is not eliminated as it is a typical feature of prescription drug markets in general.[94]

Looking at the cases examined, commonly there is no allegation that the introduction of a reformulated product itself is harmful to competition. Rather, they identify the harm from combining the introduction of the new version with conduct ancillary to that introduction.[95] In the US cases, as stated above, primary importance appears to be attributed to whether the case implies a hard or a soft switch, ie whether or not the prior version of the drug is removed from the market with the introduction of the new version, and to the effects of the conduct on consumer choice.

In the European *AstraZeneca* case, the crux of the case involving the introduction of a new product is centred on the behaviour of the firm aimed at removing the regulatory recognition of the original version. In order to establish the abuse, the European Courts relied on the concept of competition on the merits, from which they distinguished the use of regulatory procedures in such a way as to prevent or make more difficult market entry for competitors, absent an objective justification or a legitimate interest to take the measures at issue. It has been already mentioned that this case has been the subject of various comments by European scholars, in particular with regard to the main principle affirmed by the Courts, ie that a dominant undertaking may commit an abuse even when exercising legal rights. This raised the question of what rights holders are allowed to do with their rights and which obligations can be imposed upon them.[96] However, in particular after this landmark ruling, it is well-established that competition rules apply irrespective of requirements imposed by other areas of law, so that they may be well be enforced against conducts that turns out to be anti-competitive even if they are lawful under other disciplines.

V. CONCLUDING REMARKS

In the case of product hopping, the main problem is managing the fact that minimally innovative products may gain substantial sales at the expense of much cheaper generic medicines and as a result can substantially reduce consumer

[93] Shadowen et al, 'Bringing Market Discipline', 721.

[94] See ch 3.

[95] LE Battaglia, 'Drug Reformulation Regulatory Gaming in Pharmaceuticals: Enforcement & Innovation Implications' (2011) 7 *European Competition Journal* 379, 391.

[96] For a comment, see R Podszun, 'Can Competition Law Repair Patent Law and Administrative Procedures? AstraZeneca' (2014) 51 *CML Rev* 281, 290–91.

welfare. The difficult policy problem is to sort out those cases in which, on balance, the reformulation benefits consumers from those cases in which the reformulation harms them.[97] Whether and how this trade-off should be managed as a matter of regulatory or competition policy is an important question. There are sound arguments for considering this conduct first of all a regulatory problem to be addressed in this area, whereas adopting a general antitrust doctrine that imposes antitrust liability on firms that introduce a new product may result in dampening incentives to innovate.

It should also be noted that proposals of specific legislative action in the US have been supported by some scholars as the best option to address product hopping too, in particular due to the lenient approach towards soft switches. In particular, the Affordable Prescriptions for Patients Act of 2021 would provide a cause of action under section 5 of the FTC Act.[98] This initiative may be framed along the same lines of the interventions discussed for pay-for-delay. This approach, by questioning in fact the ability of existing rules in effectively tackling anti-competitive behaviours in the pharmaceutical sector, contributes to the thinking on whether more legislative action is needed in this area.

[97] Dickey et al, 'Pharmaceutical Product Hopping', 688.

[98] Affordable Prescriptions for Patients Act of 2021, § 1435. See MA Carrier, 'A Simple Solution to the Problem of "Product Hopping"' [2021] *Harvard Health Policy Review*. This legislation would give only the FTC authority to file suit under s 5 of the FTC Act. The legislation addresses: hard switches in which the company (i) withdraws its drug (or destroys inventory) and impedes competition and (ii) markets or sells a follow-on drug; and soft switches in which the firm (i) unfairly disadvantages the original and impedes competition and (ii) markets or sells a follow-on drug. The drug company benefits from exclusions from liability for 'truthful, non-misleading promotional marketing' and 'ceasing promotional marketing'. It also can offer justifications showing that it (i) would have taken the actions regardless of the effect on competition and (ii) had safety or supply-disruption reasons for the reformulation (for hard switches) or 'had legitimate pro-competitive reasons, apart from the financial effects of reduced competition' (for soft switches).

7

Excessive Drug Pricing

I. THE RESURGENCE OF EXCESSIVE PRICING CASES IN THE PHARMACEUTICAL SECTOR

THE PROLIFERATION OF high-cost medicines and rising drug prices are increasing the pressure on health spending and calling into question the pharmaceutical industry's pricing strategies. Despite the attention of scholarship so far being focused on patented prescription drugs, the narrative of patents as the main cause of skyrocketing prices must be re-read taking into account how recent practice testifies that price spikes of non-patented products are an emerging trend in the pharmaceutical markets. This has caused concern in both the EU and the US.

In the last years, controversial cases of price hikes have been documented in several European Member States and recently one of these has been the subject of investigation by the European Commission too. The most widely known cases are those that were prosecuted against Aspen, initially started in Italy, and against Pfizer and Flynn Pharma in the UK.

In Italy, in September 2016, the Italian Competition Authority (ICA) fined the multinational pharmaceutical company Aspen more than €5 million for allegedly having set unfair price increases of up to 1500 per cent on off-patent, branded, life-prolonging and non-substitutable drugs (specifically, medicines with the active ingredients chlorambucil, melphalan, mercaptopurine and thioguanine) acquired by GlaxoSmithKline and used in the treatment of patients affected by cancer, including children and elderly patients in particular, in breach of Article 102(a) of the Treaty on the Functioning of the European Union (TFEU).[1] Such drugs had been developed long before and had been sold over time in niche markets at their original prices. The strategy adopted by Aspen included aggressive behaviour in negotiating with the national regulatory agency, using the threat of instrumental delisting (ie the removal of a medicine from the reimbursement list, thus leaving the cost of the drug to the patients) and withdrawal of the products. Court appeals have confirmed both the findings

[1] *Incremento prezzi farmaci/Aspen* (Case A480) Autorità garante della concorrenza e del mercato (ICA) Decision [2016] *Bollettino* 36.

and the fine imposed by the ICA.[2] Following the ICA's investigation, the Spanish national competition authority and the Commission have both opened investigations concerning Aspen's pricing practices. The investigation conducted by the European Commission will be analysed in detail in the next section.[3]

A different outcome resulted from the decision adopted in the same year in the UK by the Competition and Markets Authority (CMA), whereby Pfizer and Flynn Pharma were fined for the imposition of excessive and unfair prices for Epanutin (prices increasing by up to 2600 per cent overnight after the drug was de-branded in September 2012).[4] Here, the anti-competitive strategy consisted of the de-branding of the product phenytoin sodium capsules, an anti-epilepsy drug with a narrow therapeutic index, as patients who were already undergoing treatment with that brand's product could not be switched to other products without risks of failure or toxicity. This case also included the acquisition of distribution rights of the medicines by Flynn Pharma from Pfizer, with no research and development (R&D) effort or high commercial risk being involved. In particular, under rules that were applicable at the time of the infringement, the de-branding of a product, ie making it a generic drug, allowed the companies to put the medicines outside the statutory price control. Two years later, on appeal, the Competition Appeals Tribunal (CAT) did not uphold the decision of the CMA.[5] Afterwards, following the Court of Appeal's judgment released in 2020, the CMA decided to reinvestigate the matters remitted by the CAT and in July 2022, following additional evidence gathering and analysis, determined that both companies abused their dominant positions.[6] Moreover, the CMA has issued infringement decisions in two other investigations, regarding price hikes for hydrocortisone (*Auden McKenzie & others*)[7] and liothyronine tablets (*Advanz Pharma*), which are under appeal at the time of writing.[8]

[2] TAR Lazio, judgment No 8948/2017 of 26 July 2017; Council of State, judgment No 01832/2020 of 13 March 2020.

[3] *Aspen* (Case AT.40394) Commission Decision [2021].

[4] *Pfizer/Flynn Pharma* (Case CE/9742-13) CMA Decision [2016].

[5] *Flynn Pharma Ltd and Flynn Pharma (Holdings) Ltd v Competition and Markets Authority* [2018] CAT 11. The CAT has also affirmed that: 'Cases of pure unfair pricing are rare in competition law. Authorities find them difficult to bring and are, rightly, wary of casting themselves in the role of price regulators … ex post price regulation through the medium of competition law presents many problems. However, the law prohibits unfair pricing in certain circumstances and in such cases there is no reason in principle why competition law cannot be applied, provided this is done on the correct legal basis and the analysis of evidence is sound.'

[6] *CMA v Flynn Pharma Ltd and others* [2020] EWCA Civ 339; *Pfizer/Flynn Pharma* (Case 50908) CMA Decision [2022].

[7] *Hydrocortisone tablets* (Case 50277) CMA Decision [2021]. The CMA fined Auden Mckenzie and Accord-UK (previously, Actavis UK) and parent companies £155 million for charging the NHS excessive and unfair prices for hydrocortisone tablets for almost 10 years, from 2008 to 2018, in particular by increasing the price of 10 mg and 20 mg hydrocortisone tablets by over 10,000% compared to the original branded version of the drug. The CMA has also fined Accord-UK and Allergan – as former parent – a further £66 million for paying two would-be competitors to stay out of the market.

[8] *Liothyronine tablets* (Case 50395), CMA Decision [2021]. The CMA found that from 2009 until 2017 excessive and unfair prices were charged for supplying liothyronine tablets, used to treat

Other cases include investigations conducted by the Danish Competition Council (DCC) – which, in January 2018, adopted a decision concerning CD Pharma's abuse of dominance by charging an excessive and unfair price for the off-patent drug Syntocinon, containing oxytocin[9] – and by the Dutch competition authority (ACM)[10] and the ICA[11] against companies belonging to the Leadiant group for a suspected abuse of dominant position for the production and sale of chenodeoxycholic acid (CDCA)-based medicines for the treatment of a rare disease (cerebrotendinous xanthomatosis), involving an orphan drug.

These investigations share some features and have renewed attention on a type of abusive behaviour by dominant companies, ie excessive pricing, targeted under EU competition rules in the category of exploitative abuses and whose application has been generally sporadic and particularly controversial.

Despite differences that will be analysed in the following sections, the issue is not unknown in the US too. According to recent data, more than 90 per cent of prescriptions dispensed in the US each year are for off-patent drugs.[12] In 2016, an investigation into dramatic price increases in off-patent prescription drugs started by the bipartisan Senate Special Committee on Aging revealed some key elements of the strategies observed in practice by companies to exploit market failures: acquiring a sole-sourced gold standard drug, with only one manufacturer and no immediate competition, serving a small market which would be unattractive to competitors; creating a closed distribution system or other means to block competitors; and engaging in price gouging by charging as much as possible.[13]

thyroid hormone deficiency. This strategy, which began in 2007, involved an overall price increase for liothyronine tablets of more than 6000%. The CMA has fined the firms involved a total of over £100 million for the relevant periods.

[9] *CD Pharma* (Case 14/08469) DCC Decision [2018]. Oxytocin is an active substance given to pregnant women in connection with childbirth. The decision of the DCC, finding CD Pharma – which was dominant on the Danish market for the sale of oxytocin due to an exclusive distribution agreement with the manufacturer of the product – to have increased the price of the drug by 2000% in 2014, was upheld by the Danish Competition Appeals Tribunal in 2018 and subsequently in 2020 by the Danish Maritime and Commercial Court. Case No KL-2-2018, *CD Pharma v The DCC; Danish Maritime and Commercial Court*, Case BS-3038/2019-SHR, judgment of 2 March 2020.

[10] *Leadiant* (Case ACM/20/041239). The ACM closed its own investigation in July 2021, finding Leadiant liable for abuse of dominant position in the period from mid-2017 to the end of 2019 by the imposition of excessive prices for CDCA-Leadiant, which received orphan designation for which no alternatives existed in that period, and imposing a fine of €19,569,500. As a result, the drug costed approximately €153,000 per patient per year. Leadiant charged the price of €14,000 in the Netherlands until Amsterdam UMC succeeded in manufacturing the drug in its own pharmacy in January 2020.

[11] *Leadiant Bioscences/Farmaco per la cura della Xantomatosi Cerebrotendinea* (Case A524) ICA Decision [2022].

[12] Association for Accessible Medicines, 'The US Generic & Biosimilar Medicines Savings Report' (2021) https://accessiblemeds.org/resources/reports/2021-savings-report.

[13] Senate Special Committee on Aging, 'Sudden Price Spikes in Off-Patent Prescription Drugs: The Monopoly Business Model that Harms Patients, Taxpayers, and the US Healthcare System' (2016) www.congress.gov/114/crpt/srpt429/CRPT-114srpt429.pdf. For details, see P FitzGerald, 'State Regulation of Generic Drug Price Gouging' (2019) 2 *Belmont Health Law Journal*.

Perhaps the most widely known case is the one concerning Daraprim, a decades-old drug used primarily to treat toxoplasmosis. In 2015, Turing Pharmaceuticals (now Vyera Pharmaceuticals) purchased from Impax the rights to Daraprim (pyrimethamine), which were 62 years old and no longer protected by patent, and soon thereafter raised the price from $13.50 per tablet to $750. Despite the fact that there were no patents or other forms of market exclusivity protecting the drug, Turing could implement this price hike due to the relatively small market in the US for pyrimethamine, which had attracted no entry by other generic manufacturers.[14] The features of this case are not so different from some of those discussed in the European context mentioned above, as it concerns a post-acquisition strategy involving a substantial and unjustified increase in price of a long off-patent drug – without any innovative effort pursued by Turing – in a market where there were no competitors.[15] Cases other than Turing (which also employed tactics leading to an antitrust lawsuit in 2020) have signalled this worrying trend, which has led to increased scrutiny and concern.[16]

[14] At the same time, apparently as a condition of the sale to Turing, pyrimethamine was switched to a controlled distribution system (called Daraprim Direct), in which prescriptions or supplies of the product could be obtained only from a single source, Walgreen's Specialty Pharmacy. As a consequence, Daraprim was available only through this new system and only registered clients could obtain it: patients could receive the drug only by mail order and not through a local pharmacy, and hospitals were prevented from obtaining the drug from general wholesalers. This system also affected other manufacturers wishing to obtain samples of the drug for use in bioequivalence studies supporting an ANDA, thereby undermining efforts by generic firms to enter the market. On these points, see MA Carrier, N Levidow and AS Kesselheim, 'Using Antitrust Law to Challenge Turing's Daraprim Price Increase' (2017) 31 *Berkeley Technology Law Journal* 1379. In 2020, the FTC filed a complaint in federal court against Vyera Pharmaceuticals (formerly Turing) alleging an elaborate anti-competitive scheme to preserve a monopoly on Daraprim.

[15] H First, 'Excessive Drug Pricing as an Antitrust Violation' (2019) 82 *Antitrust Law Journal* 701, 728.

[16] Another case that has gained the attention of scholars and media concerned EpiPen, an injector delivering epinephrine typically used for emergency treatments for anaphylaxis. In 2007, Mylan acquired Merck's generic pharmaceutical business and the exclusive right to market and distribute the EpiPen, whereas Meridian, a Pfizer subsidiary, retained the manufacturing of the device. Whereas epinephrine is not patented, the injector is. The events are rather complex, so only the main elements relevant for our purposes will be mentioned here. In 2012, Mylan and the holders of the patent on the injector settled a patent infringement suit they brought against Teva, a generic manufacturer that had agreed not to enter the market until 2015, which was 10 years before the patent's expiration. However, Teva had production problems and did not enter the market at the agreed upon time. In 2013, the School Access to Emergency Epinephrine Act (called the EpiPen bill, even though no direct mention of the EpiPen was included in the bill itself) gave funding preferences for schools maintaining emergency supplies of epinephrine, which had a strong impact on both the sales and the reputation of the EpiPen. Between 2009 and 2016, Mylan raised the price of this life-saving device by more than 400%. EpiPen faced little competition (from Auvi-Q and Adrenaclick). In 2018, the Food and Drug Administration (FDA) finally approved Teva's application to produce a generic version of the EpiPen. On this case, see MA Carrier and CJ Minniti III, 'The Untold EpiPen Story: How Mylan Hiked Prices by Blocking Rivals' (2017) 102 *Cornell Law Review Online* 53.

II. EXCESSIVE PRICING UNDER EU COMPETITION LAW

As seen in chapter four, the notion of 'abuse' under Article 102 TFEU comprises two categories: exclusionary abuses and exploitative abuses. This traditional distinction between exclusionary and exploitative abuses has typically confined the latter to being a residual category (being used only rarely and as a last resort), its application by competition agencies being particularly controversial.[17]

Excessive pricing prohibition under Article 102(a) TFEU represents one of the most striking differences between European and US antitrust laws, as the latter does not consider the charging of profit-maximising monopoly prices per se to be an antitrust violation.[18] However, the Commission has also been reluctant to treat it as such. The reason is based on two main points. Firstly, with regard to the long-standing debate on the application of competition law versus sector-specific regulation, there is a dispute over whether it is appropriate for competition agencies to act as price regulators. Secondly, determining when a price is considered to be unfair is an extremely difficult task.

This also constitutes a typical area of contention among scholars. In brief, the main arguments supporting the abstention of antitrust intervention in this area are based on the following arguments: that excessive prices may be profitable for the dominant undertaking only in the short term; that sanctioning excessive pricing may negatively affect dynamic efficiency; and that a high risk of errors exists, taking into account that competition authorities – unlike sectoral regulators – are typically not equipped to regulate prices and that such control requires a complex, time-consuming and costly intervention by the public authorities.[19] On the other side, excessive prices have been shown to not always be self-correcting,[20] in particular in markets where high and non-transitory barriers to entry exist.[21]

[17] For an analysis of the rationales for the prohibition, see M Gal, 'Abuse of Dominance – Exploitative Abuses' in D Geradin and I Lianos (eds), *Research Handbook in EU Antitrust Law* (Chelthenham, Edward Elgar, 2013) 385.

[18] With regard to the differences between US and EU approaches, see, eg M Gal, 'Monopoly Pricing as an Antitrust Offense in the US and the EC: Two Systems of Belief About Monopoly?' (2004) 49 *Antitrust Bulletin* 343.

[19] See D Evans and J Padilla, 'Excessive Prices: Using Economics to Define Administrable Legal Rules' (2005) 1 *Journal of Competition Law and Economics* 97; D Geradin, 'The Necessary Limits to the Control of "Excessive" Prices by Competition Authorities – A View from Europe' (2007) Tilburg University Legal Studies Working Paper, http://ssrn.com/abstract = 1022678. For an overview, see F Jenny, 'Abuse of Dominance by Firms Charging Excessive or Unfair Prices: An Assessment' in Y Katsoulacos and F Jenny (eds), *Excessive Pricing and Competition Law Enforcement* (Cham, Springer, 2018) 5; see also OECD, 'Excessive Pricing in Pharmaceutical Markets' (2018) www.oecd.org/daf/competition/excessive-pricing-in-pharmaceuticals.htm.

[20] A Ezrachi and D Gilo, 'Are Excessive Prices Really Self-Correcting?' (2009) 5 *Journal of Competition Law and Economics* 249 (arguing that in a majority of cases and irrespective of whether entry barriers are high or low, excessive prices alone are insufficient to attract new entry, and that intervention on the basis of excessive prices may encourage rather than discourage entry as it may allow undertakings a better understanding of post-entry prices, which are the elements that

In this debate, the costs of errors that antitrust enforcement may involve are of great importance. There is a risk of both Type I, or over-enforcement, errors and Type II, or under-enforcement, errors. However, the main concerns generally regard the former, which entails potentially high costs, especially in terms of negative effects on dynamic inefficiency related to low investment and innovation.[22] A number of economists have proposed screens aimed at limiting the intervention of antitrust agencies to stringent conditions. For instance, Evans and Padilla have proposed a test with three conditions for antitrust intervention: (i) that the firm enjoys a (near) monopoly position in the market, which is not the result of past investments or innovations and is protected by very high legal barriers to entry; (ii) that the prices charged by the firm widely exceed its average total costs; and (iii) that there is a risk that those prices may prevent the emergence of new goods and services in adjacent markets.[23] Motta and de Streel have elaborated another test requiring the following three cumulative conditions: (i) that high and non-transitory barriers exist, so that it is only 'super-dominant' or 'quasi-monopolistic' firms which should be subjected to excessive price actions; (ii) that the quasi-monopolistic position has been achieved through special and exclusive rights or through not previously condemned past exclusionary anti-competitive practices rather than market competition; and (iii) that no sectoral regulator has the jurisdiction to solve the matters.[24] Röller has proposed a test with five cumulative conditions: (i) that significant entry barriers exist; (ii) that the market is unlikely to self-correct; (iii) that no (structural) remedy is available; (iv) that no regulator exists or regulatory failure occurs; and (v) that 'gap cases' or 'mistake cases' occur (ie cases where dominance is a result of exclusionary conduct that has not been prosecuted).[25] Fletcher and Jardine have suggested a

potential entrants consider when deciding whether to enter). See also OECD, 'Excessive Pricing' 10 (mentioning that the difficulties in the assessment of excessive prices required by antitrust agencies should not be overestimated either).

[21] See, eg Geradin, 'The Necessary Limits' (affirming that antitrust enforcement on excessive prices by dominant firms should only be applied in exceptional circumstances, including situations where (i) significant and long-lasting barriers to entry and expansion exist; (ii) it is impossible to remove them; and (iii) investments and innovation tend to be limited).

[22] See Jenny, 'Abuse of Dominance', 41–43. With regard to the pharmaceutical sector, see C Calcagno, A Chapsal and J White, 'Economics of Excessive Pricing: An Application to the Pharmaceutical Industry' (2019) 10 *Journal of European Competition Law & Practice* 166, 171 (affirming that, in the case of a Type II error resulting from a competition authority failing to intervene against a pharmaceutical price that was actually excessive, it is assumed that, while higher prices may result in the short run, price and market access regulations across Europe provide governments and regulators with alternative tools to affect prices and to address concerns in the longer term; on the other hand, Type I errors may reduce prices in the short run, but may also affect a company's ability to recoup its investment if the price was, in fact, not excessive).

[23] DS Evans and J Padilla, 'Excessive Prices'.

[24] M Motta and A de Streel, 'Excessive Pricing in Competition Law: Never Say Never?' in Swedish Competition Authority, *The Pros and Cons of High Prices* (Konkurrensverket, 2007).

[25] LH Röller, 'Exploitative Abuses' in C-D Ehlermann and M Marquis (eds), *European Competition Law Annual 2007 – A Reformed Approach to Article 82 EC* (Oxford, Hart Publishing, 2008) 525. Gap cases are related to the fact that Art 102 TFEU only applies to firms that are already dominant, and anti-competitive conduct that leads to a dominant position cannot be caught as an exclusionary

policy approach which would: (i) limit intervention when there is no possibility of successful new entry within a reasonable period; (ii) consider carefully the pricing of other elements of the undertaking's portfolio, the competition it faces in those other markets and the impact on consumers' choices; (iii) exclude fines and private damages action; (iv) not intervene during the patent period of an innovative product; (v) consider carefully the effect of any ex post intervention on ex ante investment incentives; and (vi) seek alternative structural remedies to price regulation.[26] In any case, the application of excessive pricing has been defined as a messy and difficult business.[27]

The main reasons supporting the antitrust intervention against exploitative conduct in the EU are adduced making reference, in addition to the wording of Article 102(a) and the supposed legislative intent behind it, to the (direct and indirect) protection of consumer welfare as the goal of competition policy.[28] Moreover, such prohibition may serve the so-called 'gap cases', deriving from the fact that Article 102 does not prohibit the acquisition of dominance (as the Sherman Act does), but only the abusive conduct of firms already holding a dominant position; in other words, there may be cases where intervention against unilateral exclusionary conduct is not legally possible without the intervention against exploitative conduct (for example, in the cases of excessive royalties charged by a company which has obtained its dominant position as a result of patent ambush, ie not disclosing its patent in the context of a standard-setting process).[29]

Despite this, in practice, the Commission has been reluctant to resort to excessive pricing decisions and the existing jurisprudence on the matter is not very well developed. The main jurisprudential point of reference for these cases is *United Brands*, which has not been questioned in the subsequent case law.[30] According to the Court of Justice, the crucial point of the abuse is charging a price which is excessive because it has no reasonable relation to the economic

abuse (which would be an enforcement 'gap'); mistake cases refer to those situations where, for some reason, an antitrust authority may not have effectively prosecuted an exclusionary abuse.

[26] A Fletcher and A Jardine, 'Towards an Appropriate Policy for Excessive Pricing' in C-D Ehlermann and M Marquis (eds), *European Competition Law* 533. See also E Paulis, 'Article 82 EC and Exploitative Conduct' in ibid 515 (arguing that the only reasonable criterion to identify markets that could be candidates for interventions against excessive prices is the presence of very high and long-lasting barriers to entry and expansion).

[27] C Calcagno and M Walker, 'Excessive Pricing: Towards Clarity and Economic Coherence' (2010) 6 *Journal of Competition Law and Economics* 891, 910.

[28] European Union, 'Article 102 and Excessive Prices' (2011) Contribution to the 2011 OECD Roundtable, 309ff. See also T Ackermann, 'Excessive Pricing and the Goals of Competition Law' in D Zimmer (ed), *The Goals of Competition Law* (Cheltenham, Edward Elgar, 2012) 349ff (affirming that in the EU there are institutional reasons to believe that the prevention of undeserved monopoly profits can be a legitimate subject of competition law through the application of Art 102(a) if regulatory measures fail). See also P Akman and L Garrod, 'When Are Excessive Prices Unfair?' (2011) 7 *Journal of Competition Law and Economics* 403, 407; P Akman, *The Concept of Abuse in EU Competition Law* (Oxford, Hart Publishing, 2012) 187ff.

[29] See, eg *Rambus* (COMP/C-3/38626) Commission Decision [2009].

[30] Case C-27/76 *United Brands Company and United Brands Continentaal BV v Commission* EU:C:1978:22, [1978] ECR 00207.

value of the product.[31] Such excess could be determined objectively by assessing the excessiveness of the 'profit margin', ie by making a comparison between the selling price of the product in question and its cost of production ('cost-plus' method)[32] to show the unfairness of the price. Thus, the Court elaborated a two-limb test, according to which it is first necessary to determine

> whether the difference between the costs actually incurred and the price actually charged is excessive; and, if the answer to this question is in the affirmative, whether a price has been imposed which is either unfair in itself or when compared to competing products.[33]

Uncertainties and difficulties in applying this test have been highlighted in the literature. Analysing the jurisprudence and the academic debate on the matter is beyond the scope of this chapter.[34] Suffice it to say that the Commission explained that the economic value had to be determined with regard to the circumstances and by taking into account non-cost-related factors, in particular demand-side aspects.[35] Moreover, methods other than the price–cost test are available, including comparator tests, as confirmed by Advocate General Wahl in his Opinion in the *AKKA/LAA* case.[36] In this case, the choice of the most appropriate method is down to the competition authority, which must ensure that the comparison that is being carried out is based on comparators selected in accordance with objective, appropriate and verifiable criteria and are made on a consistent basis.[37] In the same judgment, the Court of Justice further clarified that the price difference between the product in question and similar comparator products is appreciable, and thus may be indicative of an abuse of a dominant position when it is 'both significant and persistent on the facts, with respect, in particular, to the market in question', without there being

[31] ibid para 250.

[32] ibid para 251.

[33] ibid para 252. Note the position expressed by Motta and de Streel, 'Excessive Pricing', 39 (disagreeing with the majoritarian view of many commentators – including Commission officials – and arguing that 'the test imposed by the Court is not necessarily cumulative and both parts of the test aimed to prove the same thing: that a price is above its competitive level').

[34] For an updated overview on the case law and the methods that can be employed under Art 102(a), see M Botta, 'Sanctioning Unfair Pricing under Art 102(a) TFEU: Yes, We Can!' (2021) 17 *European Competition Journal* 156.

[35] *Scandlines Sverige AB v Port of Helsingborg* (COMP/A.36.568/D3) Commission Decision [2004], paras 226–27.

[36] See Case C-177/166 *Autortiesību un komunicēšanās konsultāciju aģentūra/Latvijas Autoru apvienība v Konkurences padome* EU:C:2017:286, Opinion of AG Wahl, para 19 (and the case law cited therein) (according to whom a comparison may be conducted 'between, on the one hand, the price charged for the product in question by the dominant undertaking and, on the other hand, the prices charged in the same market by non-dominant undertakings (comparison across competitors) or by the same dominant undertaking at different points in time (comparison across time), or the prices charged in other geographic markets by the same dominant undertaking or by other undertakings (geographic comparison)').

[37] Case C-177/16 *Autortiesību un komunicēšanās konsultāciju aģentūra/Latvijas Autoru apvienība v Konkurences padome* ECLI:EU:C:2017:689 (*AKKA/LAA*), paras 41 and 44.

any specific or fixed minimum threshold.[38] Once it has been ascertained that an excess exists between the price actually charged by the dominant undertaking and the benchmark price, one must determine the extent to which that actual price is unfair, either in itself or when compared to competing products, in order to investigate whether the difference in price is the result of an abusive use of market power by the dominant undertaking or is the consequence of other legitimate reasons. Put differently, if the high profit margin results from the dominant company being very efficient, it cannot be said that the prices are unfair in themselves.

A. *Aspen*

The *Aspen* case is the first – and so far the only – decision issued by the Commission concerning excessive pricing in the pharmaceutical sector.

The Commission started its investigation concerning the pharmaceutical company Aspen in 2017, covering the entire European Economic Area except Italy, where, as mentioned before, a separate infringement decision was issued by the ICA in 2016. The proceedings were closed four years later, after the Commission had accepted the commitments proposed by Aspen.

The contested conduct started in some Member States in mid-2012 with high price increases, often by several hundred per cent, and resulted in very high price and profitability levels of the prescription drugs sold under the brand names Alkeran IV and Alkeran Oral (melphalan), Purinethol (mercaptopurine), Leukeran (chlorambucil), Lanvis (tioguanine) and Myleran (busulfan), used as essential and non-substitutable medicines for the treatment of certain types of cancer and for specific group of patients, including elderly persons and children. Aspen acquired the products from GlaxoSmithKline in 2009 as part of a bundle of transactions paid for with Aspen shares. In line with its business model, Aspen has been outsourcing the manufacturing and packaging of the drugs, as well as most of the commercialisation and distribution to third parties. When it took over the management of the products in 2011, it developed a plan to increase their prices.

In its preliminary assessment, the Commission found that, in the vast majority of the relevant markets, Aspen maintained very high market shares during the period from 1 July 2012 until 30 June 2019. In these markets, there was no entry – or, if entry did happen, it was limited and did not lead to a decrease in prices.[39]

[38] ibid para 55.

[39] European Commission, *Aspen*, paras 66–68. The Commission estimated Aspen has maintained market shares amounting very often to 90–100% or between 70–80% and 90–100%. The Commission considered general regulatory requirements for entering the market, such as marketing authorisation, and difficulty in arranging supply as barriers that, in view of the limited market size, may have rendered entry by certain potential entrants less attractive.

This case has proved first and foremost to be peculiar for the pan-European strategy implemented by the undertaking with the aim of increasing prices. Confirming what had already been observed in the Italian context, the strategy included attempts made by Aspen to overcome the resistance of national regulatory authorities to accept the price increase by means of threats – and, in some cases, the effective implementation of delisting and withdrawals.[40] Moreover, Aspen employed a strategic sequencing of price increases in order to defeat the external reference pricing system and avoid parallel trade. The pharmaceutical company started the price increase in Germany, as, under German law, Aspen had the freedom to unilaterally set new list prices for the products. Although a statutory claw-back applied, with the aim of preventing increases of real net prices in Germany itself, Aspen could influence the price formation process elsewhere by using the increased German list prices in its applications in other Member States, considering that many of them actually used the German official list price as the reference in their external reference pricing system. Moreover, through delistings or withdrawals, Aspen could prevent Member States from including low prices, which the company itself did not manage to increase, in their reference pricing basket. Finally, a stock allocation system, consisting of allocating quotas and, if necessary, withholding deliveries for the products in some Member States, was in place.[41]

With regard to the methodological aspects, the Commission relied on the framework of analysis of the *United Brands* test and found Aspen's prices to be unfair in themselves. Under the first limb of the test, the Commission compared the costs of production to the revenues earned by Aspen from the drugs concerned, then assessed the excessiveness of the resulting profits by carrying out a comparison of Aspen's profitability with that of a sample of other undertakings selling similar products and having a profile similar to Aspen's.[42] From this analysis, Aspen was found to achieve profitability levels much higher than those of the comparators and earned revenues exceeding the cost-plus level with each product in almost all of the relevant markets. On the basis of the specific circumstances of the case, the Commission used two measures of profitability,

[40] ibid paras 87ff.

[41] ibid paras 97–101. In the Italian investigation, the ICA found that Aspen's whole strategy also included the adoption of an 'oncology allocation mechanism', used for the creation of an artificial scarcity of Cosmos drugs in the markets concerned and employed as a means to exercise the company's bargaining power with national regulators.

[42] ibid paras 127ff. The Commission clarified that, depending on the circumstances of each case, different methods may be suitable to determine a reasonable rate of return for the purposes of establishing a benchmark to be used in assessing the potential excessiveness of profit levels. In this investigation, the sample of undertakings that are similar to Aspen has been identified on the basis of a number of objective criteria and IQVIA data for the period 2017–18, considering that the Commission had no indications that they do not operate under conditions of sufficiently effective competition ('Profitability Comparators').

namely the gross margin and the earnings before interest, tax, depreciation and amortisation (EBITDA) margin.[43]

Under the second limb, the Commission considered that the high profits gained by the pharmaceutical company appeared to derive from the exercise of market power arising from a lack of effective competition, whereas no legitimate reasons – for example, in terms of commercial risk-taking activity, innovation, investment or any improvement of the products – could be found.[44] The elements considered by the Commission included: whether Aspen had carried out any particular activity in relation to the concerned products; the characteristics of the drugs that had been off-patent for decades, but on which a number of cancer patients still depended; and the stark disproportion between the limited increases in the costs of the products, the very high price increases and the magnitude of the excessiveness of Aspen's profits.

Moreover, the Commission added a further element. It affirmed that the analysis also has to take into account the dominant undertaking's conduct and its economic motives, and that the objective reasons behind its pricing policy are highly relevant.[45] On this basis, the Commission found that Aspen's internal documents suggested that after having acquired the products, Aspen became conscious of the market power that it enjoyed and decided to exploit it. The particular means through which Aspen imposed the higher prices and the likely harm those prices may have caused to patients and the national health budgets are considered additional factors confirming the unfairness in itself.[46]

It should be noted that the Commission stressed that the two ways provided by the *United Brand* test to assess unfairness (ie whether the price is unfair in itself or unfair when compared to competing products) are alternatives, so only one must be fulfilled.[47] Nonetheless, the preliminary assessment also considered

[43] ibid paras 103ff and paras 144ff. While gross margin refers to net sales minus direct costs (and thus not considering indirect costs), EBITDA margin is a net profitability measure that takes into account all direct costs and all indirect costs, with the exception of depreciation and amortisation costs (which cover impairment costs, and are thus also excluded). The preliminary assessment used the latter as the main profitability measure to assess the profitability of the products, since it accounts for a broader set of costs and therefore provides a more complete picture of the costs required to carry out a given economic activity. See paras 117–21.

[44] ibid paras 165ff.

[45] ibid para 186. The Commission made reference to AG Wahl Opinion in *AKKA/LAA*, point 118. No case law is cited on this point.

[46] European Commission, *Aspen*, paras 191ff. In this respect, the Commission reached the conclusion that potential generic and innovative price comparator products put forward by Aspen do not challenge the preliminary finding that Aspen's prices are in themselves unfair.

[47] ibid paras 196ff. The application of this part of the test is one of the most controversial arguments opposing the ruling adopted in *Pfizer/Flynn* by the CAT, according to which, in assessing unfairness, an authority can apply either alternative of the *United Brands* test but must give due consideration to any prima facie convincing argument that the pricing is actually fair under either alternative. See also the Commission's amicus curiae observations pursuant to Art 15(3) of Regulation 1/2003 of 14 June 2019 to the UK Court of Appeal in *Pfizer/Flynn*. The Commission intervened to support the CMA, taking the position that the Tribunal erred in law in its articulation of the test for abuse of dominance and arguing that if the law were as laid down by the Tribunal it would be impracticable

the potential suitability of some other products for assessing unfairness to reply to Aspen's arguments in this respect and reached the preliminary conclusion that the potential generic and innovative price comparator products put forward by Aspen did not challenge the preliminary finding that Aspen's prices are in themselves unfair.

The final commitment decision includes a price commitment and a supply one: the reduction of Aspen's prices across Europe for the six cancer medicines by, on average, approximately 73 per cent, which is on average below the prices of 2012, before Aspen's price increases started (with reduced net prices applying for a period of 10 years); and the guaranteed supply of the medicines for the next five years, with the continuation of supply or the availability of its marketing authorisation to other suppliers for an additional five-year period. A peculiarity of the price commitments is that they include a retroactive element, as the reduction in net prices is fixed to be effective as from 1 October 2019, the date when Aspen first approached the Commission with a concrete commitment proposal, until such time as Aspen has effectively implemented the price reductions to the public and private entities that ultimately pay or reimburse medicine prices in the Member States.

The adoption of a commitment decision as an alternative remedy to prohibition decisions has the advantage of typically having a quicker effect on the market, more tailored remedies and a swifter implementation by the undertakings concerned, which avoid fines and the formal finding of infringement.[48] However, it also allows the Commission to apply Article 102 TFEU without an extensive economic and legal assessment but provides no sufficient legal certainty and only a limited chance of judicial review. For these reasons, the recourse to commitment decisions raises strong criticism in novel and complex competition cases. In *Aspen*, this precluded the release of a full assessment by the Commission, which would eventually be scrutinised before courts in order to give further guidance to the industry and enforcers.

The *Aspen* case is meaningful for various reasons. The main features of the case – including the magnitude of the price hikes, the absence of R&D and investment, recoupment or innovation justifications for it, the absence of self-correction of the market and of therapeutic alternative products, and the inability of regulators to provide an appropriate response to the price increase – confirm the justification of the antitrust intervention, which in these

and unworkable. In more detail, the CMA and the Commission claimed that the test mandated by the Tribunal interferes with the margin of manoeuvre or discretion that a competition authority should have (i) in choosing the methods or tests to apply and (ii) as to the evidence it wishes to evaluate, in that it compels or requires that authorities perform certain tests in all cases. Furthermore, according to the Commission, the Tribunal misinterpreted the general scheme of *United Brands* and of the *AKKA/LAA* case, and this led it to impose a number of additional requirements and a further test of applying demand side considerations to the 'economic value' of the product in determining whether the price was unfair.

[48] See Art 9 of Council Regulation (EC) No 1/2003 on the implementation of the rules on competition laid down in Articles 81 and 82 of the Treaty [2003] OJ L 1/1.

circumstances meets the stringent screens and tests elaborated in the literature, as mentioned above.[49]

In the view of the role of competition rules and their intersection with regulation, it is worth stressing that a peculiar aspect of this case concerns the strategy, and the means adopted by the undertaking, to which the antitrust decision gives particular relevance, despite it not being essential for the finding of unfair pricing.[50] On closer inspection, this distinctive element resembles a type of regulatory gaming behaviour.[51] In *Aspen*, the pharmaceutical company was able to strategically exploit the failures of the existing sectoral regulatory framework and exercise its bargaining power towards the regulators as the dispute concerned drugs that, although off-patent, were still essential and non-substitutable for patients, and were thus indispensable for the national health systems.

III. THE US APPROACH

As anticipated, excessive prices are not an issue under US antitrust law, which does not restrict the prices charged by a firm that has lawfully acquired market power. A famous quote from the *Trinko* judgment clearly explains the traditional stance:

> The mere possession of monopoly power, and the concomitant charging of monopoly prices, is not only not unlawful; it is an important element of the free-market system. The opportunity to charge monopoly prices–at least for a short period–is what attracts 'business acumen' in the first place; it induces risk taking that produces innovation and economic growth. To safeguard the incentive to innovate, the possession of monopoly power will not be found unlawful unless it is accompanied by an element of anticompetitive *conduct*.[52]

This approach has recently come under discussion after the cases of extraordinary price increases in the pharmaceutical sector mentioned above. In the

[49] M Colangelo and C Desogus, 'Antitrust Scrutiny of Excessive Prices in the Pharmaceutical Sector: A Comparative Study of the Italian and UK Experiences' (2018) 41 *World Competition* 225.

[50] See also G Monti, 'Excessive Pricing: Competition Law in Shared Regulatory Space' (TILEC, 2019) 12–13, www.tilburguniversity.edu/research/institutes-and-research-groups/old-tilec/events/work-progress-giorgio-monti (referring to the ICA's decision in *Aspen* and arguing that two theories of harm are utilised, when one would have been sufficient: one strand of reasoning focuses on the improper manner in which the undertakings dealt with the regulator combined with evidence of anti-competitive intent, while a second considers the unfairness of the prices charged; as a result, it is not clear if this is a 'monopoly-broth' approach).

[51] See N Dunne, 'The Role of Regulation in EU Competition Law Assessment' (2021) 44 *World Competition* 287, 301 (arguing that regulatory gaming is ultimately about corruption of the underlying regulatory regime, and this would also explain why intention may become a critical component of theory of harm).

[52] *Verizon Communications, Inc v Law Offices of Curtis V Trinko, LLP* 540 US 398, 407 (2004). See also *Pacific Bell Telephone Co v linkLine Communications, Inc* 555 US 438, 454 (2009).

literature, a number of scholars have called for an antitrust intervention in this area. For instance, First, making explicit reference to the European experience and to the *Aspen* and *Pfizer/Flynn Pharma* cases conducted by national competition authorities, has claimed that the existing approach makes the US an 'international outlier'.[53] More specifically, First challenges the conventional wisdom regarding the ability of section 2 of the Sherman Act to cover excessive pricing. According to his opinion, the failure to address excessive pharmaceutical prices under US antitrust law is based on policy grounds rather than on legal problems, and excessive pricing could satisfy the monopolistic conduct requirement. In support of this argument, reference is made to cases in which exploitation of consumers through the charging of high prices has been asserted as a type of competitive harm, in particular to the scrutiny by the Federal Trade Commission (FTC) on standard-essential patents (SEPs) and fair, reasonable and non-discriminatory (FRAND) licensing.[54]

In the academic and political debate, the issue of which means could be used for antitrust intervention has mainly concerned the possibility of relying on section 5 of the FTC Act, which gives the FTC the authority to address both 'unfair or deceptive acts or practices' and 'unfair methods of competition'. Scholars supporting this solution claim that this tool would allow the FTC to bring administrative proceedings specifically against those companies that engage in this kind of exploitative conduct, while not against those that raise prices in response to normal market forces.[55]

Up to now, such positions have not been upheld by antitrust agencies. In their note sent to OECD in 2018 in the occasion of the roundtable devoted to excessive pricing in pharmaceutical sector, the FTC and Antitrust Division of the US Department of Justice have confirmed that 'limiting the freedom to set prices may well conflict with the underlying premise of antitrust policy, ie promoting a robust competitive process that produces high-quality, innovative goods at low prices'.[56] Moreover, in 2019, in response to a directive from Congress, the FTC issued a report to the House and Senate Appropriations Committees on the use of its stand-alone authority under section 5 of the FTC Act to address high

[53] First, 'Excessive Drug Pricing', 737. See also FM Abbott, 'Excessive Pharmaceutical Prices and Competition Law: Doctrinal Development to Protect Public Health' (2016) 6 *UC Irvine Law Review* 281.

[54] See First, 'Excessive Drug Pricing', 719–20 (affirming that 'The SEP holders in these cases were able to extract monopoly rents because they controlled something "essential" to their licensees and then acted either deceptively or opportunistically to exploit that power. Put in an antitrust framework, there was monopoly power, plus anti-competitive conduct, and harm to consumer welfare'). See also JL Graber, 'Excessive Pricing of Off-Patent Pharmaceuticals: Hatch It or Ratchet?' (2017) 92 *New York University Law Review* 1146, 1184.

[55] Graber, 'Excessive Pricing', 1183. See also H First, 'Unfair Drug Prices and Section 5' [2015] (November) *Competition Policy International Antitrust Chronicle*.

[56] United States submission to the OECD, 'Excessive Pricing' (2018) DAF/COMP/WD(2018)111, 3.

pharmaceutical prices.[57] Specifically, the Committees requested the FTC, in consultation with the FDA, to examine Congress's intent regarding unfair methods of competition in the FTC's stand-alone section 5 authority with regard to unreasonable price increases, including those that occur, over multiple years, on off-patent pharmaceutical drugs and biologics when there are no alternatives available to the consumer, and when price increases are unreasonable, unavoidable and not due to increased manufacturing costs of the product. The majority of FTC commissioners agreed that the use of section 5 alone is not an effective tool for prohibiting unreasonable price increases of pharmaceutical drugs, unless the increase is accompanied by some other exclusionary or collusive conduct, or in an extreme circumstance where the FTC can show that the price increase constitutes an unfair or deceptive act or practice. In particular, this solution would hardly be successful before courts, which typically decline to impose antitrust liability for unilateral pricing decisions and consider that determining the reasonableness of prices charged by lawful monopolists goes beyond their competence.[58] The report lists several factors that would limit the use of stand-alone section 5 authority to challenge high drug prices, including the following considerations: limiting unilateral freedom to set prices diminishes companies' incentives to compete and innovate; interfering with market pricing mechanisms may distort supply and demand, and could lead to reduced supply rather than lower pricing; both courts and the FTC would find it extremely difficult to set up and enforce an accurate and meaningful standard for what constitutes an excessive price increase; and market conditions and government-granted barriers to entry may inhibit the ability of the FTC to police drug pricing. This position was not shared by Commissioners Chopra and Slaughter, who, in their dissenting statement, claimed that the FTC needs to consider the full breadth of its statutory authority under section 5. They suggested the use of the tool through the prohibition on unfair or deceptive acts or practices in situations where (i) a price increase involves off-patent drugs that lack therapeutic alternatives, and where research, production, and regulatory barriers would prevent near-term entry, (ii) the price increase bears no reasonable relationship to manufacturing or production cost increases or changes in supply and demand conditions, and (iii) the harm to patients is not outweighed by other benefits.[59]

It is worth noting that the scope of section 5 of the FTC Act is an issue that has been debated for years between those supporting a broad interpretation of the rule

[57] Federal Trade Commission, 'Report on Standalone Section 5 to Address High Pharmaceutical Drug and Biologic Prices' (2019) www.ftc.gov/system/files/documents/reports/ftc-report-standalone-section-5-address-high-pharmaceutical-drug-biologic-prices/p180101_drug_prices_appropriations_report_6-27-19.pdf.

[58] ibid 5–7.

[59] Statement of Commissioners R Chopra and RK Slaughter (24 June 2019) 2, www.ftc.gov/system/files/documents/reports/ftc-report-stand-alone-section-5-address-high-pharmaceutical-drug-biologic-prices/p180101_section_5_report_dissenting_statement_by_chopra_and_slaughter_6-27-19.pdf.

and those claiming for a restrictive approach.[60] The position expressed by the FTC in its 2019 report is compliant with the 2015 Statement of Enforcement Principles Regarding 'Unfair Methods of Competition' under Section 5 of the FTC Act (2015 UMC Statement), adopted on a bipartisan basis during the Obama administration and aimed at addressing the requests for clear guidance on the issue. The 2015 UMC Statement indicated three principles apt to guide the decision on whether to challenge an act or practice as an unfair method of competition, ie: the promotion of consumer welfare as guidance; evaluation of the act or practice at issue under a framework similar to the rule of reason; and no likelihood of use of section 5 if enforcement of the Sherman or Clayton Act is sufficient to address the competitive harm arising from the act or practice concerned.[61] The topic is currently once more under attention, and 2015 UMC statement, which has been generally considered as narrowing the FTC's ability to bring more expansive antitrust claims, was subject to withdrawal by the FTC in July 2021 in its current composition and in November 2022 a new Statement was released.[62] Thus, it remains to be seen if the recently announced changes will lead to a shift in the antitrust approach to high drug prices too.

[60] See WE Kovacic and M Winerman, 'Competition Policy and the Application of Section 5 of the Federal Trade Commission Act' (2010) 20 *Minnesota Journal of International Law* 274 (noting that 'several factors explain why Section 5 has played so small a role in the development of US competition policy principles. Probably the most important is that the Sherman Act proved to be a far more flexible tool for setting antitrust rules than Congress expected in the early 20th century'); MK Ohlhausen, 'Section 5 of the FTC Act: Principles of Navigation' (2014) 2 *Journal of Antitrust Enforcement* 1; MK Ohlhausen, 'The Procrustean Problem with Prescriptive Regulation' (2014) 23 *Communications Law Conspectus* 1 (calling for regulatory humility and arguing that consumer welfare must be among the guiding lights for the FTC to apply its section 5 authority to cases outside the reach of traditional antitrust laws and, before taking action, the FTC ought to establish substantial harm to competition or the competitive process, and thus to consumers, relying on robust economic evidence that the challenged conduct is anti-competitive and reduces consumer welfare). A different approach is sponsored by R Chopra and L Kahn, 'The Case for "Unfair Methods of Competition" Rulemaking' (2020) 87 *University of Chicago Law Review* 357. For an overview, see HJ Hovenkamp, 'The Federal Trade Commission and the Sherman Act' (2010) 62 *Florida Law Review* 1. One of the arguments supporting the expansion of the FTC authority is based on the fact that the prohibition of monopolising conduct under section 2 of the Sherman Act is narrower that the prohibitions used, for example, in the EU, which address abuses of a dominant position. Hovenkamp (at 5) clarifies that this difference 'can become quite important when conduct is not reasonably calculated to maintain or create a monopoly but rather represents the dominant firm's attempt to use its power in some complementary or collateral market in which monopoly cannot be proven to result'. In his view, 'the FTC Act's "unfair methods of competition" seem well suited for such applications, provided that they are limited to situations in which competitive harm is likely'.

[61] FTC, 'Statement of Enforcement Principles Regarding "Unfair Methods of Competition" under Section 5 of the FTC Act' (13 August 2015) www.ftc.gov/system/files/documents/public_statements/735201/150813section5enforcement.pdf. See also Dissenting Statement of Commissioner Ohlhausen, www.ftc.gov/public-statements/2015/08/dissenting-statement-commissioner-ohlhausen-ftc-act-section-5-policy.

[62] FTC, 'Statement of Chair Lina M Khan Joined by Commissioner Rohit Chopra and Commissioner Rebecca Kelly Slaughter on the Withdrawal of the Statement of Enforcement Principles Regarding "Unfair Methods of Competition" under Section 5 of the FTC Act' (1 July 2021) www.ftc.gov/system/files/documents/public_statements/1591498/final_statement_of_chair_khan_joined_by_rc_and_rks_on_section_5_0.pdf; FTC, 'Policy Statement Regarding the Scope of Unfair Methods of Competition Under Section 5 of the Federal Trade Commission Act' (10 November 2022) https://www.ftc.gov/system/files/ftc_gov/pdf/P221202Section5PolicyStatement.pdf.

However, due to the rising number of cases of excessively priced prescription drugs, several initiatives have been taken outside the antitrust scope. As anticipated in chapter three, they include bills addressing the issue proposed before Congress and some measures have been adopted in the recent Inflation Reduction Act of 2022.[63] However, the most relevant efforts have been taken at state level, where concerns about the rising costs of drugs have led to the adoption of specific legislative measures specifically targeting 'price gouging' or 'unconscionable' price increases.[64] Such kinds of legislation include several types of laws.[65] Here, only those legislations aimed directly at regulating drug prices are considered, including price gouging, rate setting and unsupported price increase laws.

The main problem with state laws is that they are particularly exposed to challenges and have been challenged in reality, for example by industry organisations, under the dormant Commerce Clause, patent law, trade secret law, the Takings Clause, the First Amendment and the Due Process Clause.[66] Price gouging laws, generally adopted in case of price increases on necessary goods during emergency situations, have been applied to 'unconscionable' or 'excessive' prices for prescription drugs. Through this kind of legislation – also called fair pricing bills in the literature – drug manufacturers may be required to justify certain price increases or face penalties, or to provide rebates when prices exceed a

[63] HR 5376 – Inflation Reduction Act of 2022, PL 117-169 (16 August 2022).

[64] For an overview, see P FitzGerald, 'State Regulation of Generic Drug Price Gouging' (2019) 2 *Belmont Health Law Journal* Art 7; WV Padula, 'State and Federal Policy Solutions to Rising Prescription Drug Prices in the US' (2019) 22 *Journal of Health Care Law & Policy* 15; S Reed, 'Preventing Drug Price Gouging: Government Power and Initiatives' (2019) 19 *Houston Journal of Health Law & Policy* 167; MM Mello and RE Wolitz, 'Legal Strategies for Reining In "Unconscionable" Prices for Prescription Drugs' (2020) 114 *Northwestern University Law Review* 859.

[65] Mello and Wolitz, 'Legal Strategies', 873, reporting data according to which, in 2019, more than 300 bills were filed at the state level to address prescription drug costs. An updated database of this kind of initiatives is the legislative tracker provided by the National Academy for State Health Policy (NASHP) www.nashp.org/rx-legislative-tracker/. For an overview, see KL Gudiksen and JS King, 'The Burden of Federalism: Challenges to State Attempts at Controlling Prescription Drug Costs' (2019) 39 *Journal* of *Legal Medicine* 95 (identifying the following main ways state bills try to address pharmaceutical costs: (i) requiring biosimilar substitution; (ii) eliminating gag-clauses for pharmacists, preventing them from informing customers when their insurance copay or cost-sharing exceeds the price of the drug without insurance; (iii) restricting when insurers and PBMs can change formularies or require step therapy; (iv) overseeing PBMs; (v) increasing transparency in drug pricing and its impact on insurance premiums – such laws, which provide information to the public, must be distinguished from 'reporting' legislation, which provides information to regulators alone; (vi) importing drugs from other countries; (vii) prohibiting price gouging for drugs; and (viii) regulating drug prices).

[66] See Mello and Wolitz, 'Legal Strategies', 863; R Feldman, BC Rowe, R Oral, AJ Gu and K Gudiksen, 'The Patent Act and the Constitutionality of State Pharmaceutical Regulation' (2019) 45 *Rutgers Computer and Technology Law Journal* 40 (2019) (analysing takings and patent-pre-emption challenges).

certain threshold.[67] After earlier efforts made in 2005 by the District of Columbia to regulate the prices of patented medications through the Prescription Drug Excessive Pricing Act were invalidated on the grounds of the patent pre-emption clause,[68] subsequent state-level price gouging bills have typically focused on off-patent or generic drugs.[69] One of the most notable examples is HB 631, the Prohibition Against Price Gouging for Essential Off-Patent or Generic Drugs, adopted by Maryland in 2017, which addressed 'unconscionable increases', meaning an increase in the price of a prescription drug that is excessive and not justified by the cost of producing the drug or the cost of appropriate expansion of access to the drug to promote public health, resulting in patients who need the drug having no choice but to purchase the drug at the increased price because of the importance of the drug to their health, and a lack of sufficient competition in the market concerned.[70] Maryland's legislation has been challenged too. Finally, the 4th Circuit Court of Appeals held Maryland's law unconstitutional under the dormant Commerce Clause (for reaching transactions outside the state territory), whereas the vagueness argument (in violation of the Due Process Clause of the Fourteenth Amendment) was not fully litigated,[71] and in 2019 the Supreme Court denied certiorari for Maryland's appeal.[72]

Maryland's legislation – and its unsuccessful enactment – has been particularly influential on other states' efforts to introduce similar bills and has inspired

[67] Yale Global Health Justice Partnership, 'Curbing Unfair Drug Prices: A Primer for States' (2017) 6, https://law.yale.edu/sites/default/files/area/center/ghjp/documents/curbing_unfair_drug_prices-policy_paper-080717.pdf.

[68] Prescription Drug Excessive Pricing Act of 2005, DC Code Ann §§ 28-4551 to 28-4555 (LexisNexis 2001 & Suppl 2008), declared unconstitutional by *Biotechnology Industry Org v District of Columbia* 496 F3d 1362, 1374 (Fed Cir 2007). The Act prohibited drug manufacturers and licensees from selling patented medications in the District of Columbia for an excessive price, stating: 'It shall be unlawful for any drug manufacturer or licensee thereof, excluding a point of sale retail seller, to sell or supply for sale or impose minimum resale requirements for a patented prescription drug that results in the prescription drug being sold in the District for an excessive price.' The law defined an 'excessive price' by referencing prices paid in high-income foreign countries. It established a prima facie case of excessive pricing if the wholesale price of a patented medication was more than 30% higher than that medicine's price in any high-income country in which the product is protected by patents or other exclusive rights. For a comment, see S Lipski, 'Excessive Pricing and Pharmaceuticals: Why the Federal Patent Act Does Not Preempt State Regulation of Pharmaceutical Prices' (2008) 39 *University of Toledo Law Review* 913.

[69] DC Code § 28-4551 (2005); *Biotechnology v Columbia*, 1374. For a thorough analysis, see Mello and Wolitz, 'Legal Strategies', 873ff.

[70] HB 631, Gen Assembly MD (28 November 2017).

[71] After the district court dismissed the dormant Commerce Clause claim but preserved the vagueness claim, the Fourth Circuit reversed the dismissal of the dormant Commerce Clause claim and invalidated the statute on that basis. *Association for Accessible Medicines v Frosh* 887 F 3d 664, 673–74 (4th Cir 2018). According to the dormant Commerce Clause doctrine, which is a corollary of the Commerce Clause, states cannot interfere with or burden interstate commerce (which is a federal competence).

[72] *Frosh v Association for Accessible Medicines* 139 S Ct 1168 (2019). For details, see Mello and Wolitz, 'Legal Strategies', 881 (noting that 'Maryland's price gouging law remains void until it is reworked to be consistent with the Fourth Circuit's ruling. Because the vagueness argument was not fully litigated, it remains a viable basis for legal challenges to future statutes like HB 631').

imitators.[73] Different tools, which are not intended to be confined to non-patented products, are: rate-setting laws, providing 'drug affordability boards' to address unconscionable pricing by setting a cap or upper limit on the amount that public and private payers may be required to pay within a state;[74] and legislation regulating excessive or unsupported price increases (UPIs), which, although new and not yet widely adopted, impose a tax or penalty when a drug's price increases by more than a specified percentage (such as the rate of general inflation) over a defined period.[75]

Thus, efforts by states to pass legislation to address rising drug costs have been aggressively challenged by industry and the lack of a federal intervention crucially matters. There is an acknowledgement that, despite widespread recognition of the problems related to drug pricing, legislative and regulatory reform attempts have failed up to now to address the problem. Different approaches have been proposed in the literature, relying on different comparison factors, including: systems based on the cost of developing a drug; affordability-based rate-setting models; reference pricing; value-based pricing; and price capping.[76] In addition to the problems mentioned above concerning the application of state legislations to patented products, challenges based on vagueness deserve particular attention, as they reproduce the recurrent problem of what constitutes an excessive or unfairly high price, showing how defining and evaluating a 'fair' price represents the main controversial task.[77]

[73] Gudiksen and King, 'The Burden of Federalism', 111 (reporting that 16 states considered legislation in 2018 and none of these passed state legislatures, and in 2019 only five states considered similar bills).

[74] ibid 112 (reporting that in 2018, eight states – California, Florida, Maryland, Minnesota, New Jersey, New Mexico, Ohio and Rhode Island – considered such legislation and three of those states (Maryland, Minnesota and New Jersey) introduced bills based on the NASHP's Rate-Setting Model Legislation). In 2019, the NASHP legislative tracker listed 15 bills introduced in nine states. For details on the NASHP model legislation, see Mello and Wolitz, 'Legal Strategies', 883ff (clarifying that in the NASHP model legislation the determination of whether a drug's cost is excessive is not primarily made by reference to the manufacturer; rather, the primary criterion pertains to 'commercial payor, provider, and consumer costs').

[75] MM Mello and T Riley, 'To Address Drug Affordability, Grab the Low-Hanging Fruit' (*JAMA Health Forum*, 2021) https://jamanetwork.com/journals/jama-health-forum/fullarticle/2777036?widget=personalizedcontent&previousarticle=2768092 (explaining that the underlying logic of UPI laws is that, given the freedom to set launch prices, base prices represent a fair return on companies' investment in research and development, so if companies are not able to justify large price increases – for example, by presenting new evidence about the drug's clinical value or by showing that an ingredient became more expensive – most of the revenue generated from the disallowable portion of the price increase is taxed).

[76] See Mello and Wolitz, 'Legal Strategies', 888ff, 950 and 962ff; Yale Global Health Justice Partnership, 'Curbing Unfair Drug Prices' 13; G Persad, 'Pricing Drugs Fairly' (2021) 62 *William & Mary Law Review* 929, 942ff. In addition to the initiatives mentioned in this section, it should be noted that many states are adopting aggressive laws setting caps on insulin costs, as life-saving treatment, through a variety of methods. See JK Paradise, 'Insulin Federalism' (2021) 27 *Boston University Journal of Science and Technology Law* 102, 158 (arguing that it seems an appropriate and equitable public health action to cap insulin costs at the federal level). With regard to insulin, see also HR 5376 – Inflation Reduction Act of 2022, providing for a cap on monthly cost sharing for insulin products, as mentioned in ch 3.

[77] On void-for-vagueness challenges, see Mello and Wolitz, 'Legal Strategies', 888ff.

IV. THE ROLE OF ANTITRUST ENFORCEMENT ON EXCESSIVE DRUG PRICES

Regulation, where in place, rather than antitrust, has typically dealt with pharmaceutical pricing. In general, price regulation, whose effects in pharmaceutical markets have been the subject of extensive economic literature,[78] is inherently distant from and often in contrast with antitrust policy, as it is at odds with the idea of the free formation of prices as a result of the interaction between supply and demand, which is deemed essential for the efficient functioning of the markets and the allocation of resources.[79] The increasing attention and concern for high prices and price hikes of prescription drugs has fuelled the thinking on whether and how competition policy may play a fundamental role in this area. Nonetheless, the traditional view supporting the intervention of antitrust as a last resort relies on sound arguments.

This issue concerns not only the European context, but also the US one, as seen in the previous section. In the EU, the difficulties in applying an appropriate methodology for excessive prices appear particularly challenging in the pharmaceutical context. To date, the main experience has dealt with off-patent products, and a resurgence of excessive pricing prohibition has been observed within the EU. The willingness of the Commission to apply this prohibition, although exploitative abuse cases fall outside its enforcement priorities in the Guidance Paper,[80] has led to questioning whether this could indicate a shift towards a 'fairness' agenda.[81] In reality, it still remains to be seen whether and to what extent such a resurgence will effectively spread.

Aspen is significant not only as an excessive pricing case, but also as recalling a sort of regulatory gaming behaviour. Further insights can be found in the national investigations in *Aspen* and *Pfizer/Flynn Pharma*. With regard to the former, under Italian rules, if the negotiations on prices between the regulator and the pharmaceutical company concerned are unsuccessful, drugs are then classified in the class of non-reimbursable ones, ie they are delisted: in other words, the Italian Medicines Agency (AIFA) was held hostage to the negotiation strategy enacted by the pharmaceutical company and turned out to have no adequate bargaining power to counter it. In *Pfizer/Flynn*, the antiepilepsy

[78] See, eg MK Kyle, 'Pharmaceutical Price Controls and Entry Strategies' (2007) 89 *Review of Economics and Statistics* 88; PM Danzon and LW Chao, 'Does Regulation Drive Out Competition in Pharmaceutical Markets?' (2000) 43 *Journal of Law and Economics* 311.

[79] See, eg M Motta, *Competition Policy: Theory and Practice* (Cambridge, Cambridge University Press, 2004) 69.

[80] European Commission, 'Guidance on the Commission's Enforcement Priorities in Applying Article 82 of the EC Treaty to Abusive Exclusionary Conduct by Dominant Undertakings' (Guidance Paper) [2009] OJ C45/7.

[81] N Dunne, 'Fairness and the Challenge of Making Markets Work Better' (2021) 84 *MLR* 230, 256–57. Recently, the Commission took another excessive pricing decision in gas market (*Upstream gas supplies in Central and Eastern Europe* (Case AT.39816) [2018] Commission Decision).

medicine Epanutin (based on phenytoin sodium) was de-branded and this, according to the rules applicable at the time of the infringement, permitted the pharmaceutical companies to put the medicines outside the statutory price control. It is worth noting that in the UK the loophole in the sectoral regulation has been addressed: the Health Service Medical Supplies (Costs) Act 2017 was introduced to give the government additional powers to control the price of drugs, particularly unbranded generic products, and to prevent manufacturers from de-branding in order to significantly increase prices.[82]

In this context, it is clear that antitrust intervention has served as an aid to regulators rather than acting in conflict with them, and there is no room for possible concerns about overlapping or trespassing by competition agencies in their area of competence. Given the EU pharmaceutical regulatory system, with its extensive price regulation based on national public policy, regulatory failure that results in unfairly high prices could be properly addressed through regulatory intervention, including remedying the existing failure or providing alternative bargaining strategies between the buyer and the seller.[83] In this perspective, antitrust intervention, where needed, might work as a pathway to help regulation address the failures, fostering effective coordination between competent agencies.[84]

Where a system of price regulation is not in place, as in the US, one might ask whether a sporadic antitrust intervention could help avoid more invasive measures. On the one side, it has been argued that the implementation of antitrust enforcement may allow regulators to not resort to more intrusive regulatory schemes, such as more general pharmaceutical price regulation, which may carry larger risks to innovation and entrepreneurial freedom.[85] However, the possible adoption of price control mechanisms and specific legislative measures addressing high drug prices are already present in the political agenda, as seen above. On the other side, the prosecution of exploitative conduct under US antitrust enforcement would require a clear indication of a rethinking of the traditional stance excluding exploitation through high prices as an antitrust offence.

[82] Health Service Medical Supplies (Costs) Act 2017, s 4, amending NHS Act 2006, s 262(2). In Italy, at the time of the investigation, the applicable rule was Article 6 of CIPE resolution No 3/2001. However, the loophole at issue has not been addressed yet, although a recent reform concerning the negotiation process and establishing new criteria for pricing and reimbursement entered into force in 2021 (Decree 2 August 2019 'Criteri e modalità con cui l'Agenzia italiana del farmaco determina, mediante negoziazione, i prezzi dei farmaci rimborsati dal Servizio sanitario nazionale').

[83] See Calcagno et al, 'Economics of Excessive Pricing', 171.

[84] See Monti, 'Excessive Pricing', 16–17. It is also worth mentioning that in Italy in 2017 the ICA and the AIFA signed a memorandum of understanding in order to strengthen cooperation in areas of mutual interest, including negotiations with pharmaceutical companies, and also to make the ICA duly informed about possible business conducts of antitrust relevance (Procollo d'intesa, www.aifa.gov.it/-/aifa-e-agcm-firmano-protocollo-d-intesa-a-tutela-della-salute-pubblica). See also OECD, 'Excessive Pricing', 25 and 31 (affirming that, among the various tools that competition authorities have at their disposal, important ones are market studies, which would help competition agencies to understand market developments and fine-tune the most appropriate response, and advocacy for the adoption of appropriate regulation or the adoption of initiatives in tandem with sectoral regulators).

[85] First, 'Excessive Drug Pricing', 739–40.

V. CONCLUDING REMARKS

This chapter has analysed the issue of high drug pricing and the possible roles and interface between regulation and antitrust enforcement in this area through the recent experience in the EU and the US concerning exponential price increases for off-patent drugs. Both types of intervention face various issues. The European *Aspen* case provides an interesting example of regulatory gaming behaviours in the context of an exploitative abuse.

A final consideration should be given to the case of patented drugs. Despite the fact that no cases of excessive pricing concerning medicines covered by patents have been prosecuted to date, the potential widening of the scope of competition enforcement against unfair prices to patented drugs requires careful consideration. In recent years, some authors have suggested that the existence of patent protection should not be seen as a reason to absolutely exclude the enforcement of excessive pricing prohibition, which might take the incentives for innovation into account.[86] According to this approach, this can be done by looking at the ex ante probability of success, which is especially important in the pharmaceutical context, where only a limited percentage of products reach the market. It has been argued that the cost of developing and approving a new product must include a risk factor, ie the R&D that goes into the discovery and refinement of the product, including the costs inherent to clinical assessment and potential failures to develop a successful drug.[87]

However, generally, antitrust intervention in situations where innovative efforts are at stake is excluded, also in compliance with the screens mentioned above.[88] In addition to the main argument relating to the likely detrimental effects on investments and the development of innovative products, it is affirmed that estimating the cost of developing and bringing a new medicine to the market may be a very complex exercise, and no widely accepted methodological

[86] C Fonteijn, I Akker and W Sauter, 'Reconciling Competition and IP Law: The Case of Patented Pharmaceuticals and Dominance Abuse' (2018) ACM Working Paper, 14–15, https://www.acm.nl/sites/default/files/documents/2018-03/acm-working-paper-reconciling-competition-and-ip-law-2018-03-07.pdf.

[87] Abbott, 'Excessive Pharmaceutical Prices', 303 (also criticising, at 316–17, the *United Brands* test). Moreover, some authors propose methodological adjustments, arguing that applying the prohibition on excessive prices, eg above the quality-adjusted life year (QALY), would not necessarily harm investment incentives but rather improve and drive investment decisions on socially relevant products. See Fonteijn et al, 'Reconciling Competition', 14–15.

[88] See, eg Fletcher and Jardine, 'Towards an Appropriate Policy', 541–42; R O'Donoghue and J Padilla, *The Law and Economics of Art 102 TFEU*, 3rd edn (Oxford, Hart Publishing, 2020) 742. In general, on the application of Art 102(a) to patented products, see SD Anderman and H Schmidt, 'EC Competition Policy and IPRs' in SD Anderman (eds), *The Interface between Intellectual Property Rights and Competition Policy* (Cambridge, Cambridge University Press, 2007) 37, 52ff.

standard exists.[89] In general, as excessive pricing cases are by their nature hard to build and often difficult to prosecute, it is also unlikely that a case concerning a patented product would succeed in court.

In any case, antitrust intervention, which operates ex post and includes risks of errors, can work only as a fact-specific tool in limited circumstances rather than be a viable solution to high price increases in the pharmaceutical markets. A very cautious approach in considering whether to further expand antitrust enforcement on exploitative conduct concerning drug prices is appropriate.

[89] Calcagno et al, 'Economics of Excessive Pricing', 170. The authors have noted, especially with regard to the assessment of excessive profitability, that many costs in the pharmaceutical industry are shared across multiple products and allocating these costs to specific products can be complicated. Moreover, they add that: (i) the profitability of any given product within a company's portfolio depends on what countries it is sold in, the size of the treatment population and price regulation; and (ii) product development in the pharmaceutical industry requires high levels of profitability on successful products to attract appropriate investments.

Part III

8

Further Interactions: Pharmaceutical Markets, Intellectual Property and Human Rights

I. THE RIGHT TO HEALTH AND ACCESS TO MEDICINES AND THE RELATIONSHIP WITH INTELLECTUAL PROPERTY RIGHTS: AN OVERVIEW

HIGH PRICES FOR prescription drugs are a crucial concern around the globe. As access to medicines is a fundamental element of the right to health, this issue is the subject of urgent debate with regard to developing and least developed countries (LDCs), which typically lack both the ability to produce the drugs on their own and the bargaining power to buy them at affordable prices. However, in a different way, it also concerns developed countries, in particular in those cases where patients cannot afford life-saving medications, and in general with regard to public expenditure funded by citizens' taxes. In such countries, controversies regarding pricing of prescription drugs are focused on identifying the appropriate tools and the competent actors to implement them.

In this context, most efforts are directed towards government regulation. At the same time, much criticism is addressed to intellectual property (IP) law, and attempts to employ competition rules are gaining ground in the overall discussion. Hence, this is another area where intersections between legal disciplines deserve attention, ultimately including the nexus with the right to health, which distinguishes pharmaceutical markets from others.

The relationship between patents and the right to health is a controversial one. Recurrent arguments in the debate on this issue revolve around criticism of the negative impact of patent law on the right to health and on interventions aimed at limiting the remit and scope of patents on the basis of human rights law.[1]

[1] In general, see RE Gold, 'Patents and Human Rights: A Heterodox Analysis' (2012) 41 *Journal of Law, Medicine and Ethics* 185, 186 (identifying three broad approaches to the conceptualisation of the relationship between patent rights and human rights: (i) the 'subjugation approach', which states that when patent rights and human rights conflict, human rights considerations should trump patent rights; (ii) the 'integrated approach', which views patents as a human right; and (iii) the 'coexistence approach', which asserts that patent law and human rights law are distinct but share a basic concern in defining the optimal amount of patent protection required to incentivise and practise socially useful innovation).

Access to patented medicines is the pivotal issue that clearly embodies the clash between human rights and intellectual property. Patent protection is deemed to adversely affect access to medicines first by increasing the cost of pharmaceuticals and thus limiting their availability to individuals unable to afford the prices charged by patent owners, and second by channelling private firms to research treatments for diseases prevalent in developed countries, which represent more lucrative markets. On the one side, the idea of denying or restricting life-saving drugs to people suffering from life-threatening or debilitating illnesses has been defined as 'anathema to all notions of morality'.[2] On the other side, the fundamental role of IP law in incentivising and preserving risky and costly innovative research, without which it is doubtful the private sector would have invested much in the discovery or development of medicines, is acknowledged as such in the view of the principles and objectives of the international human rights regime.[3] Studies and debates on how to maximise both medical innovations and access to medicines have been – and still are – widespread and vigorous, and involve national governments, international organisations, academics and expert bodies, industry representatives and public interest non-governmental organisations.

The right to access to medicines forms part of the right to health and the right to life, which are well established in international law and regional human rights agreements.[4] A human right to health is identified in numerous human rights instruments. Fundamental sources include Article 25 of the Universal Declaration of Human Rights, which refers to health, well-being and medical care as the objectives of an adequate standard of living.[5]

[2] L Helfer and G Austin, *Human Rights and Intellectual Property: Mapping the Global Interface* (Cambridge, Cambridge University Press, 2011) 90.

[3] ibid.

[4] In general, see J Wolff, *The Human Right to Health* (New York, WW Norton & Company, 2012); J Tobin, *The Right to Health in International Law* (Oxford, Oxford University Press, 2012); T Murphy, *Health and Human Rights* (Oxford, Hart Publishing, 2013). For an analysis of normative evolution of human rights and a historical overview of the relationship between human rights and global health, see BM Meier, T Murphy and LO Gostin, 'The Birth and Development of Human Rights for Health' in LO Gostin and BM Meier (eds), *Foundations of Global Health and Human Rights* (Oxford, Oxford University Press, 2020). The right to health is recognised, inter alia, in Art 5(e)(iv) of the International Convention on the Elimination of All Forms of Racial Discrimination of 1965, in Arts 11.1(f) and 12 of the Convention on the Elimination of All Forms of Discrimination against Women of 1979 and in Art 24 of the Convention on the Rights of the Child of 1989. Moreover, the right to health has been proclaimed by the Commission on Human Rights in its Resolution 1989/11, as well as in the Vienna Declaration and Programme of Action of 1993 and other international instruments. It is also included in Art 10 of the Additional Protocol to the American Convention on Human Rights in the Area of Economic, Social, and Cultural Rights (the Protocol of San Salvador), Art 16 of the African Charter and Art 11 of the European Social Charter. For an overview, see J-Y Lee, *A Human Rights Framework for Intellectual Property, Innovation and Access to Medicines* (London, Routledge, 2015) 124.

[5] Universal Declaration of Human Rights (adopted 10 December 1948) UNGA Res 217 A(III).

Reference to 'the enjoyment of the highest attainable standard of health' as a fundamental right is also contained in the Constitution of the World Health Organization (WHO).[6] In addition to many national constitutions in which the right to health is set,[7] in the EU, Articles 31(1) and 35 of the EU Charter of Fundamental Rights must be mentioned.[8] The US has no formally codified right to health but has ratified, though not signed, the International Covenant on Economic, Social and Cultural Rights (ICESCR), which is the most important covenant in terms of the right to health and was sponsored by the United Nations (UN) in 1960s, together with the International Covenant on Civil and Political Rights, with the aim of articulating the human rights recognised in the Universal Declaration of Human Rights.[9] Article 12(1) ICESCR provides states parties to recognise 'the right of everyone to the enjoyment of the highest attainable standard of physical and mental health', which is also related to the progressive realisation of the right at issue. According to General Comment 14 provided by the Committee on Economic, Social and Cultural Rights, this right must be understood as 'a right to the enjoyment of a variety of facilities, goods, services and conditions necessary for the realization of the highest attainable standard of health'.[10] In detailing the 'core obligations' of states,[11] the Committee confirms the inclusion in them, inter alia, of the provision of essential drugs, as defined under the WHO Action Programme.[12] Among the elements contained

[6] Constitution of the World Health Organization, 22 July 1946, www.who.int/governance/eb/who_constitution_en.pdf.

[7] For an overview, see ED Kinney and BA Clark, 'Provisions for Health and Healthcare in the Constitutions of the Countries of the World' (2004) 37 *Cornell International Law Journal* 287.

[8] Charter of Fundamental Rights and Freedoms of the European Union [2012] OJ C326/02.

[9] See ED Kinney, 'The International Human Right to Health: What Does This Mean for Our Nation and World?' (2001) 34 *Indiana Law Review* 1457, 1465–66 (mentioning some constitutions of individual American states that expressly recognise a right to health). With regard to the right to healthcare, see D Orentlicher, 'Rights to Health Care in the United States: Inherently Unstable' (2012) 38 *American Journal of Law & Medicine* 326.

[10] Committee on Economic, Social and Cultural Rights, 'General Comment 14: The Right to the Highest Attainable Standard of Health (Art 12)', UN Doc E/C.12/2000/4 (11 August 2000), para 9 (General Comment 14).

[11] The concept of core rights is introduced because a number of human rights are subject to 'progressive realisation' (ie governments are obligated to take steps consistent with their means to realise these rights progressively). Core rights refer to the existence of an irreducible core obligation that governments are bound to fulfil. See FM Abbott, 'The "Rule of Reason" and the Right to Health: Integrating Human Rights and Competition Principles in the Context of TRIPS' in T Cottier, J Pauwelyn and E Bürgi Bonanomi (eds), *Human Rights and International Trade* (Oxford, Oxford University Press, 2005) 279, 280.

[12] See WHO, *WHO Model List of Essential Medicines* – 22nd list, 2021, www.who.int/publications/i/item/WHO-MHP-HPS-EML-2021.02. In addition, the Committee interprets the right to health to incorporate an obligation on states, inter alia, to foster medical research. See General Comment 14, para 36. With regard to the obligation to pursue research, as emphasised by the Report of the High Commissioner on Human Rights and the TRIPS Agreement, see FM Abbott, 'TRIPS and Human Rights: Preliminary Reflections' in FM Abbott, C Breining-Kaufmann and T Cottier (eds), *International Trade and Human Rights. Foundations and Conceptual Issues* (Ann Arbor, University of Michigan Press, 2001).

in this notion, accessibility in its economic dimension implies affordability for all health facilities, goods and services.[13] The affirmation of the inclusion of the right to access to life-saving medicines into the right to health has resulted from several factors, such as the spread of global pandemics including HIV/AIDS, malaria and tuberculosis, and appears in a series of statements adopted by UN bodies.[14] While the WHO list has been considered to provide the starting point for identifying the core obligations of a state in respect of essential medicines, states also have progressive obligations with regard to the provision of all effective drugs.

The precise scope of the right to access to medicines and its relationship with patent protection remains controversial. Public health interests are affected by various provisions of the 1994 Agreement on Trade-Related Aspects of Intellectual Property Rights (the TRIPS Agreement).[15] The Doha Declaration was adopted in part to address criticism and clarify the relationship of the Agreement with the right to health and the right of World Trade Organization (WTO) members to adopt measures necessary to protect public health.[16]

[13] General Comment 14, para 12. The essential elements of the right to health include availability, accessibility (in the four dimensions of non-discrimination, physical accessibility, economic accessibility and information accessibility), acceptability and quality.

[14] eg UN Declaration of Commitment on HIV/AIDS [2001] GA Res 33/2001, para 15; UN Committee on the Rights of the Child, 'General Comment No 3: HIV/AIDS and the Rights of the Child' [2003] UN Doc CRC/GC/2003/3, para 28. For further details, see Helfer and Austin, *Human Rights*, 113–15.

[15] Agreement on Trade-Related Aspects of Intellectual Property Rights, 15 April 1994, Marrakesh Agreement Establishing the World Trade Organization, Annex 1C, 1869 UNTS 299, 33 ILM 1197 (1994) (TRIPS Agreement). The enforcement of patent rights was elevated to a globally enforceable regime in 1994 when the US and European Community shifted negotiations over intellectual property from the WIPO to the WTO and linked the result of those negotiations (the TRIPS Agreement) to the new WTO dispute settlement system. As a result, any nation seeking to join the international trade club was required to accept a package deal that included strong IPRs and relative international enforcement. See D Gervais, *The TRIPS Agreement: Drafting History and Analysis*, 4th edn (London, Sweet & Maxwell, 2012); LR Helfer, 'Regime Shifting: The TRIPs Agreement and the New Dynamics of International Intellectual Property Making' (2004) 29 *Yale Journal of International Law* 1; LR Helfer, 'Regime Shifting in the International Intellectual Property System' (2009) 7 *Perspectives on Politics* 39 (clarifying that the TRIPS Agreement created tension points with both substantive and procedural dimensions in various areas – such as human rights, public health, biodiversity and plant genetic resources – that acted as catalysts for new intellectual property rules in parallel and overlapping international institutions). On the criticism of the expansion of the IP ecosystem as increasing the global divide in terms of inequality and disparities, *ex multis*, see J Braithwaite and P Drahos, *Global Business Regulation* (Cambridge, Cambridge University Press, 2000). For an in-depth analysis of the controversial relationship between international trading system and human rights, see HP Hestermeyer, *Human Rights and the WTO. The Case of Patents and Access to Medicines* (Oxford, Oxford University Press, 2007). For a wide treatment of the TRIPS Agreement in this context, see CM Ho, *Access to Medicine in the Global Economy* (Oxford, Oxford University Press, 2011) 56ff.

[16] Declaration on the TRIPS Agreement and Public Health, adopted on 14 November 2001, para 4, WT/MIN(01)/DEC/2 (20 November 2001) (Doha Declaration). See para 4, according to which 'the Agreement can and should be interpreted and implemented in a manner supportive of WTO Members' right to protect public health and, in particular, to promote access to medicines for all'. For an overview of the history and the negotiations surrounding the adoption of the TRIPS

As already mentioned in chapter two, patents are national in scope and differences among national patent laws were greater prior to the TRIPS Agreement, which binds members of the WTO to implement patent laws meeting certain minimum standards. In general, the TRIPS Agreement requires that patents must be available for all 'inventions' if they are 'new, involve an inventive step and are capable of industrial application', and considers patent protection as extending to both products and processes, thereby marking at the time an important expansion of international patent rules. Prior to the adoption of the TRIPS Agreement, approximately 50 countries did not recognise any patent protection for pharmaceuticals.[17] The TRIPS Agreement has provided a 10-year period during which LDCs were exempted from most TRIPS obligations in order to facilitate their transition to the new regime.[18] The transition period for LDC members has been extended in 2005 and 2013, and lastly in 2021 until 1 July 2034.[19] With regard to pharmaceutical products, members agreed in the Doha Declaration to extend the transitional arrangements for LDCs with respect to patents and data protection for pharmaceutical products, and further extensions have been subsequently provided up to 1 January 2033.[20] These last extensions also follow the adoption of the new UN Sustainable Development Goals, which affirm the right of developing countries to utilise TRIPS flexibilities to ensure access to medicines for all.[21]

While providing for minimum standards, the TRIPS Agreement leaves some room for WTO members to implement its provisions in different ways. The general principle is explicitly set forth in Article 1.1, according to which 'Members may, but shall not be obliged to, implement in their law more extensive protection than is required by this Agreement, provided that such protection does not contravene the provisions of this Agreement'.

The impact of the TRIPS Agreement on public health and, particularly, access to medicines has been fundamental in promoting debates and analyses on the TRIPS flexibilities, although they are also important in relation to other

Agreement and the Doha Declaration and the implications for developing countries, see FM Abbott, 'The Doha Declaration on the TRIPS Agreement and Public Health: Lighting a Dark Corner at the WTO' (2002) 5 *Journal of International Economic Law* 469; FM Abbott and JH Reichman, 'Doha Round's Public Health Legacy: Strategies for the Production and Diffusion of Patented Medicines under the Amended TRIPS Provisions' (2007) *Journal of International Economic Law* 921.

[17] See Helfer and Austin, *Human Rights and Intellectual Property*, 119ff.

[18] TRIPS, Art 66.1.

[19] Council for TRIPS, Extension of the Transition Period under Article 66.1 for Least-developed country Members (IP/C/88) 29 June 2021 (allowing LDCs to delay the implementation of the TRIPS Agreement other than the core non-discrimination provisions – Arts 3, 4 and 5 – until 1 July 2034; first extension: IP/C/40, 29 November 2005; second extension: IP/C/64, 11 June 2013).

[20] General Council WTO, WT/L/478, 12 July 2002; WT/L/971, 2 December 2015; Council for TRIPS, IP/C/73, 6 November 2015.

[21] See General Assembly of UN, 'Transforming Our World: The 2030 Agenda for Sustainable Development', Resolution adopted on 25 September 2015, A/RES/70/1, Goal 3.b.

public interests.[22] There is no agreed-upon definition of 'TRIPS flexibilities'. Since the adoption of the Doha Declaration, the concept of TRIPS flexibilities has been referenced in a vast body of literature, but also in numerous resolutions of UN agencies and bodies.[23] The flexibilities include the exemption for LDCs, but also encompass possible variations in the manner in which the provisions of the TRIPS Agreement are interpreted and implemented. In fact, there is no universal option in the use of flexibilities by each government. A taxonomy of the main public health-related TRIPS flexibilities includes, for example: flexibility in the choice of patentability criteria, including for chemical entities and biologics; compulsory licences; government use; use of competition law to address the misuse of intellectual property rights (IPRs); Bolar exception; and research or experimentation exception.[24]

Thus, the TRIPS Agreement specifies the economic exploitation rights of patent owners, which include the right to exclude others from making, using, selling, offering to sell or importing the patented invention into a country where it is protected. In addition to rules for patentability, term of protection and economic exploitation, the TRIPS Agreement contains exceptions and limitations to patents. First, Article 30 rules that WTO members may provide limited exceptions to the exclusive rights conferred by a patent, provided that such exceptions 'do not unreasonably conflict with a normal exploitation of the patent and do not unreasonably prejudice the legitimate interests of the

[22] In accordance with WIPO, the term 'flexibilities' means that there are 'different options through which TRIPS obligations can be transposed into national law so that national interests are accommodated and yet TRIPS provisions and principles are complied with'. See WIPO, 'CDIP/5/4 Rev – Patent Related Flexibilities in the Multilateral Legal Framework and Their Legislative Implementation at the National and Regional Levels' (18 August 2010) para 34 www.wipo.int/meetings/en/doc_details.jsp?doc_id=142068. See also WIPO, 'Constraints Faced by Developing Countries and Least Developed Countries (LDCs) in Making Full Use of Patent Flexibilities and Their Impacts on Access to Affordable Especially Essential Medicines for Public Health Purposes in Those Countries: Supplement to Document SCP/26/5' (20 November 2017) www.wipo.int/edocs/mdocs/scp/en/scp_27/scp_27_6.pdf. According to WIPO, the TRIPS flexibilities may be grouped as follows: (i) the application of the customary rules of interpretation of public international law, in particular, reading each provision of the TRIPS Agreement in the light of its objective and purpose (eg interpretation of Art 30 with respect to exceptions to patent rights); (ii) each member's range of options to interpret and apply explicit, non-defined expressions in the TRIPS Agreement in line with the general rules of treaty interpretation as applied in WTO dispute settlement practice; (iii) each member's freedom to choose whether and how it implements explicit options (permissive provisions) in the TRIPS Agreement (eg rules for the grant of compulsory licences, establishment of exhaustion regime); and (iv) each member's freedom to determine matters on which the TRIPS Agreement is silent (eg the grounds for compulsory licences or procedural aspects related to patent prosecution which are not included in the TRIPS Agreement).

[23] On the topic, see also CM Correa, 'Interpreting the Flexibilities under the TRIPS Agreement' in CM Correa and RM Hilty (eds), *Access to Medicines and Vaccines* (Cham, Springer 2022) 1, 4 and the documents cited therein.

[24] ibid 7–8 (referring to South Centre, 'A Public Health Approach to Intellectual Property Rights: Public Health Related Flexibilities in the TRIPS Agreement' https://ipaccessmeds.southcentre.int/wp-content/uploads/2018/12/Public-Health-Related-Flexibilities-in-the-TRIPSAgreement.pdf).

patent owner, taking account of the legitimate interests of third parties'.[25] Second, Article 31 TRIPS is widely understood to refer to compulsory licences, although it does not adopt this terminology, thereby permitting governments to issue tools that authorise the use of a patented product or process without the patent owner's consent but subject to the payment of 'adequate remuneration'.

Some scholars have elaborated on the role of competition rules relying on TRIPS provisions to deal with anti-competitive practices both in general and specifically in the pharmaceutical sector, considering that the TRIPS Agreement provides WTO members with substantial discretion in the development and application of competition law to arrangements and conduct in the field of IPRs.[26] As mentioned above, competition law is part of the flexibility tools of the IP system.[27] The TRIPS Agreement recognises the balancing role of competition law[28] and does not prescribe substantive rules, but just states that WTO members acknowledge the right of governments to use competition law to restrain potential excesses. Articles 8, 31(k) and 40 are usually referred to as the provisions of the TRIPS Agreement addressing competition.[29] Article 8(2) acknowledges the right of members to act against abuse of IPRs, provided such action is consistent with the provisions of the Agreement. Article 40 is a more detailed provision that refers to anti-competitive licensing practices or conditions and provides that, consistently with the other TRIPS provisions, members may specify in their legislation licensing practices or conditions that may in particular cases constitute an abuse of IPRs having an adverse effect on competition in the relevant market and adopt appropriate measures to prevent or control such practices (which may include, for example, exclusive grant-back conditions, conditions preventing challenges to validity and coercive package

[25] With regard to Art 30, two provisions of Canada's patent law have been the subject of a WTO decision (*Canada – Patent Protection of Pharmaceutical Products*, WTO, WT/DS114/R (17 March 2000)). Such provisions were adopted by Canada to encourage the prompt marketing of generic drugs, and specifically: (i) permitted generic drug producers to use patented pharmaceuticals to obtain regulatory approval of generic medicines before the patent term expired; and (ii) authorised the stockpiling of generic drugs during the patent term so that the drugs could be released immediately after the expiration of the patent. The WTO panel interpreted the patent exceptions clause as having three distinct and cumulative requirements and held that the regulatory review exception, but not the stockpiling exception, was consistent with the TRIPS Agreement. On this topic, see R Howse, 'The Canadian Generic Medicines Panel: A Dangerous Precedent in Dangerous Times' (2000) 3 *Journal of World Intellectual Property* 493.

[26] Abbott, 'The "Rule of Reason" and the Right to Health', 286–87.

[27] M Bakhoum, 'Intellectual Property Rights (IPRs), Competition Law and Excessive Pricing of Medicines' in Correa and Hilty, *Access to Medicines and Vaccines* 277, 279–80 (emphasising that in the case of pharmaceuticals, the effectiveness of using competition law as a flexibility tool depends on the institutional framework of each country and that TRIPS competition-related provisions may also be used as an access-to-medicines tool).

[28] FM Abbott, 'Health and Intellectual Property Rights' in GL Burci and B Toebes (eds), *Research Handbook on Global Health Law* (Cheltenham, Edward Elgar, 2018) 135, 151.

[29] Abbott, 'The "Rule of Reason" and the Right to Health', 284.

licensing). Article 31(k) concerns compulsory licensing: it acknowledges the use of the subject matter of a patent without the authorisation of the right holder 'to remedy a practice determined after judicial or administrative process to be anti-competitive'. It provides that in such cases members are not obliged to apply the conditions stated by Article 31(b) and (f), respectively requiring the proposed user to make efforts to obtain a licence previously to the grant of a compulsory licence and limiting the licence predominantly to the domestic market. It also states that the need to correct anti-competitive practices may be taken into account in determining the amount of remuneration.

It has been argued that the competition-related provisions of the TRIPS Agreement, while representing an essential element of balance in the Agreement itself, leave important questions unanswered. As they do not define the evaluative standard to be employed and leave competition policy to be addressed in domestic law, some authors have stressed that a broader approach might have been more effective in putting the provisions to use and also avoid potential international coordination problems.[30] According to this view, there could be merit in a policy analysis at the multilateral level to further elucidate the relationship between competition policy and IPRs and to promote international policy coherence in this important area.[31]

[30] RD Anderson, WE Kovacic, AC Müller and N Sporysheva, 'Competition Policy, Trade and the Global Economy: Existing WTO Elements, Commitments in Regional Trade Agreements, Current Challenges and Issues for Reflection' (2018) WTO Working Paper No 2018/12; RD Anderson, AC Müller and AS Taubman, 'The WTO TRIPS Agreement as a Platform for Application of Competition Policy to the Contemporary Knowledge Economy' in RD Anderson, N Pires de Carvalho and A Taubman (eds), *Competition Policy and Intellectual Property in Today's Global Economy* (Cambridge, Cambridge University Press, 2021) 62, 69. It must be considered that the national competition laws of WTO member states have not been harmonised in the same way as their IP regimes have converged upon the standards enshrined within the TRIPS Agreement (in particular, developed countries have considerably more sophisticated competition law regimes compared to the least developed countries, which might not even have such laws in place as yet). On this point, see B Ong, 'Compulsory Licences of Pharmaceutical Patents to Remedy Anti-competitive Practices under Article 31(k) of the TRIPS Agreement: Can Competition Law Facilitate Access to Essential Medicines?' in RM Hilty and K-C Liu (eds), *Compulsory Licensing. Practical Experiences and Ways Forward*, MPI Studies on Intellectual Property and Competition Law 22 (Berlin Heidelberg, Springer-Verlag, 2015) 235, 247. See also J Berger, 'Advancing Public Health by Other Means: Using Competition Policy to Increase Access to Essential Medicines' in P Roffe and G Tansey (eds), *Negotiating Health. Intellectual Property and Access to Medicines* (London, Routledge, 2015) 181 (arguing that the TRIPS Agreement provides significant scope within which competition policy may be employed to advance a public health agenda that may be compromised if IP protection is left unchecked). See also Abbott, 'The "Rule of Reason" and the Right to Health', 297 (claiming that 'the application of competition law principles is part of an overall arsenal of useful measures to rebalance aspects of the TRIPS Agreement in favour of the right to health, but it is not likely an adequate solution in itself').

[31] See generally E Fox, 'International Antitrust: Edging Towards a Global Framework with Our Feet on the Ground' in Anderson et al, *Competition Policy and Intellectual Property in Today's Global Economy*, 809 (arguing that it would be important for the trade and competition law community together to explore further the interstices of trade, competition and intellectual property law as they are already embodied in the TRIPS Agreement). Others advocating for the strengthening of policy coherence between IP system and competition law argue that the latter is under-utilised and that,

II. COMPULSORY LICENSING

Unsurprisingly, compulsory licensing is a very controversial tool, as it precisely affects the property rationale of patent protection.[32] Unlike a voluntary licence, a compulsory one forces the patent owner to accept its use as well as a fee that is likely far less than what the owner would like to charge in a free market. Under the TRIPS Agreement, a number of procedural requirements govern the issuance of such licences. In general, prior attempts to negotiate with the patent owner for a voluntary licence are required, but this condition 'may be waived by a Member in the case of a national emergency or other circumstances of extreme urgency or in cases of public non-commercial use'.[33] Other restrictions include considering the 'individual merits' of each compulsory licence,[34] limiting the duration and scope of the licence to its authorised purpose, and enabling a court or other independent body to review the licence and the amount of the royalty awarded. Article 31(f) TRIPS provides that uses under a compulsory licence must be 'predominantly for the supply of the domestic market'. After criticism of this provision and following substantial international discussion, the TRIPS Council introduced a formal waiver of the requirement of domestic use for compulsory licensing, according to which a country can issue such a licence predominantly for export to a country in need so long as additional requirements are met.[35] The new waiver regime, which entered into force in 2017, requires that both the exporting and importing members issue compulsory licences and further requires the exporting country to pay remuneration to the patent holder. However, several WTO member states, mainly high-income

when in-built flexibilities in the TRIPS Agreement are employed to facilitate access to medicines, it could assist in ensuring expeditious measures, in particular when the issuance of compulsory licensing is provided (D Matthews and O Gurgula, 'Patent Strategies and Competition Law in the Pharmaceutical Sector: Implications for Access to Medicines' (2016) 38 *European Intellectual Property Review* 661).

[32] Debates about compulsory licensing are multi-factored and their analysis is beyond the scope of this book. Suffice it to recall that one of the main critical arguments against compulsory licensing generally points to the unsuitability of this tool as a long-term solution to the problem of access to medicines due to its negative effect in terms of reduction of incentives for research and development (R&D). See, eg RA Epstein and F Scott Kieff, 'Questioning the Frequency and Wisdom of Compulsory Licensing for Pharmaceutical Patents' (2011) 78 *University of Chicago Law Review* 71.

[33] TRIPS, Art 31(b).

[34] TRIPS, Art 31(a).

[35] This is a particularly controversial clause, as countries with little or no local pharmaceutical manufacturing capacity such as LDCs may not be able to produce generic drugs themselves and such provision largely prohibits supply from another country in which a compulsory licence has been granted. To address this, a system known as Paragraph 6 was implemented after Doha and Art 31bis TRIPS was introduced. This new provision was incorporated in August 2003, and came into force in January 2017 (see WTO, Decision of the General Council, 'Implementation of Paragraph 6 of the Doha Declaration on the TRIPS Agreement and Public Health', 1 September 2003, WT/L/540 and corr 1). For an analysis of the 2003 waiver and its negotiating history, see FM Abbott, 'The WTO Medicines Decision: World Pharmaceutical Trade and the Protection of Public Health' 99 *American Journal of International Law* 317 (2005). In general, on Art 31bis, see Ho, *Access to Medicine in the Global Economy*, 195ff.

countries, including the United States and EU Member States, opted out from the Article 31bis mechanism, and undertook not to make use of the system to import generic pharmaceuticals manufactured under compulsory licence elsewhere.

The effective resort to compulsory licensing has been limited in practice by burdens included in the provisions mentioned above and further requirements deriving from subsequent regional and bilateral free trade agreements (so-called TRIPS-plus agreements)[36] on the one side, and by criticism from foreign countries as well as retaliation from pharmaceutical firms towards states that have used this tool on the other side.[37]

Compulsory licensing is an issue that is debated not only at the international level, but also at the national one. In TRIPS-related debates on compulsory licensing, the goal is focused on lessening the negative impact of patent rights on public health in low- and middle-income countries. However, it has been argued that since the Agreement was adopted, there has been growing awareness that compulsory licensing can be a valuable instrument for wealthy countries with mature patent systems too.

It should be noted that most countries have inserted compulsory licences into their IP laws, providing different grounds for granting them.[38] Article 5 of the Paris Convention provides compulsory licensing to prevent patent abuse.[39] In the EU, there is no EU-wide compulsory licensing mechanism, except for the specific regime provided for in Regulation (EC) 816/2006 concerning the manufacture of pharmaceutical products for export to countries with public

[36] 'TRIPS Plus' treaties contain more expansive IP protection rules than those found in the TRIPS Agreement. The US and EU have negotiated such treaties with developing nations to expand IP protection rules at a faster pace than is possible within the WTO. See J-F Morin and J Surbeck, 'Mapping the New Frontier of International IP Law: Introducing a TRIPs Plus Dataset' (2020) 19 *World Trade Review* 109.

[37] R Eisenberg, 'Intellectual Property and Public Health' in R Dreyfuss and J Pila (eds), *The Oxford Handbook of Intellectual Property Law* (Oxford, Oxford University Press, 2018) 931, 955–56.

[38] O Gurgula and WH Lee, 'COVID-19, IP and Access: Will the Current System of Medical Innovation and Access to Medicines Meet Global Expectations?' (2021) 17 *Journal of Generic Medicines* 61, 64 (specifying that the typical grounds include the following: (i) market demand not sufficiently satisfied; (ii) exploitation of patent rights violating competition law (eg excessive prices); (iii) patentees' abuse of their exclusive rights; (iv) public interest (eg health, environment, economic development, national security); and (v) dependent patents (eg technical improvement). For a comparative study on compulsory licensing, see Hilty and Liu, *Compulsory Licensing*. See also J Tudor, 'Compulsory Licensing in the European Union' (2013) 4 *George Mason Journal of International Commercial Law* 222.

[39] The Paris Convention, Art 5 (WIPO, Paris Convention for the Protection of Industrial Property, 828 UNTS 303, Art 5.A(2)) provides that 'Each country of the Union shall have the right to take legislative measures providing for the grant of compulsory licences to prevent the abuses which might result from the exercise of the exclusive rights conferred by the patent, for example, failure to work'. For an analysis of the relationship between the TRIPS Agreement and the Paris Convention, see S Frankel and JC Lai, 'Recognised and Appropriate Grounds for Compulsory Licences: Reclaiming Patent Law's Social Contract' in Hilty and Liu, *Compulsory Licensing*, 149, 153ff (clarifying that other than incorporating the Paris Convention, the TRIPS Agreement does not expressly refer to the ground of failure to work or insufficient working, but Art 31 TRIPS implicitly provides other grounds for compulsory licences).

health problems.[40] At the national level, many states have typically included specific provisions on compulsory licensing. However, in practice, the use of compulsory licences is very rare.[41] As one of the few examples, in the pharmaceutical sector in Germany, a case involving the grant of a compulsory licence was decided by the Federal Patent Court in 2016, and then confirmed by the Federal Court of Justice, citing the urgent public interest of patients and the health risks associated with the potential nonavailability of the drug.[42]

The US Patent Act does not contain a provision introducing compulsory licensing. However, compulsory licences have been granted under antitrust consent decrees.[43] Two statutes allow agencies and their contractors to produce drugs without patent-holder permission: 28 USC § 1498 and the Bayh-Dole Act.[44] The former has been used many times by the US government, especially for federal programmes involving defence equipment as well as medicines, and provides 'reasonable and entire compensation' to patent holders whose inventions are used by the government or its contractors.[45] It should be noted that some scholars have proposed using section 1498 to lower drug prices in the US, such as those of hepatitis C antiviral drugs for Medicaid patients.[46] For instance, this tool was invoked in 2001, when the threat of anthrax being used as a widespread biological weapon led the government to

[40] Regulation (EC) No 816/2006 of the European Parliament and of the Council on compulsory licensing of patents relating to the manufacture of pharmaceutical products for export to countries with public health problems [2006] OJ L157/1.

[41] For an overview on the effective use of TRIPS flexibilities, including compulsory licensing, see EF 't Hoen, J Veraldi, B Toebes and HV Hogerzeil, 'Medicine Procurement and the Use of Flexibilities in the Agreement on Trade-Related Aspects of Intellectual Property Rights, 2001–2016' (2018) 96 *Bulletin of the World Health Organization* 185. It should be noted that a particular case occurred in Italy, where, in 2017, due to the high price of hepatitis C medicines, the government granted its citizens the right to import more affordable generic versions for their personal use (see Ministry of Health, circular of 23 March 2017 clarifying that the ministerial decree of 11 February 1997 must be interpreted as the lack of a valid therapeutic alternative, as a precondition to request the importation of a drug, may also occur when a similar medicinal product duly authorised in Italy is available but is excessively expensive).

[42] BGH, judgment of 11 July 2017, ref: X ZB 2/17, GRUR 2017, 1017 – *Raltegravir*. Before this case, there was only one case in which the Federal Patent Court granted a compulsory licence, but this decision was reversed by the Federal Court of Justice (BGH, judgment of 5 December 1995, ref: X ZR 26/92, GRUR 1996, 190 – *Polyferon*). This case also related to pharmaceuticals.

[43] For an overview, see FM Scherer and J Watal, 'Competition Policy and Intellectual Property: Insights from Developed Country Experience' in Anderson et al, *Competition Policy and Intellectual Property*, 396, 403ff.

[44] See, eg CV Chien, 'Cheap Drugs at What Price to Innovation: Does the Compulsory Licensing of Pharmaceuticals Hurt Innovation?' (2003) 18 *Berkeley Technology Law Journal* 853, 875. The government may also facilitate drug production by utilising the Defense Production Act (PL 81-774, 50 USC §4501ff) to acquire raw materials and obtain access to manufacturing facilities.

[45] The 'government use' provision is a form of governmental immunity from patent claims: under it, patent holders can demand royalties but cannot stop the government from producing the medicine or allowing others (eg generic manufacturers) to produce or import the medicine.

[46] See A Kapczynski and AS Kesselheim, '"Government Patent Use": A Legal Approach to Reducing Drug Spending' (2016) 15 *Health Affairs* 791 (acknowledging that the profits earned by pharmaceutical companies would diminish in cases where the government use provision is deployed, but would still ensure a reasonable return on investment as long as there were no sizeable errors in

seek to stockpile the antibiotic ciprofloxacin (Cipro) as treatment. On that occasion, the Secretary of Health and Human Services threatened to break the Bayer patents on ciprofloxacin in order to import less expensive generic copies for US government stockpiles to treat anthrax poisoning. In the end, this government threat caused Bayer to agree to cut its prices considerably. The federal government had previously relied on this provision numerous times to procure cheaper generic drugs in the 1960s (eg for the antibiotic tetracycline). However, the resort to government patent use for pharmaceuticals faces numerous practical and legal hurdles, the most challenging of which are non-patent exclusivities.[47]

With regard to the second provision, the Bayh-Dole Act provides that in case of patents granted on inventions developed with the use of government funds, the government retains the ability to 'march in' if the patented technology is not made available to the public on reasonable terms. It should be noted that this option is relevant in the pharmaceutical context only if there is a formal government interest in all of the relevant Food and Drug Administration (FDA)-listed patents and the company at issue does not also hold some of its own patents that could independently allow it to block generic entry.[48] To date, this tool has never been used.

Instruments of the compulsory licensing kind are, of course, an extreme option, and this is also the reason why the use of such tool is very sporadic and generally only considered under very limited, extraordinary circumstances. One possible use of compulsory licensing in high-income countries is as a price negotiation tool.[49] Further thoughts on this issue have recently been raised due

the estimates of risk or of R&D costs; to avoid this, courts can compel disclosure of information on R&D costs and risks, which can be used to fine-tune the amount of royalties awarded). See also A Kapczynski, 'Realizing Public Rights Through Government Patent Use' (2021) 49 *Journal of Law, Medicine & Ethics* 34; H Brennan, A Kapczynski, CH Monahan and Z Rizvi, 'A Prescription for Excessive Drug Pricing: Leveraging Government Patent Use for Health' (2016) 18 *Yale Journal of Law and Technology* 275.

[47] See RE Wolitz, AS Kesselheim and JJ Darrow, 'Government Patent Use to Promote Public Health in the United States: Overcoming Nonpatent Exclusivities' (2022) 8 *American Journal of Public Health* 1110. The authors mention (at 1111) two significant examples where discussions on the possible application of government patent use took place: (i) after sofosbuvir (Sovaldi) for the hepatitis C virus was first approved in 2013, its initial price was set at $84,000 for a 12-week course of treatment; then, by 2016, competition led the prices that US private payors negotiated for drugs in this class to decline by up to 85%; (ii) the FDA approved remdesivir (Veklury) for COVID-19 in October 2020 and the price was set at $3120 for a five-day course of therapy; by January 2022, alternative COVID-19 medicines became available at lower costs. In both cases, operation of the five-year new drug Hatch-Waxman exclusivity would have been a possible sticking point if the government had decided to manufacture or procure products in the absence of the patent holder's authorisation. More recently, access concerns have surfaced relating to Merck's new COVID-19 antiviral drug molnupiravir, which received FDA emergency use authorisation in December 2021.

[48] Kapczynski and Kesselheim, 'Government Patent Use', 794 (arguing, moreover, that historically there has been some aversion in considering the use of march-in rights on the ground of drug pricing, due to the idea that reasonable terms cover only product availability).

[49] KB Son, 'Importance of the Intellectual Property System in Attempting Compulsory Licensing of Pharmaceuticals: A Cross-Sectional Analysis' (2019) 15 *Global Health* 42.

to the rising cost of prescription drugs and the excessive pricing cases mentioned in chapter seven of this book.[50] Moreover, new attention has been given due to the COVID-19 pandemic, with the debate on the appropriate instrument to use to manage the emergency questioning the role of compulsory licensing and an IP waiver to grant access to vaccines.[51]

Finally, this is a classical topic in the interface between IP and competition rules. The issue has been the subject of a number of cases concerning the unilateral refusal to supply patented technology in EU and US antitrust practice. Irrespective of the requirements of patent law, the non-voluntary grant of a licence may result from competition law enforcement. This is particularly the case if a refusal to grant a licence or the enforcement of the patent constitutes an abuse of a dominant position or an unfair restraint or discrimination on the part of a dominant undertaking. Very briefly, the academic debate has seen two main positions: on the one side are the advocates for introducing more competition policy considerations into the patent system itself; on the other side are those who seek to defend patent exclusivity against the application of antitrust laws that would result in imposing licensing duties on the patentee where that patentee is market dominant.[52] In particular, when a competition authority or a court imposes a duty to supply or license, which is the usual remedy in a unilateral refusal to license case, it overrides patent rights to exclude and is thus a direct affront to patent protection.[53] Looking back at the pharmaceutical sector, as mentioned above, there have been a few cases in which compulsory licensing has been used for antitrust purposes.[54] In the contemporary debate on

[50] It should be noted that in Belgium a legislative proposal was submitted by parliamentary members aimed at expanding the existing system of compulsory licensing in cases of relevant disproportion between sales prices and costs of production. For details, see the report commissioned by the Committee for Health and Equal Opportunities of the Federal Chamber of Representatives: E Van Zimmeren, T Minssen, L Paemen, W Van Dyck, J Luyten, R Janssens, L Barbier, S Simoens, C Pouppez, I Cleemput and I Vinck, 'Compulsory Licensing for Expensive Medicines' (2022) Belgian Health Care Knowledge Centre (KCE) Reports 356, D/2022/10.273/35.

[51] See, eg B Kianzad and J Wested, '"No-One Is Safe until Everyone Is Safe" – Patent Waiver, Compulsory Licensing and COVID-19' (2021) 5 *European Pharmaceutical Law Review* 71. In the case of COVID-19 vaccines, compulsory licensing of trade secrets in addition to that of patents and of the waiver has been discussed (see, eg O Gurgula and J Hull, 'Compulsory Licensing of Trade Secrets: Ensuring Access to COVID-19 Vaccines via Involuntary Technology Transfer' (2021) 16 *Journal of Intellectual Property Law & Practice* 1242).

[52] In general, see H Ullrich, 'Mandatory Licensing under Patent Law and Competition Law: Different Concerns, Complementary Roles' in Hilty and Liu, *Compulsory Licensing*, 333, 336, 357 and the bibliography cited therein. See also T Cheng, *The Patent–Competition Interface in Developing Countries* (Oxford, Oxford University Press, 2021) 95ff.

[53] Cheng, *The Patent–Competition Interface in Developing Countries*, 95.

[54] Among the cases, the Italian Competition Authority (ICA) found an abuse of a dominant position through the refusal by the multinational pharmaceutical company Merck to grant to Dobfar, a chemical–pharmaceutical company, a licence to produce the active ingredient needed for the manufacture of certain drugs and ordered Merck, by means of an interim measure, to grant the licence (ICA, *Merck – Principi Attivi* [2005] decision A364; the interim measure was confirmed upon appeal by the administrative court of first instance TAR Lazio 7 March 2006, No 1713).

the responsiveness of antitrust enforcement in this sector, proposals to consider stringent remedies have been put forward; according to this view, resorting to robust instruments such as compulsory licences by competition authorities would be justified by the unacceptability of non-ethical behaviour in the health-care sector.[55]

III. CONCLUDING REMARKS

The innovation–access trade-off is a dominant theme in discussions on patent law, health policy and human rights. This chapter has provided an overview on the main relevant issues at the intersection of IP rules and human rights at the international level. Such rules are not analysed *in toto*, as only those aspects and rules in the TRIPS Agreement which may be affected by the most relevant intersections mentioned above are highlighted.

Public health considerations have been put forward as a powerful argument for giving governments flexibility in the implementation of exclusionary rights to medicines. Among the instruments available to governments, compulsory licensing has gained attention, but very limited application in practice. Both patent and antitrust policy hold strong arguments against compulsory licensing of IPRs. Most compulsory licences that have been awarded in the past were granted in developing countries faced with limited access to many medicines. Only a few examples exist where compulsory licensing has been granted for health reasons in high-income countries; these are not necessarily related to high prices, but rather to the availability of the medicines and shortages.

Whether changes in the approach towards compulsory licensing will be implemented remain to be seen. However, it should be noted that the issue is under consideration in the EU.

As part of the policy response to the COVID-19 pandemic, in its recent IP Action Plan, the European Commission affirmed the need to ensure that effective systems for issuing compulsory licences are in place, to be used as a means of last resort and a safety net, when all other efforts to make IP available have failed.[56] Thus the Commission has called on Member States to: (i) ensure that the tools they have are as effective as possible (for example, by putting in place fast-track procedures for issuing compulsory licences in emergency situations); and (ii) implement stronger co-ordination in this area, to avoid distortive effects

[55] W Sauter, 'Towards Responsive Enforcement of EU Antitrust in Pharmaceuticals' in W Sauter, M Canoy and J Mulder (eds), *EU Competition Law and Pharmaceuticals* (Cheltenham, Edward Elgar, 2022) 246, 254 (arguing that in the context of the pharmaceutical sector, compulsory licensing based on healthcare law is a significant sanction and 'would go to the root of the competitive issue by facilitating market entry at the expense of the incumbent').

[56] European Commission, 'Making the Most of the EU's Innovative Potential. An Intellectual Property Action Plan to Support the EU's Recovery and Resilience' (Communication) COM/2020/760 final.

on innovation and trade (for example, on the duration of and royalties on any such licences). The European Parliament, in its resolution of November 2021, therefore called on the Commission to analyse and explore possible options to ensure effectiveness and better co-ordination of compulsory licensing in the EU, and the Council conclusions on IP policy of June 2021 confirmed that the EU stood ready to discuss the flexibilities provided for in Articles 31 and 31bis of the TRIPS Agreement.[57] It also confirmed the need to explore possible IP tools and options to better coordinate the management of cross-border crises. In July 2022, the Commission has launched a consultation on the issue with a view of presenting an initiative for an EU framework on compulsory licensing in 2023.

[57] European Parliament, 'An Intellectual Property Action Plan to Support the EU's Recovery and Resilience' (Resolution) 2021/2007(INI); Council of the EU, 'Council Conclusions on Intellectual Property Policy' (18 June 2021) 9932/21.

9

Public Health and Public Interest in Competition Law

I. PUBLIC HEALTH AND COMPETITION LAW

THE RELATIONSHIP BETWEEN competition law and public health has not been investigated widely. However, different approaches to the topic and interconnections between them can be identified.

A reading of the issue may be centred on the interactions with international IP rules and human rights principles. One approach elaborates on the idea that competition law should be used as a tool for the realisation of the right to health. It is clear that access to medications concerns several areas, including pharmaceutical policy, trade, intellectual property rights (IPRs) and human rights law. It has been argued that the last of these may be seen as providing a workable framework for influencing the way in which adjudicative and legislative bodies make decisions that affect access to medicines. A rights-based approach would imply that access to medications is considered a priority to be taken into account in competition, pricing and licensing.[1] Even if the impact of human rights thinking has not yet been subjected to deep analysis, some authors have affirmed that the right to health may be a point of reference informing competition law enforcement.[2] These hints have been elaborated in a wider effort of reconceptualisation of competition law in a broader narrative, considering

[1] AE Yamin, 'Not Just a Tragedy: Access to Medications as a Right under International Law' (2003) 21 *Boston University International Law Journal* 325, 327. The author explains that from a public health perspective, access to essential drugs depends on several factors, including: rational selection and use of medicines; sustainable adequate financing; affordable prices; and reliable health and supply systems. In this context, understanding access to basic medications as a human rights issue implies that governments have not only moral or humanitarian responsibilities, but also legal obligations to undertake measures to ensure access to essential drugs.

[2] I Lianos, T Minssen and C Kollmar, 'Tackling Grand Challenges with Competition Law: Lessons from the Pandemic' in W Sauter, M Canoy and J Mulder (eds), *EU Competition Law and Pharmaceuticals* (Cheltenham, Edward Elgar, 2022) 279, 283 (arguing that 'the right to health may provide both a context to and content for the norms of competition law and could be a guideline in its enforcement'). A similar argument has been put forward with regard to the right to food (see A Darr and I Lianos, 'Hunger Games: Connecting the Right to Food and Competition Law' in I Lianos, A Ivanov and D Davis (eds), *Global Food Value Chains and Competition Law* (Cambridge, Cambridge University Press, 2022) 420, 426).

antitrust not only as an instrument for achieving economic efficiency, innovation and consumer welfare, but also as a tool to pursue further aims, as will be discussed later in this chapter.

Among the approaches to the issue, a proposal advanced in the literature argues that an interpretation of the right to health as a right to consumer protection might affect the application of competition rules. According to Abbott, since the right to health pertains to the individual, it would inform competition law to the extent of elevating consumer protection interests over industrial policy ones.[3] Abbott applies this approach to the categories of per se rules and the rule of reason, arguing that the competent authorities of each World Trade Organization (WTO) member state (including legislators) might determine which acts fall into which category, asking themselves whether there is a 'right to health' interest that would mandate a per se approach or rather a rule or reason analysis to a certain type of conduct.[4] Abbott affirms that practices that might be considered a per se unreasonable interference with the right to health might include abusive licensing, such as exclusive grant-backs and tying arrangements, but also submission of false or misleading information to regulatory authorities regarding the patent status of medicines. Moreover, he claims that the right to health may inform the rule of reason in the evaluation of potentially anti-competitive practices by taking into account the interests that are affected by the conduct and distinguishing between different forms of potentially anti-competitive conduct depending on the effect on public health.[5]

The idea that the full realisation of access to medicines may be read in the light of the maximisation of consumer welfare in the pharmaceutical sector

[3] FM Abbott, 'The "Rule of Reason" and the Right to Health: Integrating Human Rights and Competition Principles in the Context of TRIPS' in T Cottier, J Pauwelyn and E Bürgi Bonanomi, *Human Rights and International Trade* (Oxford, Oxford University Press, 2005) 279, 289.

[4] ibid 290–91. According to Abbott, developing country regulators may benefit from a comparative approach, looking to the existing practices of developed and developing countries' competition authorities, supplemented by a historical approach (ie considering how competition laws have evolved to address different phases of economic development).

[5] ibid 293. Abbott elaborates that the WTO Appellate Body has indirectly adopted a rule-of-reason approach in cases such as *European Communities – Measures Affecting Asbestos and Asbestos-Containing Products* (AB-2000-11 WT/DS135/AB/R, 12 March 2001). According to Abbott, 'the notion of protecting consumer interests in the competition law context might be "softer" than importing the human right to health. That is, governments are basically free to choose the basis of their competition policy, and might elect to pursue an industrial policy approach over a consumer protection approach. However, because the right to health is established by international law, it may be argued that competition authorities are compelled to take it into account in rule of reason analysis. This might even be seen to limit the flexibility of WTO Members in deciding whether to address anticompetitive conduct in the field of TRIPS. If the right to health demands progressive realization, and if anti-competitive conduct interferes with that path, then Members may be obligated to act' (at 294). For a critique of this view, see A Darr, 'Competition Law and Human Rights: a Complex Relationship' [2021] *Wirtschaft und Wettbewerb*, https://ssrn.com/abstract=3915662 (arguing that from a purely competition law perspective, Abbott's suggestion includes a non-exhaustive consideration of the consumer welfare standard and does not engage with the possible contradiction that may arise for competition authorities if attempts on their part to regulate the pharmaceutical sector in a way that secures the right to health results in consumers paying higher prices for these products).

relies on the sources mentioned in the previous chapter, such as Article 12 of the International Covenant on Economic, Social and Cultural Rights and General Comment 14, which could be interpreted as requiring states to protect the right to health by means of taking all necessary measures to safeguard consumers against human rights infringements by third parties, including preventing pharmaceutical companies from engaging in practices detrimental to health.[6] Patent strategies as reverse payment patent settlements and product switching, treated in Part II of this book, are recurrent examples of such types of practice used also in the literature engaging with human rights principles.[7]

Approaches grounded on human rights principles may take into consideration not only the primary responsibility of states for the right to health and access to medicines, but also the idea that such responsibility is shared with other non-state actors, including pharmaceutical companies.[8] Such views are mainly based on the UN Guiding Principles on Business and Human Rights, which were meant to effectuate the UN 'Respect, Protect and Remedy' Framework, developed by Secretary-General Ruggie and centred on three core pillars: i) States' existing obligations to respect, protect and fulfill human rights from abuse by third parties through appropriate law, policy, regulation, and adjudication; ii) the responsibility of business enterprises to respect human rights; iii) the need to provide access to effective remedies in case of breach.[9]

While not providing formally binding obligations, these Guiding Principles constitute an international standard-setting tool.[10] They must be considered together with the Guidelines advanced by the past UN Special Rapporteur on the Right to Health Paul Hunt, dealing specifically with pharmaceutical companies and access to medicines.[11] In particular, Hunt argues that patent holders have a special set of obligations or right-to-health responsibilities linked to the

[6] K Yoo, 'Interaction of Human Rights Law and Competition Law: The Right to Access to Medicines and Consumer Welfare in the US Pharmaceutical Sector' (2018) 43 *Vermont Law Review* 123, 130.

[7] ibid. See also D Matthews and O Gurgula, 'Patent Strategies and Competition Law in the Pharmaceutical Sector: Implications for Access to Medicines' (2016) 38 *European Intellectual Property Review* 661.

[8] Committee on Economic, Social and Cultural Rights, 'General Comment 14: The Right to the Highest Attainable Standard of Health (Art 12)', UN Doc E/C.12/2000/4 (11 August 2000), para 42.

[9] J Ruggie, 'Protect, Respect and Remedy: A Framework for Business and Human Rights' (2008) Report of the Special Representative of the Secretary-General on the Issue of Human Rights and Transnational Corporations and Other Business Enterprises, UN Doc A/HRC/8/5; J Ruggie, 'Guiding Principles on Business and Human Rights: Implementing the United Nations "Protect, Respect and Remedy" Framework' (2011) UN Doc No A/HRC/17/31. For a comment, see S Moon, 'Respecting the Right to Access to Medicines: Implications of the UN Guiding Principles on Business and Human Rights for the Pharmaceutical Industry' (2013) 15 *Health & Human Rights Journal* 32.

[10] See J James-Eluyode, *Corporate Responsibility and Human Rights: Global Trends and Issues* (London, Lexington Books, 2020) (discussing, at 70–72, how such guidelines set forth the ambits of the due diligence duty incurred by corporations with regard to human rights).

[11] P Hunt, 'Report of the Special Rapporteur on the Right of Everyone to the Enjoyment of the Highest Attainable Standard of Physical and Mental Health', UN General Assembly A/63/263 (2008)

legitimate expectations that society may have on a patent covering a life-saving medicine. These responsibilities are reinforced when the patented life-saving medicine benefited from research and development undertaken in publicly funded laboratories. While Ruggie's Guiding Principles focus on company responsibility to avoid causing or contributing to human rights impacts and preventing or mitigating such impacts when directly linked to their activities,[12] Lee and Hunt further elaborate on the basis of the Hunt Guidelines that companies must not only prevent or address negative impacts of their pricing and licensing policies on access to medicines, but must also do everything possible, within a viable business, to fulfil their social function and human rights responsibilities.[13] To conclude, it is worth briefly mentioning that, in addition to the the discussion over the consistency and the applicability of the principles mentioned above, the idea that special obligations may be placed on pharmaceutical companies has been envisaged by scholars in health law, business ethics and bioethics in terms of the application of a duty to rescue as a moral imperative,[14] which may be applied to donating medications or reducing prices, but also to licensing drugs to generic firms or not enforcing patent protections. This issue is also relevant in both corporate social responsibility and business and human rights fields, and is particularly topical due to the current call for sustainability practices to be prioritised by for-profit corporations.

An alternative approach considers the possibility of integrating public health and its protection into the broader narrative around sustainable development.[15] The most commonly agreed definition of sustainable development comes from the Brundtland Report of the World Commission on Environment and Development, which refers to it as 'development that meets the needs of the present without compromising the ability of future generations to meet

(Hunt Report), paras 23, 26, containing Annex 'Human Rights Guidelines for Pharmaceutical Companies in Relation to Access to Medicines' (Hunt Guidelines). See also P Hunt, 'Report of the Special Rapporteur on the Right of Everyone to the Enjoyment of the Highest Attainable Standard of Physical and Mental Health', UN General Assembly A/61/338 (2006); P Hunt, 'Report of the Special Rapporteur on the Right of Everyone to the Enjoyment of the Highest Attainable Standard of Health', Annex: Mission to GlaxoSmithKline, UN Doc No A/HRC/11/12/Add.2 (2009).

[12] Ruggie, 'Guiding Principles', principles 11 and 13.

[13] J-Y Lee and P Hunt, 'Human Rights Responsibilities of Pharmaceutical Companies in Relation to Access to Medicines' (2012) 40 *Journal of Law, Medicine & Ethics* 220, 231. For a wide discussion, see MK Land and L Nesselhauf, 'Business and Human Rights Approaches to Intellectual Property' in I Bantekas and MA Stein (eds), *The Cambridge Companion to Business and Human Rights Law* (Cambridge, Cambridge University Press, 2021) 380, 387 et seq (explaining, at 390, that the Hunt Guidelines also envision company responsibility in the competitive context, considering disputes that may arise regarding the disclosure of information relating to access to medicines, which may encompass disputes over test data or issues of cross-licensing for dependent technologies).

[14] For an analysis of such approaches, see RE Wolitz, 'A Corporate Duty to Rescue: Biopharmaceutical Companies and Access to Medications' (2019) 94 *Indiana Law Journal* 1163.

[15] See Lianos et al, 'Tackling Grand Challenges with Competition Law', 281. From a terminological point of view, 'sustainability' and 'sustainable development' are usually used interchangeably. See OECD, 'Sustainability and Competition' (2020) OECD Competition Committee Discussion Paper, www.oecd.org/daf/competition/sustainability-and-competition-2020.pdf.

their own needs'.[16] The essence of this concept is that it involves a balance between the needs of the current generation and those of future generations, taking into account environmental, societal and economic limits. The attention on the topic has been reinvigorated, as in 2015 the UN General Assembly adopted Resolution 70/1, often referred to simply as the 2030 Agenda or the UN Sustainable Development Goals (SDGs), defining broader development targets for both developed and developing countries.[17] Among those targets, good health and well-being are important SDG goals and 'access to safe, effective, quality and affordable essential medicines and vaccines for all' has been established as a specific target.[18]

The European Commission committed to implement the 2030 Agenda through its internal and external policies.[19] Sustainable development may be considered a foundational legal principle, grounded in rights and bound up with universalistic moral values.[20] Scholars envisioning this approach underline that provisions of EU Treaties – such as Articles 3(3) and 13(1) of the Treaty on European Union (TEU) and Article 7 of the Treaty on the Functioning of the European Union (TFEU) – also encompass sustainable development objectives in the light of the principle of consistency between EU policies and activities and all their goals, including competition law.[21] Following these arguments, the principles of competition should be enforced in a way that is congruent with the aims and structure of the legal system as a whole, of which competition law is a part. In other words, competition authorities and courts enforcing antitrust rules should seek to interpret the law in accordance with the broader moral and legal principles that underpin the legal system as a result of a process of 'regulatory osmosis'.[22] Moreover, in the context of the SDGs, several instruments are supposed to work in a coordinated manner in order to provide systemic responses at the national, supranational and international levels, in particular when fundamental rights are at stake. Thus, according to this view, competition law is to be seen as just one policy tool among many which must necessarily operate together with other instruments, such as IP, public procurement and pharmaceutical regulation, in view of these shared objectives.[23]

[16] UN World Commission on Environment and Development, 'Our Common Future' (1987) 43 (also known as the Brundtland Report).

[17] General Assembly of UN, 'Transforming Our World: The 2030 Agenda for Sustainable Development', Resolution adopted on 25 September 2015, A/RES/70/1. The Resolution created 17 sustainable development goals with 169 associated targets, all grounded in the economic, social and environmental dimensions of sustainable development.

[18] SDG Goal 3, target 3.8.

[19] See, eg European Commission, 'Next steps for a sustainable European future: European action for sustainability' (Communication) COM(2016) 0739 final; European Commission, Directorate-General for Communication, 'Towards a Sustainable Europe by 2030: Reflection Paper' (2019) https://data.europa.eu/doi/10.2775/676251.

[20] Lianos et al, 'Tackling Grand Challenges with Competition Law', 282.

[21] ibid.

[22] ibid. The authors define 'regulatory osmosis' as 'the absorption of regulatory aims into the enforcement of competition law'.

[23] ibid 291.

II. COMPETITION LAW AND NON-COMPETITION INTERESTS

Consumer welfare is the most commonly stated goal of the antitrust laws. This standard is both widely used and subject to criticism and diverse interpretations, as shown in the last section. The adoption of the welfarist approach by competition authorities, including EU and US ones, traditionally tends to favour the interests of those who benefit from higher output, including consumers. In other words, antitrust intervention is aimed at encouraging markets in which output – measured by quantity, quality or innovation – is, as large as possible, consistent with sustainable competition. The justification and the boundaries of such intervention are based on purely economic grounds.[24]

The use of this standard and the preponderant role of economics in antitrust law is a matter of debate, as clarified in chapter four. In this context, there are two main elements that are relevant for the topic of this book. First, the revival of the attack on corporate 'bigness', which has been popular since the beginning of the antitrust movement and has been renewed by the Neo-Brandeisian School developed in the US, currently has a wide echo with regard to large digital platforms but includes several sectors.[25] This thinking appears to target big corporations as the evil of the markets and the society. 'Bigness' in antitrust rhetoric is often depicted in the famous 'Octopus metaphor' recalling the ability of large corporations to expand their dominance over institutions and secondary markets.[26] Needless to say, this popular image has been applied to Big Pharma too and readily couples with the reputational issues and negative perception of pharmaceutical companies (especially big originators), which – as already stressed many times – are considered to mainly engage in strategies detrimental to consumers and society in general (including strategic patenting, excessive pricing and killer acquisitions). Neo-Brandeisians advocate for a resizing or dismissal of economics, arguing that a concern with efficiency lacks support from legislative history.[27] Despite the criticisms mentioned in chapter four, the direction indicated by this approach informs current enforcement by the antitrust agencies in the US. Moreover, the idea that the protection of competition should be concerned not only with efficiency can be also found in the recent European Commission's policy.[28]

[24] HJ Hovenkamp, 'Is Antitrust's Consumer Welfare Principle Imperiled?' (2019) 45 *Journal of Corporation Law* 101, 103.

[25] See T Wu, *The Curse of Bigness: Antitrust in the New Gilded Age* (New York, Columbia Global Reports, 2018).

[26] See, eg H Hovenkamp, 'The Slogans and Goals of Antitrust Law' (2022) University of Penn, Institute for Law & Economics Research Paper No 22-33, https://ssrn.com/abstract=4121866 (recalling, at 9, antitrust popular history of the Octopus, used to depict Standard Oil).

[27] LM Khan, 'Amazon's Antitrust Paradox' (2016) 126 *Yale Law Journal* 710, 739ff.

[28] See, eg M Vestager, 'Fairness and Competition Policy' (Speech) (2022) https://ec.europa.eu/commission/presscorner/detail/en/SPEECH_22_6067 (making also reference to Commissioner A Bedoya 'Returning to Fairness', Remarks to the Midwest Forum of the FTC (2022) https://www.ftc.gov/system/files/ftc_gov/pdf/returning_to_fairness_prepared_remarks_commissioner_alvaro_bedoya.pdf).

Second, as well as these new approaches, many authors have dealt with the general question of whether policy goals other than that of protecting competition should be able to influence the outcomes of competitive assessments. Alternative thinking that conceives the purpose of antitrust in terms of non-economic goals has been developed in the past, but in general these stances have not claimed broad consensus.[29]

In the EU, a discussion about the appropriate approach to adopt and the relevance of economics was particularly relevant at the time of the modernisation process.[30] The European Treaties set a variety of objectives to be pursued through the Union's policies, as listed in Article 3 TEU, but do not provide a hierarchy between these goals. Some policy goals, including health policy (Article 9 TFEU), must be considered in implementing policies and activities even if not directly aimed at pursuing those objectives. Moreover, the Treaty explicitly excludes the application of some provisions when specific values are involved, such as in the case of essential interests of state security (Article 346 TFEU). This would suggest that non-competition-related objectives connected to the protection of other public interests may influence the enforcement of competition rules in accordance with the principles of the Treaty. In a limited number of cases, the European Commission has taken broader non-competition goals into account, for example environmental goals, cultural policy goals, the protection of public health and industrial policy goals. The Court of Justice has generally endorsed the Commission's practice and acknowledged that the Commission enjoyed broad discretion in applying Article 101(3) TFEU, including the authority to reconcile competition with 'objectives of a different nature'.[31]

[29] With regard to the US context, see R Pitofsky, 'The Political Content of Antitrust' (1979) 127 *University of Pennsylvania Law Review* 1051, 1052 (stating that one political value underlying the Sherman Act was a 'fear that excessive concentration of economic power will breed antidemocratic political pressures'); LB Schwartz, '"Justice" and Other Non-economic Goals of Antitrust' (1979) 127 *University of Pennsylvania Law Review* 1076 (affirming that 'putative economic gains should not be the exclusive or decisive factor in resolving antitrust controversies'); ME Stucke, 'Reconsidering Antitrust's Goals' (2012) 53 *Boston College Law Review* 551 (disputing all economic statements of antitrust goals, including competitive process and consumer welfare); M Steinbaum and ME Stucke, 'The Effective Competition Standard: A New Standard for Antitrust' (2020) 87 *University of Chicago Law Review* 595; S Paul, 'Recovering the Moral Economy Foundations of the Sherman Act' (2021) 131 *Yale Law Journal* 175.

[30] The term 'modernisation' often refers to the major reform in the EU competition law enforcement that took place in 2004 as a consequence of the entry into force of Regulation 1/2003. In general, it indicates a wider phenomenon, encompassing the changes in the interpretation and application of substantive law through the implementation of the so-called 'more economic approach', ie the implementation of efficiency/consumer welfare standard.

[31] *Metro SB-Großmärkte GmbH & Co KG v Commission* (*Metro I*) ECLI:EU:C:1977:167, [1977] ECR 1875, para 21; see also Joined Cases T-528/93, T-542/93, T-543/93 and T-546/93 *Metropole télévision SA and Reti Televisive Italiane SpA and Gestevisión Telecinco SA and Antena 3 de Televisión v Commission* ECLI:EU:T:1996:99, [1996] ECR II-649, para 118: 'in the context of an overall assessment, the Commission is entitled to base itself on considerations connected with the pursuit of the public interest in order to grant exemptions under Art 81(3)'. For further details, see H Schweitzer, 'Competition Law and Public Policy: Reconsidering an Uneasy Relationship – The Example of Article 81' in J Drexl, L Idot and J Monéger (eds), *Economic Theory and Competition Law* (Cheltenham, Edward Elgar, 2009) ch 9.

Since the middle of the 1990s, a change in the role of economics in competition law has been implemented and the Commission has progressively emphasised the adoption of the consumer welfare standard through the endorsement of a more economics-based approach.[32] The current framework on which the Commission operates the analysis of the agreements is set out in its Guidelines on the Application of Article 101(3).[33] Here, the Commission states that consumer welfare should be the benchmark against which agreements are tested under Article 101 and that Article 101(3) provides the forum for weighing the restrictions identified against the economic benefits and efficiencies created by the agreement.[34] The adoption of such standard by the Commission implies the rejection of broader objectives and the concern with redistributive effects, as the wording of Article 101(3) – demanding a fair share of the efficiency gains to be passed on to consumers – suggests.[35]

An important question is to determine whether the criteria of Article 101(3) should be interpreted in a narrow or a broad manner. According to the narrow view, the Guidelines on the Application of Article 101(3) are drafted explicitly in terms of economic efficiency and both the Commission and the European Courts have adopted such a restrictive approach in several cases. An example, again, in the pharmaceutical sector derives from the *Lundbeck* case, where the General Court rejected the potential efficiency gains claimed by the parties and refused to consider the alleged wider public interest in avoiding litigation as a justification for pay-for-delay agreements.[36]

Authors supporting this narrow view consider it consistent with both the wording of Article 101(3) and the recitals of the various block exemptions existing in the EU system and aimed at permitting certain agreements under the Article purely in terms of economic efficiency.[37] This would also be in line with the Guidance on the Commission's enforcement priorities in applying Article 102 TFEU.[38] However, the Commission in the Guidelines on the application of Article 101(3) also affirms that goals pursued by other Treaty provisions

[32] For an extensive treatment, see A Witt, *The More Economic Approach to EU Antitrust Law* (Oxford, Hart Publishing, 2016).

[33] Commission, 'Guidelines on the Application of Article 81(3) of the Treaty' [2004] OJ C101/97.

[34] ibid paras 13 and 33.

[35] See A Jones, B Sufrin and N Dunne, *Jones and Sufrin's EU Competition Law*, 7th edn (Oxford, Oxford University Press, 2019) 47. It is worth remembering that the notion of 'consumer' in EU competition law includes all direct and indirect users, thus comprising customers on intermediate markets.

[36] Case T-472/13 *H Lundbeck A/S and Lundbeck Ltd v European Commission* ECLI:EU:T:2016:449, paras 706–20. The issue was not then challenged in the appeal before the Court of Justice (Case C-591/16 P, ECLI:EU:C:2021:243, para 138).

[37] R Whish and D Bailey, *Competition Law*, 10th edn (Oxford, Oxford University Press, 2021) 165–66; O Odudu, *The Boundaries of EC Competition Law: The Scope of Article 81* (Oxford, Oxford University Press, 2007) ch 6; O Odudu, 'The Wider Concerns of Competition Law' (2010) 30 *OJLS* 559; G Monti, 'Article 81 EC and Public Policy' (2002) 39 *CML Rev* 1057.

[38] See European Commission, 'Guidance on the Commission's Enforcement Priorities in Applying Article 82 of the EC Treaty to Abusive Exclusionary Conduct by Dominant Undertakings' (Guidance Paper) [2009] OJ C45/7, paras 19, 30 and 86.

can be taken into account to the extent that they can be subsumed under the conditions of Article 101(3).[39] On the other hand, other scholars have put forward the idea that other public policy considerations should be taken into account when applying competition rules.[40]

As mentioned above, this debate has been reinvigorated in recent years. Whether to extend competition enforcement to further objectives is a normative question, which is strictly related to the definition of the goals of competition law. How it can take these considerations into account is a more technical issue. Firstly, considering normative concerns about whether specific public interest objectives should be relevant in competition law and policy implies a definition of what constitutes 'public interest', which is hard to give and is inevitably vague and imprecise. Attention is currently given mostly to environmental protection and related sustainability issues.[41] Other concerns regard societal inequality,[42] labour practices,[43] the influence of big firms on political elections[44] and various issues related to the digital economy (including very different topics, such as data privacy and fake news).[45] In such a debate, the possible goals of antitrust may be intended to comprise various objectives, such as dispersal of economic

[39] European Commission, Guidelines on the Application of Article 81(3), para 42, citing Case T-17/93, *Matra Hachette SA v Commission* ECLI:EU:T:1994:89, [1994] ECR II-595, para 139 and Case 26/76 *Metro I*, para 43.

[40] See, eg C Townley, *Article 81 and EC Public Policy* (Oxford, Hart Publishing, 2009); H Schweitzer, 'Competition Law and Public Policy'; I Lianos, 'Polycentric Competition Law' (2018) *Current Legal Problems* 161; O Brook, 'Struggling with Article 101(3) TFEU: Diverging Approaches of the Commission, EU Courts, and Five Competition Authorities' (2019) 56 *CML Rev* 121; A Gerbrandy, 'Rethinking Competition Law within the European Economic Constitution' (2019) 57 *Journal of Common Market Studies* 127.

[41] See, eg G Monti and J Mulder, 'Escaping the Clutches of EU Competition Law Pathways to Assess Private Sustainability Initiatives' (2017) 42 *EL Rev* 635; A Gerbrandy, 'Solving a Sustainability-Deficit in European Competition Law' (2017) 40 *World Competition* 539; H Hovenkamp, 'Are Agreements to Address Climate Change Anticompetitive?' (2019) *The Regulatory Review* www.theregreview.org/2019/09/11/hovenkamp-are-regulatory-agreements-to-addressclimate-change-anticompetitive/; OECD, 'Sustainability and Competition'; MC Iacovides and C Vrettos, 'Falling through the Cracks No More? Article 102 TFEU and Sustainability: The Relation between Dominance, Environmental Degradation, and Social Injustice' (2022) 10 *Journal of Antitrust Enforcement* 32.

[42] See, eg JB Baker and SC Salop, 'Antitrust, Competition Policy, and Inequality' (2015) 104 *Georgetown Law Journal* 1; LM Khan and S Vaheesan, 'Market Power and Inequality: The Antitrust Counterrevolution and Its Discontents' (2017) 11 *Harvard Law & Policy Review* 235; I Lianos, 'The Poverty of Competition Law – the Short Story' in D Gerard and I Lianos (eds), *Reconciling Efficiency and Equity: A Global Challenge for Competition Law?* (Cambridge, Cambridge University Press, 2022) 45.

[43] See, eg H Hafiz, 'Labor Antitrust's Paradox' (2020) 87 *University of Chicago Law Review* 381; I Lianos, N Countouris and V de Stefano, 'Rethinking the Competition Law/Labour Law Interaction: Promoting a Fairer Labour Market' (2019) 10 *European Labour Law Journal* 291; OECD, 'Competition Concerns in Labour Markets', www.oecd.org/daf/competition/competition-concerns-in-labour-markets.htm; M Maggiolino, 'Even Employees Are Undertakings in the Labour Market, but Granting Social Rights Is Not Antitrust's Job' (2022) 10 *Journal of Antitrust Enforcement* 365.

[44] Z Teachout, *Break 'Em Up: Recovering Our Freedom from Big Ag, Big Tech, and Big Money* (New York, All Points Books, 2020) 109–25.

[45] See, eg A Ezrachi, 'EU Competition Law Goals and the Digital Economy' (2018) Oxford Legal Studies Research Paper No 17.

power, economic equity, fairness, reasonable employment standards and sustainability, including the realisation of the right to health and public health interests.

Secondly, some authors elaborating on the use of competition law to achieve public health policy objectives in the broader narrative of sustainability have taken the role that competition authorities have played in COVID-19 pandemic as a useful example.[46] In particular, they argue that competition authorities had to be ready to use competition rules both as a 'sword', to achieve public health goals in the case of restrictions on competition (in particular, in the event of excessive pricing by dominant undertakings and cartel activity), and as a 'shield', to enable and promote specific collaboration if necessary for public health reasons.[47] On the basis of this approach, welcoming the proactive steps taken by the Commission in re-assessing the treatment of sustainability in the revision process of Horizontal Block Exemption Regulations and related Guidelines, they advocate for a change in addressing broader sustainability challenges.[48] According to this view, sustainable development should be a guiding legal principle according to which assessing the effects of potentially restrictive agreements can take into account factors other than pure economic welfare considerations, under certain circumstances, and encompass broader social objectives, such as the right to health or the societal interest of public health.

[46] See 'European Competition Network (ECN),'Joint Statement on Application of Competition Law during the Corona Crisis' (23 March 2020); European Commission, 'Temporary Framework for Assessing Antitrust Issues Related to Business Cooperation in Response to Situations of Urgency Stemming from the Current COVID-19 Outbreak' (Communication) [2020] OJ C116 I/7; Commission, 'Guidelines on the Optimal and Rational Supply of Medicines to Avoid Shortages during the COVID-19 Outbreak' (Communication) [2020] OJ C116 I/01. With regard to EU competition law and COVID-19, see G Monti, 'Business Cooperation in Times of Emergency: The Role of Competition Law' [2020] *Competition Policy International* www.competitionpolicyinternational.com/business-cooperation-in-times-of-emergency-the-role-of-competition-law/; F Costa-Cabral, L Hancher, G Monti and A Ruiz Feases, 'EU Competition Law and COVID-19' (2020) TILEC Discussion Paper No DP2020-007, https://papers.ssrn.com/sol3/papers.cfm?abstract_id=3561438.

[47] Lianos et al, 'Tackling Grand Challenges with Competition Law', 284ff. Similarly, with regard to sustainability, OECD, 'Sustainability and Competition', 19.

[48] Lianos et al, 'Tackling Grand Challenges with Competition Law', 293, 295–6. On 1 March 2022, the Commission published drafts of the revised R&D and Specialisation Block Exemption Regulations (HBERs) and Horizontal Guidelines for stakeholder comments, repealing the previous ones which are set to expire by the end of 2022. The draft Guidelines introduce the category of 'sustainability agreements', defined as any type of horizontal cooperation agreement that genuinely pursues one or more sustainability objectives (including activities that support economic, environmental and social development). According to the draft Guidelines, the genuine pursuance of a sustainability objective may be taken into account in determining whether the restriction in question is a restriction by object or by effect within the meaning of Article 101(1). A more limited reference to sustainability objectives as qualitative criteria in the assessment is also included in the Guidelines on new Vertical Block Exemption Regulation. See European Commission, 'Guidelines on vertical restraints' (Communication) [2022] OJ C248/1, paras 8–9, 144 and 316. In general, on the relevance of public policy considerations in block exemption regulations, see O Brook, 'Block Exemption Regulations and Public Policy: In the Defence of BERS' [2022] *Cambridge Yearbook of European Legal Studies* 1, 3 (arguing that block exemption regulations are 'also the expression of a clearly defined political consensus on the appropriate balance between competition and public policy considerations').

Taking these stances into consideration, fundamental normative questions arise about which public policy factors may count, how they can be addressed in competition cases and whether all public policy factors should be appraised in the same way or some should 'count' more than others.[49] Moreover, substantive antitrust assessment is centred on competition problems deriving from firm behaviour: challenges to the possibility of including other non-market public interests – ie permitting restrictive practices on the basis that they nonetheless further other socially valuable goals or, conversely, condemning behaviour that is not anti-competitive but nonetheless conflicts with such values – clearly occur.[50]

III. CONCLUDING REMARKS

There is a tendency in the academic debate to reconsider the role of competition law and question its applicability as a viable tool to address objectives beyond those typically linked to economic efficiency. This discussion has a general scope and involves several aspects and sectors. The pharmaceutical sector as related to the fundamental right to health represents one of the main cases in which such theses matter.

The inclusion of public non-economic interests in competition law has been a subject of study in the antitrust literature in the past. Nowadays, this issue needs to be re-read in the current rethinking of competition law in a broader narrative. This chapter has illustrated the main approaches envisaged in the literature considering the relationship between competition law and public health, and placed them in such discussion.

As clarified in the previous chapters of this book, in the pharmaceutical sector, several competing (and sometimes conflicting) public interests occur, from the need to secure access to medicines to the containment of prices, the need to preserve innovation for future products delivering new and more effective medical treatments and the industrial policy considerations related to the central role of this sector in the EU and US economies. When dealing with proposals aimed at rethinking and reconsidering the role of antitrust, it appears difficult to clearly identify which public interests merit accommodation within the competition framework and which do not. The main criticism of these proposals relies on the consistency of antitrust intervention on the basis of a clear legal standard and the feared risk of using competition rules as a remedy for all problems where other legal disciplines may more appropriately intervene. However, it is clear that these issues cannot be ignored but require careful and thorough consideration.

[49] Monti, 'Article 81 EC and Public Policy', 1058.
[50] N Dunne, 'Public Interest and EU Competition Law' (2020) 65 *The Antitrust Bulletin* 256, 263.

Conclusion

IN INNOVATION-INTENSIVE INDUSTRIES, law enforcers and regulators are confronted with the severe and unavoidable problem of maintaining and enhancing incentives to innovate while granting competitive markets and prosecuting harmful conducts. In the case of the pharmaceutical sector, the pervasive role of regulation informing the entire life cycle of medicinal products makes the picture still more complex. Enhancing innovation requires not only intellectual property rights (IPRs) and regulatory tools, but also that the competitive pressure is maintained. However, strong IPRs may also undermine competition raising market entry barriers. Regulatory failures may give room to opportunistic behaviours having anti-competitive effects too. Although there are some differences in the specific regulatory choices of the European and US systems, these features are common. Moreover, one cannot ignore the relevance of the international legal environment for pharmaceutical markets. The growing awareness of the need to grant access to medicines as a global challenge fuels the debate on the role that regulatory frameworks, intellectual property (IP) rules and competition law must play in international settings.

This book argues that the first challenge is to develop a coherent interplay between the different areas of law involved. An overview of antitrust policy in prescription drug markets shows that this is an area in which enforcement in general has been attentive and effective. Competition law has traditionally played an important role, prosecuting a wide range of exclusionary practices, both collusive and unilateral ones. Recent experience in the EU also testifies its readiness to intervene against exploitative conducts. Despite the differences between them, the relevance of the practices treated in this book (reverse payment patent settlements, product hopping, excessive pricing of off-patent drugs) must be contextualised in the efforts directed at promoting competition in the pharmaceutical sector with the declared aim of fostering a competitive and innovative marketplace together with the reduction of governments' expenditure and prices for final consumers.

Competition problems in pharmaceutical markets are often complex and imply a variety of considerations. This must be traced mainly to the overall regulatory landscape governing this sector. Anti-competitive behaviours by pharmaceutical firms are often facilitated by the existing framework and the institutional setting. The practices analysed show that there can be hypotheses of conflicting concurrent application of competition rules and other rules, where formal compliance with the latter may correspond to liability under the former. Moreover, there are cases in which regulatory failures may occur, when the sectoral regime and/or the tools at the disposal of regulatory agencies are inadequate to address opportunistic behaviour that turns out to be anti-competitive. Should one attempt to summarise the role of competition law in this context, it would be right to affirm that antitrust intervention is prominent, given that preconditions exist for the application of competition rules.

In this perspective, the analysis conducted in this book does not advocate for a greater place for antitrust law or, alternatively, for a resizing of it. Rather, it is aimed at highlighting some insights on the interface with other areas of law with a view to ensuring consistent interplay between them. In this perspective, some final observations may be put forward.

Anti-competitive effects facilitated by IP and regulatory systems require further intervention. With regard to patents, the approval process by patent offices does not perform a sufficiently effective screening function to warrant a presumption that a patent is valid or that, in the case of follow-on products, genuine improvement has taken place. In particular, the problem of the issuance of a high number of 'weak' or 'bad' patents by patent offices is routinely complained about.[1] Here, the alternative between investing in ex ante regulation or focusing on judicial inquiry into the validity of patents is a matter of debate.[2] However, in this discussion, the uncertainty and costs that patent litigation entails must be taken into account, as the practice of pay-for-delay suggests. On the other hand, medicine agencies have neither the mandate nor the power to take into consideration patent law or competition concerns during the approval process of pharmaceutical products.

It should be certainly agreed that, as a first best option, improving patent law and sector-specific regulation is the most appropriate solution rather than resorting to competition rules.[3] A viable option to be explored is that of enhancing coordination between public agencies. This approach would imply an improved collaboration ex ante among agencies having complementary tasks and would help ex post competition authorities to identify cases to be investigated and

[1] See, eg MD Frakes and MF Wasserman, 'Investing in Ex Ante Regulation: Evidence from Pharmaceutical Patent Examination' (2020) Working Paper 27579, www.nber.org/papers/w27579 (arguing that time constraints facing US patent examiners may currently be leading to the issuance of invalid secondary pharmaceutical patents that delay generic entry). See also R Feldman, 'May Your Drug Price Be Evergreen' (2018) 5 *Journal of Law and the Biosciences* 590, 600 (reporting that, on average, the patent office spends only 18 hours across a two-year period examining a patent application and that, although the number of patent examiners has doubled since 2005, the number of patents approved each year has doubled as well, rising to over 300,000 new patents in the fiscal year ending August 2017; the author also refers to the problem of patents invalidly applied).

[2] See, eg MA Lemley, 'Rational Ignorance at the Patent Office' (2001) 95 *Northwestern University Law Review* 1495 (arguing that patent litigation is rare so that it may be more cost effective to rely upon the courts to execute the screening function on patent validity rather than paying for a more protracted examination of all patents ex ante); MA Lemley, 'Fixing the Patent Office' (2013) 13 *Innovation Policy and the Economy* 83.

[3] See, eg MK Kyle, 'Competition Law, Intellectual Property, and the Pharmaceutical Sector' (2016) 81 *Antitrust Law Journal* 1, 16 and 32.

courts in their rulings, while minimising the risk of clashing with other areas of law. The idea of fostering collaboration between agencies has been envisaged both in recent scholarship and practice.[4] For instance, pursuant to the Executive Order issued by the President of the United States in July 2021, the Food and Drug Administration (FDA) identified strategies, such as patent thickets, evergreening and product hopping, where a greater engagement between the FDA and the US Patent and Trademark Office (USPTO) could be established in order to improve the examination process for pharmaceutical patent applications and patent term extension.[5] Further types of coordination may be established between competition agencies and regulators. At the investigation level, a range of public actors may be involved in this effort (such as the USPTO and FDA in the US, the European Patent Office, the European Medicines Agency and national regulators in Europe) providing information directly relevant to the antitrust analysis. Moreover, also coherently with its advocacy function, antitrust intervention may signal deficiencies of sectoral rules and work as a pathway to help regulation addressing the failures and loopholes.[6]

The issue might then be translated in broader terms and applied to the supposed role of competition law to address a range of public non-economic interests, as supported by recent calls for its redirection towards non-efficiency considerations. Among those non-economic interests, one could argue for considering public health to be paramount. Of course, antitrust enforcement intervenes to break up agreements or punish dominant drug manufacturers that block generic entry and thereby impede access to cheaper medicines. This, however, does not mean that competition law is the appropriate tool to address public objectives irrespective of whether or not they coincide with its general task of promoting effective competition against abuses of private market power.

Considering the impact of high prices on public health and the circumstance that public funds often contribute to research and development activity,

[4] See DA Hyman and WE Kovacic, 'Risky Business: Should the FDA Pay Attention to Pharmaceutical Prices?' (2017) GWU Law School Public Law Research Paper No 2017-37; GWU Legal Studies Research Paper No 2017-37, https://ssrn.com/abstract=2970683 (calling, among the various proposals, for the FDA and the FTC to work together more closely). See, eg Food and Drug Administration and Federal Trade Commission, 'Joint Statement Regarding a Collaboration to Advance Competition in the Biologic Marketplace' (2020) https://www.ftc.gov/system/files/documents/public_statements/1565273/v190003fdaftcbiologicsstatement.pdf.

[5] Executive Order No 14036 on Promoting Competition in the American Economy, 86 Fed Reg 36,987 (9 July 2021). The USPTO and the FDA have recently announced collaboration initiatives (www.uspto.gov/initiatives/fda-collaboration).

[6] See G Monti, 'Excessive Pricing: Competition Law in Shared Regulatory Space' (2019) TILEC Working Paper, 16–17, www.tilburguniversity.edu/research/institutes-and-research-groups/old-tilec/events/work-progress-giorgio-monti; OECD, 'Excessive Prices in Pharmaceutical Markets' (2018) 25 and 31, www.oecd.org/daf/competition/excessive-pricing-in-pharmaceuticals.htm (affirming that, among the various tools that competition authorities have at their disposal, an important one is market studies, which would help them to understand market developments and fine-tune the most appropriate response, and advocacy for the adoption of appropriate regulation, or the adoption of initiatives in tandem with sectoral regulators).

competition agencies may be under strong public pressure to prosecute actions in the pharmaceutical sector. This pressure, together with the severe criticism and reputational issues that have concerned the pharmaceutical companies for years, is widely perceived, and resorting to antitrust in situations where other approaches have failed may seem an appealing solution. However, competition law is not a panacea that can make up for the shortcomings of other disciplines.[7]

There is an urgent need for novel regulatory approaches in the pharmaceutical sector. Proposals on the matter may vary, but a consensus about the need to improve the system can be found. Some insights as to future possible paths can be gained by looking at the current topics on the regulatory agendas.

In the US, the main focus is currently on prescription drug prices: absent price regulation, measures able to put a brake on exponential price increases are on the table, although they have typically faced political and legal challenges that are difficult to overcome. The impact of the most recent legislative initiatives taken by the Congress and the likely adoption of further measures are yet to be seen.[8]

In the EU, in addition to initiatives such as the IP Action Plan, a new Pharmaceutical Strategy for Europe was adopted in November 2020.[9] Among its ambitious key initiatives, it prioritises the need to fulfil unmet medical needs and declares that a process of reflection has begun on how to tailor the system of incentives provided by the EU framework better in order to stimulate innovation in such areas. The Strategy also includes the consideration of targeted policies enhancing greater generic and biosimilar competition, and the employment of health technology assessment to support the analysis and information on clinical added-value and cost-effectiveness of new medicinal products relevant to informing national pricing and reimbursement decisions. Importantly, affordability and accessibility are indicated as principles informing overall reform. Complementing these principles with the need to secure the availability of drugs is a major policy knot for any system. Such objectives require a coordinated approach that takes into account the relationship with IPRs and includes the complementary role of competition rules.

[7] N Dunne, 'Public Interest and EU Competition Law' (2020) 65 *The Antitrust Bulletin* 256, 281.

[8] The most recent effort has been addressed through HR5376 – Inflation Reduction Act (2022), which includes a broad package of health, tax and climate change provisions.

[9] European Commission, 'Making the Most of the EU's Innovative Potential. An Intellectual Property Action Plan to Support the EU's Recovery and Resilience' (Communication) COM/2020/760 final; European Commission, 'Pharmaceutical Strategy for Europe' (Communication) COM(2020) 761 final.

Bibliography

Abbott, FM, 'TRIPS and Human Rights: Preliminary Reflections' in FM Abbott, C Breining-Kaufmann and T Cottier (eds), *International Trade and Human Rights. Foundations and Conceptual Issues* (Ann Arbor, University of Michigan Press, 2001).

Abbott, FM, 'The Doha Declaration on the TRIPS Agreement and Public Health: Lighting a Dark Corner at the WTO' (2002) 5 *Journal of International Economic Law* 469.

Abbott, FM, 'The WTO Medicines Decision: World Pharmaceutical Trade and the Protection of Public Health' (2005) 99 *American Journal of International Law* 317.

Abbott, FM, 'The "Rule of Reason" and the Right to Health: Integrating Human Rights and Competition Principles in the Context of TRIPS' in T Cottier, J Pauwelyn and E Bürgi Bonanomi, *Human Rights and International Trade* (Oxford, Oxford University Press, 2005) 279.

Abbott, FM, 'Parallel Importation: Economic and Social Welfare Dimensions' (International Institute for Sustainable Development, 2007) www.iisd.org/system/files/publications/parallel_importation.pdf.

Abbott, FM, 'Excessive Pharmaceutical Prices and Competition Law: Doctrinal Development to Protect Public Health' (2016) 6 *UC Irvine Law Review* 281.

Abbott, FM, 'Parallel Trade in Pharmaceuticals: Trade Therapy for Market Distortions' in I Calboli and E Lee (ed), *Research Handbook on Intellectual Property Exhaustion and Parallel Imports* (Cheltenham, Edward Elgar, 2016), 145.

Abbott, FM, 'Health and Intellectual Property Rights' in GL Burci and B Toebes (eds), *Research Handbook on Global Health Law* (Cheltenham, Edward Elgar, 2018) 135.

Abbott, FM and Reichman, JH, 'Doha Round's Public Health Legacy: Strategies for the Production and Diffusion of Patented Medicines under the Amended TRIPS Provisions' (2007) 10 *Journal of International Economic Law* 921.

Ackermann, T, 'Excessive Pricing and the Goals of Competition Law' in D Zimmer (ed), *The Goals of Competition Law* (Cheltenham, Edward Elgar, 2012) 349.

Actis Perinetto, P, 'A Formalistic Approach to Competition Law and Its Risks: The Curious Case of Roche/Novartis' (2020) 43 *World Competition* 319.

Addanki, S, 'Antitrust and IP: Developments in Pharmaceuticals' in RD Blair and DD Sokol, *The Cambridge Handbook of Antitrust, Intellectual Property, and High Tech* (Cambridge, Cambridge University Press, 2017) 21.

Ahlborn, C and Padilla, J, 'From Fairness To Welfare: Implications for the Assessment of Unilateral Conduct under EC Competition Law' in C-D Ehlermann and M Marquis (eds), *European Competition Law Annual 2007: A Reformed Approach to Article 82 EC* (Oxford, Hart Publishing, 2008) 55.

Akman, P, 'Searching for the Long-Lost Soul of Articles 82 EC' (2009) 29 *OJLS* 267.

Akman, P, *The Concept of Abuse in EU Competition Law* (Oxford, Hart Publishing, 2012).

Akman, P and Garrod, L, 'When are Excessive Prices Unfair?' (2011) 7 *Journal of Competition Law and Economics* 403.

Allison, JR, Lemley, MA and Schwartz, DL, 'Our Divided Patent System' (2015) 82 *University of Chicago Law Review* 1072.

Anderman, SD (ed), *The Interface between Intellectual Property Rights and Competition Policy* (Cambridge, Cambridge University Press, 2007).

Anderman, SD and Ezrachi, A (eds), *Intellectual Property and Competition Law: New Frontiers* (Oxford, Oxford University Press, 2011).

Anderman, SD and Schmidt, H, 'EC Competition Policy and IPRs' in SD Anderman (eds), *The Interface between Intellectual Property Rights and Competition Policy* (Cambridge, Cambridge University Press, 2007) 37.

Anderson, RD, Kovacic, WE, Müller, AC and Sporysheva, N, 'Competition Policy, Trade and the Global Economy: Existing WTO Elements, Commitments in Regional Trade Agreements, Current Challenges and Issues for Reflection' (2018) WTO Working Paper No 2018/12.

Anderson, RD, Müller, AC and Taubman, AS, 'The WTO TRIPS Agreement as a Platform for Application of Competition Policy to the Contemporary Knowledge Economy' in RD Anderson, N Pires de Carvalho and A Taubman (eds), *Competition Policy and Intellectual Property in Today's Global Economy* (Cambridge, Cambridge University Press, 2021) 62.

Angell, M, *The Truth About the Drug Companies: How They Deceive Us and What to Do About It* (New York, Random House, 2004).

Aronson, JK and Green, AR, 'Me-Too Pharmaceutical Products: History, Definitions, Examples, and Relevance to Drug Shortages and Essential Medicines Lists' (2020) 86 *British Journal of Clinical Pharmacology* 2114.

Arrow, KJ, 'Economic Welfare and the Allocation of Resources for Invention' in R Nelson (ed), *The Rate and Direction of Economic Activities: Economic and Social Factors* (Princeton, Princeton University Press, 1962) 609.

Association for Accessible Medicines, 'The US Generic & Biosimilar Medicines Savings Report' (2021) https://accessiblemeds.org/resources/reports/2021-savings-report.

Athanasiadou, A, *Patent Settlements in the Pharmaceutical Industry under US Antitrust and EU Competition Law* (Alphen aan den Rijn, Kluwer, 2018).

Athanasiadou, A, 'Rethinking Pharmaceutical Product Reformulations' [2020] (May) *Competition Policy International Antitrust Chronicle* 6.

Ayres, I and Klemperer, P, 'Limiting Patentees' Market Power Without Reducing Innovation Incentives: The Perverse Benefits of Uncertainty and Non-injunctive Remedies' (1999) 97 *Michigan Law Review* 985.

Bagley, MA, 'Patent Term Restoration and Non-patent Exclusivity in the US' in G Muscolo and G Pitruzzella (eds), *Competition and Patent Law in the Pharmaceutical Sector: An International Perspective* (Alphen aan den Rijn, Kluwer, 2016) 111.

Baker, JB and Salop, SC, 'Antitrust, Competition Policy, and Inequality' (2015) 104 *Georgetown Law Journal* 1.

Bakhoum, M, 'Intellectual Property Rights (IPRs), Competition Law and Excessive Pricing of Medicines' in CM Correa and R Hilty (eds), *Access to Medicines and Vaccines* (Cham, Springer, 2022) 277.

Banakas, EK, 'The Method of Comparative Law and the Question of Legal Culture Today' (1994) 3 *Tilburg Law Review* 113.

Baquero Cruz, J, *Between Competition and Free Movement: The Economic Constitutional Law of the European Community* (Oxford, Hart Publishing, 2002).

Battaglia, LE, 'Drug Reformulation Regulatory Gaming in Pharmaceuticals: Enforcement & Innovation Implications' (2011) 7 *European Competition Journal* 379.

Baumann, MG, Bigelow, JP, Harris, BC, Murphy, KM, Ordover, JA, Willig, RD and Wright, MB, 'Activating *Actavis* With a More Complete Model' (2014) 28 *Antitrust* 83.

Beherens, P, 'The Ordoliberal Concept of "Abuse" of a Dominant Position and Its Impact on Article 102 TFEU' in F Di Porto and R Podszun (eds), *Abusive Practices in Competition* Law (Cheltenham, Edward Elgar, 2018) 5.

Berger, J, 'Advancing Public Health by Other Means: Using Competition Policy to Increase Access to Essential Medicines' in P Roffe and G Tansey (eds), *Negotiating Health. Intellectual Property and Access to Medicines* (London, Routledge, 2015) 181.

Bessen, J and Meurer, MJ, *Patent Failure. How Judges, Bureaucrats, and Lawyers Put Innovators at Risk* (Princeton, Princeton University Press, 2009).

Bignami, F, 'A New Field: Comparative Law and Regulation' in F Bignami and D Zaring (eds), *Comparative Law and Regulation. Understanding the Global Regulatory Process* (Cheltenham, Edward Elgar, 2016) 1.

Blair, RD and Sokol, D (eds), *Antitrust, Intellectual Property, and High Tech* (Cambridge, Cambridge University Press, 2017).

Boldrin, M and Levine, DK, *Against Intellectual Monopoly* (Cambridge, Cambridge University Press, 2008).

Boldrin, M and Levine, DK, 'The Case against Patents' (2013) 27 *Journal of Economic Perspectives* 3.

Bork, RH, *The Antitrust Paradox: A Policy at War with Itself* (New York, Basic Books, 1978).

Boscheck, R, 'Constraining Drug Supply: Product Positioning, Patent Protection and Regulatory Standards' (2008) 31 *World Competition* 485.

Botta, M, 'Sanctioning Unfair Pricing under Art. 102(a) TFEU: Yes, We Can!' (2021) 17 *European Competition Journal* 156.

Bradford, A, *The Brussels Effect. How the European Union Rules the World* (Oxford, Oxford University Press, 2020).

Braithwaite, J and Drahos, P, *Global Business Regulation* (Cambridge, Cambridge University Press, 2000).

Brennan, H, Kapczynski, A, Monahan, CH and Rizvi, Z, 'A Prescription for Excessive Drug Pricing: Leveraging Government Patent Use for Health' (2016) 18 *Yale Journal of Law and Technology* 275.

Brook, O, 'Struggling with Article 101(3) TFEU: Diverging Approaches of the Commission, EU Courts, and Five Competition Authorities' (2019) 56 *CML Rev* 121.

Brook, O, 'Block Exemption Regulations and Public Policy: In the Defence of BERS' [2022] *Cambridge Yearbook of European Legal Studies* 1.

Bruzzone, G and Capozzi, S, 'The Procompetitive and Anticompetitive Impact of Patent Settlements' in G Muscolo and G Pitruzzella (eds), *Competition and Patent Law in the Pharmaceutical Sector: An International Perspective* (Alphen aan den Rijn, Kluwer, 2016) 15.

Budish, E, Roin, BN and Williams, H, 'Do Firms Underinvest in Long-Term Research? Evidence from Cancer Clinical Trials' (2015) 105 *American Economic Review* 2044.

Busse, R, Blümel, M, Knieps, F and Bärnighausen, T, 'Statutory Health Insurance in Germany: A Health System Shaped by 135 Years of Solidarity, Self-Governance, and Competition' (2017) 390 *Lancet* 882.

Calboli, I, 'Corporate Strategies, First Sale Rules, and Copyright Misuse: Waiting for Answers from Kirstsaeng v Wiley and Omega v Costco (II)' (2013) 11 *Northwestern Journal of Technology and Intellectual Property* 221.

Calboli, I, 'Intellectual Property Exhaustion and Parallel Imports of Pharmaceuticals: A Comparative and Critical Review' in CM Correa and R Hilty (eds), *Access to Medicines and Vaccines* (Cham, Springer, 2022) 31.

Calcagno, C and Walker, M, 'Excessive Pricing: Towards Clarity and Economic Coherence' (2010) 6 *Journal of Competition Law and Economics* 891.

Calcagno, C, Chapsal, A and White, J, 'Economics of Excessive Pricing: An Application to the Pharmaceutical Industry' (2019) 10 *Journal of European Competition Law & Practice* 166.

Cárdena-Navia, JF, 'Thirty Years of Flawed Incentives: An Empirical an Economic Analysis of Hatch-Waxman Patent-Term Restoration' (2014) 29 *Berkeley Technology Law Journal* 1301.

Carlton, DW, Flyer, F, and Shefi, Y, 'Does the FTC's Theory of Product Hopping Promote Competition?' (2016) 12 *Journal of Competition Law & Economics* 495.

Caro De Sousa, P, 'Free Movement and Competition in the European Market for Pharmaceuticals' in P Figueroa and A Guerrero (eds), *EU Law of Competition and Trade in the Pharmaceutical Sector* (Cheltenham, Edward Elgar, 2019) 431.

Carrier, MA, 'Unsettling Drug Patent Settlements: A Framework for Presumptive Illegality' (2009) 108 *Michigan Law Review* 37.

Carrier, MA, 'A Real-World Analysis of Pharmaceutical Settlements: The Missing Dimension of Product Hopping' (2010) 62 *Florida Law Review* 1009.

Carrier, MA (ed), *Intellectual Property and Competition* (Cheltenham, Edward Elgar, 2011).

Carrier, MA, 'Why the "Scope of the Patent" Test Cannot Solve the Drug Patent Settlement Problem' (2012) 16 *Stanford Technology Law Review* 1.

Carrier, MA, 'A Response to Chief Justice Roberts: Why Antitrust Must Play a Role in the Analysis of Drug Patent Settlements' (2014) 15 *Minnesota Journal of Law, Science & Technology* 31.

Carrier, MA, 'How Not To Apply Actavis' (2014) 109 *Northwestern University Law Review Online* 113.

Carrier, MA, 'Payment after *Actavis*' (2014) 100 *Iowa Law Review* 7.

Carrier, MA, 'Eight Reasons Why "No-Authorized-Generic" Promises Constitute Payment' (2015) 67 *Rutgers University Law Review* 697.

Carrier, MA, 'Why a "Large and Unjustified" Payment Threshold Is Not Consistent with Actavis' (2016) 91 *Washington Law Review* 109.

Carrier, MA, 'Sharing, Samples, and Generics: An Antitrust Framework' (2017) 103 *Cornell Law Review* 1.

Carrier, MA, 'Five Actions to Stop Citizen Petition Abuse' (2018) 118 *Columbia Law Review Online* 81.

Carrier, MA, 'The Four-Step Rule of Reason' (2019) 33 *Antitrust* 50.

Carrier, MA, 'Product Hopping: the US Approach' in P Figueroa and A Guerriero (eds), *EU Law of Competition and Trade in the Pharmaceutical Sector* (Cheltenham, Edward Elgar, 2019) 716.

Carrier, MA, 'Don't Die! How Biosimilar Disparagement Violates Antitrust Law' (2020) 115 *Northwestern University Law Review* 119.

Carrier, MA, 'The US District Court for the Northern District of Illinois Dismisses Antitrust Case Challenging Patent Thicket (Humira)' [2020] *e-Competitions* No 96364.

Carrier, MA, 'A Simple Solution to the Problem of "Product Hopping"' [2021] *Harvard Health Policy Review*.

Carrier, MA, 'Pharmaceutical Settlements and Judicial Error' [2022] (May) *Competition Policy International Antitrust Chronicle* 5.

Carrier, MA and Minniti, CJ, 'Citizen Petitions: Long, Late-Filed, and At-Last Denied' (2016) 66 *American University Law Review* 305.

Carrier, MA and Minniti, CJ, 'The Untold EpiPen Story: How Mylan Hiked Prices by Blocking Rivals' (2017) 102 *Cornell Law Review Online* 53.

Carrier, MA and Minniti, CJ, 'Biologics: The New Antitrust Frontier' (2018) 2 *University of Illinois Law Review* 3.

Carrier, MA and Shadowen, S, 'Product Hopping: A New Framework' (2016) 92 *Notre Dame Law Review* 167.

Carrier, MA and Shadowen, SD, 'A Non-coercive Economic Approach to Product Hopping' (2018) 33 *Antitrust* 102.

Carrier, MA and Shadowen, SD, 'Don't Ditch Antitrust's Role in Product Hopping: A Response to Pace and Adam' (2019) 33 *Antitrust* 72.

Carrier, MA, Lemley, MA and Miller, SP, 'Playing Both Sides: Branded Sales, Generic Drugs, and Antitrust Policy' (2020) 71 *Hastings Law Journal* 307.

Carrier, MA, Levidow, N and Kesselheim, AS, 'Using Antitrust Law to Challenge Turing's Daraprim Price Increase' (2017) 31 *Berkeley Technology Law Journal* 1379.

Castanheira, M, Ornaghi, C and Siotis, G, 'The Unexpected Consequences of Generic Entry' (2019) 68 *Journal of Health Economics* 22.

Cengiz, F, *Antitrust Federalism in the EU and the US* (London, Routledge, 2012).

Cheng, T, *The Patent–Competition Interface in Developing Countries* (Oxford, Oxford University Press, 2021).

Chien, CV, 'Cheap Drugs at What Price to Innovation: Does the Compulsory Licensing of Pharmaceuticals Hurt Innovation?' (2003) 18 *Berkeley Technology Law Journal* 853.

Chopra, R and Kahn, L, 'The Case for "Unfair Methods of Competition" Rulemaking' (2020) 87 *University of Chicago Law Review* 357.

Chowdhury, A and Gaigl, A, 'The Economics of Competition Law and of Pharmaceutical Patents' in Coates, K (ed), *Competition Law and Regulation of Technology Markets* (Oxford, Oxford University Press, 2011).

Colangelo, M, 'Reverse Payment Patent Settlements in the Pharmaceutical Sector under EU and US Competition Laws: A Comparative Analysis' (2017) 40 *World Competition* 471.

Colangelo, M, 'The Dissemination of Misleading Information in the Pharmaceutical Market: The Italian Experience' in W Sauter, M Canoy and J Mulder (eds), *EU Competition Law and Pharmaceuticals* (Cheltenham, Edward Elgar, 2022) 197.

Colangelo, M and Desogus, C, 'Antitrust Scrutiny of Excessive Prices in the Pharmaceutical Sector: A Comparative Study of the Italian and UK Experiences' (2018) 41 *World Competition* 225.

Correa, CM, 'Guidelines for the Examination of Pharmaceutical Patents: Developing a Public Health Perspective – A Working Paper' (ICTSD, WHO, UNCTAD, 2006).

Correa, CM, 'Guidelines for Pharmaceutical Patent Examination: Examining Pharmaceutical Patents from a Public Health Perspective' (UNDP, 2015).

Correa, CM, 'Interpreting the Flexibilities under the TRIPS Agreement' in CM Correa and RM Hilty (eds), *Access to Medicines and Vaccines* (Cham, Springer, 2022) 1.

Coscelli, A and Overd, A, 'Market Definition in the Pharmaceutical Sector' (2007) 28 *European Competition Law Review* 294.

Costa-Cabral, F, Hancher, L, Monti, G and Ruiz Feases, A, 'EU Competition Law and COVID-19' (2020) TILEC Discussion Paper No DP2020-007, https://papers.ssrn.com/sol3/papers.cfm?abstract_id=3561438.

Cotter, T, 'Refining the "Presumptive Illegality" Approach to Settlements of Patent Disputes Involving Reverse Payments: A Commentary on Hovenkamp, Janis & Lemley' (2003) 87 *Minnesota Law Review* 1789.

Cotter, TF, 'FTC v Actavis, Inc: When Is the Rule of Reason Not the Rule of Reason?' (2014) 15 *Minnesota Journal of Law, Science & Technology* 41.

Crane, DA, 'Actavis, the Reverse Payment Fallacy, and the Continuing Need for Regulatory Solutions' (2014) 15 *Minnesota Journal of Law, Science & Technology* 51.

Cseres, K, 'The Controversies of the Consumer Welfare Standard' (2007) 3 *Competition Law Review* 121.

Cunningham, C, Ederer, F and Ma, S, 'Killer Acquisitions' (2021) 129 *Journal of Political Economy* 649.

Dabbah, MM, *International and Comparative Competition Law* (Cambridge, Cambridge University Press, 2010).

Danzon, PM, 'Regulation of Price and Reimbursement for Pharmaceuticals' in PM Danzon and S Nicholson (eds), *The Oxford Handbook of the Economics of the Biopharmaceutical Industry* (Oxford, Oxford University Press, 2012) 266.

Danzon PM, 'Competition and Antitrust Issues in the Pharmaceutical Industry: Final Report' (2014) https://faculty.wharton.upenn.edu/wp-content/uploads/2017/06/Competition-and-Antitrust-Issues-in-the-Pharmaceutical-IndustryFinal7.2.14.pdf.

Danzon, PM, 'Pricing and Reimbursement of Biopharmaceuticals and Medical Devices in the USA' in AJ Culyer (ed), *Encyclopedia of Health Economics* (Cheltenham, Edward Elgar, 2014) vol 3, 127.

Danzon, PM and Chao, LW, 'Does Regulation Drive Out Competition in Pharmaceutical Markets?' (2000) 43 *Journal of Law and Economics* 311.

Darr, A, 'Competition Law and Human Rights: A Complex Relationship' [2021] *Wirtschaft und Wettbewerb*, https://ssrn.com/abstract=3915662.

Darr, A and Lianos, I, 'Hunger Games: Connecting the Right to Food and Competition Law' in I Lianos, A Ivanov and D Davis (eds), *Global Food Value Chains and Competition Law* (Cambridge, Cambridge University Press, 2022) 420.

de Margerie, S, '"Pay-for-Delay" Settlements: In Search of the Right Standard' (2013) 36 *World Competition* 85.

Devlin, AJ, 'Exclusionary Strategies in the Hatch-Waxman Context' (2007) 2007 *Michigan State Law Review* 631.

Dickey, BM and Rubinfeld, DL, 'Would the Per Se Illegal Treatment of Reverse Payment Settlements Inhibit Generic Drug Investment?' (2012) 8 *Journal of Competition Law & Economics* 615.

Dickey, BM, Huang, K and Rubinfeld, DL, 'Pharmaceutical Product Hopping: Is There a Role for Antitrust Scrutiny?' (2019) 82 *Antitrust Law Journal* 679.

DiMasi, JA, Grabowski, HG and Hansen, RW, 'Innovation in the Pharmaceutical Industry: New Estimates of R&D Costs' (2016) 47 *Journal* of *Health Economics* 20.

Dogan, SL and Lemley, MA, 'Antitrust Law and Regulatory Gaming' (2009) 87 *Texas Law Review* 685.

Dolin, G, 'Reverse Settlements as Patent Invalidity Signals' (2011) 4 *Harvard Journal of Law & Technology* 281.

Dolin, G, 'Non-Price Competition in "Substitute" Drugs: The FTC's Blind Spot' (2014) 59 *Antitrust Bulletin* 579.

Domeij, B, 'Anticompetitive Marketing in the Context of Pharmaceutical Switching in Europe' in J Drexl and N Lee (eds), *Pharmaceutical Innovation, Competition and Patent Law: A Trilateral Perspective* (Cheltenham, Edward Elgar, 2013) 273.

Dorbeck-Jung, B, 'Transcending the Myth of Law's Stifling Technological Innovation: How Adaptive Drug Licensing Processes Are Maintaining Legitimate Regulatory Connections' in R Brownsword, E Scotford and K Yeung (eds), *The Oxford Handbook of Law, Regulation and Technology* (Oxford, Oxford University Press, 2016) 929.

Drexl, J (ed), *Research Handbook on Intellectual Property and Competition Law* (Cheltenham, Edward Elgar, 2008).

Drexl, J, 'Real Knowledge Is to Know the Extent of One's Own Ignorance: On the Consumer Harm Approach in Innovation-Related Competition Cases' (2010) 76 *Antitrust Law Journal* 677.

Drexl, J, 'AstraZeneca and the EU Sector Inquiry: When Do Patent Filings Violate Competition Law?' (2012) Max Planck Institute for Intellectual Property & Competition Law Research Paper No 2.

Dreyfuss, R, 'Protecting the Public Domain of Science: Has the Time for an Experimental Use Defense Arrived?' (2004) 46 *Arizona Law Review* 457.

Dreyfuss, R, 'Reconsidering Experimental Use' (2017) 50 *Akron Law Review* 699.

Duggan, M and Scott Morton, FM, 'The Distortionary Effects of Government Procurement: Evidence from Medicaid Prescription Drug Purchasing' (2006) 121 *Quarterly Journal of Economics* 1.

Dunne, N, *Competition Law and Economic Regulation* (Cambridge, Cambridge University Press, 2015).

Dunne, N, 'Public Interest and EU Competition Law' (2020) 65 *The Antitrust Bulletin* 256.

Dunne, N, 'Fairness and the Challenge of Making Markets Work Better' (2021) 84 *MLR* 230, 256–257.

Dunne, N, 'Potential Competition in EU Law' (2021) 42 *European Competition Law Review* 638.

Dunne, N, 'The Role of Regulation in EU Competition Law Assessment' (2021) 44 *World Competition* 287.

Duns, J, Duke, A and Sweeney, B (eds), *Comparative Competition Law* (Cheltenham, Edward Elgar, 2017).

Edlin, A, Scott Hemphill, C, Hovenkamp, HJ and Shapiro, C, 'Activating Actavis' [2013] *Antitrust* 16.

Edlin, A, Scott Hemphill, C, Hovenkamp, HJ and Shapiro, C, 'Actavis and Error Costs: A Reply to Critics' [2014] (October) *Antitrust Source* 1.

Edlin, A, Scott Hemphill, C, Hovenkamp, H and Shapiro, C, 'The Actavis Inference: Theory and Practice' (2015) 67 *Rutgers University Law Review* 1.

Elhauge, E and Krueger, A, 'Solving the Patent Settlement Puzzle' (2012) 91 *Texas Law Review* 283.

Ehlermann, C-D, 'The Contribution of EC Competition Policy to the Single Market' (1992) 29 *CML Rev* 257.
Eisenberg, RS, 'Patents and the Progress of Science: Exclusive Rights and Experimental Use' (1989) 56 *University of Chicago Law Review* 1017.
Eisenberg, RS, 'The Shifting Functional Balance of Patents and Drug Regulation' [2001] *Health Affairs* 119.
Eisenberg, RS, 'The Role of the FDA in Innovation Policy' (2007) 13 *Michigan Telecommunications and Technology Law Review* 345.
Eisenberg, RS, 'Intellectual Property and Public Health' in R Dreyfuss and J Pila (eds), *The Oxford Handbook of Intellectual Property Law* (Oxford, Oxford University Press, 2018) 931.
EMA and European Commission, 'Biosimilars in the EU' (2019) www.ema.europa.eu/en/documents/leaflet/biosimilars-eu-information-guide-healthcare-professionals_en.pdf.
Epstein, RA and Scott Kieff, F, 'Questioning the Frequency and Wisdom of Compulsory Licensing for Pharmaceutical Patents' (2011) 78 *University of Chicago Law Review* 71.
European Commission, 'Pharmaceutical Sector Inquiry: Final Report' (2009).
European Commission, 'Study on the Economic Impact of Supplementary Protection Certificates, Pharmaceutical Incentives and Rewards in Europe: Final Report' (2018) 14, https://data.europa.eu/doi/10.2873/886648.
European Commission, 'Competition Enforcement in the Pharmaceutical Sector (2009–2017): European Competition Authorities Working Together for Affordable and Innovative Medicines' (2019) https://data.europa.eu/doi/10.2763/218954.
European Commission, 'Joint Report on Health Care and Long-Term Care Systems & Fiscal Sustainability' (2019) Institutional Paper 105, https://ec.europa.eu/info/sites/default/files/economy-finance/ip105_en.pdf.
European Commission, Romandini, R, Slowinski, P, Wright, G et al, 'Study on the Legal Aspects of Supplementary Protection Certificates in the EU: Final Report' (2018) https://data.europa.eu/doi/10.2873/680006.
European Federation of Pharmaceutical Industries Associations, 'The Pharmaceutical Industry in Figures – Key Data' (2020) https://www.efpia.eu/media/554521/efpia_pharmafigures_2020_web.pdf.
Evans, D and Padilla, J, 'Excessive Prices: Using Economics to Define Administrable Legal Rules' (2005) 1 *Journal of Competition Law and Economics* 97.
Ezrachi, A, 'EU Competition Law Goals and the Digital Economy' (2018) Oxford Legal Studies Research Paper No 17.
Ezrachi, A and Gilo, D, 'Are Excessive Prices Really Self-Correcting?' (2009) 5 *Journal of Competition Law and Economics* 249.
Fackelmann, CR, 'Clinical Data, Data Exclusivity and Private Investment Protection in Europe' in G Muscolo and G Pitruzzella (eds), *Competition and Patent Law in the Pharmaceutical Sector: An International Perspective* (Alphen aan den Rijn, Kluwer, 2016) 141.
Federal Trade Commission, 'Generic Drug Entry Prior to Patent Expiration' (2002) www.ftc.gov/sites/default/files/documents/reports/generic-drug-entry-prior-patent-expiration-ftc-study/genericdrugstudy_0.pdf.
Federal Trade Commission, 'Report on Standalone Section 5 to Address High Pharmaceutical Drug and Biologic Prices' (2019) www.ftc.gov/reports/ftc-report-standalone-section-5-address-high-pharmaceutical-drug-biologic-prices.
Feldman, R, *Rethinking Patent Law* (Cambridge, MA, Harvard University Press, 2012).
Feldman, R, 'Ending Patent Exceptionalism and Structuring the Rule of Reason: The Supreme Court Opens the Door for Both' (2014) 5 *Minnesota Journal of Law, Science & Technology* 61.
Feldman, R, 'May Your Drug Price Be Evergreen' (2018) 5 *Journal of Law and the Biosciences* 590.
Feldman, R, *Drugs, Money, and Secret Handshakes. The Unstoppable Growth of Prescription Drug Prices* (Cambridge, Cambridge University Press, 2019).
Feldman, R, 'The Devil in the Tiers' (2021) 8 *Journal of Law and the Biosciences* 1.
Feldman, R, 'The Price Tag of "Pay-for-Delay"' (2022) 23 *Columbia Science and Technology Law Review* 1.

Feldman, R and Frondorf, E, 'Drug Wars: A New Generation of Generic Pharmaceutical Delay' (2016) 53 *Harvard Journal on Legislation* 499.

Feldman, R and Frondorf, E, *Drug Wars. How Big Pharma Raises Prices and Keeps Generics Off the Market* (Cambridge, Cambridge University Press, 2017).

Feldman, R and Misra, P, 'The Fatal Attraction of Pay-for-Delay' (2019) 18 *Chicago-Kent Journal of Intellectual Property* 249.

Feldman, R, Rowe, BC, Oral, R, Gu, AJ and Gudiksen, K, 'The Patent Act and the Constitutionality of State Pharmaceutical Regulation' (2019) 45 *Rutgers Computer and Technology Law Journal* 40.

Fink, C, 'Entering the Jungle of Intellectual Property Rights Exhaustion and Parallel Imports' in KE Maskus and C Fink (eds), *Intellectual Property and Development: Lessons from Recent Economic Research* (Washington, World Bank and Oxford University Press, 2005) 171, 172.

First, H, 'Unfair Drug Prices and Section 5' [2015] (November) *Competition Policy International Antitrust Chronicle*.

First, H, 'Excessive Drug Pricing as an Antitrust Violation' (2019) 82 *Antitrust Law Journal* 701.

FitzGerald, P, 'State Regulation of Generic Drug Price Gouging' (2019) 2 *Belmont Health Law Journal* Art 7.

Fletcher, A and Jardine, A, 'Towards an Appropriate Policy for Excessive Pricing' in C-D Ehlermann and M Marquis (eds), *European Competition Law Annual 2007: A Reformed Approach to Article 82 EC* (Oxford, Hart Publishing, 2008) 533.

Fonteijn, C, Akker, I and Sauter, W, 'Reconciling Competition and IP Law: The Case of Patented Pharmaceuticals and Dominance Abuse' (2018) ACM Working Paper, www.acm.nl/sites/default/files/documents/2018-03/acm-working-paper-reconciling-competition-and-ip-law-2018-03-07.pdf.

Fox, EM, 'Monopolization and Dominance in the United States and the European Community: Efficiency, Opportunity, and Fairness' (1986) 61 *Notre Dame Law Review* 981.

Fox, EM, 'International Antitrust: Edging towards a Global Framework with Our Feet on the Ground' in RD Anderson, N Pires de Carvalho and A Taubman (eds), *Competition Policy and Intellectual Property in Today's Global Economy* (Cambridge, Cambridge University Press, 2021) 809.

Frakes, MD and Wasserman, MF, 'Investing in Ex Ante Regulation: Evidence from Pharmaceutical Patent Examination' (2020) Working Paper 27579, www.nber.org/papers/w27579.

Frankel, S and Lai, JC, 'Recognised and Appropriate Grounds for Compulsory Licences: Reclaiming Patent Law's Social Contract' in RM Hilty and K-C Liu (eds), *Compulsory Licensing. Practical Experiences and Ways Forward*, MPI Studies on Intellectual Property and Competition Law 22 (Berlin, Springer-Verlag, 2015) 149.

Gaessler, F and Wagner, S, 'Patents, Data Exclusivity, and the Development of New Drugs' (2019) Rationality and Competition Discussion Paper Series 176, https://rationality-and-competition.de/wp-content/uploads/discussion_paper/176.pdf.

Gal, M, 'Monopoly Pricing as an Antitrust Offense in the US and the EC: Two Systems of Belief about Monopoly?' (2004) 49 *Antitrust Bulletin* 343.

Gal, M, 'Abuse of Dominance – Exploitative Abuses' in D Geradin and I Lianos (eds), *Research Handbook in EU Antitrust Law* (Chelthenham, Edward Elgar, 2013) 385.

Gal, MS and Miller, A, 'Patent Challenge Clauses: A New Antitrust Offense?' (2017) 102 *Iowa Law Review* 1477.

Gavil, AI, 'Moving beyond Caricature and Characterization: The Modern Rule of Reason in Practice' (2012) 85 *Southern California Law Review* 733.

Gavulic, KA and Dusetzina, SB, 'Prescription Drug Priorities under the Biden Administration' (2021) 46 *Journal of Health Politics, Policy and Law* 599.

Geradin, D, 'The Necessary Limits to the Control of "Excessive" Prices by Competition Authorities – A View from Europe' (2007) Tilburg University Legal Studies Working Paper, http://ssrn.com/abstract = 1022678.

Geradin, D, Ginsburg, DH and Safty, G, 'Reverse Settlements in the European Union and the United States' in G Pitruzzella and G Muscolo (eds), *Competition and Patent Law in the Pharmaceutical Sector. An International Perspective* 125 (Alphen aan den Rijn, Kluwer Law International, 2016).

Gerbrandy, A, 'Solving a Sustainability-Deficit in European Competition Law' (2017) 40 *World Competition* 539.

Gerbrandy, A, 'Rethinking Competition Law within the European Economic Constitution' (2019) 57 *Journal of Common Market Studies* 127.

Gervais, D, *The TRIPS Agreement: Drafting History and Analysis*, 4th edn (London, Sweet & Maxwell, 2012).

Ghidini, G, *Rethinking Intellectual Property. Balancing Conflicts of Interests in the Constitutional Paradigm* (Cheltenham, Edward Elgar, 2018).

Ghosh, S, 'Convergence?' (2014) 15 *Minnesota Journal of Law, Science & Technology* 95.

Ghosh, S and Calboli, I, *Exhausting Intellectual Property Rights: A Comparative Law and Policy Analysis* (Cambridge, Cambridge University Press, 2019).

Gilbert, RJ, 'Not Another Drug: Antitrust for Drug and Other Innovations' (2015) 30 *Antitrust* 38.

Ginsburg, DH, Wong-Ervin, K and Wright, JD, 'Product Hopping and the Limits of Antitrust: The Danger of Micromanaging Innovation' [2015] (December) *Competition Policy International Antitrust Chronicle* 1.

Giraud, A, Raffaitin, J and Dobelmann, C, 'Disparagement: The European Union and France' in W Sauter, M Canoy and J Mulder, *EU Competition Law and Pharmaceuticals* (Cheltenham, Edward Elgar, 2022) 173.

Gitter, DM, 'International Conflicts over Patenting Human DNA Sequences in the United States and the European Union: An Argument for Compulsory Licensing and a Fair-Use Exemption' (2001) 76 *New York University Law Review* 1623.

Gold, R, 'Patents and Human Rights: A Heterodox Analysis' (2012) 41 *Journal of Law, Medicine and Ethics* 185.

Gold, R and Joly, Y, 'The Patent System and Research Freedom: A Comparative Study' (2010) prepared for WIPO, SCP/15/3.

Goldman, D and Lakdawalla, D, 'The Global Burden of Medical Innovation' (2018) https://healthpolicy.usc.edu/wp-content/uploads/2018/01/01.2018_Global20Burden20of20Medical20Innovation.pdf.

Gordley, J, 'The Functional Method' in PG Monateri (ed), *Methods of Comparative Law* (Cheltenham, Edward Elgar, 2012) 107.

Graber, JL, 'Excessive Pricing of off-Patent Pharmaceuticals: Hatch It or Ratchet?' (2017) 92 *New York University Law Review* 1146.

Graziadei, M, 'The Functionalist Heritage' in P Legrand and R Munday (eds), *Comparative Legal Studies: Traditions and Transitions* (Cambridge, Cambridge University Press, 2003) 100.

Gudiksen, KL and King, JS, 'The Burden of Federalism: Challenges to State Attempts at Controlling Prescription Drug Costs' (2019) 39 Journal *of Legal* Medicine 95.

Guimarães de Lima e Silva, V, 'Sham Litigation in the Pharmaceutical Sector' (2011) 7 *European Competition Journal* 455.

Gupta, R, Morten, CJ, Zhu, AY, Ramachandran, R, Shah, ND and Ross, JS, 'Approvals and Timing of New Formulations of Novel Drugs Approved by the US Food and Drug Administration between 1995 and 2010 and Followed through 2021' (2022) 3 *JAMA Health Forum* e221096.

Gurgula, O and Hull, J, 'Compulsory Licensing of Trade Secrets: Ensuring Access to COVID-19 Vaccines via Involuntary Technology Transfer' (2021) 16 *Journal of Intellectual Property Law & Practice* 1242.

Gurgula, O and Lee, WH, 'COVID-19, IP and Access: Will the Current System of Medical Innovation and Access to Medicines Meet Global Expectations?' (2021) 17 *Journal of Generic Medicines* 61.

Hacohen, UY, 'Evergreening at Risk' (2020) 33 *Harvard Journal of Law & Technology* 480.

Hafiz, H, 'Labor Antitrust's Paradox' (2020) 87 *University of Chicago Law Review* 381.

Hancher, L, 'The EU Pharmaceutical Market: Parameters and Pathways' in E Mossialos, G Permanand, R Baeten and TK Hervey (eds), *Health Systems Governance in Europe: The Role of European Union Law and Policy* (Cambridge, Cambridge University Press, 2010) 640.

Hancher, L and Sauter, W, 'A Dose of Competition: EU Antitrust Law in the Pharmaceuticals Sector' (2016) 4 *Journal of Antitrust Enforcement* 381.

Hantman, RD, 'Experimental Use as an Exception to Patent Infringement' (1986) 67 *Journal of the Patent and Trademark Society* 617.

Heled, Y, 'Regulatory Competitive Shelters' (2015) 76 *Ohio State Law Journal* 299.

Helfer, LR, 'Regime Shifting: The TRIPs Agreement and the New Dynamics of International Intellectual Property Making' (2004) 29 *Yale Journal of International Law* 1.

Helfer, LR, 'Regime Shifting in the International Intellectual Property System' (2009) 7 *Perspectives on Politics* 39.

Helfer, LR and Austin, G, *Human Rights and Intellectual Property: Mapping the Global Interface* (Cambridge, Cambridge University Press, 2011).

Heller, MA and Eisenberg, RS, 'Can Patents Deter Innovation? The Anticommons in Biomedical Research' (1998) 280 *Science* 698.

Hemel, DJ and Ouellette, LL, 'Bayh-Dole beyond Borders' (2017) 4 *Journal of Law and the Biosciences* 282.

Hervey, TK and Orentlicher, D, 'Editors' Introduction' in TK Hervey and D Orentlicher (eds), *The Oxford Handbook of Comparative Health Law* (Oxford, Oxford University Press, 2021) 2.

Hestermeyer, HP, *Human Rights and the WTO. The Case of Patents and Access to Medicines* (Oxford, Oxford University Press, 2007).

Hilty, RM and Liu, K-C (eds), *Compulsory Licensing. Practical Experiences and Ways Forward*, MPI Studies on Intellectual Property and Competition Law 22 (Berlin, Springer-Verlag, 2015).

Ho, CM, *Access to Medicine in the Global Economy* (Oxford, Oxford University Press, 2011).

Ho, CM, 'Should All Drugs Be Patentable?: A Comparative Perspective' (2015) 17 *Vanderbilt Journal of Entertainment and Technology Law* 295, 312.

Hoen, EF 't, Veraldi, J, Toebes, B and Hogerzeil, HV, 'Medicine Procurement and the Use of Flexibilities in the Agreement on Trade-Related Aspects of Intellectual Property Rights, 2001–2016' (2018) 96 *Bulletin of the World Health Organization* 185.

Hoerner, RJ, 'The Decline (and Fall?) of the Patent Misuse Doctrine in the Federal Circuit' (2001) 69 *Antitrust Law Journal* 669.

Holman, CM, Minssen, T and Solovy, EM, 'Patentability Standards for Follow-On Pharmaceutical Innovation' (2018) 37 *Biotechnology Law Report* 131.

Holzapfel, H and Sarnoff, JD, 'A Cross-Atlantic Dialog on Experimental Use and Research Tools' (2008) 48 *IDEA Intellectual Property Law Review* 123.

Hovenkamp, HJ, 'The Federal Trade Commission and the Sherman Act' (2010) 62 *Florida Law Review* 1.

Hovenkamp, HJ, 'Patent Exclusions and Antitrust after Therasense' (2013) Faculty Scholarship at Penn Law 1870, https://scholarship.law.upenn.edu/faculty_scholarship/1870.

Hovenkamp, HJ, 'The Rule of Reason and the Scope of the Patent' (2015) 52 *San Diego Law Review* 515.

Hovenkamp, HJ, *Federal Antitrust Policy: The Law of Competition and Its Practice*, 5th edn (St Paul, West Academic Publishing, 2016).

Hovenkamp, HJ, 'The Rule of Reason' (2018) 70 *Florida Law Review* 81.

Hovenkamp, HJ, 'Is Antitrust's Consumer Welfare Principle Imperiled?' (2019) 45 *Journal of Corporation Law* 101.

Hovenkamp, HJ, 'Are Agreements to Address Climate Change Anticompetitive?' (*The Regulatory Review*, 11 September 2019) www.theregreview.org/2019/09/11/hovenkamp-are-regulatory-agreements-to-address-climate-change-anticompetitive/.

Hovenkamp, HJ, 'President Biden's Executive Order on Promoting Competition: An Antitrust Analysis' (2021) https://ssrn.com/abstract=3887776.

Hovenkamp, HJ, 'The Slogans and Goals of Antitrust Law' (2022) University of Penn, Institute for Law & Economics Research Paper No 22-33, https://ssrn.com/abstract=4121866.

Hovenkamp, HJ, Janis, MD and Lemley, MA, 'Anticompetitive Settlement of Intellectual Property Disputes' (2003) 87 *Minnesota Law Review* 1719.

Hovenkamp, H, Janis, MD, Lemley, MA and Leslie, CR, *IP and Antitrust: An Analysis of Antitrust Principles Applied to Intellectual Property* 2 edn (New York, Wolter Kluwers, 2013).

Howse, R, 'The Canadian Generic Medicines Panel: A Dangerous Precedent in Dangerous Times' (2000) 3 *Journal of World Intellectual Property* 493.

Hyman, DA and Kovacic, WE, 'Risky Business: Should the FDA Pay Attention to Pharmaceutical Prices?' (2017) GWU Law School Public Law Research Paper No 2017-37; GWU Legal Studies Research Paper No 2017-37, https://ssrn.com/abstract=2970683.

Hull, D, 'The AstraZeneca Judgment: Implications for IP and Regulatory Strategies' (2010) 1 *Journal of European Competition Law & Practice* 500.

Hunt, P, 'Report of the Special Rapporteur on the Right of Everyone to the Enjoyment of the Highest Attainable Standard of Physical and Mental Health', UN General Assembly A/61/338 (2006).

Hunt, P, 'Report of the Special Rapporteur on the Right of Everyone to the Enjoyment of the Highest Attainable Standard of Physical and Mental Health', UN General Assembly A/63/263 (2008).

Hunt, P, 'Report of the Special Rapporteur on the Right of Everyone to the Enjoyment of the Highest Attainable Standard of Health', Annex: Mission to GlaxoSmithKline, UN Doc No A/HRC/11/12/Add.2 (2009).

Husa, J, 'Metamorphosis of Functionalism – Or Back to Basics' (2011) 18 *Maastricht Journal of European & Comparative Law* 548.

Husa, J, 'Comparative Law, Legal Linguistics and Methodology of Legal Doctrine' in M VanHoecke (ed), *Methodologies of Legal Research* (Oxford, Hart Publishing, 2011) 209.

Husa, J, 'Functional Method in Comparative Law – Much Ado about Nothing?' (2013) 2 *European Property Law Journal* 4.

Iacovides, MC and Vrettos, C, 'Falling through the Cracks No More? Article 102 TFEU and Sustainability: The Relation between Dominance, Environmental Degradation, and Social Injustice' (2022) 10 *Journal of Antitrust Enforcement* 32.

Ibáñez Colomo, P, 'On the Application of Competition Law as Regulation: Elements for a Theory' (2010) 29 *Yearbook of European Law* 261.

Ibáñez Colomo, P, 'Beyond the "More Economics-Based Approach": A Legal Perspective on Article 102 TFEU Case Law' (2016) 53 *CML Rev* 709.

Ibáñez Colomo, P, 'Restrictions on Innovation in EU Competition Law' (2016) 41 *EL Rev* 201.

Ibáñez Colomo, P, *The Shaping of EU Competition Law* (Cambridge, Cambridge University Press, 2018).

Ibáñez Colomo, P, 'The Legal Status of Pay-for-Delay Agreements in EU Competition Law: Generics (Paroxetine)' (2020) 57 *CML Rev* 1933.

Ibáñez Colomo, P, 'What Is an Abuse of a Dominant Position? Deconstructing the Prohibition and Categorizing Practices' in P Akman, O Brook and K Stylianou (eds), *Research Handbook on Abuse of Dominance and Monopolization* (Cheltenham, Edward Elgar, forthcoming).

Jaenichen, H-R and Pitz, J, 'Research Exemption/Experimental Use in the European Union: Patents Do Not Block the Progress of Science' (2015) 5 *Cold Spring Harbor Perspectives in Medicine* 1.

James-Eluyode, J, *Corporate Responsibility and Human Rights: Global Trends and Issues* (London, Lexington Books, 2020).

Janis, MD and Lemley, MA, 'Balancing Ease and Accuracy in Assessing Pharmaceutical Exclusion Payments' (2004) 88 *Minnesota Law Review* 712.

Jenny, F, 'Abuse of Dominance by Firms Charging Excessive or Unfair Prices: An Assessment' in Y Katsoulacos and F Jenny (eds), *Excessive Pricing and Competition Law Enforcement* (Cham, Springer, 2018) 5.

Joliet, R, *Monopolization and Abuse of Dominant Position. A Comparative Study of the American and European Approaches to the Control of Economic Power* (Leiden, Martinus Nijhoff, 1970).

Jones, A and Nazzini, R, 'The Effect of Competition Law on Patent Remedies' in B Biddle, JL Contreras, BJ Love and NV Siebrasse (eds), *Patent Remedies and Complex Products: Towards a Global Consensus* (Cambridge, Cambridge University Press, 2019).

Jones, A, Sufrin, B and Dunne, N, *Jones and Sufrin's EU Competition Law*, 7th edn (Oxford, Oxford University Press, 2019).

Kanavos, P, Vandoros, S, Irwin, R, Nicod, E and Casson, M, 'Differences in Costs of and Access to Pharmaceutical Products in the EU' (European Parliament, 2011) IP/A/ENVI/ST/2010-12, www.europarl.europa.eu/document/activities/cont/201201/20120130ATT36575/20120130ATT36575EN.pdf.

Kapczynski, A, 'Realizing Public Rights through Government Patent Use' (2021) 49 *Journal of Law, Medicine & Ethics* 34.

Kapczynski A and Kesselheim, AS, '"Government Patent Use": A Legal Approach to Reducing Drug Spending' (2016) 15 *Health Affairs* 791.

Karas, L, Anderson, GF and Feldman, R, 'Pharmaceutical "Pay-for-Delay" Reexamined: A Dwindling Practice or a Persistent Problem?' (2020) 71 *Hastings Law Journal* 959.

Karas, L, Sachs, R and Anderson, G, 'Legal Obstacles to Biosimilar Market Entry' (2021) *Harvard Public Health Review* 28.

Keisler-Starkey, K and Bunch, LN, 'Health Insurance Coverage in the United States: 2021' (US Census Bureau, 2022) Current Population Report P60-278, www.census.gov/content/dam/Census/library/publications/2022/demo/p60-278.pdf.

Khan, LM, 'Amazon's Antitrust Paradox' (2016) 126 *Yale Law Journal* 710.

Khan, LM, 'The Ideological Roots of America's Market Power Problem' (2018) 127 *Yale Law Journal Forum* 960.

Khan, LM, 'The New Brandeis Movement: America's Antimonopoly Debate' (2018) 9 *Journal of European Competition Law and Practice* 131.

Khan, L and Vaheesan, S, 'Market Power and Inequality: The Antitrust Counterrevolution and its Discontents' (2017) 11 *Harvard Law & Policy Review* 235.

Kianzad, B and Wested, J, '"No-One Is Safe until Everyone Is Safe" – Patent Waiver, Compulsory Licensing and COVID-19' (2021) 5 *European Pharmaceutical Law Review* 71.

Kinney, ED, 'The International Human Right to Health: What Does This Mean for Our Nation and World?' (2001) 34 *Indiana Law Review* 1457.

Kinney, ED and Clark, BA, 'Provisions for Health and Healthcare in the Constitutions of the Countries of the World' (2004) 37 *Cornell International Law Journal* 287.

Kip Viscusi, W, Harrington, JE Jr and Sappington, DEM, *Economics of Regulation and Antitrust*, 5th edn (Cambridge, MA, MIT Press, 2018).

Kirchner, C, 'Competition Policy versus Regulation: Administration versus Judiciary' in M Neumann and J Weigand (eds), *The International Handbook of Competition* (Cheltenham, Edward Elgar, 2004).

Kischel, U, *Comparative Law* (Oxford, Oxford University Press, 2019).

Kjølbye, L, 'Article 82 EC as Remedy to Patent System Imperfections: Fighting Fire with Fire?' (2009) 32 *World Competition* 163.

Klaus Patel, KK and Schweitzer, H, (eds), *The Historical Foundations of EU Competition Law* (Oxford, Oxford University Press, 2013).

Klimenta, T and Sauter, W, 'An Eye for an Eye: Off-Label Use and Misleading Information: Hoffmann-La Roche v AGCM' (2018) 2 *European Pharmaceutical Law Review* 100.

Kovacic, WE, 'The Intellectual DNA of Modern US Competition Law for Dominant Firm Conduct: The Chicago/Harvard Double Helix' (2007) 2007 *Columbia Business Law Review* 1.

Kovacic, WE and Winerman, M, 'Competition Policy and the Application of Section 5 of the Federal Trade Commission Act' (2010) 20 *Minnesota Journal of International Law* 274.

Kupecz, A et al, 'Safe Harbors in Europe: An Update on the Research and Bolar Exemptions to Patent Infringement' (2015) 33 *Nature Biotechnology* 710.

Kyle, MK, 'Pharmaceutical Price Controls and Entry Strategies' (2007) 89 *Review of Economics and Statistics* 88.

Kyle, MK, 'Parallel Trade in Pharmaceuticals: Firm Responses and Competition Policy' in B Hawk (ed), *International Antitrust Law & Policy: Fordham Competition Law 2009* (Huntington, Juris Publishing, 2009).

Kyle, MK, 'Competition Law, Intellectual Property, and the Pharmaceutical Sector' (2016) 81 *Antitrust Law Journal* 1.

Kyle, MK, 'Economic Analysis of Supplementary Protection Certificates in Europe' (2017) https://ec.europa.eu/docsroom/documents/25621/attachments/1/translations/en/renditions/native.

Kyle, MK and McGahan, AM, 'Investments in Pharmaceuticals Before and After TRIPS' (2012) 94 *Review of Economics and Statistics* 1157.

Kyle, MK and Scott Morton, F, 'Markets for Pharmaceutical Products' in MV Pauly, TG Mcguire and PP Barros (eds), *Handbook of Health Economics* (Oxford, Elsevier, 2012) vol 2, 763.

Land, MK and Nesselhauf, L, 'Business and Human Rights Approaches to Intellectual Property' in I Bantekas and MA Stein (eds), *The Cambridge Companion to Business and Human Rights Law* (Cambridge, Cambridge University Press, 2021) 380.

Laser, CJ, 'Continuing the Conversation of "The Economic Irrationality of the Patent Misuse Doctrine"' (2012) 11 *Chicago-Kent Journal of Intellectual Property* 104.

Lee, J-Y, *A Human Rights Framework for Intellectual Property, Innovation and Access to Medicines* (London, Routledge, 2015).

Lee, J-Y and Hunt, P, 'Human Rights Responsibilities of Pharmaceutical Companies in Relation to Access to Medicines' (2012) 40 *Journal of Law, Medicine & Ethics* 220.

Lemley, MA, 'The Economic Irrationality of the Patent Misuse Doctrine' (1990) 78 *California Law Review* 1599.

Lemley, MA, 'Rational Ignorance at the Patent Office' (2001) 95 *Northwestern University Law Review* 1495.

Lemley, MA, 'Fixing the Patent Office' (2013) 13 *Innovation Policy and the Economy* 83.

Lemley, MA, 'Expecting the Unexpected' (2017) 92 *Notre Dame Law Review* 1369.

Lemley, MA and Shapiro, C, 'Probabilistic Patents' (2005) 19 *Journal of Economic Perspectives* 75.

Lianos, I, 'Polycentric Competition Law' (2018) *Current Legal Problems* 161.

Lianos, I, 'The Poverty of Competition Law – the Short Story' in D Gerard and I Lianos (eds), *Reconciling Efficiency and Equity: A Global Challenge for Competition Law?* (Cambridge, Cambridge University Press, 2022) 45.

Lianos, I, Countouris, N and de Stefano, V, 'Rethinking the Competition Law/Labour Law Interaction: Promoting a Fairer Labour Market' (2019) 10 *European Labour Law Journal* 291.

Lianos, I, Minssen T and Kollmar, C, 'Tackling Grand Challenges with Competition Law: Lessons from the Pandemic' in W Sauter, M Canoy and J Mulder (eds), *EU Competition Law and Pharmaceuticals* (Cheltenham, Edward Elgar, 2022) 279.

Lietzan, E, 'The "Evergreening" Metaphor in Intellectual Property Scholarship' (2019) 53 *Akron Law Review* 805.

Lietzan, E and Zettler, PJ, 'Regulating Medicines in the United States' in D Orentlicher and TK Hervey (eds), *The Oxford Handbook of Comparative Health Law* (Oxford, Oxford University Press, 2020) 690.

Lietzan, E, Mahalatchimy, A and Zettler, PJ, 'Introduction to Medical Products Law' in D Orentlicher and TK Hervey (eds), *The Oxford Handbook of Comparative Health Law* (Oxford, Oxford University Press, 2020) 684.

Lipski, S, 'Excessive Pricing and Pharmaceuticals: Why the Federal Patent Act Does Not Preempt State Regulation of Pharmaceutical Prices' (2008) 39 *University of Toledo Law Review* 913.

Maggiolino, M, *Intellectual Property and Antitrust. A Comparative Economic Analysis of US and EU Law* (Cheltenham, Edward Elgar, 2011).

Maggiolino, M, 'Even Employees Are Undertakings in the Labour Market, but Granting Social Rights Is not Antitrust's Job' (2022) 10 *Journal of Antitrust Enforcement* 365.

Maggiolino, M and Montagnani, ML, 'Astrazeneca's Abuse of IPR-Related Procedures: A Hypothesis of Antitrust Offence, Abuse of Rights, and IPR Misuse' (2011) 34 *World Competition* 245.

Mahalatchimy, A, 'Regulating Medicines in the European Union' in D Orentlicher and TK Hervey (eds), *The Oxford Handbook of Comparative Health Law* (Oxford, Oxford University Press, 2020) 721.

Maier-Rigaud, F, Blalock, N and Gannon, O, 'Reverse Payments: An EU and US Perspective' in P Figueroa and A Guerrero (eds), *EU Law of Competition and Trade in the Pharmaceutical Sector* (Cheltenham, Edward Elgar, 2019) 35.

Maini, L and Pammolli, F, 'Reference Pricing as a Deterrent to Entry: Evidence from the European Pharmaceutical Market' (2020) https://ssrn.com/abstract=3694471.

Marco Colino, S, Dunne, N, Fournier, K, Pais, S and Ritzmann, D, 'The Lundbeck Case and the Concept of Potential Competition' (2017) 2 *Concurrences*.

Markham, JW Jr, 'Sailing a Sea of Doubt: A Critique of the Rule of Reason in US Antitrust Law' (2012) 17 *Fordham Journal of Corporate & Financial Law* 591.

Marsden, P, 'Some Outstanding Issues from the European Commission's Guidance on Article 102 TFEU: Not-So-Faint Echoes of Ordoliberalism' in F Etro and I Kokkoris (eds), *Competition Law and the Enforcement of Article 102* (Oxford, Oxford University Press, 2010) ch 3.

Matthews, D and Gurgula, O, 'Patent Strategies and Competition Law in the Pharmaceutical Sector: Implications for Access to Medicines' (2016) 38 *European Intellectual Property Review* 661.

Mazzucato, M, *The Entrepreneurial State: Debunking Public vs. Private Sector Myths* (London, Anthem Press, 2013).

Meier, BM, Murphy, T and Gostin, LO, 'The Birth and Development of Human Rights for Health' in LO Gostin and BM Meier (eds), *Foundations of Global Health and Human Rights* (Oxford, Oxford University Press, 2020).

Mejer, M, '25 Years of SPC Protection for Medicinal Products in Europe: Insights and Challenges' (2017) https://ec.europa.eu/docsroom/documents/26001.

Mello, MM and Riley, T, 'To Address Drug Affordability, Grab the Low-Hanging Fruit' (*JAMA Health Forum*, 2021) https://jamanetwork.com/journals/jama-health-forum/fullarticle/2777036?widget=personalizedcontent&previousarticle=2768092.

Mello, MM and Wolitz, RE, 'Legal Strategies for Reining In "Unconscionable" Prices for Prescription Drugs' (2020) 114 *Northwestern University Law Review* 859.

Meunier, V and Padilla, J, 'Should Reverse Payment Patent Settlements Be Prohibited Per Se?' (2016) 3 *Concurrences*.

Michaels, R, 'The Functional Method of Comparative Law' in M Reimann and R Zimmermann (eds), *The Oxford Handbook of Comparative Law*, 2nd edn (Oxford, Oxford University Press, 2019) 350.

Mische, H, Kamilarova, E and Schnichels, D, 'Pharma' in J Faull and Nikpay (eds), *The EU Law of Competition*, 3rd edn (Oxford, Oxford University Press, 2014) 1869.

Monti, G, 'Article 81 EC and Public Policy' (2002) 39 *CML Rev* 1057.

Monti, G, 'Managing the Intersection of Utilities Regulation and EC Competition Law' (2008) 4 *Competition Law Review* 123.

Monti, G, 'Excessive Pricing: Competition Law in Shared Regulatory Space' (2019) TILEC Working Paper, www.tilburguniversity.edu/research/institutes-and-research-groups/old-tilec/events/work-progress-giorgio-monti.

Monti, G, 'Business Cooperation in Times of Emergency: The Role of Competition Law' (*Competition Policy International*, 2020) www.competitionpolicyinternational.com/business-cooperation-in-times-of-emergency-the-role-of-competition-law/.

Monti, G and Mulder, J, 'Escaping the Clutches of EU Competition Law Pathways to Assess Private Sustainability Initiatives' (2017) 42 *EL Rev* 635.

Moon, S, 'Respecting the Right to Access to Medicines: Implications of the UN Guiding Principles on Business and Human Rights for the Pharmaceutical Industry' (2013) 15 *Health & Human Rights Journal* 32.

Morin, J-F and Surbeck, J, 'Mapping the New Frontier of International IP Law: Introducing a TRIPs Plus Dataset' (2020) 19 *World Trade Review* 109.

Morse, MH, 'Product Market Definition in the Pharmaceutical Industry' (2003) 71 *Antitrust Law Journal* 633, 642.

Mossialos, E, Mrazek, M and Walley, T, 'Regulating Pharmaceuticals in Europe: An Overview' in E Mossialos, M Mrazek and T Walley (eds), *Regulating Pharmaceuticals in Europe: Striving for Efficiency, Equity and Quality* (Maidenhead, Open University Press, 2004) 7.

Motta, M, *Competition Policy: Theory and Practice* (Cambridge, Cambridge University Press, 2004).

Motta, M and de Streel, A, 'Excessive Pricing in Competition Law: Never Say Never?' in Swedish Competition Authority, *The Pros and Cons of High Prices* (Konkurrensverket, 2007).

Moufang, R, 'Patentability of Pharmaceutical Innovation: The European Perspective' in J Drexl and N Lee, *Pharmaceutical Innovation, Competition and Patent Law. A Trilateral Perspective* (Cheltenham, Edward Elgar, 2013) 54.

Mueller, JM, 'No "Dilettante Affair": Rethinking the Experimental Use Exception to Patent Infringement for Biomedical Research Tools' (2001) 76 *Washington Law Review* 1.

Mulcahy, AW, Christopher, MW, Mahlet, G, Schwam, D, Edenfield, N and Becerra-Ornelas, AU, 'International Prescription Drug Price Comparisons: Current Empirical Estimates and Comparisons with Previous Studies' (RAND Corporation, 2021) www.rand.org/pubs/research_reports/RR2956.html.

Murphy, T, *Health and Human Rights* (Oxford, Hart Publishing, 2013).

Muscolo, G and Pitruzzella, G (eds), *Competition and Patent Law in the Pharmaceutical Sector: An International Perspective* (Alphen aan den Rijn, Kluwer, 2016).

Naci, H and O'Connor, AB, 'Assessing Comparative Effectiveness of New Drugs before Approval Using Prospective Network Meta-analyses' (2013) 66 *Journal of Clinical Epidemiology* 812.

Navarro Varona, E and Caballero Candelairo, C, 'The Pharmaceutical Sector and Parallel Trade' in P Figueroa and A Guerriero (eds), *EU Law of Competition and Trade in the Pharmaceutical Sector* (Cheltenham, Edward Elgar, 2019) 405.

Nazzini, R, *The Foundations of European Union Competition Law: The Objective and Principles of Article 102* (Oxford, Oxford University Press, 2011).

Neven, D and Siotis, G, 'Dominance and Market Definition in the Pharmaceutical Industry Following the ECJ Paroxetine Judgment' (2020) 11 *Journal of European Competition Law & Practice* 194.

O'Connor, SM, 'Enabling Research or Unfair Competition? De Jure and De Facto Research Use Exceptions in Major Technology Countries' in T Takenaka (ed), *Patent Law & Theory: A Handbook of Contemporary Research* (Cheltenham, Edward Elgar, 2009) ch 19.

O'Donoghue, R and Padilla, J, *The Law and Economics of Article 102 TFEU*, 3rd edn (Oxford, Hart Publishing, 2020) 742.

O'Rourke, MA, 'Toward a Doctrine of Fair Use in Patent Law' (2000) 100 *Columbia Law Review* 1177.

Odudu, O, *The Boundaries of EC Competition Law: The Scope of Article 81* (Oxford, Oxford University Press, 2007).

Odudu, O, 'The Wider Concerns of Competition Law' (2010) 30 *OJLS* 559.

Ohlhausen, MK, 'Section 5 of the FTC Act: Principles of Navigation' (2014) 2 *Journal of Antitrust Enforcement* 1.

Ohlhausen, MK, 'The Procrustean Problem with Prescriptive Regulation' (2014) 23 *Communications Law Conspectus* 1.

Ong, B, 'Compulsory Licences of Pharmaceutical Patents to Remedy Anti-competitive Practices under Article 31(k) of the TRIPS Agreement: Can Competition Law Facilitate Access to Essential Medicines?' in RM Hilty and K-C Liu (eds), *Compulsory Licensing. Practical Experiences and Ways Forward*, MPI Studies on Intellectual Property and Competition Law 22 (Berlin, Springer-Verlag, 2015) 235.

Orbach, BY, 'The Antitrust Consumer Welfare Paradox' (2010) 7 *Journal of Competition Law & Economics* 133.

Orentlicher, D, 'Rights to Health Care in the United States: Inherently Unstable' (2012) 38 *American Journal of Law & Medicine* 326.

Organisation for Economic Co-operation and Development, 'Excessive Pricing in Pharmaceutical Markets' (Paris, OECD, 2018) www.oecd.org/daf/competition/excessive-pricing-in-pharmaceuticals.htm.

Organisation for Economic Co-operation and Development, 'Pharmaceutical Innovation and Access to Medicines' (Paris, OECD, 2018).

Organisation for Economic Co-operation and Development, 'Competition Concerns in Labour Markets' (Paris, OECD, 2020) www.oecd.org/daf/competition/competition-concerns-in-labour-markets.htm.

Organisation for Economic Co-operation and Development, 'Sustainability and Competition' (2020) OECD Competition Committee Discussion Paper, www.oecd.org/daf/competition/sustainability-and-competition-2020.pdf.

Örücü, E, *The Enigma of Comparative Law: Variations on a Theme for the Twenty-first Century* (Leiden, Springer, 2004).

Örücü, E, 'Methodology of Comparative Law' in JM Smits (ed), *Elgar Encyclopedia of Comparative Law* (Cheltenham, Edward Elgar, 2012) 442.

Ouellette, L and Hemel, D, 'Licensing in the Shadow of Impression Products' (2017) https://law.stanford.edu/2017/05/31/licensing-in-the-shadow-of-impression-products/.

Pace, JE and Adam, KC, 'Doryx, Namenda, and Coercion: Understanding and Un-tying Product Hopping Litigation' (2018) 32 *Antitrust*.

Pace, JE and Adam, KC, 'Understanding and Un-tying Product Hopping Litigation, Part II: A Reply to Carrier and Shadowen' (2019) 33 *Antitrust* 68.

Padula, A and Garattini, L, 'Health Technology Assessment for Pharmaceutical Regulation in the European Union: Do We Need Another Body?' (2019) 113 *Journal of the Royal Society of Medicine* 12.

Padula, WV, 'State and Federal Policy Solutions to Rising Prescription Drug Prices in the US' (2019) 22 *Journal* of *Health Care Law & Policy* 15.

Papadopoulou, F, *Evergreening Patent Exclusivity in Pharmaceutical Products. Supplementary Protection Certificates, Orphan Drugs, Paediatric Extensions and ATMPs* (Oxford, Hart Publishing, 2021).

Paradise, JK, 'Insulin Federalism' (2021) 27 *Boston University Journal of Science and Technology Law* 102.

Paul, S, 'Recovering the Moral Economy Foundations of the Sherman Act' (2021) 131 *Yale Law Journal* 175.

Paulis, E, 'Article 82 EC and Exploitative Conduct' in C-D Ehlermann and M Marquis (eds), *European Competition Law Annual 2007: A Reformed Approach to Article 82 EC* (Oxford, Hart Publishing, 2008) 515.

Peeperkorn, L, 'Coherence in the Application of Articles 101 and 102: A Realistic Prospect or an Elusive Goal?' (2016) 39 *World Competition* 389.

Persad, G, 'Pricing Drugs Fairly' (2021) 62 *William & Mary Law Review* 929.

Pitofsky, R, 'The Political Content of Antitrust' (1979) 127 *University of Pennsylvania Law Review* 1051.

Podszun, R, 'Can Competition Law Repair Patent Law and Administrative Procedures? AstraZeneca' (2014) 51 *CML Rev* 281.

Posner, RA, 'The Rule of Reason and the Economic Approach: Reflections on the Sylvania Decision' (1977) 45 *University of Chicago Law Review* 1.

Prosser, T, *The Limits of Competition Law* (Oxford, Oxford University Press, 2004).

Raimond, VC, Feldman, WB, Rome, BN and Kesselheim, AS, 'Why France Spends Less Than the United States on Drugs: A Comparative Study of Drug Pricing and Pricing Regulation' (2021) 99 *Milbank Quarterly* 240.

Rasi, G and Bonini, S, 'Innovative Medicines: New Regulatory Procedures for the Third Millennium' (2015) 15(Suppl 1) *Expert Opinion on Biological Therapy* 5.

Reed, S, 'Preventing Drug Price Gouging: Government Power and Initiatives' (2019) 19 *Houston Journal of Health Law & Policy* 167.

Rodwin, MA, 'Common Pharmaceutical Price and Cost Controls in the United Kingdom, France, and Germany: Lessons for the United States' [2021] *International Journal of Health Services* 1.

Roin, BN, 'Unpatentable Drugs and the Standards of Patentability' (2009) 87 *Texas Law Review* 503.

Röller, LH, 'Exploitative Abuses' in C-D Ehlermann and M Marquis (eds), *European Competition Law Annual 2007: A Reformed Approach to Article 82 EC* (Oxford, Hart Publishing, 2008) 525.

Ross, SA, 'The Economic Theory of Agency. The Principal's Problem' (1973) 63 *American Economic Review* 134.

Ruggie, J, 'Protect, Respect and Remedy: A Framework for Business and Human Rights' (2008) Report of the Special Representative of the Secretary-General on the Issue of Human Rights and Transnational Corporations and Other Business Enterprises, UN Doc A/HRC/8/5.

Ruggie, J, 'Guiding Principles on Business and Human Rights: Implementing the United Nations "Protect, Respect and Remedy" Framework' (2011) UN Doc No A/HRC/17/31.

Sarpatwari, A, Avorn, J and Kesselheim, AS, 'Using a Drug-Safety Tool to Prevent Competition' (2014) 370 *New England Journal of Medicine* 1476.

Sauter, W, 'Towards Responsive Enforcement of EU Antitrust in Pharmaceuticals' in W Sauter, M Canoy and J Mulder, *EU Competition Law and Pharmaceuticals* (Cheltenham, Edward Elgar, 2022), 246.

Scherer, FM and Watal, J, 'Competition Policy and Intellectual Property: Insights from Developed Country Experience' in RD Anderson, N Pires de Carvalho and A Taubman (eds), *Competition Policy and Intellectual Property in Today's Global Economy* (Cambridge, Cambridge University Press, 2021) 396.

Schwartz, LB, '"Justice" and Other Non-economic Goals of Antitrust' (1979) 127 *University of Pennsylvania Law Review* 1076.

Schweitzer, H, 'The History, Interpretation and Underlying Principles of Section 2 Sherman Act and Article 82 EC' in C-D Ehlermann and M Marquis (eds), *European Competition Law Annual 2007: A Reformed Approach to Article 82 EC* (Oxford, Hart Publishing, 2008) 119.

Schweitzer, H, 'Competition Law and Public Policy: Reconsidering an Uneasy Relationship – The Example of Article 81' in J Drexl, L Idot and J Monéger (eds), *Economic Theory and Competition Law* (Cheltenham, Edward Elgar, 2009) ch 9.

Scott Hemphill, C, 'An Aggregate Approach to Antitrust: Using New Data and Rulemaking to Preserve Drug Competition' (2009) 109 *Columbia Law Review* 629.

Scott Hemphill, C, 'Unjustified Delays in Generic Competition' (2014) OECD Expert Paper DAF/COMP/WD(2014)7.

Scott Hemphill, C, 'Less Restrictive Alternatives in Antitrust Law' (2016) 116 *Columbia Law Review* 927.

Scott Hemphill, C and Lemley, MA, 'Earning Exclusivity: Generic Drug Incentives and the Hatch-Waxman Act' (2011) 77 *Antitrust Law Journal* 947.

Scott Hemphill, C and Sampat, BN, 'Drug Patents at the Supreme Court' (2013) 339 *Science* 1386.

Scott Morton, F and Boller, LT, 'Enabling Competition in Pharmaceutical Markets' (2017) Hutchins Center Working Paper #30.

Scott Morton, F, Stern, AD and Stern, S, 'The Impact of the Entry of Biosimilars: Evidence from Europe' (2018) 53 *Review of Industrial Organization* 173.

Shadowen, SD, Leffler, KB and Lukens, JT, 'Anticompetitive Product Changes in the Pharmaceutical Industry' (2009–10) 41 *Rutgers Law Journal* 1.

Shadowen, SD, Leffler, KB and Lukens, JT, 'Bringing Market Discipline to Pharmaceutical Product Reformulations' (2011) 42 *International Review of Intellectual Property and Competition Law* 698.

Shapiro, C, 'Antitrust Limits to Patent Settlement' (2003) 34 *RAND Journal of Economics* 391.

Shelanski, H, 'Antitrust and Deregulation' (2018) 127 *Yale Law Journal* 1922.

Shepherd, JM, 'Deterring Innovation: New York v Actavis and the Duty to Subsidize Competitors' Market Theory' (2016) 17 *Minnesota Journal of Law, Science & Technology* 663.

Siebrasse, N and Culver, K, 'The Experimental Use Defence to Patent Infringement: A Comparative Assessment' (2006) 56 *University of Toronto Law Journal* 333.

Siems, M, *Comparative Law*, 3rd edn (Cambridge, Cambridge University Press, 2022).

Siotis, G, Ornaghi, C and Castanheira De Moura, M, 'Market Definition and Competition Policy Enforcement in the Pharmaceutical Industry' (Université Libre de Bruxelles, 2020) Working Papers ECARES 2020-49.

Smith, RL and Duke, A, 'Pharmaceuticals and Market Definition: A Cautionary Tale' (2021) 17 *European Competition Journal* 593.

Smits, JM, 'Taking Functionalism Seriously: On the Bright Future of a Contested Method' (2011) 18 *Maastricht Journal of European & Comparative Law* 554.

Son, KB, 'Importance of the Intellectual Property System in Attempting Compulsory Licensing of Pharmaceuticals: A Cross-Sectional Analysis' (2019) 15 *Global Health* 42.

South Centre, 'A Public Health Approach to Intellectual Property Rights: Public Health Related Flexibilities in the TRIPS Agreement', https://ipaccessmeds.southcentre.int/wp-content/uploads/2018/12/Public-Health-Related-Flexibilities-in-the-TRIPSAgreement.pdf.

Steinbaum, M and Stucke, ME, 'The Effective Competition Standard: A New Standard for Antitrust' (2020) 87 *University of Chicago Law Review* 595.

Stern, AD, Pietrulla, F, Herr, A, Kesselheim, AS and Sarpatwari, A, 'The Impact of Price Regulation on the Availability of New Drugs in Germany' (2019) 38 *Health Affairs* 1182.

Stothers, C, *Parallel Trade in Europe: Intellectual Property, Competition and Regulatory Law* (Oxford, Hart Publishing, 2007).

Stotland Weiswasser, E and Danzis, SD, 'The Hatch-Waxman Act: History, Structure, and Legacy' (2003) 71 *Antitrust Law Journal* 585.

Strandburg, KJ, 'What Does the Public Get? Experimental Use and the Patent Bargain' (2004) 2004 *Wisconsin Law Review* 81.

Strandburg, KJ, 'The Research Exemption to Patent Infringement: The Delicate Balance between Current and Future Technical Progress' in PK Yu (ed), *Intellectual Property and Information Wealth* (Westport, Praeger, 2007) 107.

Stucke, ME, 'Does the Rule of Reason Violate the Rule of Law?' (2009) *UC Davis Law Review* 1375.

Stucke, ME, 'Reconsidering Antitrust's Goals' (2012) 53 *Boston College Law Review* 551.

Subiotto, R, 'The Implications of the Imperfect European Patent System on the Assessment of Reverse Payment Settlemets', Expert Paper, in OECD, 'Generic Pharmaceuticals', DAF/COMP/WD(2014)75.

Tapia, J and Mantzari, D, 'The Regulation/Competition Interaction' in I Lianos and D Geradin (eds), *Handbook on European Competition Law-Substantive Aspects* (Cheltenham, Edward Elgar, 2013) ch 14.

Teachout, Z, *Break, 'Em Up: Recovering Our Freedom from Big Ag, Big Tech, and Big Money* (New York, All Points Books, 2020).

Teachout, Z and Khan, L, 'Market Structure and Political Law: A Taxonomy of Power' (2014) 9 *Duke Journal of Constitutional Law & Public Policy* 37.

Thomas, JR, 'The End of "Patent Medicines"? Thoughts on the Rise of Regulatory Exclusivities' (2015) 70 *Food & Drug Law Journal* 39.

Thomas, JR, 'Pharmaceutical Patents' in T Takenaka (ed), *Research Handbook on Patent Law and Theory*, 2nd edn (Cheltenham, Edward Elgar, 2019) 353.

Tobin, J, *The Right to Health in International Law* (Oxford, Oxford University Press, 2012).

Todino, M and Colombo, N, 'Case C-179/16 Hoffmann-La Roche: By Object Restrictions Still Bitter Pills to Swallow? A Close Watch on the Pharmaceutical Sector' (2018) 9 *Journal of European Competition Law & Practice* 376.

Townley, C, *Article 81 and EC Public Policy* (Oxford, Hart Publishing, 2009).

Tridico, A, Jacobstein, J and Wall, L, 'Facilitating Generic Drug Manufacturing: Bolar Exemptions Worldwide' (2014) WIPO Magazine www.wipo.int/wipo_magazine/en/2014/03/article_0004.html.

Tucker, DS, Wells, GF and Sheer, ME, 'REMS: The Next Pharmaceutical Enforcement Priority?' (2014) 28 *Antitrust Magazine*.

Tudor, J, 'Compulsory Licensing in the European Union' (2013) 4 *George Mason Journal of International Commercial Law* 222.

Ullrich, H, 'Strategic Patenting by the Pharmaceutical Industry: Towards a Concept of Abusive Practices of Protection' in J Drexl and N Lee (eds), *Pharmaceutical Innovation, Competition and Patent Law* (Cheltenham, Edward Elgar, 2013) 241.

Ullrich, H, 'Mandatory Licensing under Patent Law and Competition Law: Different Concerns, Complementary Roles' in RM Hilty and K-C Liu (eds), *Compulsory Licensing. Practical*

Experiences and Ways Forward, MPI Studies on Intellectual Property and Competition Law 22 (Berlin, Springer-Verlag, 2015) 333.

US Federal Trade Commission, 'Generic Drug Entry Prior to Patent Expiration: An FTC Study' (2002) www.ftc.gov/sites/default/files/documents/reports/generic-drug-entry-prior-patent-expiration-ftc-study/genericdrugstudy_0.pdf.

US Senate Special Committee on Aging, 'Sudden Price Spikes in Off-Patent Prescription Drugs: The Monopoly Business Model that Harms Patients, Taxpayers, and the US Healthcare System' (2016) www.congress.gov/114/crpt/srpt429/CRPT-114srpt429.pdf.

Vaishnav, A, 'Product Market Definition in Pharmaceutical Antitrust Cases: Evaluating Cross-Price Elasticity of Demand' (2012) 2011 *Columbia Business Law Review* 586.

Van den Bergh, R, *Comparative Competition Law and Economics* (Cheltenham, Edward Elgar, 2017).

Van Zimmeren, E, Minssen, T, Paemen, L, Van Dyck, W, Luyten, J, Janssens, R, Barbier, L, Simoens, S, Pouppez, C, Cleemput, I and Vinck, I, 'Compulsory Licensing for Expensive Medicines' (2022) Belgian Health Care Knowledge Centre (KCE) Reports 356, D/2022/10.273/35.

Vidal-Quadras, M, 'Analysis of EU Regulation 2019/933 on the SPC Manufacturing Waiver Exception' (2019) 50 *International Review of Intellectual Property and Competition Law* 971.

Vogler, S and Martikainen, JE, 'Pharmaceutical Pricing in Europe' in Z-U-D Babar (ed), *Pharmaceutical Prices in the 21st Century* (Cham, Springer, 2015) 343.

Vogler, S, Zimmermann, N and Haasis, MA, 'PPRI Report 2018 – Pharmaceutical Pricing and Reimbursement Policies in 47 PPRI Network Member Countries' (Vienna, Gesundheit Österreich, 2019) https://ppri.goeg.at/sites/ppri.goeg.at/files/inline-files/PPRI%20Report2018_2nd_edition_final.pdf.

Wenzl, M and Paris, V, 'Pharmaceutical Reimbursement Pricing in Germany' (Paris, OECD, 2018).

Whish, R and Bailey, D, *Competition Law*, 10th edn (Oxford, Oxford University Press, 2021).

Williams, HL, 'How Do Patents Affect Research Investments?' (2017) 9 *Annual Review of Economics* 441.

Willig, RD and Bigelow, JP, 'Antitrust Policy towards Agreements That Settle Patent Litigation' [2004] *Antitrust Bulletin* 655.

Witt, A, *The More Economic Approach to EU Antitrust Law* (Oxford, Hart Publishing, 2016).

Wolff, J, *The Human Right to Health* (New York, WW Norton & Company, 2012).

Wolitz, RE, 'The Pay-Twice Critique, Government Funding, and Reasonable Pricing Clauses' (2019) 39 *Journal of Legal Medicine* 177.

Wolitz, RE, 'A Corporate Duty to Rescue: Biopharmaceutical Companies and Access to Medications' (2019) 94 *Indiana Law Journal* 1163.

Wolitz, RE, Kesselheim, AS and Darrow, JJ, 'Government Patent Use to Promote Public Health in the United States: Overcoming Nonpatent Exclusivities' (2022) 8 *American Journal of Public Health* 1110.

World Intellectual Property Organization, 'Exceptions and Limitations to Patent Rights: Experimental Use and/or Scientific Research' (2013) SCP/20/4.

Wright, JD and Ginsburg, DH, 'Comment on the Canadian Competition Bureau's Draft Updated Intellectual Property Enforcement Guidelines' (2015) George Mason University Law & Economics Research Paper Series Paper No 15-31.

Wright, JD, Dorsey, E, Klick, J and Rybnicek, JM, 'Requiem for a Paradox: The Dubious Rise and Inevitable Fall of Hipster Antitrust' (2019) 51 *Arizona State Law Journal* 292.

Wu, T, 'After Consumer Welfare, Now What? The "Protection of Competition" Standard in Practice' [2018] *Competition Policy International*.

Wu, T, *The Curse of Bigness: Antitrust in the New Gilded Age* (New York, Columbia Global Reports, 2018).

Yale Global Health Justice Partnership, 'Curbing Unfair Drug Prices: A Primer for States' (2017) 6 https://law.yale.edu/sites/default/files/area/center/ghjp/documents/curbing_unfair_drug_prices-policy_paper-080717.pdf.

Yamin, AE, 'Not Just a Tragedy: Access to Medications as a Right under International Law' (2003) 21 *Boston University International Law Journal* 325.

Yelderman, S, 'Do Patent Challenges Increase Competition?' (2016) 83 *University of Chicago Law Review* 1943.

Yoo, K, 'Interaction of Human Rights Law and Competition Law: The Right to Access to Medicines and Consumer Welfare in the US Pharmaceutical Sector' (2018) 43 *Vermont Law Review* 123.

Zeno-Zencovich, V, 'Lessons from a Traffic Light. A Juridical Scherzo' (2016) 3 *European Journal of Comparative Law and Governance* 3.

Zeno-Zencovich, V, *Comparative Legal Systems. A Short and Illustrated Introduction* (Rome, Roma TrE-Press, 2019).

Zweigert, K and Kötz, H, *An Introduction to Comparative Law*, 3rd edn (T Weir tr, Oxford, Oxford University Press, 1998).

Index

www.ingramcontent.com/pod-product-compliance
Lightning Source LLC
Chambersburg PA
CBHW071351220926
51613CB00008B/71
9781509965519